GW00771251

Tracing the Criminal

For Anne

Adieu, dit le renard. Voici mon secret. Il est très simple: on ne voit bien qu'avec le cœur. L'essentiel est invisible pour les yeux.

—Antoine de Saint-Exupéry, *Le Petit Prince* (1943)

the Tracing Criminal

The Rise of Scientific Criminology in Britain 1860–1918

Neil Davie

with a foreword by Bryan S. Turner

The Bardwell Press
Oxford

Published by:

The Bardwell Press
6 Bardwell Road
Oxford OX2 6SW
www.bardwell-press.co.uk

British Library Cataloguing in Publication Data
A catalogue record for this book is available from the British Library

ISBN 0-9548683-1-5

Typeset by The Bardwell Press, Oxford, UK
Printed in Great Britain by Athenaeum Press Ltd., Gateshead, Tyne & Wear

Contents

Acknowledgements

I have incurred many debts in the researching and writing of this book. First of all, my understanding of crime, criminology and penal policy in the Victorian and Edwardian periods has benefited immeasurably from the work of other historians and criminologists. Although singling out names is a pernicious business, I would like to acknowledge a particular intellectual debt to the researches of Victor Bailey, Bill Forsythe, David Garland, Sean McConville, Nicole Hahn Rafter, and Martin J. Wiener. Despite their differences on other points, each shares an ability, all too rare in my experience, to combine meticulous empirical research with a capacity to stand back and consider the bigger picture (Michel Foucault's work reveals the danger of jumping straight to the bigger picture without that solid empirical foundation). Although my own work reaches conclusions which in some respects differ from theirs, without the latter, we would still be thrashing around in the dark on a wide range of subjects.

Mention should also be made of an earlier influence on my work, that of two sociologists, Huw Beynon and the late Philip Abrams, whose paths I was fortunate to cross some twenty-five years ago while a sociology and anthropology undergraduate at the University of Durham. Their enthusiastic advocacy of a historically-informed sociology or a sociologically-informed history (which amounts to much the same thing) set me on a course which has provided nothing but pleasure and intellectual fulfilment. Professor Abrams, who died suddenly in 1981, left behind him the still highly relevant *Historical Sociology* (Open Books, 1982). My thanks to them both.

Closer to the present, a large number of scholars and institutions have generously shared their expertise with me during the researching and writing of this book, responding with courtesy and efficiency to my persistent inquiries. I would like to thank Clare Anderson; Peter Becker; Ivan Crozier; Lesley A. Hall; Anne Hardy, Her Majesty's Prison Service Museum; John

Kingsbury of Parkhurst Heritage Museum, Isle of Wight; Nicky Rafter; Perth and Kinross Council Archives; University Art Museum, New York; John Van Wyhe; John Waller; Richard Wetzell and the members of that unique electronic community, the Victoria Research Web. Peter Becker and Nicky Rafter were kind enough to give me access to work of theirs in advance of its publication.

My many cross-Channel hops were always a pleasure thanks in no small part to the warm welcome provided by my sister-in-law Irène, her husband Michael and their children in Oxford. I look forward to more such occasions in the future, complete with the obligatory curries! The efficiency and good humour of the staff of the Bodleian Library, Oxford, of the British Library, of the Public Record Office at Kew, and of the University College Library, London were also much appreciated.

I should equally like to record my gratitude to my former colleague at Paris 7 University, Professor Michel Prum, a continuing source of guidance and encouragement over many years. His Eugenics and Racism Research Group (GRER), based at Paris 7, financed a number of important research trips to Britain, as well as providing a stimulating sounding board for many of the ideas contained in this book. My thanks both to Michel and the other members of the group.

My warm thanks also to Peter Hamilton, Bryan Turner, Toby Matthews and their colleagues at Bardwell Press for having backed this project from the word go.

Thanks too to my son, Luke, who in a moment of Eureka-like inspiration, came up with the title: *Tracing the Criminal.*

Finally, this book would never have been written without the unflagging support, encouragement and stimulating discussion provided by my wife extraordinaire, Anne. *Tracing the Criminal* is dedicated to her.

Neil Davie,
Lyons and Bozel, France, November 2005

Author's Note

Some of the material in this book first appeared in my article "Criminal Man Revisited? Continuity and Change in British Criminology, *c.*1865–1918", *Journal of Victorian Culture*, vol. 8, no. 1, Spring 2003, pp. 1–32. I would like to thank the journal's editor and Edinburgh University Press for permission to reproduce it here.

Foreword

The Victorian period produced a wealth of new ideas about criminology, criminal behaviour, prison reform, prison architecture, and mental health. It saw the rise of new disciplines such as criminal anthropology and the use of technologies such as photography to record the details of the criminal body. These developments can be treated as aspects of a more general movement towards social reform that expressed the general optimism of Victorian society and its commitment to organised social change. Its programme of social reform can be seen alongside an equally deep commitment to scientific advancement, technological investment and medical inquiry. It is within this optimistic project of social development that the figure of 'the criminal type' was deeply problematic. As in all societies that have been significantly influenced by Enlightenment values, the Victorians discovered that legal and penal reform was certainly possible, but criminal statistics characteristically presented irrefutable evidence of the stubborn presence of criminal behaviour, and the widespread growth in urban crime and deviance. The criminal type was a recidivist whose behaviour appeared to be resistant to rational treatment and obdurately failed to respond to penal management. In an era of rapid social change, it is hardly surprising that the criminal appeared to be atavistic.

Neil Davie provides a magnificent overview of the long and complex history of scientific, legal and medical responses to the criminal type, demonstrating the heterogeneous sources of thinking about the criminal that have shaped and occasionally misshaped social policy towards criminal behaviour. In recent years, Michel Foucault's *Discipline and Punish* (1977)[1975] has perhaps been one of the most influential accounts of attempts to manage crime in the modern period. Foucault in particular showed how the utilitarian philosophy of Jeremy Bentham conceived of the penitentiary as a project designed to provide an efficient, economy and effective management of the criminal by exposing the criminal mind to the moral regulation of public opinion. But the most significant intellectual figure in the modern history of criminology that unfolds in *Tracing the Criminal* is Cesare Lombroso (1835–1909). In the great debate over whether inherited characteristics or social environment (nature or nurture) was the causal matrix within which criminal behaviour was to be adequately understood and explained, Lombroso, who embraced a thorough-going positivistic stance towards social science, claimed from his own observations of the physical make-up of known criminals, that there was a definite 'criminal type'. More importantly, the criminal was an atavistic specimen—a throwback to a pre-social figure whose stooping frame, large hands, and low brow marked him out as different from the rest of society. The criminal was born, not socialised within a deviant environment. These arguments created new professional opportunities for criminal anthropology, forensic medicine and the hospital doctor, and for the use of photography as an instrument of scientific investigation into the stigmata that were the telltale signs of criminal degeneracy.

Lombroso's positivistic criminology promised to resolve definitively the puzzle of criminal behaviour, and more importantly it claimed to be demonstrably grounded in a scientific methodology that delivered unambiguous results. Criminal Man had stigmata that could be read by the criminologist with the same clarity as reading an English text. Nineteenth century positivism was a deterministic and reductionist doctrine that broke with the classical tradition of criminology, which had been much more closely associated with legal theory, the doctrine of free will and philosophical liberalism. The conventional criticism of positivism has been that, if criminal behaviour is caused by the genetic make-up of the criminal, then there can be no legitimate reason to punish criminal behaviour. Legal theory typically assumes that punishment of the criminal must demonstrate that the criminal was responsible for his or her behaviour. In short, the criminal law assumes that criminals have freedom and rational motivation, and therefore they can be held responsible for their actions, and suitably punished. Positivist criminology in fact places 'crime' in a category that is outside the criminal law, in the sense that the criminal needs treatment not punishment. We should no more punish the criminal than we would punish the patient for his illness. If Lombroso was correct in thinking that 70% of criminals were programmed from birth to lead a life of crime, then correction was an inadequate social policy, because criminality has the same ontological status as disease.

There is some dispute as to the extent of the influence of the Italian school of positivist criminology. In retrospect we can see that Lombroso's positivist theory of the criminal type had more impact on the development of American than European criminology. Lombroso's account of the criminal type was challenged by for example Enrico Ferri, who, in a review of *L'Uomo delinquente* in 1878, claimed that up to 60% of criminals exhibited no obvious defective stigmata. By contrast, Lombroso's influence over American social science was recognised by Lombroso himself in his 1893 introduction to Arthur MacDonald's *Criminology*, in which Lombroso noted the neglect of his work in 'the old world'. Despite Lombroso's own assessment, his *L'Uomo delinquente* (1876) had a powerful influence on emerging criminology in continental Europe. One might have imagined that Lombrosian positivism would have also been welcomed enthusiastically in Great Britain where the scientific principles of Darwinian evolution were having an important impact on the social sciences. Certainly Henry Maudsley the influential English alienist was also committed to a theory of degeneration in explaining criminal behaviour. However, British scientists working in the field of criminology remained sceptical about Lombroso's sweeping generalisations. As Davie shows so clearly, the intellectual roots of British criminology in the period from 1890 to 1918 were diverse and complex, including phrenology, psychiatry, biology, jurisprudence and sociology.

What is striking however about criminology at the end of the century was the concentration not on the criminal type but on the idea of the feeble-minded criminal. Crime was a product, not of the robust atavistic man, but of the feeble-minded simpleton, who could not cope independently with the exigencies of urban life in a social world that was rapidly changing. The problem with the feeble-minded criminal was his unfortunate capacity to reproduce. If the feeble-minded man had been infertile, he would have been less problematic in the social landscape of late Victorian England. There is a connection between the Victorian horror of masturbatory insanity, which resulted in feeble-mindedness, and the propensity to wasteful reproduction on the part of the criminal. With Darwinian presuppositions, one can see how the persistent criminal was not only a danger to healthy society, but also a danger to himself. The criminal type within the moral framework of Victorian values was not so much a vicious and dangerous fellow, but a sad and pathetic figure in need of regulation and restraint, and medical guidance. The prison medical officers therefore played an important role in offering regular and reliable surveillance of physical degeneracy and mental illness in the profile of these inferior types. Criminal anthropology offered a classification of social class and ethnic identity in which the upper classes were dominated by the Norman type, the middle classes by the legacy of the Saxon world, and the working class by the troublesome Celtic type. These criminal classifications were a feature of Victorian science with its predilection for evolutionary chains and developmental types, and for the quest to find the missing link.

As Davie shows, Charles Goring's *The English Convict* (1913) provided a critique of the positivistic legacy of scientific criminology, but while he was critical of the specific legacy of Lombroso, Goring concluded that there was a clear association between poor physique, defective mental abilities and anti-social tendencies. Goring's approach was a stepping stone between Victorian assumptions about moral and mental feeble-mindedness and the more encompassing world of scientific eugenics. The work of Francis Galton on positive eugenics supported the conclusion that there was a propensity for the weak-minded person of low intellect to multiple through unrestrained reproduction. There was therefore an interesting convergence between evolutionary thought, medical science, eugenics and criminology in the Edwardian period. Galton, who was Darwin's cousin, developed a social philosophy in which national salvation was to be sought through selective breeding. Against the sanitarians, positive eugenics argued that breeding stock was more important than environmental conditions—housing stock, wage levels and water supply—in determining the health of the nation. Poverty and unemployment were the consequences, not the causes, of social incapacity, and therefore the eugenically sound should be encouraged to breed more. These eugenic ideas had significant consequences as illustrated by the Mental Deficiency Act of 1913 which increased medical powers to sequester defective individuals, and in the United States fifteen thousand individuals had been sterilised following eugenic criteria by 1930.

Lombroso and the Italian *Scuola Positiva* held out the promise in the late nineteenth century of bringing about a revolution in criminology and hence in the treatment of criminals. As we have seen, positivist criminology eventually joined hands with eugenics in recommending that breeding not punishment or education was the real solution to the presence of the criminal type. After the Second World War, revelations about the role of German scientists in the technological innovations that were necessary for the Holocaust, the involvement of scientific medicine in Nazi social policies towards mental health, and the controversial role of medicine in social control in the Soviet Union resulted in general disgust towards eugenics as an aspect of the social policies of the modern state. Eugenics involved a significant intervention into the private lives of citizens by an authoritarian state. In liberal theory, the separation between the private and the public is intended to guarantee the sanctity of freedom of choice in matters that are deemed to be intimate. In the famous case of *Griswold vs. Connecticut,*

381 U.S.479 (1965), the Court upheld the legal position that there is a fundamental right to privacy that, for example, prohibits laws criminalising birth control. This case has become an influential precedent in the defence of privacy, but this ruling has produced many legal battles over the constitutional right to privacy in which states have sought for example to make homosexual sodomy a criminal offence. Generally speaking, the state has retained the right to proscribe certain types of sexual behaviour in private as illegal. While direct interference in breeding as an aspect of eugenics is rarely upheld by the modern state, all societies have eugenic strategies that are designed to improve or have the consequence of improving the breeding stock. By supporting contraception or by making abortion legal or by making an amniocentesis test available to pregnant women, the state supports what we might call an indirect eugenics policy. The one-child policy of the Chinese state is perhaps the most far-reaching policy of eugenic regulation in modern history. However, stem cell research, the human genome project and regenerative medicine are also indicators of the role of eugenics in modern medicine and the capitalist economy.

While *Tracing the Criminal* is overtly an historical account of the emergence of criminology, it is very relevant to contemporary social debates about appropriate social policy towards crime. As I have indicated, the contemporary excitement about genetic research is promoted by the quest to find the gene that will explain some social problem, deviance or criminal behaviour. Positivist and reductionist explanations of human behaviour are seen to be appropriate, and treated as if they will produce effective strategies. There is of course less talk about 'the criminal type' in official discourse and criminals are no longer defined in medical science as atavistic throwbacks, but there is as much anxiety now about 'offensive behaviour' and its treatment as there was in the Edwardian period about the persistent offender who was feeble minded and inclined towards degeneracy. Neil Davie's comprehensive and skilful history of the complex evolution of fashions and fads in criminology is a useful reminder that our own preoccupations with genetic explanations and the social offence of 'laddish' behaviour is not that far removed from the world of Lombroso, Grove and Maudsley. The scientific quest to discover the cause of crime in the atavistic figure of the criminal type is characterised more by its continuity rather than its disruptions.

Bryan S. Turner
National University of Singapore
November 2005

Introduction

"It is certain", wrote Henry Maudsley, leading alienist and specialist on the criminal mind in 1874,

> ... that lunatics and criminals are as much manufactured articles as are steam engines and calico-printing machines, only the processes of the organic manufactury are so complex that we are not able to follow them. They are neither accidents nor anomalies in the universe, but come by law and testify to causality; and it is the business of science to find out what the causes are and by what laws they work.[1]

If Victorian science did not yet have the ability to observe this "organic manufactury" at first-hand, it did consider itself perfectly capable of producing a detailed description of the finished article. But what was to be gained from such an enterprise? There was of course the desire to satisfy scientific curiosity; part of that quintessentially Victorian passion for measurement, classification and precise visual representation which swept through a whole raft of scientific disciplines of the period, a passion which left its lasting monument in the great nineteenth-century museums as well as countless private collections.[2]

This is part of the story, as we shall see, but not its entirety. There was not just a desire to *describe* criminals, but also to *explain* them. What gripped the minds of a wide range of Victorians and Edwardians was thus not simply a taxonomic desire to pin a label on "The Criminal" and place him or her under a bell jar, but to explore the very springs of crime itself. These two were very much complementary approaches of course, for it was an article of faith of Victorian inductive science that theory followed naturally from careful observation. Thus providing the object of study was approached with sufficient scientific rigour, the "facts" would speak for themselves. As leading French anthropologist Paul Broca put it in 1868, "it is the axiom of all observational sciences that facts must precede theories."[3] What was required was the methodological equivalent of Sherlock Holmes's magnifying glass; when brought to bear on the problem by a well-trained observer, the facts would miraculously spring into focus, just like a fingerprint at the scene of a crime. Only after such meticulous data collection could cautious generalisations be made.

If the elusive criminal diathesis could be distilled, bottled and rendered accessible to the scientist's gaze, a first and important step would have been made on the road to penetrating the workings of Maudsley's "organic manufactury". Further analysis should then logically permit hypotheses to be formulated concerning the cause—or causes—of crime. This was no mere academic conundrum, for upon its successful resolution depended the very life, limb and property of each of Her Majesty's subjects. At a time when the ingenuity and economic power of this, the first Industrial Nation, seemed capable of resolving any problem, intellectual or practical, criminal behaviour continued to stubbornly resist the best efforts of the country's greatest minds. Even when overall crime levels began to fall in the last quarter of the nineteenth century, there remained a rump of "habituals"—or "recidivists" as the fashionable new term from across the Channel would have it—apparently immune to both the punitive and reformatory elements in the penal system.

In the British case, research on the causes of criminal behaviour in the period covered by this book—from 1860 to 1918—would retain a fundamentally *practical* character. Its practitioners tended to shy away from grandiose, over-arching theories; speculation as to the causes of crime could safely be left to the various Continental schools of criminology with their "barren disquisitions and pretentious speculations".[4] Indeed, with only one or two exceptions, the British took no part in the wide-ranging and often acrimonious debates on the causes of crime played out at a series of international congresses on criminal anthropology in the 1880s and 1890s.

Home-grown experts, in contrast to their continental colleagues, were almost exclusively criminal justice professionals, many of them doctors, psychiatrists or civil servants working in the Home Office-run prison system. Such men were looking for what they considered to be common-sense solutions to concrete problems faced by both law enforcement agencies and by the prison system: How to tell the difference between the criminal and the law-abiding; how to unmask an inveterate "habitual" who was claiming to be a first-time offender; how to distinguish between a convict genuinely "unfit" for the rigours of punishment or forced labour and a mere malingerer?

"Common sense" is of course a fickle mistress. As Martin Wiener has perceptively noted, the British insistence on practical, value-free solutions to policing and penal problems

> ... has often served simply to obscure the sources and contexts of policy concerning criminals and others.... [I]t is obvious that even the most practical men do not act in a conceptual or moral vacuum. *Determining what constitutes practicality and common sense requires prior interpretations of experience*; and thus we are brought back to wider social and cultural questions.[5]

Thus, for "The Criminal" to be conceptualised as a worthy object of scientific study in the same way as, say, a mollusc or an unstable chemical compound, it was necessary to start from the kind of assumptions to which Wiener refers here; namely that criminals constituted a sub-category of the Human Race who differed from the law-abiding majority in other ways than simply by their lawbreaking, and that those differences were accessible to scientific investigation.

Thus, despite their emphasis on inductive method and self-evident facts "out there", in reality British criminologists[6] approached their chosen subject with a whole raft of preconceptions which coloured their view of the phenomenon. It is as if Sherlock Holmes's magnifying glass had been fitted with a variety of distorting lenses and coloured filters, thereby subtlely, almost imperceptibly, altering the image under scrutiny. The object of this book is to dust off and examine these "filters", to explore Wiener's "prior interpretations of experience" which structured the British approach to understanding criminal behaviour in this period.

Just as a particular species of mollusc has empirically demonstrable characteristics that permit a specimen to be unequivocally classified either within or outside the group, so, the Victorians reasoned, an individual could be unequivocally apportioned to one of two mutually exclusive categories: the "criminal" or the "non-criminal". It was a matter of cracking the code. That it was possible to grasp the key to this code, the Victorian mind took as read. It might take some time to flush it out, but like Alice, eager to pursue that elusive white rabbit, scientists were convinced that they would eventually succeed in tracking down the equivalent of the "drink me" potion, thereby permitting policy-makers and criminal justice professionals to unlock the secrets of the criminal mind.

The stakes were high. Most of Britain's criminologists were employed in the country's centrally-administered and publicly-financed prison system—which before 1877 meant its convict prisons[7]—and felt keenly the pressure emanating from public and politicians alike to find penal solutions that were at once effective and economical. For the first part of our period, the crime rate seemed to be rising inexorably, and the pressure to do something—*anything*—to halt it in its tracks was intense. There was a temptation in such circumstances, as historian Janet Saunders has observed[8], for prison administrators to put up their hands and claim impotence in the face of a criminal class born and bred to incorrigible lawbreaking. As we shall see, by the 1860s, they were able to marshal convincing scientific arguments drawn from a number of fields—Darwinian biology, racial anthropology and French psychiatry among them—to support such a gloomily determinist prognosis. However, such arguments carried with them a major drawback. For career prison administrators and medical officers, impotence was not a very comfortable mantle to bear, at least not for any length of time. There was professional pride at stake. If Britain's criminal class was destined from birth to break the law and end up behind bars, what role did that leave for the senior personnel of the country's penal system, except as glorified turnkeys?

There was a more sophisticated version of this fatalistic argument, according to which prison could function to *deter potential wrongdoers*—particularly young people tempted by the easy pickings of a life of crime—while having little or no power to reform those who had already embarked upon the path of the career criminal. This argument would be advanced repeatedly by Sir Edmund Du Cane, Britain's prison supremo from 1877 until his retirement in 1895. If the country's prisons contained a greater and greater proportion of habitual criminals, this was not, he argued, proof of the inability of the system to reform prisoners, but rather of the prison's increasing success at inspiring a salutary dread in the breasts of those tempted by crime. "I should rejoice", Du Cane told an audience at the Social Science Association in 1875,

> to see the day when no persons were convicted except those who had been convicted before; for if there were no fresh conviction, then clearly the criminal army would not be receiving any recruits, and we should be one step nearer to the full attainment of our object.[9]

According to such reasoning, the effectiveness of the prison as a deterrent would eventually mean that the supply of habituals would dry up altogether, and carceral institutions would render themselves obsolete (though quite how "deterrence" would operate in such circumstances with no habituals of which to make an example remains unclear).

This argument had the merit of restoring a certain positive role for the prison—if it can be called that— in that it emphasised the need for a particular carceral regime, though one whose chief objective was to make prison as thoroughly disagreeable for its inmates as possible. This regime was not chiefly for the benefit of the prisoners themselves (though "hard labour, hard fare and a hard bed" would not do them any harm, it was reasoned), but rather to deter potential criminals *outside* the prison walls. However, such a conception of the function of the prison system left little scope for intervention by prison doctors; little, that is, beyond administering to ailments real or imaginary (the latter in the form of *malingering* were considered to represent a particularly intractable problem), and distinguishing between prisoners who were "fit" for labour or punishment, and those whose poor mental and/or physical condition meant that they were "unfit" to undergo its rigours.

This latter question was of no little importance in the daily routine of the prison doctors, and we shall see that attempts to resolve it was an important impetus to research on the mental and physical characteristics of the convict population by medical officers from the 1860s onwards. These pioneering researches drew both on long-standing stereotypes of the Criminal drawn from phrenology and physiognomy, and newer biological, anthropological and psychiatric theories becoming current in mid-Victorian empirical science. Out of the blending of these intellectual influences and the practical necessities of the prison regime would emerge something closely resembling a *criminal-type*: a generic portrait of the Criminal in both his physical (particularly physiognomic) traits and behavioural aspects.

Significantly, attention would be focussed almost exclusively on establishing a *male* criminal-type. The reasons for this are complex and yet to be fully determined, but need to be considered briefly here to explain why a decision was taken to largely exclude any consideration of theories of female criminal behaviour from this book. Most important perhaps, the apparent crime wave of the 1850s and 1860s which served as a catalyst for early research on the springs of criminal behaviour was perceived as an almost exclusively male affair, linked in both the public mind and official discourse to the release of unreformed convicts back into the community. The threat posed by the "Criminal Class" was thus seen in strongly gendered terms. Female crime did of course pose its own problems to the dominant moral order —seen above all in the long-running debate on prostitution[10]—but the priority among Britain's first generation of criminologists was on doing something about the urgent "problem of the habitual criminal"; a problem seen—with some empirical justification[11]—in largely male terms.

Though the precise reasons for the increasing rarity of women in the machinery of the nineteenth-century criminal justice system are yet to be adequately explained[12], the relatively modest size of the female prison population may account in part for the relative lack of interest in the scientific study of its behavioural and physical specificities. Other factors may also be involved. Outside the specialised women's prisons (the first of which were built in the 1850s), there would have been little opportunity for medical officers to come into regular contact with female offenders, and this may have limited the opportunities for research. There was also (again) the question of professional pride. The female convict service was regarded by medical officers and officials as the least desirable posting in the Victorian prison service. Perhaps research on women prisoners would have suffered by association. At the same time, the male corps of Victorian prison doctors may have considered speculation on the behavioural and particularly *physical* characteristics of female criminals to be either of dubious moral propriety or likely to lead to allegations of prurience from their colleagues or the wider reading public. The way in which the 1895 English translation of Cesare Lombroso and Guglielmo Ferrero's anthropological study of women criminals, *La donna delinquente* (published in the UK as *The Female Offender*[13]) was heavily bowdlerised, leaving out or toning down any material of a sexually explicit nature, reveals the force of such unwritten taboos.[14]

Whatever the reasons, while there are scattered references in the literature to the physiognomy of women criminals[15], and general remarks about their "troublesome" and "unreasonable" natures[16], they were conspicuous by their absence in the criminological research produced during the period covered by this book, despite the availability from 1895 of Lombroso and Ferrero's book.[17] Only in the Edwardian period would the situation begin to change, with growing eugenics-inspired concern about the procreative capacities of "feeble-minded" female criminals.[18]

In fact in many ways, the trajectory of criminological thinking is gender-specific. A recent study has argued that *The Female Offender* "actually had a greater long-term impact on the study of female crime than *Criminal Man* did on theories of male crime."[19] It was felt that to do full justice to that specificity was beyond the scope of this book. However, if anything close to an adequate history of these early years of British criminology is to be written, the intriguing possibilities of the statement quoted above will need to be unravelled. That task still awaits its historian.[20]

In the last decades of the nineteenth century, British prison medical officers would increasingly be drawn towards a new, *therapeutic* conception of their role, one which went beyond merely sorting prisoners into one of a number of administrative boxes: "fit for punishment", "fit only for light duties", etc. As they delved deeper into the darker recesses of the criminal mind—amassing data on the physical and mental traits of the prisoners in their charge—it is not surprising perhaps that prison doctors should have sought a more rewarding, and socially more prestigious function within the prison system than that of the filing clerk, one in fact more in keeping with the growing social and professional status of the medical profession as a whole.[21] After all, medical practitioners on the outside were in a position to heal—or at least attempt to heal—their patients, and were able to draw on an increasing body of knowledge about complex psychological and psychiatric disorders in order to do so. Prison medical officers were keen to share in these exciting new developments, and adapt new treatments to the case of individual criminals, or perhaps come up with suitable treatments of their own. Such a conception of the criminal was clearly incompatible with one that emphasised the incorrigibility of large swathes of the prison population. Since British criminology was born in this medico-penal context, the occupational priorities of this small, close-knit group of practitioners is of vital importance.

David Garland has argued[22] that the therapeutic, individualising impetus of late nineteenth-century British thinking on crime can be contrasted with the approach favoured by Victorian physical anthropologists, who sought to classify individuals into discrete groups based on generic constitutional and racial attributes. Such a conception of British criminology is offered as an explanation of why home-grown practitioners remained resolutely, often vituperatively, hostile to Italian criminologist Cesare Lombroso and his conception of the atavistic *delinquente-nato* or "born criminal-type", programmed from birth to commit crime.[23] Identifiable by means of distinctive anatomical and physiognomic stigmata, here was "a group of criminals born for evil, against whom all social cures break as against a rock."[24] Such an approach was consistently lambasted in British medical journals and criminological treatises from the 1890s onwards; condemned not just for its fundamentally misguided search for an all-encompassing criminal-type instead of the case-by-case approach favoured on this side of the Channel, but also for its slapdash methodology and deductive, rather than inductive, reasoning.

According to this view, theories of the born criminal-type were at best, like phrenology and physiognomy, quaint reminders of the pre-history of scientific scrutiny of criminal behaviour. At worst, recycling old stereotypes of atavistic, low-browed born criminals pandered to what an 1894 article in the *British Medical Journal* called the "morbid love of notoriety fostered by the cheap newspapers of the present day with their blood-curdling 'bills' and their puffing paragraphs." It was one thing for penny dreadfuls, broadsheets and popular theatre to feed such unwholesome public interest in the gruesome details of violent crime and the inhuman "monsters" believed to perpetrate them. It was quite another for respectable men of science to sully their hands with notions which, in the view of the journal, represented "a greater danger to society than 'atypical confluence' of the fissures of the brain and other signs relied upon by criminological Zadigs."[25]

Indeed, British specialists in the late-Victorian and Edwardian periods frequently poured scorn not only on the biological determinism of Lombroso but also on its principle rival, the sociological model of criminal behaviour associated with the French *milieu social* school of Alexandre Lacassagne and Gabriel Tarde. Some British criminologists would even go as far as ruling out the value of generalisation *per se*.

This account of the origins of British criminology was found to raise some troubling questions however. Prison medical officers shared, we have noted, in researches in the 1860s and 1870s which conceptualised the Criminal as belonging to a relatively homogenous "criminal class", with distinctive physical and mental traits, precisely the kind of assumptions underlying Lombroso's later conception of the born-criminal type (an intellectual debt which the Italian was quite happy to acknowledge). The conventional account has the researches conducted by these "English precursors of Lombroso"[26] petering out around the mid-1870s, at which point criminological research apparently disappeared from these shores until its re-birth in the 1890s in a new therapeutic and ferociously anti-Lombrosian form. The intention in the following pages is to explore this puzzling series of events in further detail. To look at where that early research took its inspiration, and why—if such was indeed the case—this search for the criminal-type faded into obscurity barely a decade after it began. Equally, the sudden arrival of Garland's therapeutic criminology in the 1890s, with assumptions apparently in stark contrast to those of the previous generation of researchers, would require further examination.

As the foregoing remarks may already have hinted, neither the mysterious disappearance of the "precursors", nor the equally miraculous emergence of the white-coated therapeutic discipline twenty years later, proved to be quite what they seemed. It turned out that there was not in fact a fifteen-year standstill in British theorising on the causes of crime from the mid-1870s, neither was the "new" criminology of the 1890s quite as new as contemporaries—and some historians—have suggested. Equally, the opposition between continental theorising—whether clothed in French environmentalism or Italian atavism—and the home-grown variety proved to be much less clear-cut than a superficial reading might suggest. This is not to deny the existence of important differences between British criminological practice and dominant approaches in France and Italy. What tended to get lost in the heat of debate, however, was that these competing schools had a number of fundamental assumptions in common.

The search for a distinctive criminal-type—for a set of physical and mental traits believed to be common to all criminals, or at least to certain kinds of criminals—would in fact prove to be an enduring feature of British criminological discourse during the whole period from 1860 to 1918, despite wide-ranging changes in the socio-economic, political and intellectual climate in which this search was grounded, and despite the currency of comments expressing the precise opposite. The language would change, the theories mustered to justify the existence of the criminal-type would change, but many of the visual signifiers of the "gaol look" as it was sometimes called, would prove remarkably resilient during this sixty-year period. When Edwardian prison doctors and psychiatrists described the visual traits of the "feeble-minded" offender, and eugenicists sought to define those of the "unfit" or "degenerate", striking similarities can be observed with the crude physiognomic stereotypes of the 1850s and '60s. In short, Cesare Lombroso's *delinquente nato* had not after all been consigned to the history books, nor was it confined to the harmless rantings of foreign theorists, but was alive and well and safely ensconsed at the heart of British criminological practice.

Notes

1 Henry Maudsley, *Responsibility in Mental Disease*, New York, 1900 [1874], p. 30.
2 Bernard Lightman (ed.), *Victorian Science in Context*, London, University of Chicago Press, 1997.
3 Quoted in Stephen J. Gould, *The Mismeasure of Man*, 2nd edition, London, Penguin, 1997, p. 116.
4 Henry Maudsley, "Remarks on Crime and Criminals", *Journal of Mental Science*, vol. XXXIV, 1888, p. 167.
5 *England 1830–1914*, Cambridge, Cambridge University Press, 1990, p. 6 [my emphasis]. Cf. Roger Cooter, *The Cultural Meaning of Popular Science: Phrenology and the Organisation of Consent in Nineteenth Century Britain*, Cambridge, Cambridge University Press, 1984, p. 35: "… the task before the historian … is to determine how and why some conceptions of reality acquire the mantle of scientific truth and enter into the domain of common sense while others come to be regarded as arrant nonsense."
6 The term will be used in this book to denote those using scientific or pseudo-scientific methodology to investigate the causes of crime. The word "criminologist" would not in fact be used in Britain until the 1890s, and even then its use remained controversial.

7 Until 1877, prisoners serving sentences of less than three years were incarcerated in local prisons, outside Home Office control. The term "convict" applies thus to those serving longer terms, either of transportation or penal servitude.

8 Janet Saunders, "Quarantining the Weak-minded: Psychiatric Defintions of Degeneracy and the Late-Victorian Asylum", *in* W. F. Bynum *et al.* eds., *The Anatomy of Madness: Essays in the History of Psychiatry*, vol. 3, London, Routledge, 1988, p. 277.

9 Edmund Du Cane, "Address on the Repression of Crime", *Transactions of the National Association for the Promotion of Social Science*, 1875, p. 279.

10 See Judith R. Walkowitz, *Prostitution and Victorian Society: Women, Class and the State*, Cambridge, Cambridge University Press, 1980.

11 Between 1857 and 1890, the proportion of women proceeded against for indictable offences fell from 27–19% (Clive Emsley, *Crime and Society in England 1750–1900*, 2nd edition, London, Longmans, 1996, p. 152). See also Lucia Zedner, "Wayward Sisters", in Norval Morris & David Rothman (eds.), *The Oxford History of the Prison: The Practice of Punishment in Western Society*, Oxford, Oxford University Press, 1998, p. 297.

12 Emsley, *op. cit.*, ch. 6.

13 Cesare Lombroso & Guglielmo Ferrero, *The Female Offender*, London, 1895.

14 Cesare Lombroso & Guglielmo Ferrero *Criminal Woman, the Prostitute and the Normal Woman*, trans. & ed. Nicole Hahn Rafter & Mary Gibson, Durham, Duke University Press, 2004, "Editors' Introduction", pp. 4–5.

15 Lucia Zedner, *Women, Crime and Custody in Victorian England*, Oxford, Clarendon Press, 1991, p. 78.

16 Typical of such comments is that by Prisons inspector Major Arthur Griffiths, who described women prisoners as "... more troublesome because they cannot be so firmly governed; they require humouring, a lighter hand, the tact which can command while seeming to persuade. Their artifice goes deeper; defiance is not less marked, and more prolonged ... Feminine nature is more hysterical, unreasonable and uncontrollable" (Major Arthur Griffiths, *Secrets of the Prison House*, 2 vols., London, 1894, vol. 1, p. 41). See also his *Fifty Years of Public Service*, London, Cassell, n.d. [1904], pp. 205–6.

17 On the significance and subsequent influence of this work, Lombroso & Ferrero, *Criminal Woman*, "Editors' Introduction", pp. 23–29.

18 See below, Chapter Five.

19 Lombroso & Ferrero, *op. cit.*, "Editors' Introduction", p. 4.

20 It is to be hoped that the publication of this new unbowdlerised English version of *La donna delinquente*— the first English translation of one of Lombroso's criminological works in nearly a hundred years—will stimulate further research in this area. A new translation of Lombroso's *L'Uomo delinquente* ("Criminal Man"), by the same indefatigable team, is planned for 2005.

21 Joe Sim, *Medical Power in Prisons: The Prison Medical Service in England 1774–1989*, Buckingham, Open University Press, 1990, p. 56.

22 Garland, David, "British Criminology Before 1935", *British Journal of Criminology*, vol. 28, no. 2, Spring 1988, pp. 1–18.

23 First revealed in Cesare Lombroso, *L'Uomo delinquente*, Milan, Hoepli, 1876. See Chapter Three.

24 Cesare Lombroso, *Crime: Its Causes and Remedies*, Boston, Little Brown & Co., 1911, p. 447.

25 "Criminals and Criminal Anthropology", *British Medical Journal*, 24 February 1894, p. 427. See also "The 'Criminal Type' of Development", *The Lancet*, 15 February 1879, pp. 239–40.

26 C. H. S. Jayewardine, "The English Precursors of Lombroso", *British Journal of Criminology*, vol. 4, no. 1, July 1963, pp. 164–70.

Chapter One

Prologue: Bumps, Bull-terriers and Habituals

There is in the metropolis, and other large towns, a class of persons who are so inveterately addicted to dishonesty, and so averse to labour, that there is no chance of their ceasing to seek their existence by depredations on the public, unless they are compulsorily withdrawn, for a very considerable time from their accustomed haunts.

Royal Commission on Transportation and Penal Servitude, 1863[1]

There are few greater errors than to suppose that all, or even the majority of the dangerous classes are continually passing through the hands of justice.

Daily Telegraph, 14 November 1862[2]

There is a strong case for arguing that to all intents and purposes British criminology was born in the space of a few short months in 1869 and early 1870. It may be considered perverse to attempt such precision when talking about the origins of a mode of scientific discourse, when it is customary to erect around such statements a dense thicket of caveats about "precursors", "influences" and so on. Certainly, criminology textbooks—like the influential collection of biographical essays edited by Herman Mannheim[3]—often take the story back much further, to Enlightenment penal theorists like Cesare Beccaria (1738–1794) and Jeremy Bentham (1748–1832). More recently American criminologist Nicole Hahn Rafter has put a strong case for tracing the discipline's origins back to the turn of the eighteenth and nineteenth centuries, when psychiatrists like Benjamin Rush, James Prichard and Philippe Pinel developed their conceptions of "moral insanity".[4]

The second group of theorists are certainly more likely suspects than the first, with their championing of rigorous scientific method—dispassionate observation, precise measurement and indicative reasoning—in order to explore the darker recesses of the criminal psyche. Practitioners of physiognomy and phrenology, at the peak of their influence in Britain in the 1820s and '30s, could also be placed in this category, even if their theories would later be dismissed by mainstream medical science as mere quackery. Like the psychiatrists (or "alienists" as they were known at this period), physiognomists and phrenologists insisted on the scientific credentials of their claims that the close observation of the proportions of the face or of the contours of the skull (the latter involving literally a "hands-on" approach to data gathering) could afford vital clues to the working of the human mind—including the *criminal* mind.

There is a fundamental difficulty, however, in describing these early practitioners as "criminologists". Neither the alienists nor the physiognomists and phrenologists were *primarily* interested in investigating the causes of criminal behaviour. Their interest in crime and criminals, though real enough, was in terms of a possible contribution to a larger project: the construction of an all-encompassing theory of the workings of the human mind, or in the case of the alienists, the *abnormal* human mind. "None of these discourses", as David Garland points out, "was struggling to create a distinctive criminological enterprise, though once such a subject was created, each formed a resource to be drawn upon, usually in a way which wrenched its insights about crime apart from the framework which originally produced them."[5]

It is revealing in this context that no British alienist or physiognomist working in the first half of the nineteenth century produced a book-length study of criminal behaviour. There is phrenologist Marmaduke B. Sampson's *Criminal Jurisprudence Considered in Relation to Mental Organisation* (1841)[6], a work perhaps better-known in its expanded American version of 1846, edited by Eliza Farnham, matron of Mount Pleasant State Prison, New York.[7] (Interestingly, the American edition of Sampson's book, with footnotes and appendices by Miss Farnham, also carried a small number of engravings based on daguerreotypes of criminals, which she had commissioned from future Civil War photographer Matthew Brady.[8] Readers were invited to compare the images of the prison inmates—bearing captions like "B. F. is vicious, cruel and apparently incapable of any elevated or humane sentiments"—with a number of "heads of persons possessing superior intellect".[9] The reader's attention was directed to the "striking contrast" between the two. Indeed, Eliza Farnham's edition of Sampson's book may well be the first published instance of photography being used, albeit indirectly, to portray the "criminal type".[10]) However, there is no evidence that the author of the original British work—unlike Eliza Farnham, or French contemporary Hubert Lauvergne (1796–1859)[11]—considered himself in any sense a specialist in the scientific study of crime.[12] Surely, such endeavours, important though they are to later developments, cannot in any meaningful sense be termed the work of "criminologists".

If we consider the term *criminology*, as I have argued elsewhere[13], to denote the self-conscious application of scientific principles to the study of crime and criminals, embracing such issues as causation, correction and prevention, and a criminologist as someone whose efforts to apply these principles are a *central* and not merely peripheral aspect of his or her research, then in the British case at least, we are drawn ineluctably towards the end of the 1860s. January 1870 saw the publication in the *Journal of Mental Science* of an article by Dr J. Bruce Thomson (1810–1873), resident surgeon at Scotland's Perth convict prison. He had occupied the post since 1858 and would remain there until his death in 1873. The article, just eleven pages long, was called "The Hereditary Nature of Crime".[14] A second, longer article appeared in the same journal later the same year.[15] The first of Thomson's articles contains the author's reflections on the physical and mental characteristics of the criminal class (a point to which we will return later), and his gloomy assertion that crime is "intractable to the highest degree and must be so because it is hereditary." "Is it be marvelled", he asks with a rhetorical flourish, "if these premises are correct, that all modes of criminal treatment, severe or mild, have failed in giving anything like satisfactory results?" There was some hope of catching juvenile offenders before they succumbed to these hereditary impulses, but for "old offenders", the prospects were all but hopeless.[16]

Dr Thomson's pessimistic emphasis on what alienist Dr Henry Maudsley would shortly refer to as "the tyranny of a bad organisation"[17] was far from unique, either within the prison medical service or without. The previous year, Dr George Wilson, assistant surgeon at Woking convict prison, had read a paper to a meeting of the British Association for the Advancement of Science, entitled "On Moral Imbecility of Habitual Criminals as Exemplified by Cranial Measurement".[18] We shall return presently to the medical, penological and broader scientific context in which these two prison doctors were working, but first of all something should be said about the roots of this dyed-in-the-wool pessimism, for it was in fact fairly recent in origin.

Just forty years earlier, great hopes were still being held out for a very different—and much more optimistic—conception of the Criminal, and of the institution in which his permanent reformation would be effected. The significantly-named *Penitentiary* would, it was argued, function, in Jeremy Bentham's grimly memorable phrase, as a "mill for grinding rogues honest and idle men industrious."[19] While Bentham's own favoured solution, the *Panopticon*, a circular glass and iron structure with a free-standing central observation tower casting its unblinking gaze over a ring of individual cells, had been turned down by a parliamentary inquiry in 1811[20], the penitentiary principle was retained[21], and by the end of the following year the Home Office had begun construction of the country's first purpose-built convict prison. Situated on a sixteen-acre site at Millbank on the banks of the Thames below Westminster, the new penitentiary received its first batch of prisoners in 1816.[22] For the next thirty-five years or so, the penitentiary ideal would remain intact, though it had to cope with sniping from local justices (who resented being excluded from this Home Office project) as well as from those who, for a variety of reasons, considered *transportation* an altogether more satisfactory way of dealing with the country's more serious criminals.

The credo of the penal reformers supporting the penitentiary project was a resolutely optimistic one. Providing criminals were isolated both from their corrupting environment and from each other, were exposed to the morally-invigorating rigours of hard physical labour and left for long periods in the sole company of their Maker to contemplate the enormity of their crimes, they could be successfully cleansed of their criminal propensities and would in time be ready to be re-born as useful members of the community. Here was an unashamedly environmentalist theory of criminal causation, one in keeping with the intense evangelical faith which drove many reformers.[23] Just as no sinner was beyond redemption, so no criminal heart was entirely devoid of Christian impulses. It was a matter of stripping off the filth accumulated by a life of moral degradation and nurturing what George Laval Chesterton, former governor at Cold Bath Fields House of Correction, called the "innate, but long concealed virtue". The existence of the latter, Chesterton noted in his memoirs of 1856, was "a fact too largely observed to admit any doubt whatsoever."[24]

The reformers were under no illusions as to the difficulty of the task. Governor Chesterton again:

> It seems almost superfluous to affirm how largely the lowest neighbourhoods of the metropolis and of our populous manufacturing towns contribute their quota to the pests and outcasts which infest society, and how above all things, those foetid localities engender that fertile parent of every vice, *idleness*. ... Thus the dens of Westminster, the Borough, Cow Cross, the alleys of Grays Inn Lane, and Whitechapel, stand attested in the mere gait and sinister aspect of these degraded beings ... they present the example of creatures swathed in vice, nurtured in the foulest degeneracy, and at length, launched into an active participation in fraud and spoliation.[25]

Like an unruly horse unused to the bit and the saddle, these "degraded beings" would have to be "broken" before they could become receptive to the Christian message. The Reverend John Burt, sometime assistant chaplain at Pentonville (the country's second purpose-built penitentiary, opened in 1842), put across this point clearly in an article of 1852:

> The passions of the criminal by which he is chiefly actuated, are usually excessive and malignant. Penal discipline finds the will vigorous, but vicious, propelled powerfully, but lawlessly. It is this vicious activity that is subjugated by protracted seclusion and wholesome discipline. ... The will is ... subdued ... bent or broken, and the moral character is ... made plastic by the discipline ... The will is bent in its direction; it is broken in its resistance to virtue, its vicious activity is suppressed only to leave it open to the control of better motives.[26]

Exactly how moral character was to be "made plastic by the discipline" was a matter of longstanding and often acrimonious disagreement. Was each prison inmate to be kept entirely separated from his fellows, his cell serving as "his workshop by day and his bed-room by night", as leading prison official Sir Joshua Jebb urged, an arrangement which "effectively prevented [him] from holding communication with, or even being sufficiently recognised by other prisoners"?[27] Or was this regime of near-total isolation—known as "the separate system"—a recipe for insanity and/or suicide, and therefore to be avoided at all costs?

Supporters of the main alternative to separation, the so-called "silent system", clearly thought so. Their preferred regime involved limited association among prisoners but in an atmosphere of total silence, with immediate punishment for any infringement of the silent rule. Advocates of the silent system included Chesterton and a young Charles Dickens, who penned a fierce condemnation of separate confinement after visiting Pennsylvania's Eastern Penitentiary in 1842.[28] However, it was the rival separate system which won the day, and following the appointment of the country's first prison inspectors in 1835, it was a regime of close confinement which became official policy both for the country's penitentiaries and the many local prisons being constructed or adapted to accommodate the new regime.[29]

Millbank had initially been saddled with a mixture of the two systems, with complete isolation for newly-arrived inmates and the silent rule for those in the latter stages of their sentences. The hybrid regime had been adopted (following the recommendations of the same parliamentary select committee which had dashed Bentham's hopes for the Panopticon) to blend the best of both systems, but ended up pleasing no-one. The

Reverend Daniel Nihill, chaplain-governor of the penitentiary between 1837 and 1843, summed up what had by now become official orthodoxy in a book published in 1839:

> In spite of the most vigilant superintendence, they [the prisoners] will sip enough of communication to defeat discipline and to subserve bad purposes, while the hindrance of harmless communication excites a sense of injustice, or confounds their moral notions, taking off the conscience from real guilt, and occupying it with that which is local, temporary and artificial.[30]

When reformation of prisoners was achieved, Nihill argued, it was uniquely thanks to the rigours of separate confinement, while the silent system

> … prevent[s] much of the good that would otherwise accrue from separation; … much which is actually accomplished, is marred and counteracted from the same cause. In short, *the intercourse of prisoners is the bane of the General Penitentiary*.[31]

Where a fully-fledged separate system was put in place, as in the early years of Jebb's Model Prison at Pentonville, care was taken to limit as far as possible both "communication" and "recognition". This was achieved by such devices as stalled chapels and classrooms in which prisoners, each in their own personal cubicle or "upright coffin"[32], could see the chaplain or schoolmaster, but not each other. In a similar spirit, plans were made for exercise yards to be partitioned. At Pentonville, Jebb approved a structure resembling a large cartwheel, one hundred feet in diameter, placed on the ground. The triangle-shaped compartments, created by the "spokes" were separated from each other by ten-foot walls. In each compartment, a prisoner could be exercised in isolation for an hour.[33]

Such cumbersome arrangements, often involving an infernally complex series of partitions, gates and covered walkways, not only taxed the ingenuity of prison architects but also tugged at the purse-strings of the prison authorities as well, requiring as they did both a large capital outlay, and high levels of manpower to operate.[34] There were other problems too. One long-serving prison guard at Millbank recalled that the only way he had avoided getting lost in the penitentiary's warren of tunnels and walkways was to leave a trail of marks in chalk to indicate the route he had taken.[35]

In practice, despite such elaborate precautions, enforcing complete isolation was to prove well nigh impossible. Indeed, as Randall McGowen observes:

> Prisoners were inventive in discovering ways to subvert the penal regime. … They developed a form of ventriloquism, the art of talking without moving one's lips [and] the prison at night was filled with the sounds of tapping as pipes became the medium for telegraphic communication. Some prisoners created chat holes through which they could speak to each other. They relayed information on where to find nails that would make oakum picking, the separation of strands of old rope, easier. They told how to step on the treadwheel so as to make the ordeal less exhausting.[36]

There was thus a constant battle of wits between prison officials and their charges to respectively limit and subvert Jebb's twin banes of "communication" and "recognition". As far as the latter was concerned, the solution adopted for a time was to provide prisoners with a brown cap, equipped with a long peak, so fashioned as to hide the face. Two holes were cut to allow the wearer to see where he was going. In principle, the caps were to be worn whenever the prisoner had to leave his cell, principally in the exercise yard.[37]

Talking was strictly forbidden during exercise time, as the masked prisoners, all identically dressed in prison tunic and trousers, followed a prearranged circuit around the prison yard. A route of concentric circles might be marked on the ground to keep the shuffling prisoners apart, or in some cases a long rope, with knots at regular intervals, served the same purpose. *Morning Chronicle* journalist Henry Mayhew (1812–1887) witnessed such a scene at Pentonville when he visited the prison with colleague John Binny in the late 1850s (by which time Jebb's cartwheel-like arrangement had presumably been abandoned).[38] The following extract from Mayhew and Binny's book, *The Criminal Prisons of London and Scenes of Prison Life* (1862), represents an interesting verbal counterpoint to Gustave Doré's well-known visual image of the prison exercise yard, sketched at Newgate a decade later[39]:

> … each of the prisoners is not only clad alike—and brown as so many bees pouring forth from the countless cells of a hive—but every one wears a peculiar brown cap … [which] cover[s] the face like a mask, the eyes alone of the individual appearing through the two holes cut in the front, and seeming almost like phosphoric lights shining through the sockets of the skull. This gives to the prisoners a half-spectral look … the costume of the men seems like the outward vestment to some wandering soul rather than that of a human being; for the eyes glistening through the apertures in the mask give one the notion of a spirit peeping out behind it, so that there is something positively terrible in the idea that these are men whose crimes have caused their very features to be hidden from the world.[40]

Mayhew and Binny's description of Pentonville, as indeed their book as a whole, is indicative of that "potent mixture of ill-digested scientific concept and unmistakable fear" which, W. J. Forsythe points out, characterised much contemporary writing on the criminal class.[41] A second passage from the Pentonville chapter of *Criminal Prisons*, concerning a murderer observed in the exercise yard, illustrates this point forcefully:

> … we saw sufficient of the features of the felon—for he returned our glance with a savage stare—to teach us, or rather to make us believe (and it is astonishing what physiognomical foresight we obtained *after* such traits of character), that he was thoroughly capable of the act for which he was suffering. He had been a pitman in the north, and had the peculiar freckled, iron-mouldy, Scottish complexion, whilst his cheek bones were high, his face broad and flat, and his neck short and thick as a bull-terrier's to which animal, indeed, he appeared to be a kind of human counterpart. As we saw him prowling there, round and round within his deep, narrow yard, he reminded us of a man-beast caged up in some anthropo-zoological gardens.[42]

Interestingly, Mayhew and Binny were well aware of the danger of simply recycling the kind of physiognomic stereotypes already current in popular depictions of the Criminal in the 1850s and '60s. In fact, it had become axiomatic by that time, as art historian Mary Cowling explains, that an individual's criminal character could be "read" from a "disproportionate" and/or "irregular" face;[43] or in the jargon of the physiognomist, that "The configuration of the head of all criminals diverges in a greater or lesser ratio, from the fixed geometrical quantities that each section of the brain should possess."[44]

The general notion that a criminal's face was less pleasing to the eye, that in Roy Porter's phrase, the body was "the signature of the soul"[45], was nothing new of course—it went back at least to Classical times—but in its scientific garb, it is associated above all with the writings of Swiss theologian Johann Kaspar Lavater (1741–1801). In his *Essays on Physiognomy*, first published in English in 1789, Lavater had defined physiognomy as "the science of knowledge of the correspondence between the external and internal man, the visible superficies, and the invisible contents."[46] He divided the human face into three zones: the mouth and chin represented Man's "animal nature"; the nose and cheeks his "moral nature" and the forehead and eyebrows his "intellectual nature".[47] Lavater had insisted that

> Precision in observation is the very soul of physiognomy. The physiognomist must possess a most delicate, swift, certain, most extensive spirit of observation … To observe, to be attentive, to distinguish what

> is similar, what dissimilar, to discover proportion, and disproportion, is the office of his understanding.[48]

In practice, almost any physical deformity could be given as evidence of criminal propensities, but, Cowling observes,

> … the one most frequently cited [in the Victorian period] is the extreme form associated with low development; that is a disproportionately large jaw and face in relation to the higher faculties of the mind, indicated by the size of the forehead and skull. Such an imbalance suggested a predominance of the senses and, at least, a disposition to crime.[49]

This was "the criminal type of head" described by British physiognomist W. Hatfield in his book *Face Reading* (1870): low and broad, with wide lips, and a short and thick or "bullish" neck. Gapped teeth and a convex chin were also frequently mentioned in contemporary accounts.[50]

Illustrations from the period also played an important role in reinforcing such stereotypes. Just as Sydney Paget's illustrations for the *Strand Magazine* would later fix in the minds of its readers the chisel-featured appearance of Sherlock Holmes, so illustrations in popular magazines like *Punch* or the *Illustrated London News*—whether explicitly caricatured or purportedly "realistic"—served, as it were, to fix stereotypical images of the criminal.[51]

"High" culture of the period was also suffused with images of criminals inspired by physiognomic principles. Mary Cowling has made a detailed study of two paintings by one of the most respected artists of the mid-Victorian period, William Powell Frith (1819–1909).[52] A fellow of the Royal Academy, Frith's speciality was the panorama of contemporary life, as seen for example in *Derby Day* (1858) and *The Railway Station* (1862). In the latter case, the artist's depiction of one of the characters on his crowded canvas as a man with heavy brows, wide nostrils, and protruding and sensual lips clearly sent out the appropriate physiognomic signals in order to identify him as a reprobate. Cowling quotes ten different newspapers and magazines whose reviews of the painting came to virtually identical conclusions about the character's "low", "brutish", "hardened" and "dissipated" nature, simply on the basis of a close scrutiny of his face. We were clearly, as one particularly damning review put it, in the presence of a future "gallows bird". Only one art critic, writing in the *Sunday Times*, begged to differ, describing him as "a healthy, hardy, upstanding *rough*, who … will make an excellent soldier."[53] Even here however, Frith's character was correctly identified as a member of the working classes, indicative of widespread agreement as to the physical characteristics of each social class "type". According to one physiognomist, it was possible to determine "the rank of each in the social scale as readily as you can tell a general from a captain by his shoulder straps."[54]

Physiognomy was not, of course, the only science which made such claims on the basis of external—particularly facial—differences. Since the publication in French in 1809 of the works by German anatomist Franz Joseph Gall (1758–1828) and his Austrian assistant John Caspar Spurzheim (1776–1832)[55], the science of "phrenology" had claimed to provide a window on Man's soul through expert palpation of the head. Whether the subject was living or dead (and phrenologists examined both), the skull offered up purportedly unequivocal evidence concerning the innermost workings of the human brain. Three fundamental assumptions lay behind the discipline's claim to scientific truth. First, that the exterior conformation of the skull matched both its interior surface and the conformation of the brain. Second, that the mind could be analysed in terms of innate faculties or functions. Third, that the shape and size of protuberances on the surface of the skull reflected the development of these faculties (hence the term "bumpology" used by phrenology's detractors).

Gall—whose research methods included stopping people in the street if he noticed their heads had "any distinct protuberance"[56]—believed that each psychological character or "power" (he initially identified twenty-seven[57]) had its physiological counterpart in a specifically located organ or "seat" of the brain. It was after establishing the size of these various organs—via giveaway bumps—on a particular skull that the trained phrenologist was able to construct a psychological profile of the individual in question.[58] Like its sister science, physiognomy, phrenology adopted a three-way division of the human mind. Instead of Lavater's "animal", "moral" and "intellectual" regions of the face, Gall provided us with "propensities", "sentiments" and "intellectual" powers. What physiognomists had mapped onto the human face, phrenologists ascribed to precise regions of the skull.[59]

Possibly because of its scientific lineage—with a respected anatomist rather than an obscure theologian as its inventor—phrenology was of greater interest to the medical profession than physiognomy's recycling of handed-down folk wisdom.[60] Indeed, leading phrenologists were at pains to distinguish their discipline from the work of "mere" physiognomists. In his book *On the Functions of the Brain* (1822–1825), Gall dismissed the work of Lavater in the following terms:

> A physiognomist, Lavater for example, is not at all guided by the knowledge of anatomy and of physiology; the laws of the organisation of the nervous system in general, and of the brain in particular, are unknown

> to them; they have no idea of the different composition of the brain in different species of animals; they take no account of the different results of the different development of the cerebral parts. They know not the influence, which the brain exerts on the form of the head …[61]

However, the fact that its subtleties could apparently be mastered by practitioners without any formal medical training made phrenology a potential threat as well. It is significant in this context that Britain's first phrenological society was founded in 1820 not by a doctor but by George Combe (1788–1858), an Edinburgh lawyer. After having been introduced to Dr Spurzheim at an dinner party in the Scottish capital (where the latter produced a brain from a paper bag, and proceeded to dissect it in front of the assembled guests), Combe went on to become Britain's leading authority on the subject. His book, *The Constitution of Man and its Relation to External Objects*, published in 1828 had, by 1860, sold over 100 000 copies. (By way of comparison, Darwin's *On the Origin of Species* would only sell half that number over an equivalent period). A whole network of phrenological societies and journals soon sprung up all over the country.[62]

Phrenology's heyday in Britain was in the 1820s and 1830s, although both the medical profession and educated opinion in general remained divided on the validity of its claims. Doctors were impressed by the range of Gall and Spurzheim's knowledge of anatomy, which by association gave added weight to their phrenological deductions. The scientific study of mental illness was in its infancy, and here again, phrenology claimed to provide the key to unlocking the "unbalanced mind". There were of course examples of outright rejection of Combe's boast that phrenology could provide the "clearest, the most complete, and the best supported system of human nature"[63], but probably a more common reaction among doctors and surgeons was to see in it at least some elements of truth which would, in time, be integrated into mainstream medical science.[64]

As for lay opinion, phrenology's aspiration to provide an agreeably comprehensive explanation for the workings of the human mind, with rational laws just as structured as those governing any other aspect of the natural world, couched in language that did not demand specialised scientific knowledge, and based on studies of individual conduct recorded by reputable (often non-phrenological) authorities, all help account for its popularity.[65] Historian of British phrenology, Roger Cooter, compares its attraction for the Victorian middle-class public to that obtained from

> … gazing through the open front of a Victorian doll's house. [… One is confronted] not only with order and classification par excellence, but also (just as with the actual workings of the middle-class

> Victorian home) with a clear hierarchy of spaces for specialised functions and duties.[66]

With much of Franz Gall's early examination of heads carried out among subjects found in jails and lunatic asylums, it is understandable that he was led to reflect on the "causes" of criminal behaviour. Given our earlier discussion of criminal stereotypes, it should come as no surprise to learn that Gall and his fellow phrenologists considered that it was the so-called "lower propensities" which provided the key to understanding criminal nature. Of particular importance, according to phrenologists, were the propensities of amativeness, philoprogenitiveness, combativeness, secretiveness, and acquisitiveness. There was also a specific organ on the side of the head above the ear, "destructiveness", which, if unduly developed, could lead to murder.[67] The possession in an individual of such lower propensities was considered sufficient to account for criminal behaviour, though phrenologists were at pains to point out that in most cases they could be held in check by higher "sentiments" or ruled by intellectual powers.[68]

Spurzheim played a key role in the development of this more optimistic strand of phrenological thinking. "Bring men into favourable situations calculated to call forth their feelings", he wrote in 1828, "and these will be strengthened."[69] Thus,

> ... because post-Gall phrenologists conceived of the brain as malleable and capable of change, they were able to combine their determinism with an optimistic rehabilitative approach to crime and other social problems without a sense of contradiction. Conceiving of character traits as heritable but not fixed, they could simultaneously argue that criminals are not responsible for their crimes *and* that, with treatment, they can be cured of criminality.[70]

A good example of such thinking is Frederick Bridges's *Criminals, Crimes and their Governing Laws, as Demonstrated by the Sciences of Physiology and Mental Geometry* (1860). In addition to singing the praises of a mathematical instrument of his own invention, the "Phreno-physiometer", Bridges cautions his readers as follows:

> There is one remarkable feature connected with Criminals and Crimes, which those who condemn would do well to keep in view; and that is, that if they had received a brain of a quality and formation similar to that of the unfortunate criminal, and had been surrounded by the same external influences, they would have acted in precisely a similar manner.[71]

Phrenological societies were commonly sent skulls for examination from all over Britain, including those of executed criminals. Where original crania were not available, a cast would be provided instead. Not only were such skulls relatively easy to obtain, they were also considered to be of enormous value to phrenology, offering as they did the opportunity to correlate cranial observations with known details of the individual criminal's character. The heads of living criminals were also examined to this end, both among Britain's prison population, and among those transported to the country's penal colonies overseas.[72]

Flora Tristan's *London Journal* (1840) recalls a chance encounter in Newgate Gaol between the author and Dr John Elliotson, leading London phrenologist and close friend of Charles Dickens.[73] Elliotson, who could apparently "always be found in prisons and insane asylums studying convex protuberances and divining concave ones", proceeded to explain to the young Frenchwoman why a young soldier she had just seen had murdered an officer of his regiment. "He killed him", she was told, "because he has two pronounced protuberances, that of *pride*, and that of *revenge*." Case closed, at least as far as Dr Elliotson was concerned.

In similar fashion, the phrenological examination of a prisoner at Newcastle jail in 1835 by George Combe produced the following portrait:

> T. S., aged 18. … Destructiveness is very large; Combativeness, Secretiveness, and Acquisitiveness are large; intellectual organs fairly developed; Amativeness is large; Conscientiousness rather moderate; Benevolence is full, and Veneration rather large. This boy is considerably different from the last. He is more violent in his dispositions; he has probably been committed for assault connected with women. He has also large Secretiveness and Acquisitiveness, and may have stolen, although I think this less probable. He has fair intellectual talents, and is an improveable subject.[74]

As Combe's closing remark suggests, phrenologists conceived of their science as furnishing a useful therapeutic tool for the reform of prisoners. Captain Alexander Maconochie (1787–1860) sought to put in place a regime based partly on phrenological principles when he was appointed superintendent of the infamous penal station at Norfolk Island, Australia, in 1840.[75] The system of "kindness without weakness" he put in place there during his four-year appointment, was based on the principle of "stimulating mental exertion" in those parts of the brain where the organs of "benevolence" were located.[76] In fact, he favoured abandoning fixed terms of imprisonment altogether, in favour of a system in which prisoners would be sentenced to earn a defined number of "marks", to be awarded by prison staff for good conduct and taken away for misdemeanours. W. J. Forsythe explains:

> In consequence, the entire energies of the prisoner would be harnessed to success in all the tasks required of him, because his predicament and release date would wholly depend on his efforts. The prisoners would learn that 'exertion and good conduct' were inevitably associated with reward and pleasure and they would go out with 'habits and … intentions and views founded upon ... an inseparable connection in the mind of the prisoner between industry and self denial and advantage to himself'.[77]

Maconochie eschewed specifically phrenological language in his published works. However, as David De Giustino has shown, he maintained a correspondence with Combe and other leading phrenologists in the 1840s and '50s, often expressing—in private—his support for their theories. His public reticence (which some phrenologists, including Combe, seemed to have held against him) may well have been prompted by an awareness that giving overt backing to "bumpology" would have seriously damaged his chances of promotion in the convict prison service.[78]

According to phrenologists, there was a category of prisoners incapable of reform, whatever the skill of the phrenological therapist. Such "Irredeemables", they argued, were unsuitable for transportation overseas to penal colonies like Norfolk Island. Instead, it was felt that such criminals should remain in the Mother Country, held in specialised prisons where they could be observed and further classified according to the tenets of phrenological science by appropriately trained experts.[79]

Such a sifting of candidates for transportation was the intention of the plan mooted in 1836 by aristocrat and phrenology buff, Sir George Stewart Mackenzie. Among the forty-six letters supporting his proposal addressed to Secretary for the Colonies, Lord Glenelg, were testimonials from the surgeon of Portsmouth Prison, and the governors of two of Glasgow's penal institutions. In a letter to George Combe written in April 1836, William Brebner, governor of the County and City Bridewell, Glasgow, wrote:

> About two thousand persons pass through this establishment yearly, and I have had the charge for upwards of twenty-five years. During that period, and long before I heard anything of Phrenology, I was often struck with the extraordinary shape of the heads of most of the criminals. … I have no hesitation in saying that the most notoriously bad characters have a confirmation of head very different from those of the common run of mankind.[80]

Brebner added that after witnessing Combe, Spurzheim and other phrenological experts at work in his prison, he had been impressed by the "very remarkable manner" in which they had "described the character and told the leading propensities of the inmates."[81] George Salmond,

Procurator-Fiscal of Lanarkshire, also saw Combe in action in April 1836, this time at Glasgow Jail. The following account of what he witnessed, again contained in a letter to Combe, was counter-signed by both the governor of the prison, and the Sheriff-Substitute of Lanarkshire:

> I was very much pleased to observe, that while your examination of each did not average more than a minute, you instantly and without hesitation stated the character, not generally but with specialities of feelings and propensities, surprisingly justified by what I knew of them; and being aware that you had no access to them, nor means of knowing them previously, as they were taken at the moment promiscuously from numbers of other criminals, I was at once led to a conviction of the truth of the science ...[82]

Despite such pleas to harness phrenological expertise to protect colonists in New South Wales from the worst elements of Britain's criminal classes, neither Mackenzie nor Maconochie had any success in changing official policy.[83]

There were similar theories circulating in the USA at this period. We have already referred to Eliza Farnham, matron of Mount Pleasant State Prison, New York, and her influential 1846 edition of Marmaduke Sampson's *Treatise on Criminal Jurisprudence,* one of the relatively few works in English devoted entirely to the phrenological approach to crime. Possibly influenced by George Combe, who had examined the heads of prisoners during a visit to America in 1838–1940 and written on the subject on his return[84], she urged the case for phrenological "treatment" as an alternative to capital punishment. She read books to her inmates and brought in musicians and lecturers in a belief that, through practice, underused organs could be returned to normality.[85]

"No sound system of criminal legislation and prison discipline", wrote Combe in 1854, "can be reached while the influence of the organism on the dispositions and capacities of men continues to be ignored."[86] Approbation for such claims from within the penal system was unusual, at least on this side of the Atlantic.[87] There was, though, a great deal of common ground between the phrenologists and those voices calling for root and branch reform of Britain's penal institutions. Thus many of the causes championed by Combe and his circle in the 1820s and '30s (including the separation of different categories of prisoners, the importance of manual labour for prisoners, and the value of separate confinement) would later find their way into official government policy.[88]

Although phrenology's star had waned by the 1850s and '60s, the kind of assumptions on which both it and physiognomy were based continued to influence mainstream descriptions of the Criminal. The following extract from William Hepworth Dixon's *The London Prisons* (1850) is typical:

> A man who has not seen masses of men in a great prison, cannot conceive how hideous the human countenance can become. Looking in the front of these benches, one sees only demons. … the vast mass of heads and faces seem made and stamped by nature for criminal acts. Such low, misshapen brows; such animal and sensual mouths and jaws; such cunning, reckless, or stupid looks—hardly seem to belong to anything that can by courtesy be called human.[89]

These are the precisely kind of descriptions that Mayhew and Binny claimed to eschew. Observing a Sunday church service in Pentonville prison, the authors note:

> The general run of the countenances and skulls are very far from being of that brutal or semi-idiotic character, such as caricaturists love to picture as connected with the criminal race … whilst a few are certainly remarkable for the coarse and rudely-mouthed features—the high cheek-bones and prognathous mouths—that are often associated with the *hard-bred* portion of our people, … there is hardly one [head] that bears the least resemblance to the vulgar baboon-like types that unobservant artists still depict as representative of the convict character … even the keenest eye for character would be unable to distinguish a photograph of the criminal from the non-criminal congregation.[90]

However, despite their best intentions, they appear unable to shake off entirely the physiognomist's mind-set.[91] Here is how they describe the arrival of a new batch of prisoners at Pentonville:

> On descending from the omnibus, the new prisoners were drawn up in five rows on one side of the court-yard. They were of all ages—from mere boys to old men of between fifty and sixty. Nor were their expressions of features less various; some looked as bad as a physiognomist would say, 'really bad fellows', whilst others appeared to have even a 'respectable' countenance, the features being well-formed rather than coarse, and the expression marked by frankness rather than cunning, so that one could not help wondering what hard pressure of circumstance had brought *them* there.

Thus, the authors make instant judgments about the "respectability" or otherwise of particular prisoners on the basis of established physiognomical criteria. It is assumed that those with "well-formed rather than coarse" features had been pushed into crime by force of circumstance, rather than being "natural" criminals. This distinction is made explicit in the continuation of the previous passage:

> It did not require much skill in detecting character to pick out the habitual offender from the casual criminal, or to distinguish the simple, broad brown face of the agricultural convict from the knowing, sharp, pale features of the town thief.[92]

This distinction made by Mayhew and Binny between the "habitual" and the "casual" or "accidental" offender alludes to one of several systems of classification juxtaposed rather confusingly by the authors; all part of an "attempt at a scientific classification of the criminal classes".[93] In fact, the end result provides a good example of the kind of "ill-digested" scientific concepts referred to earlier by W. J. Forsythe. Thus in addition to the dichotomous habitual-casual division, they also refer to "three distinct families" of criminals (beggars, cheats and thieves) and later three "classes" of criminal: a "well-educated class" of casual criminals (forgers, embezzlers etc.); an "imperfectly educated class" ("town criminals", including pickpockets, burglars etc.); and a "comparatively uneducated class" (the "lower kind of city thieves", "agricultural labourers turned sheep-stealers", etc.).[94] It is the second of these three "classes"—more or less conterminous with their earlier "habitual" category—that clearly worries the authors the most. While the first and third groups provide "the greater number of cases of reformation", the second "is exceedingly difficult of real improvement, though the most ready of all to *feign* conversion."[95]

This last remark picks up a point made elsewhere in *The Criminal Prisons of London*, that of an almost animal "cunning" attributed to the intractable habitual criminal. The authors describe for example the "strong animal passions" of the "'brutal violence' class of prisoners", with their "peculiar lascivious look"—"... a trait which is as much developed in the attention paid to the hair, as in the look of the eyes or the play of the mouth." Such views are symptomatic of what Martin Wiener calls the "spectre of instinctualism" which shaped early- and mid-Victorian images of criminality, "a polarity between restraint, frequently identified with civilisation itself, and instincts or impulses, identified with 'barbarism' or 'savagery'."[96]

Mayhew and Binny's prisoners clearly fall into the latter category, seeming "as if they were ready to burst into laughter at the least frivolity, thus denoting that it is almost impossible to excite in their minds any deep or lasting impression."[97] Similarly, during a visit to Newgate jail, the deputy-governor showed the authors a series of busts of murderers executed on the premises. The bust of James Greenacre, a notorious early-Victorian murderer (later to be immortalised in Madame Tussaud's Chamber of Horrors[98]), is described by Mayhew and Binny as having "a very sinister appearance. The brow is narrow and low, and the underface sensual, strongly indicative of a man of low, passionate character."[99]

Mayhew and Binny's criminals were then clearly conceived as "a distinct race of individuals, as distinct as the Malay is from the Caucasian tribe."[100] Like Mayhew's earlier, and better-known, study of the working class of the Capital, *London Labour and the London Poor*, published in four volumes between 1851 and 1862, *Criminal Prisons* sought to identify criminals with that class of "human parasites" which preys on "every civilised and barbarous community".[101] This conception, no doubt influenced by Mayhew's reading of the accounts of contemporary ethnologists and travel writers, is made more explicit in *London Labour*. In volume 1, published in 1851, he wrote:

> Of the thousand millions of human beings that are said to constitute the population of the entire globe, there are—socially, morally, and perhaps even physically considered—but two distinct and broadly marked races, viz., the wanderers and the settlers—the vagabond and the citizen—the nomadic and the civilised tribes.[102]

Every civilised race, Mayhew suggested, had its parasitic nomads: the Hottentots had the Bushmen and Sonquas, the Arabs had the Bedouins, and the Finns had the Lapps. So far, he went on, no-one had sought to apply such an analysis to "certain anomalies in the present state of society among ourselves." Mayhew returned on several occasions to this ethnological parallel, describing himself as a "traveller in the undiscovered country of the poor" and his object of study a country "of whom the public has less knowledge than of the most distant tribes of the earth."[103] Contemporary reviewers responded in similar vein, praising Mayhew for having "travelled through the unknown regions of our metropolis, and returned with full reports concerning the strange tribes of men which he may be said to have discovered."[104] Indeed, the author of *London Labour and the London Poor* can be seen as the first in a long line of social explorers, ready to venture into what George Sims would call that "dark continent that is within easy walking distance of the General Post Office."[105]

Like other civilised tribes, the English had their cross to bear, in the form of hordes of "paupers, beggars, and outcasts, possessing nothing but what they acquire by depredation from the industrious, provident, and civilised portion of the community."[106] He went on to describe the physical and mental characteristics of this wandering class, among whom were:

> ... the pickpockets—the beggars—the prostitutes—the street-sellers—the street-performers—the cabmen—the coachmen—the watermen—

> the sailors and such like. In each of these classes—according as they partake more or less of the purely vagabond ... so will the attributes of the nomad tribes be more or less marked in them. ... we must all allow that in each of the classes above mentioned, there is a greater development of the animal than of the intellectual or moral nature of man, and that they are all more or less distinguished for their high cheek-bones and protruding jaws—for their use of slang language—for their lax ideas of property—for their general improvidence—their repugnance to continual labour—their disregard of female honour—their love of cruelty—their pugnacity—and their utter want of religion. [107]

The influence of anthropology can also be detected in a rather different form in Mayhew and Binny's description of the "man-beast" prowling around Pentonville exercise yard. The language they use to link his physical characteristics to a particular British regional "type" ("... the peculiar freckled, iron-mouldy, Scottish complexion, ... cheek bones ... high, ... face broad and flat, ... neck short and thick as a bull-terrier's") is strongly reminiscent of anthropological writing of the period. Many anthropologists of the mid- and late-Victorian periods saw their primary task as the uncovering of underlying "pure" racial "types" from the confusing variety observable, a variety explained essentially in terms of successive waves of migration and conquest. Measuring head shape and size (a technique known as "craniometry") was the most widely-accepted marker of racial affinity, having the advantage of remaining stable over long periods.[108] Heads, as leading practitioner Robert Dunn enthused, "speak a language which cannot be mistaken".[109]

The presumed physical contrasts which marked the three major social classes, already well-known to physiognomists, were explained by anthropologists in terms of successive waves of immigration into Britain in the distant past. Thus, the Upper Class were of the "Norman type", the middle class of the "Saxon type", and the working class (particularly in areas of Irish immigration) of the "Celt type". Typical of such work is an article by a certain D. Mackintosh published in January 1866 in *The Anthropological Review*, entitled "Comparative Anthropology of England and Wales". The article describes the physical characteristics of the "Gaelic" type of South-west England and Wales in language remarkably similar to that used by the physiognomists:

> A bulging forwards of the lower part of the face, more extreme in the upper jaw; chin more or less retreating ...; forehead retreating; large mouth and thick lips; great distance between nose and mouth; nose short, frequently concave and turned up, with yawning nostrils; cheek-bones more or less prominent; eyes generally sunk, and eyebrows

> projecting; skull narrow and very much elongated backwards; ears standing off to a very striking extent; very acute in hearing; slender or rather slender and elegantly formed body; stature short or middle-sized, though in some districts tall; hair brown or dark brown and generally straight.[110]

Mackintosh went on to describe Gaelic "mental characteristics", which included a tendency to be "deficient in reasoning power; headstrong and excitable … with a propensity to crowd together."[111]

Such work would remain the mainstay of British anthropology for the next twenty or so years, giving the discipline what its historian George Stocking Jnr. has described a "remarkably Europocentric and even Anglocentric focus" in the 1870s and '80s.[112] This in turn reflected both a preoccupation with the degenerative effects of urban living—on which more later—and a desire to prove the "Anglo-Saxon" or "Teutonic" origins of the British national character.[113] The culmination of this kind of fieldwork among Britain's melting-pot of racial types would be the influential study, *The Races of Britain: A Contribution to the Anthropology of Western Europe* (1885), written by John Beddoe, president of the Anthropological Institute.[114]

Combining freely physiognomic and craniometrical observations with generalisations about the "moral character" of the subjects under study, Beddoe embarked on a grand tour of the British Isles, identifying the various "races" as he went. He contrasts for example the "brachycephalous Celt" of the eastern and northern Highlands of Scotland, with his broad head and cheek-bones, shuffling gait and "strong attachments and feelings", with the shrewdness and honesty of the "Teutonic" Yorkshireman, "generally very vigorous" in mind and body, even if somewhat lacking in "imaginative power".[115] Despite the calliper-like precision of Beddoe's craniometrical jargon, Robert Dunn's heads were being clearly being asked to speak a "language" suffused with moral judgements about the relative merits of the different "races" under study.

We were now in a vastly different intellectual landscape from that inhabited by the early champions of the penitentiary movement. In fact, as early as 1843, following a series of disciplinary and management failures, its trail-blazing exemplar, Millbank, was converted ignominiously into a "convict depot": a humble sorting house for those awaiting transportation. As Major Arthur Griffiths, deputy-governor and unofficial historian of the prison, would wryly observe looking back from the 1870s, having hitherto presented itself as a morally superior alternative to transportation, the Penitentiary had now become "distinctly subordinate to it".[116] In

1849, a similar fate befell England's other national convict penitentiary, Pentonville, just seven years after its inauguration. Penal historian Sean McConville observes:

> Henceforth, Pentonville differed little in objectives, methods or population from Millbank convict depot; in both convicts were disciplined before being sent, as a preliminary to transportation, to labour in association at the new public works prison at Portland, thus irrevocably wrecking the scheme of careful penitential preparation followed by ejection into completely new circumstances. … the reformatory experiment was effectively abandoned.[117]

In the subsequent period, the prison system would essentially be organised around the principles of discipline and productivity; reformation, when it did occur was regarded as an "incidental benefit".[118] (It is significant in this context that religious instruction, given a central role in the penitentiary experiment at Millbank was now totally subordinated to the concerns of discipline and administration).[119] The key organising principle of the mid-century regime was the application of the so-called progressive stage system, loosely based on Captain Maconochie's suggestions. The system, as McConville points out, was intended to test, encourage, and deter.[120] "Blameless or meritorious behaviour" (defined not merely by obedience, but by "steady, hard labour") would allow access to the next stage, where conditions of imprisonment—bedding, diet, access to visits, etc.—would be somewhat less harsh. Any misdemeanour would mean demotion, Snakes and Ladders-style, to the previous stage.[121] Except for the most recalcitrant, moving through these successive levels of punishment—the earlier stages of which have been described as taking "the prisoner to the extreme limits of physical and psychological endurance"[122]—also brought an earlier release date, reducing a convict's sentence by anything up to a third.[123] Although the stages were sometimes justified in terms of crude carrot and stick psychology—teaching the prisoner to appreciate the advantages of hard work and obedience and the negative consequences of giving in to baser instincts of idleness or violence—it is clear that discipline and productivity remained the system's key objectives.[124]

It was not only within the convict prison service itself that the reformative aspirations of the penitentiary were being cut down to size. Indeed, according to W. J. Forsythe, by the beginning of the 1860s, distrust of the reformatory ideals of the previous forty years had become "a major feature of debate about the workings of the prison system."[125] The demise of transportation had no doubt contributed to popular fears. Since the early eighteenth century, convicts had been ear-marked for transportation overseas, in the first instance to penal colonies in Britain's American territories. However, with post-revolutionary America having closed its doors to Britain's criminal detritus, and Australia looking set to go the same way[126], an alternative was needed. At the same time, reformers were increasingly concerned that transportation had become, in Martin Wiener's words, both "lottery and spectacle", ill-suited to the new wind of sober rationality and uniformity blowing through the prison service.[127]

Under the influence of Enlightenment philosophy, Benthamite utilitarianism and evangelical Christianity, consistency of punishment was becoming seen as a desirable end in itself, in keeping with a modern, rational State. A "just measure of pain" was required; no more, no less.[128] A system of punishment that by turns brutalised or cosseted those in its charge—as transportation appeared to do—clearly did not meet these requirements, and risked sullying both punished and punisher. Indeed, the potentially polluting effect of degrading punishment went beyond the intimate circle of chastiser and chastised. There were the crowds that came to gawp at the chain-clad unfortunates as they shuffled past on their way to their transport ships. Should punishment be reduced to public spectacle in this way?[129]

From the 1850s, transportation would be confined mainly to fit males with the longest sentences.[130] The remainder, after a spell of separate confinement at Millbank or Pentonville, served out their sentences of "penal servitude" (as the new alternative to transportation was officially known) in the "hulks"[131], or increasingly in purpose-built public works prisons such as Portland (1848), Portsmouth and Dartmoor (1850) or Chatham (1856).[132] Transportation as a means of dealing with Britain's long-term offenders was abolished altogether in November 1867, just a few months before the last public hanging, and five years after the end of public floggings.[133]

The British public—unlike their neighbours across the Channel[134]—were no longer separated from their most dangerous criminals by a comforting stretch of salt sea. There were thus "ground[s] for fear", warned an 1847 article in *The Economist*, that the "sweltering venom" previously exported overseas would "henceforth … be confined here", making "England herself … a penal settlement".[135] In this context, the threat represented by Britain's criminal class, with its "excessive and malignant" passions, understandably took on a new urgency. There was particular public concern between the mid-1850s and early 1860s—whipped up by a campaign in *The Times* (which had never been won over to the optimism of the reformers' cause)—about the prospect of convicts being released into the community before their sentences had expired, the so-called "ticket of leave" men. The following *Times* article from January 1857 is typical. In it a case is described in which

> … it came out that three ruffians had been heard, over their supper, talking about their attempt at garrotting a man, as others talk of shooting pigeons or spearing salmon. It was just their profession, or one form of their profession. Now, it is clear that when these men, when they come out of prison, or from penal servitude, must betake themselves to robbery, burglary or some other violent misdeed. It is a law of nature, and a habit with them; and it is equally clear that when they are again convicted, they ought not to receive the same sentence as others, whose guilt is an accident rather than a trade … We have been content to impose punishment on the crime rather than on the criminal.[136]

Government responded to such concerns later that year with a tightening of the rules governing conditional release, but there were renewed calls for official action when it appeared that a rash of violent street robberies which took place between August 1862 and January 1863, all apparently committed by the same gruesome "garotting" method, were the work of ex-convicts. In fact there was little concrete evidence to support such allegations, but this did not stop them being widely described as hard fact.[137]

A good example of this can be found in volume IV of Mayhew's *London Labour and the London Poor*, a work entirely devoted to exploring "the physics and economy of vice and crime generally"—and published with timely relevance at the height of the garrotting panic in 1862.[138] In his book, Mayhew described a "class of low ruffians" who

> … frequently cohabit with low women and prostitutes, and commit highway robberies. They often follow these degraded females on the street, and attack persons who accost them, believing them to be prostitutes. At other times they garotte men on the street at midnight, or in the by-streets in the evening, and plunder them with violence. This class of persons are generally hardened with crime, and many of them are returned convicts.[139]

Mayhew's approach was typical of the period. The mid-Victorian conception of the criminal class was of a parallel world, existing alongside, and preying off, the respectable, law-abiding community. As historians like V. A. C. Gatrell, Clive Emsley and Victor Bailey have pointed out, the spectre of an idle "criminal class", sucking on the life blood of the wealth-generating portion of the community, served as a powerful receptacle for respectable fears associated with the rapid—and quite unprecedented—pace of economic, urban and demographic growth in the first half of the nineteenth century. The notion that there was a distinct "class", "race" or "tribe" of criminals, who had, as it were, excluded themselves from polite society by their rejection of respectable Victorian values—religion, social duty and sexual virtue—made sense of the otherwise inexplicable rise in the crime figures, and placed responsibility for this social plague squarely—and reassuringly—on the shoulders of the malefactors themselves.[140]

In the early part of the Victorian period, not only was the working class growing in size at an alarming rate, particularly in Britain's manufacturing towns and cities where it was posing fearful administrative and financial problems, it was also beginning to flex its collective muscles. Thus in the 1830s and early '40s, the combined effect of Chartist agitation, anti-Poor Law protests and Captain Swing riots in the countryside, had rekindled fears of revolutionary insurrection on the French model, and for a time there was a tendency to view the "working classes" and "criminal classes" as coterminous. It would appear, however, as Victor Bailey has cogently argued, that the association of "the unrestrained increase of crime" and "depravity among the working class in the manufacturing districts" (to quote the well-known alarmist comments of Scottish sheriff and Tory grandee, Archibald Allison), was confined to relatively circumscribed periods of intense political tension.[141] By the time Mayhew was writing, with economic conditions improving and fears of revolutionary violence fading, majority opinion seems to have come to the conclusion that crime was perpetrated by a distinct *criminal* class, rather than by the labouring class as a whole.

Those inhabiting this parallel world were believed to share common values, codes and rituals, and a specialised argot; in short, what modern sociologists would call a "sub-culture". There were sub-divisions (as Mayhew and Binny had striven to show) and professional specialisms (of which garrotting was believed to be one), but observers tended to emphasise the collective, almost organic structure of Britain's criminal class. Pestilential imagery was common[142], an indication perhaps of the continuing influence of Edwin Chadwick's *Report on the Sanitary Condition of the Labouring Population* (1842), which had in sensational fashion linked "atmospheric impurities" and "noxious filth" to "an adult population short-lived, improvident, reckless and intemperate, ... with habitual avidity for sensual gratifications".[143]

Thus Thomas Plint made full use of Chadwickian imagery in his 1851 book, *Crime in England, Its Relation, Character and Extent*:

> The criminal class live amongst and are dove-tailed in, so to speak, with the operative classes, whereby they constitute so many points of vicious contact with those classes—so may ducts by which the virus of a moral poison circulates through and around them. They constitute a

> pestiferous canker in the heart of every locality where they congregate, offending the sight, revolting the sensibilities, and lowering, more or less, the moral status of all who come into contact with them.[144]

Yet Plint, like George Laval Chesterton, rejected the suggestion that the criminal classes were beyond salvation. It should be possible, Plint wrote, to "establish in the hearts of the outcast race the feeling of common brotherhood", despite the fact that "a large majority of that class is so by descent, and stands as completely isolated from the other social classes, in blood, in sympathies, in its domestic and social organisation … as it is hostile to them in the whole '*ways and means*' of its temporal existence."[145]

Plint's emphasis on the "isolation" of the criminal class from the rest of society survived into the 1860s. However, his notion of a "race" whose traits, present in the very "blood" coursing through its members' veins and fixed by "descent", had in many cases hardened into a conception of a hermetically-sealed, biologically self-reproducing criminal class that left little room for "common brotherhood". An 1862 work by William Pare is a typical example of such views. Its title is revealing in itself: *A Plan for the Suppression of the Predatory Classes*.[146] This was the mood of middle class opinion which saw a garrotter at every street corner, and the tone of Pare's work is noticeably more shrill than that of Thomas Plint:

> … habitual crime [… is] the true disease, and … the offender, far from being an isolated depredator, is, in fact, one of a large bad class—a minute portion of a vast and pernicious organism, the action of which will still go on, whether he be cut off from it or not, the great predatory body having, like a huge polypus, the power to speedily replace any portion that may become injured or detached.[147]

Historical research has found precious little evidence of either a self-reproducing caste of career criminals with its own deviant sub-culture or a distinct underclass of idlers and vagrants, hermetically sealed from the broader working class. In fact, as Clive Emsley points out,

> … no clear distinction can be made between a dishonest criminal class and a poor but honest working class. … Most thefts, and most crimes of violence were not committed by professional criminals; nor is it helpful to think of these offences as committed by a group which can, in any sense, be described as a separate class.[148]

The much-vaunted crime wave of the first half of the nineteenth century has also met with scholarly scepticism. It is true that between 1805 and 1842, the number of indictable offences per 100 000 of population rose nearly four-fold from 49 to 194.[149] However, where government statistician

G. R. Porter saw in Britain's "continued progress ... in its economical relations, the still greater multiplication of criminals"[150], historians counter that "what was increasing in the first half of the nineteenth century was not crime but the prosecution rate."[151] Contemporaries saw the national figures in more unequivocal terms however. Many reached the gloomy conclusion that the reality of crime in Victorian Britain was *even worse* than official estimates suggested. Parliament's response to the apparent wave of garrotting attacks was equally unequivocal. The so-called "Garotters' Act" of 1863 added a supplementary punishment of up to fifty strokes of corporal punishment to the statutory sentence for those found guilty of armed or violent robbery.[152]

In fact, 1863 has been described as a year which saw a significant tightening of the penal screw in a number of areas.[153] In addition to the Garrotters' Act, two hard-line government reports on the prison system were published.[154] The same year also saw the death of Sir Joshua Jebb, who more than anyone had symbolised the reformatory ideals of the penitentiaries, and the appointment of Edmund Du Cane, a strict disciplinarian, as Assistant Director of Convict Prisons.[155]

A more punitive spirit was abroad, and this was reflected in the two parliamentary inquiries into the prison system which reported that year. The Lords' inquiry into the country's local prisons (catering for those serving sentences of less than three years), chaired by Lord Carnarvon, was particularly vehement in its condemnation of the reformers, declaring itself "... compelled to admit that the reformation of individual character by any known process of prison discipline is frequently doubtful."[156] Speaking in the House of Lords in February 1863, Lord Carnarvon put it even more bluntly, castigating "the intervention of well-intentioned theorists who thought it practicable to make moral influences a substitute for hard labour". Such "fanciful theories" had, he argued, led to "an insufficiency of penal discipline" in Britain's local prisons, a state of affairs more likely to attract potential criminals than strike the fear of God into them.[157]

The Carnarvon Committee placed particular emphasis on the value of punitive rather than productive labour, an issue which has been described as "the central and defining issue" of the Lords' inquiry.[158] Enthusiastic backing was given to the tread-wheel, the crank, the capstan and the shot drill. If rogues could not be ground honest, it was reasoned, at least they could be made to "grind the wind" by their exertions on the tread-wheel or crank.[159] The reduction of prisoners' food was also encouraged as a "salutary" disciplinary measure ("render[ed] plain" by "the low animal natures of too many of the criminal class"[160]); and so-called "guard-beds",

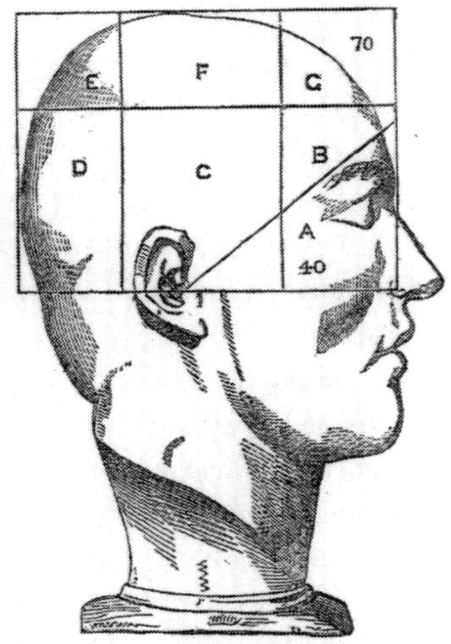

COURVIOSIER,
The Murderer of Lord William Russell.
Reduced to $\frac{1}{5}$.

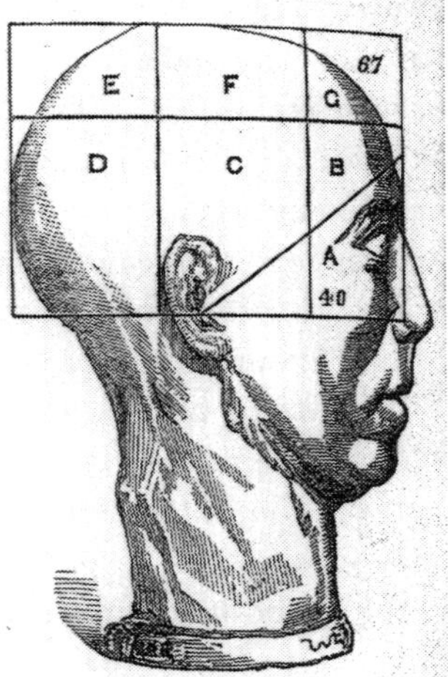

ROBERT MARLEY,
Ticket-of leave Murderer.
Reduced to $\frac{1}{5}$.

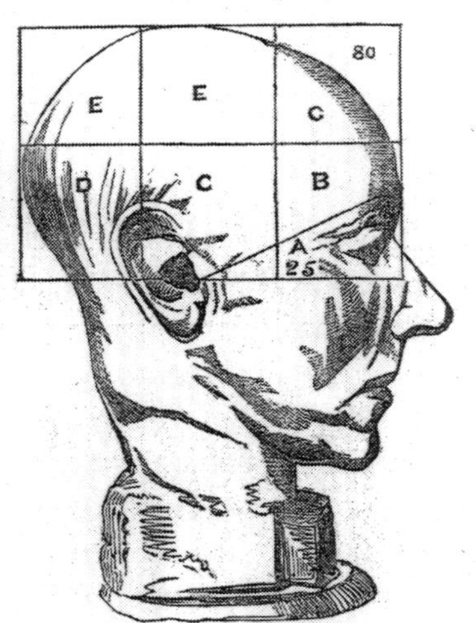

ROBERT OWEN,
Mental and moral type.
Reduced to $\frac{1}{5}$.

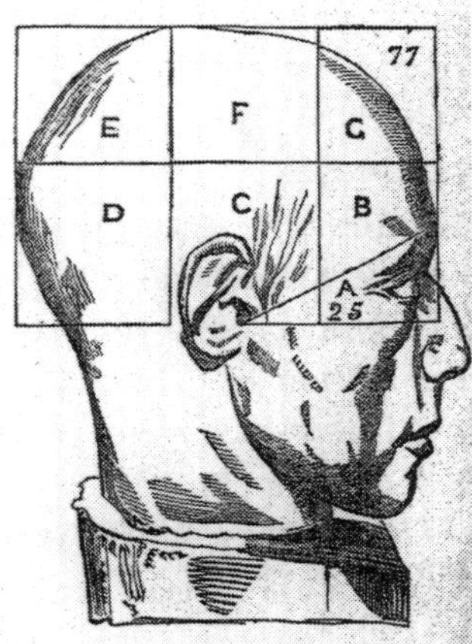

GEORGE COMBE,
Mental and moral type.
Reduced to $\frac{1}{5}$.

Phrenological Comparison of Two Criminal Skulls with those of Two "Superior" Specimens, Belonging to George Combe and Robert Owen, 1860

Frederick Bridges, *Criminals, Crimes and their Concerning Laws, as Demonstrated by the Sciences of Physiology and Mental Geometry*, London, 1860, frontispiece.

comprised only of wooden planks, competed the grim triptych of "hard labour, hard fare and a hard bed" on which the committee decided.[161] Such views were embodied in the 1865 Prison Act, a law which, in Sean McConville's words, "systematically put [all aspects of life in prison] on a footing as austere and vexatious as possible."[162] The Act followed the Carnarvon committee report in reaffirming the importance of separate confinement—principally for its punitive rather than reformatory qualities—and made clear that labour should be "penal" rather than "productive".

The Royal Commission on penal servitude, which also reported in 1863, was more receptive to the reformist aims of imprisonment than the Carnarvon committee. However, in a climate of concern about spiralling crime rates and in particular the high reconviction rate (there was even talk on both committees of bringing back branding to facilitate the identification of "habituals"[163]), the Royal Commission did advocate an increase in the minimum sentence for convicts from three to seven years, the extension of transportation to all fit adult males, and the reinforcement of police supervision for those prisoners released before the full term of their sentences had expired. In addition, the commission urged that the rules governing the granting of such tickets-of-leave be tightened up. Those benefiting from a reduction in their sentence should, it was argued, have unequivocally demonstrated spirited diligence and effort to obtain the necessary "marks", not simple a passive absence of "bad behaviour". The Penal Servitude Act, passed in 1864, converted the Commission's findings into statute law.[164]

By the mid-1860s then, there were growing doubts that "good education and the general spread of knowledge, the cultivation of habits of forethought, sobriety and frugality, …the control of the passions, [and] the promotion of habits of … self-reliance" would be enough to raise "every class of society beyond the sphere of destitution."[165] This had been replaced, as Captain Walter Crofton's significantly-titled book *The Immunity of Habitual Criminals* (1861) put it, by a widespread view that Britain's "implicit faith in Prison Training and Reformation" had been misplaced; the result being "to discharge 'Habitual Offenders' within the terms of their original sentences without any check upon their future misdeeds."[166]

Increasingly, it was not a matter of a collective heave to pull up the poorest elements in society by their bootstraps, drawing them within the sphere of Mayhew's "industrious, provident, and civilised portion of the community". Instead, a growing body of opinion was coming to the conclusion that there was a permanent "residuum"[167], stubbornly refusing to join the rest of civilised society, that as Metropolitan Police Commissioner

Sir Richard Mayne put it in 1863, "... the love of thieving and the love of criminal practices is like some other passions of human nature, and ... you cannot eradicate them."[168]

As we noted in the introduction, there was a certain appeal to beleaguered prison officials in such a prognosis, offering as it did a convenient explanation for the Prison system's apparent inability to eradicate the problem of habitual crime. The new punitive agenda did not demand any soul-searching, either of prison inmates, or among their guardians. Jeremy Bentham's dictum that "it is only from a man's acts that his disposition can be judged of"[169], while out of tune with the ethos of his Regency contemporaries, had now become enshrined in official practice. For the inmates, all that was required was outward conformity and hard, unrelenting physical effort; for those charged with their supervision, all that could be done was to find more and more effective (and preferably cheaper) ways of making prison life as thoroughly disagreeable as possible, without causing any lasting physical or mental damage. The first empirical research on the physical and mental characteristics of Britain's criminal population would be conducted with this aim in mind.

Notes

1 "Report of the Royal Commission on Transportation and Penal Servitude", *Parliamentary Papers*, 1863, vol. 21, p. 25.

2 Quoted in William Pare, A *Plan for the Suppression of the Predatory Classes*, London, 1862, p. 3.

3 Herman Mannheim (ed.), *Pioneers in Criminology*, 2nd edition, Montclair NJ, Patterson Smith, 1972. For a more recent example, see Daniel J. Curran & Claire Renzetti, *Theories of Crime*, London, Allyn & Bacon, 1994.

4 Nicole Hahn Rafter, "The Unrepentant Horse-Slasher: Moral Insanity and the Origins of Criminology", (*Criminology*, Vol. 42, 4, Nov. 2004, pp. 977–1006). I am grateful to Professor Rafter for making available an early draft of this paper.

5 David Garland, "Of Crimes and Criminals: The Development of Criminology in Britain", in Mike Maguire *et al.* (eds.), *The Oxford Handbook of Criminology*, 3rd edition, Oxford, Oxford University Press, 2002, p. 23.

6 Marmaduke B. Sampson, *Criminal Jurisprudence Considered in Relation to Mental Organisation*, London, 1841.

7 Eliza Farnham (ed.), Marmaduke B. Sampson, *Rationale of Crime, and its Appropriate Treatment; Being a Treatise on Criminal Jurisprudence Considered in Relation to Cerebral Organisation*, New York, 1846.

8 Madeline B. Stern, "Matthew Brady and the 'Rationale of Crime': A Discovery in Daguerreotypes", *Quarterly Journal of the Library of Congress*, vol. 31, 1974, pp. 127–35. I am grateful to Nicole Hahn Rafter for drawing my attention to this reference.

9 For a similar technique, see Frederick Bridges, *Criminals, Crimes and their Concerning Laws, as Demonstrated by the Sciences of Physiology and Mental Geometry*, London, 1860, frontispiece, where the author contrasts two criminal skulls with those of two "superior" specimens, belonging to George Combe and Robert Owen.

10 Allan Sekula, "The Body and the Archive", *October*, no. 39, 1986, pp. 13–15.

11 Lauvergne was naval doctor at the Toulon penal colony. In 1841, he published a phrenological study of the *bagnards* in his care (*Les Forçats considérés sous le rapport physiologique moral et intellectuel*, Paris, 1841). On French phrenology as applied to crime, see Georges Lanteri-Laura, "Phrénologie et criminalité: les idées de Gall", in Laurent Mucchielli (ed.), *Histoire de la criminologie française*, Paris, L'Harmattan, 1994, pp. 21–28.

12 There is no record of Sampson having produced any other work on crime, with the exception of a defence of his book, published in pamphlet form: *The Phrenological Treatment of Criminals Defended, in a Letter*, London, 1843. He was, however, the author of at least five other books, mostly on homeopathy.

13 Neil Davie, "Criminology", in Tom & Sara Pendergast (eds.), *Grolier Encyclopedia of the Victorian Era*, 4 vols., Danbury, Connecticut, Grolier Academic Press (2004).

14 J[ames] Bruce Thomson, "The Hereditary Nature of Crime", *Journal of Mental Science*, vol. 15, January 1870, pp. 487–98.

15 J[ames] Bruce Thomson, "The Psychology of Criminals", *Journal of Mental Science*, vol. 16, 1870, pp. 321–50.

16 Thomson, "Hereditary Nature of Crime", pp. 496–98.

17 Henry Maudsley, *Body and Mind*, London, 1870, p. 43.

18 Jayewardine, "English Precursors of Lombroso", pp. 167–68.

19 A. Taylor Milne (ed.), *The Correspondence of Jeremy Bentham*, vol. 4, London, Athlone Press, 1981, p. 342.

20 "Select Committee on Penitentiary Houses" [Holford Committee], First Report, *Parliamentary Papers*, 1810–1811, vol. 3, pp. 567–89. Bentham described his pet project as follows: "The building *circular*—an iron cage, glazed, a glass lantern, about the size of *Ranelagh*—the prisoners, in their cells, occupying the circumference—the officers, governors (chaplain, surgeon, etc.) the center. By *blinds* and other contrivances, the inspectors concealed … from the observation of the prisoners: hence the sentiment of a sort of invisible omnipresence.—The whole circuit reviewable with little, or if necessary without any, change of place" (*Proposal for a New and Less Expensive Mode of Employing and Reforming CONVICTS*, 1798). On the fascinating background to Bentham's scheme and its eventual rejection, see Janet Semple, *Bentham's Prison: A Study of the Panopticon Penitentiary*, Oxford, Clarendon Press, 1993.

21 In fact, it could be said that the penitentiary principle was *resurrected*, for it had first been approved by the Penitentiary Act of 1779. The two national convict prisons envisaged by the act were never built.

22 There is no comprehensive history of Millbank, but some clues can be garnered from Sean McConville, *A History of English Prison Administration I: 1750–1877*, London, Routledge & Kegan Paul, 1981, ch. 6; Michael Ignatieff, *A Just Measure of Pain: The Penitentiary in the Industrial Revolution*, New York, Pantheon Books, 1978, pp. 170–3, 175–76, 193–94; and David Wilson, "Millbank, the Panopticon and

their Victorian Audiences", *The Howard Journal*, vol. 41, no. 4, September 2002, pp. 364–81. There is much contemporary information in George Holford, *An Account of the General Penitentiary at Millbank*, London, 1828, and, from a late-Victorian perspective (revealing in itself), in Major Arthur Griffiths, *Memorials of Millbank and Chapters in Prison History*, London, 1884.

23 Janet Semple has argued that Bentham's lack of evangelical zeal (he once described religion as a "a very cheap drug" and privately, he expressed doubts about the usefulness of seeking to see into a Man's soul) was a major cause of the failure of the Panopticon project (*op. cit.*, p. 94).

24 George Laval Chesterton, *Revelations of Prison Life, with an Enquiry into Prison Discipline and Secondary Punishments*, 2 vols., London, 1856, vol. 1, p. 10. For other examples of this point of view, see Philip Priestley, *Victorian Prison Lives: English Prison Biography 1830–1914*, 2nd ed., London, Pimlico, 1999, p. 78.

25 Chesterton, *op. cit.*, pp. 7–8.

26 Quoted in Sean McConville, "The Victorian Prison, England 1865–1965" in Norval Morris & David Rothman (eds.), *The Oxford History of the Prison: The Practice of Punishment in Western Society*, Oxford, Oxford University Press, 1998, p. 122.

27 Sir Joshua Jebb, quoted in William J. Forsythe, *The Reform of Prisoners 1830–1900*, London, Croom Helm, 1987, p. 262.

28 "Philadelphia, and its Solitary Prison", in *American Notes and Pictures from Italy*, Oxford, Oxford University Press, 1957 [1842], pp. 97–111. Cf. Paul Schlicke (ed.), *Oxford Reader's Companion to Dickens*, Oxford, Oxford University Press, 1999, pp. 123–29; 465–68; Philip Collins, *Dickens and Crime*, London, Macmillan, 1962, chs. 3, 5.

29 Robin Evans, *The Fabrication of Virtue: English Prison Architecture 1750–1840*, Cambridge, Cambridge University Press, 1982, ch. 6; Randall McGowen, "The Well-Ordered Prison, England 1780–1865", in Morris & Rothman (eds.), *Oxford History of the Prison*, pp. 90–92.

30 Reverend Daniel Nihill, *Prison Discipline in its Relations to Society and Individuals in Deterring from Crime, and as Conducive to Personal Reformation*, London, 1839, pp. 23–24.

31 *Ibid.*, p. 45.

32 The term used by "One-who-has-tried-them" (1881), quoted in Priestley, *op. cit.*, p. 92. One enterprising Pentonville prisoner, a certain Hackett, turned this state of affairs to his advantage, making use of the time when the congregation was knelt in prayer to work loose the wooden floorboards under his pew. After a number of weeks' work, he fell to his knees in prayer one Sunday, never to reappear. He had disappeared under the chapel floor and squeezed through a ventilation hole to freedom (Donald Thomas, *The Victorian Underworld*, London, John Murray, 1998, pp. 280–81).

33 Priestley, *op. cit.*, p. 85.

34 *Ibid.*

35 Griffiths, *Memorials of Millbank*, p. 27.

36 McGowen, "The Well-Ordered Prison", p. 97.

37 Neil Davie, *Les Visages de la criminalité: à la recherché d'un criminel-type scientifique en Angleterre*, 1860–1914, Paris, Kimé, 2004, p. 31.

38 It is unclear precisely when Mayhew and Binny visited the prison. However, the stalled chapel and brown masks were both withdrawn from use in 1859, which

suggests that their visit was prior to this date (McConville, *History of English Prison Administration* pp. 405–6).

39 An engraving based on Doré's drawing was reproduced in Blanchard Jerrold's, *London: A Pilgrimage* (London, 1872). See Eric de Maré, *Victorian London Revealed: Gustave Doré's Metropolis*, London, Penguin, 2001 [1973], pp. 158–59. Vincent Van Gogh later copied the image for his painting "Prisoners Exercising" (1890). The painting is now in the Museum of Modern Art, Moscow.

40 Henry Mayhew & John Binny, *The Criminal Prisons of London and Scenes of Prison Life*, London, 1862, p. 113.

41 Forsythe, *Reform of Prisoners*, p. 185.

42 Mayhew & Binny, *op. cit.*, p. 145.

43 Mary Cowling, *The Artist as Anthropologist: The Representation of Type and Character in Victorian Art*, Cambridge, Cambridge University Press, 1989, p. 289.

44 Bridges, *Criminals, Crimes and their Governing Laws*, p. 15.

45 Roy Porter, *Bodies Politic: Disease, Death and Doctors in Britain, 1650–1900*, London, Reaktion, 2001, p. 44; S. Giora Sholam & Giora Rahav, *The Mark of Cain: The Stigma Theory of Crime and Social Deviance*, 2nd ed., St. Lucia, University of Queensland Press, 1982, p. 13.

46 Quoted in Lucy Hartley, *Physiognomy and the Meaning of Expression in Nineteenth-Century Culture*, Cambridge, Cambridge University Press, 2001, p. 33.

47 *Ibid.*, p. 34.

48 Johann Kaspar Lavater, *Essays on Physiognomy* (1789), reproduced in Jenny Bourne Taylor & Sally Shuttleworth (eds.), *Embodied Selves: An Anthology of Psychological Texts 1830–1890*, Oxford, Oxford University Press, 1998, p. 10.

49 Cowling, *op. cit.*, p. 289.

50 Quoted in *ibid.*, p. 291.

51 Tim Barringer, "Images of Otherness and the Visual Production of Difference: Race and Labour in Illustrated Texts 1850–1865", in Shearer West (ed.), *The Victorians and Race*, Aldershot, Scholar Press, 1996, pp. 34–52.

52 His first notable success was *Ramsgate Sands (Life at the Seaside)*, exhibited in 1854, and subsequently bought by Queen Victoria. Frith, an avowed physiognomist, received his early training at Sass's Academy, where plaster casts of the faces of hanged murderers were used as a teaching aid in anatomy classes. Frith recalled later being struck by the fact that eyelashes still adhered to the casts (Cowling, *op. cit.*, p. 302).

53 *Ibid.*, pp. 309–12.

54 S. R. Wells, quoted in *ibid.*, p. 122.

55 Francis Joseph Gall & Johann Caspar Spurzheim, *Recherches sur le système nerveux en général, et sur celui du cerveau en particulier*, Paris, 1809.

56 Johann Caspar Spurzheim (1815), quoted in Nicole Hahn Rafter, "The Murderous Dutch Fiddler: Criminology, History and the Problem of Phrenology" (*Theoretical Criminology*, Vol. 9, 1, Feb. 2005, p. 72.), p. 12. I am grateful to Professor Rafter for making available an early draft of this article.

57 Spurzheim, whose more accessible version of Gall's theories, *The Physionomical System of Drs Gall and Spurzheim* (London, 1815) became the basis for the phrenological movement in Britain and the USA (Rafter, *op. cit.*, p. 72), added six new organs to Gall's twenty-seven.

58 Arthur E. Fink, *Causes of Crime: Biological Theories in the United States 1800–1915*, New York, A. S. Barnes, 1962 [1st. ed. 1938], pp. 1–3.

59 Gall divided his twenty-seven powers into two broad groupings: "affective" and "intellectual". The affective powers were further sub-divided into "propensities" (characteristics shared with animals such as *adhesiveness, combativeness, destructiveness, acquisitiveness and amativeness*) and nobler, specifically human "sentiments", including *self-esteem, piety, benevolence, veneration and conscientiousness*. As for the intellectual powers, they were separated into the "perceptive" and "reflective" faculties. Among the former *were form, size, weight, colour* and *tune*; the latter included *comparison, wit, causality* and *imitation*.

60 Rafter, *op. cit.*, p. 74.

61 Franz Joseph Gall, *On the Functions of the Brain*, Boston, 1835 [1822–1825], reproduced in Bourne Taylor & Shuttleworth, *op. cit.*, p. 27.

62 George Combe, *Essays on Phrenology*, Edinburgh, 1819; *The Constitution of Man and its Relation to External Objects*, Edinburgh, 1828. On Combe, see David de Giustino, *Conquest of Mind: Phrenology and Victorian Social Thought*, London, Croom Helm, 1975. The comparison with *The Origin of Species* is based on an equivalent period following its publication in 1859 (Marc Renneville, *Le Langage des crânes: une histoire de la phrénologie*, Paris, Institut d'édition Sanofi-Synthélabo, 2000, p. 185 & note 1).

63 Combe, *The Constitution of Man*, p. viii, quoted in De Giustino, *op. cit.*, p. 9.

64 *Ibid.*, pp. 39–46; Cooter, *Cultural Meaning of Popular Science*, 1984, pp. 28–35.

65 De Giustino, *op. cit.*, pp. 32–39; Cooter, *op. cit.*, pp. 174–75. Cf. Gall, *On the Functions of the Brain*: "The physiology of the brain is entirely founded on observations, experiments, and researches for the thousandth time repeated, on man and brute animals. Here, reasoning has nothing more to do with it, than to seize the results, and deduce the principles that flow from the facts…" (reproduced in Bourne Taylor & Shuttleworth, *op. cit.*, p. 28).

66 Cooter, *op. cit.*, p. 111.

67 The term "destructiveness" was coined by Spurzheim to replace Gall's reference to a "murder" organ. Spurzheim preferred the former term to denote this organ since if less developed, it could produce, not murderous behaviour, but a tendency to "pinch, scratch, bite, cut break, pierce, [and] devastate" (Spurzheim, *The Physionomical System*, quoted in Rafter "The Murderous Dutch Fiddler", p. 76).

68 Renneville, *op. cit.*, pp. 63–75.

69 Spurzheim (1828), quoted in Rafter, *op. cit.*, p. 12.

70 *Ibid.*, pp. 17–18.

71 Frederick Bridges, *Criminals, Crimes and their Governing Laws, as Demonstrated by the Sciences of Physiology and Mental Geometry*, London, 1860, p. 32.

72 Clare Anderson, *Legible Bodies: Race, Criminality and Colonialism in South Asia*, Oxford, Berg, 2004, p. 183.

73 Flora Tristan, *Flora Tristan's London Journal, 1840*, trans. Denis Palmer & Giselle Pincentl, London, George Prior, 1980, pp. 105–7. In 1824, Dr Elliotson had founded the London Phrenological Society and became its first president. He accompanied Dickens to the execution of Courvoisier in July 1841. The experience prompted Dickens' widely-quoted letters to the *Daily News* in 1846, in which the young novelist made a powerful case for the abolition of the death penalty (Collins,

Dickens and Crime, pp. 224–26; Schlicke, *Oxford Reader's Companion to Dickens*, p. 443). On John Elliotson, see also Cooter, *op. cit.*, pp. 29, 52–53.

74 George Combe, *A System of Phrenology*, 2 vols., 5th edition, Edinburgh, 1853, vol. 2, appendix 5, p. 54.

75 The fullest discussion of Maconochie's ideas remains John Vincent Barry, *Alexander Maconochie of Norfolk Island*, London, Oxford University Press, 1958. See also *idem.*, "Alexander Maconochie 1787–1860", in Mannheim, *Pioneers in Criminology*, pp. 84–106 and the fictional treatment of US criminologist Norval Morris in his book, *Maconchie's Gentlemen: The Story of Norfolk Island and the Roots of Modern Prison Reform*, Oxford, Oxford University Press, 2002.

76 De Giustino, *op. cit.*, p. 157. Maconochie had doubts, though, that a precise list of mental faculties could be enumerated, describing such efforts as "cranial cartography" (*ibid.*, p. 159).

77 Forsythe, *Reform of Prisoners*, p. 83. The quotations from Maconochie are taken from his evidence to the 1850 Select Committee of the House of Commons on Prisons. Maconochie's marks system would subsequently be adopted in both Irish and English prisons, though shorn of one its fundamental principles, that of the indeterminate sentence (*ibid.*, p. 85; Wiener, *Reconstructing the Criminal*, pp. 114–16).

78 De Giustino, *op. cit.*, pp. 157–61. After his dismissal from Norfolk Island in 1844, Maconochie returned to England, where he became until 1851 Governor of Birmingham Borough Prison. His methods were criticised in the 1854 "Royal Commission Appointed to Inquire into the Condition and Treatment of the Prisoners Confined to Birmingham Borough Prison" (Parliamentary Papers, 1854, vol. 31). The main object of the inquiry, however, was the regime put in place by Maconochie's successor and former Deputy-Governor at Birmingham, Lieutenant George Austin. Austin was dismissed after it was discovered that he had "punished illegally and cruelly" a fifteen year-old boy who had subsequently committed suicide. The prison doctor, who was found to have regularly doused recalcitrant prisoners with buckets of cold water, was also heavily criticised by the report. He resigned before he could be sacked (Priestley, *Victorian Prison Lives*, pp. 210–13).

79 De Giustino, *op. cit.*, p. 147.

80 Combe, *op. cit.*, p. 49.

81 *Ibid.*

82 *Ibid.*, pp. 51–53.

83 Anderson, *op. cit.*

84 George Combe, *Notes on the United States of North America during a Phrenological Visit in 1838–9–40*, 3 vols., Edinburgh, 1841. In this work, Combe had sought to divide the criminal population into three "great classes": the first with "moderate" organs of the propensities, capable of exercising free will; the second with large organs and thus marked criminal impulses, but still responsible for their actions; and a third "incorrigible" group, termed "moral patients" by Combe. The latter, he wrote, "should not be punished, but restrained, and employed in useful labour during life with as much liberty as they can enjoy without abusing it." Release, in fact should only follow successful reformation (vol. 1, pp. 204–7, vol. 2, pp. 9–10, 16). See also George Combe & C. J. A. Mittermaieri, "On the Application of Phrenology to Criminal Legislation and Prison Discipline", *Phrenological Journal*, vol. 16, 1843, pp. 1–19; George Combe, "Instances of Successful Moral Treatment

of Criminals", *Phrenological Journal*, vol. 18, 1845, pp. 205–9. I am grateful to Dr John Van Wyhe of Cambridge University for these references. English lawyer James Simpson had come up with a similar three-tier phrenological conception of crime in his 1834 book *Necessity of Popular Education as a National Object; with Hints on the Treatment of Criminals and Observations on Homicidal Insanity*, Edinburgh & London, 1834 (See Rafter, "The Murderous Dutch Fiddler", pp. 77–78).

85 Nicole Hahn Rafter, "Seeing and Believing: Images of Heredity in Biological Theories of Crime", *Brooklyn Law Review*, vol. 67, no. 1, Autumn 2001, pp. 76, 78.

86 George Combe (1853), quoted in Rafter, "The Murderous Dutch Fiddler", p. 77–78.

87 Forsythe, *op. cit.*, p. 179.

88 De Giustino, *Conquest of Mind*, pp. 145–62; Cooter, *op. cit.*, pp. 124–25. During his trip to the United States in 1838–1840, Combe had visited prisons to help him make up his mind which of the various systems of penal management was most suited to his phrenological principles. Interestingly, he finally decided on a combination of the separate and silent systems, not unlike that put into operation at Millbank in 1816 (Rafter, "The Murderous Dutch Fiddler", pp. 83–84).

89 William Hepworth Dixon, *The London Prisons*, London, 1850, pp. 244–45. Cf. Thomas Carlyle's oft-quoted comments on the inmates at Pentonville: "Miserable distorted blockheads, the generality; ape-faces, imp-faces, angry dog-faces, heavy sullen ox-faces; degraded underfoot perverse creatures, sons of *in*-docility, greedy, mutinous darkness, and in one word of STUPIDITY, which is the general mother of such" ("Model Prisons", 1850, quoted in Priestley, *op. cit.*, p. 78). Leon Radzinowicz & Roger Hood note that Carlyle's "violent diatribe" had "no real impact because of its unnatural distortions" (*The Emergence of Penal Policy in Victorian and Edwardian England*, Oxford, Clarendon Press, 1990 [first published as vol. 5 of *A History of English Criminal Law*, London, Stevens & Sons, 1986], p. 504).

90 Mayhew & Binny, *op. cit.*, p. 164.

91 A point of view shared by Henry Mayhew's biographer: Anne Humpherys, *Travels into the Poor Man's Country: The Work of Henry Mayhew*, Athens, University of Georgia Press, 1977, p. 117.

92 Mayhew & Binny, *op. cit.*, pp. 147–48.

93 *Ibid.*, p. 45.

94 *Ibid.*, pp. 45, 87, 89, 90–91.

95 *Ibid.*, p. 91.

96 Wiener, *Reconstructing the Criminal*, p. 26, and ch. 1 *passim.*

97 Mayhew & Binny, *op. cit.*, pp. 164–65 (footnote).

98 Victor A.C. Gatrell, *The Hanging Tree: Execution and the English People 1770–1868*, Oxford, Oxford University Press, 1994, pp. 68–72, 114. Greenacre was hanged at Newgate in May 1837 in front of a crowd estimated at 160 000.

99 Mayhew & Binny, *op. cit.*, p. 597.

100 *Ibid.*, p. 45.

101 *Ibid.*, p. 89.

102 Henry Mayhew, *London Labour and the London Poor*, vol. 1, London, 1851, p. 1.

103 *Ibid.*, reproduced in Peter Quennel (ed.), *Mayhew's Characters*, London, Spring Books, n.d., p. xvii.

104 *The Eclectic Review*, October 1851, quoted in Gertrude Himmelfarb, *The Idea of Poverty: England in the Early Industrial Age*, London, Faber, 1984, p. 352.

105 George R. Sims, *How the Poor Live* (1881), quoted in Peter Keating (ed.), *Into Unknown England: Selections from the Social Explorers*, Manchester, Manchester University Press, 1976, p. 64. Cf. William Booth, *In Darkest England and the Way Out*, London, 1890.

106 Cf. the comments of Dr William Augustus Guy in his pamphlet, *The Evils of England Social and Economic* (1846): "My blood boils as I see the honest and hardworking English labourer, with an Irish rebel on one shoulder, an English pauper on the other, a dead weight of taxation on his back, and a crowd of beggars, thieves, and vagrants pulling at his skirts and picking his pockets" (p. 10). Dr Guy would go on to become medical superintendent at Millbank prison (1859–1865). See below, Chapter Two.

107 Mayhew, *London Labour*, vol. 1, pp. 2–3.

108 Nancy Stepan, *The Idea of Race in Science: Great Britain 1800–1860*, London, Macmillan, 1982, ch. 4.

109 Robert Dunn, quoted in Christina Bolt, *Victorian Attitudes to Race*, London, Routledge, 1971.

110 D. Mackintosh, "Comparative Anthropology of England and Wales", *The Anthropological Review*, no. 12, January 1866, pp. 15–16.

111 *Ibid.*, p. 16.

112 George W. Stocking Jr., *Victorian Anthropology*, New York, The Free Press, 1987, p. 261.

113 James R. Ryan, *Picturing the Empire: Photography and the Visualisation of the British Empire*, London, Reaktion Books, 1977, p. 167.

114 John Beddoe, *The Races of Britain: A Contribution to the Anthropology of Western Europe*, Bristol, 1885.

115 *Ibid.*, pp. 246, 252.

116 Griffiths, *Memorials of Millbank*, p. 241.

117 McConville, *History of English Prison Administration*, p. 209.

118 *Ibid.*, p. 403.

119 *Ibid.*, p. 407. The chapel's pivotal position in the prison's snowflake-shaped groundplan symbolised this in architectural terms. On the importance of religious instruction in the early days at Millbank, see Holford, *An Account of the General Penitentiary*, p. xli, and Nihill, *Prison Discipline*, p. 32.

120 McConville, "The Victorian Prison", p. 121.

121 Lord Stanley (1843) and Lieutenant-Colonel Henderson (1864), both quoted in McConville, *English Prison Administration*, pp. 400, 403.

122 McConville, "The Victorian Prison", *op. cit.*, p. 135.

123 It should be remembered that such conditional release was not available to those serving sentences of two years or less in the local prisons. Indeed, McConville points out (*ibid.*, p. 135) that most local prisoners were not in gaol long enough to benefit from the improvements in conditions—however modest—that came with promotion to one of the superior classes. At the time of the Carnarvon Report, it has been calculated that 52 000 out of the 74 000 sentences handed down by magistrates were for terms of one month or less (McGowen, "The Well-Ordered Prison", p. 95).

124 Forsythe, *The Reform of Prisoners*, pp. 73–81.

125 *Ibid.*, p. 143.

126 The last shipment of 279 convicts arrived in Western Australia in January 1869. Among their number were 63 Fenians, from the abortive 1867 uprising in Ireland.

127 Wiener, *Reconstructing the Criminal*, p. 98.
128 Cf. Michael Ignatieff, *A Just Measure of Pain: The Penitentiary in the Industrial Revolution*, London, Macmillan, 1978.
129 Wiener, *op. cit.*, ch. 3.
130 From 1853, transportation was reserved for those serving sentences of more than 14 years.
131 The last hulk to be used in home waters, the *Defence*, was destroyed by fire in July 1857 (McConville, *op. cit.*, p. 393).
132 See *ibid.*, pp. 142–55.
133 Wiener, *op. cit.*, p. 100.
134 France suspended the transportation of its own convicts to French Guyana the same year as Britain's last cargo of prisoners sailed for Australia. There had been alarming reports about the death rate in the French penal colony; in the first fourteen years of the colony's operation (1852–1864), it was estimated that 39% of the convict population had died, the victims of a combination of malnutrition, physical exhaustion and epidemic disease. Perhaps the Guyanese climate just was not appropriate for the "white race", concluded a report of 1865, doomed to "perish [there] in large numbers and certainly degenerate …" Thus while the country's Algerian and Caribbean convicts continued to be transported to Guyana, for the rest, the example of Britain's successful penal colony in Australia had suggested an alternative destination: France's own possession in the Antipodes, New Caledonia. During the next thirty-five years, 15 000 convicts and petty recidivists would be transported there, among them over 4000 for offences linked to the Paris Commune of 1871 (Michel Pierre, "La transportation (1848–1938)", in Jean-Jacques Petit *et al.*, *Histoires des galères, bagnes et prisons* XIIIe–XXe *siècles*, Toulouse, Bibliothèque historique Privat, 1991, pp. 241–41).
135 "What is to be Done with our Criminals?", *The Economist* (1847), quoted in Radzinowicz & Hood, *Emergence of Penal Policy*, p. 74.
136 *The Times*, 6 January 1857, quoted in Sir Walter Crofton, *The Immunity of Habitual Criminals, with Proposals for Reducing their Number*, London, 1861, p. 43.
137 J. Davis, "The London Garotting Panic of 1862: A Moral Panic and the Creation of a Criminal Class in Mid-Victorian England", in V. A. C. Gatrell *et al.* (eds.), *Crime and the Law: The Social History of Crime in Europe since 1500*, London, Europa, 1980, pp. 190–213.
138 Peter Quennell (ed.), *London's Underground, Being Selections from 'Those That Will Not Work', the Fourth Volume of 'London Labour and the London Poor' by Henry Mayhew*, London, Spring Books, 1950 [1862], p. 29.
139 *Ibid.*, p. 135.
140 V. A. C. Gatrell, "Crime, Authority and the Policeman State", *in* F. M. L. Thompson, ed., *The Cambridge Social History of Britain 1750–1950*, 3 vols., vol. 3: *Social Agencies and Institutions*, Cambridge, Cambridge University Press, 1990, p. 250; Emsley, *Crime and Society*, p. 175; Victor Bailey, "The Fabrication of Deviance?: 'Dangerous Classes' and 'Criminal Classes' in Victorian England", in John Rule & Robert Malcolmson (ed.), *Protest and Survival: The Historical Experience*, London, Merlin Press, 1993, p. 254.
141 Bailey, "The Fabrication of Deviance?", pp. 237–38. Archibald Allison's comments are from "Causes of the Increase of Crime", *Blackwood's Edinburgh Magazine*, vol. 56, July 1844, pp. 1–14. The following passage gives a good idea of the tone of his

article: "If the past increase and present amount of crime in the British islands be alone considered, it must afford grounds for the most melancholy forebodings … Meanwhile, destitution, profligacy, sensuality and crime advance with unheard-of rapidity in the manufacturing districts, and the dangerous classes there massed together combine every three or four years in some general strike or alarming insurrection, which, while it lasts, excites universal terror" (pp. 1–2).

142 Marie-Christine Leps, *Apprehending the Criminal: The Production of Deviance in Nineteenth-Century Discourse*, Durham & London, Duke University Press, 1992, p. 23.

143 Edwin Chadwick, *Report on the Sanitary Condition of the Labouring Population*, London, 1842, "Conclusions", quoted in Neil Tongue & Michael Quincy (eds.), *British Social and Economic History 1800–1900*, London, Macmillan, 1980, pp. 60–61. Cf. Anthony S. Wohl, *Endangered Lives: Public Health in Victorian Britain*, London, Dent, 1983.

144 Thomas Plint, *Crime in England, its Relation, Character and Extent*, London, 1851, p. 146.

145 *Ibid.*, p. 153.

146 William Pare, *A Plan for the Suppression of the Predatory Classes*, London, 1862.

147 *Ibid.*, pp. 23–24.

148 Emsley, *Crime and Society*, pp. 173, 175. See also Bailey, *op. cit.*, p. 246.

149 David Philips, "Crime, Law and Punishment in the Industrial Revolution", *in* Patrick O'Brien & Roland Quinault (eds.), *The Industrial Revolution and British Society*, Cambridge, Cambridge University Press, 1993, Table 7.1, p. 158.

150 Government statistician G. R. Porter (1847), quoted in *ibid.*, p. 158.

151 Gatrell, "Crime, Authority and the Policeman State", p. 250. Among the factors responsible for the dramatic rise in crime rates in this period was the increased speed and falling costs of prosecution (thanks, for example to the spread of summary jurisdiction) and the greater intervention of law enforcement agencies, following the creation of professional police forces from the 1820s (Clive Emsley, *The English Police: A Political and Social History*, 2nd edition, London, Longmans, 1996, chs. 2–3).

152 Emsley, *Crime and Society*, pp. 276–77; Radzinowicz & Hood, *Emergence of Penal Policy*, pp. 243–44.

153 Emsley, *op. cit.*, pp. 277–78.

154 "Report from the Select Committee of the House of Lords on the Present State of Discipline in Gaols and Houses of Correction", *Parliamentary Papers*, 1863, vol. 9; "Report of the Royal Commission on Transportation and Penal Servitude", *Parliamentary Papers*, 1863, vol. 21.

155 *Ibid.*, p. 278.

156 "Carnarvon Committee", p. 12.

157 Quoted in Forsythe, *Reform of Prisoners*, p. 145. On Lord Carnarvon's views on penal reform, see Sean McConville, *English Local Prisons 1860 to 1900: "Next Only to Death"*, London, Routledge, 1994, chs. 1, 3.

158 *Ibid.*, p. 116.

159 The expression is a contemporary one, quoted in Priestley, *Victorian Prison Lives*, pp. 125, 129. The realities of punitive labour are captured with grim effectiveness in *ibid.*, pp. 124–31; and in McConville, "The Victorian Prison", pp. 132–35. The latter describes punitive labour as "scarcely veiled torture" (p. 132).

160 Cf. the later remarks of prison medical officer Dr R. F. Quinton, who wrote: "Though it has always seemed to me a more or less barbarous and senseless proceeding to apply to human beings, [it] was nevertheless very necessary with unruly prisoners. I know of nothing approaching a scientific excuse for its use, except the principle on which a horse has its oats reduced in order to tame his spirit" (R.F. Quinton, *Crime and Criminals 1876–1910*, London, Longmans, 1910, p. 27).

161 McConville, *History of English Prison Administration*, pp. 349–64.

162 *Ibid.*, p. 349.

163 "Report from the Select Committee of the House of Lords", pp. 128, 221, 290; "Report of the Royal Commission", pp. 140, 427, 450.

164 Forsythe, *op. cit.*, pp. 160–62. In the 1864 act, the minimum sentence was raised to five not seven years, except for those with a previous conviction for felony. For such recidivists the right to remission was abolished. The latter rule remained in force until 1891 (Radzinowicz & Hood, *Emergence of Penal Policy*, p. 531 & note no. 15).

165 Frederic Hill, *Crime: Its Amount, Causes and Remedies*, London, John Murray, 1853, pp. 34–35. See also Robinson, *Prison Characters*, vol. 2, p. 249.

166 Crofton, *Immunity of Habitual Criminals*, p. 23. See also *idem.*, "The Criminal Classes", *Transactions of the National Association for the Promotion of Social Science*, 1868, pp. 299–311. Captain Crofton was Chairman of the Directors of Convict Prisons in Ireland, and an influential voice on penal matters.

167 According to the *Oxford English Dictionary*, the first use of the word in this sense dates to 1867.

168 "Report of the Royal Commission", p. 127. On this point, see Radzinowicz & Hood, *The Emergence of Penal Policy*, 1990, p. 7; Forsythe, *The Reform of Prisoners*, p. 187.

169 Quoted in Semple, *Bentham's Prison*, p. 93.

Chapter Two

"The Tyranny of Organisation": Towards a Natural History of Crime

When a race of plants is to be improved, gardeners go over their seed beds and pull up the rogues, as they call the plants that deviate from the proper standard. With cattle, this kind of selection is in fact always followed; for hardly any one is so careless as to allow his worst animals to breed. Why, then, should incorrigible criminals, at the healthy, vigorous period of life, be at large; why should they go into prison for short periods only, to be sent out again in renewed health, to propagate a race so low in physical organisation?

Dr James Bruce Thomson, Resident Surgeon,
Perth General Prison, 1870[1]

Systematic scientific study of the Criminal would only emerge in Britain with the appointment of full-time, resident medical personnel to the country's convict prisons. The first appointments had been made in the 1840s, but it was not until the passage of the Act for the Better Government of Convict Prisons (1850) and the setting up of a professional, centralised Directorate to administer the penal system, that we can talk about a prison medical service as a professional entity, with a corps of career practitioners.[2] The former penitentiaries of Millbank and Pentonville, together with the newer public works prisons at Portland, Parkhurst and Dartmoor would each have their own full-time, resident prison medical officer, usually seconded by an assistant-surgeon. Though there were some early recruits who had began life working as naval surgeons, it soon became customary for prison doctors to spend their whole professional careers behind bars, working their way up the ladder from assistant-surgeon to one of the more senior posts. Some went on to become governors or deputy-governors.[3]

As for the local prisons and houses of correction, they were not yet under central government control. The extent and nature of medical care provided thus varied enormously from prison to prison. In the majority of cases, however, a local general practitioner would devote just a few hours a week to examining prisoners and prescribing medicines. From 1865, the Prisons Act imposed a statutory weekly examination for all inmates in local prisons, but until their nationalisation in 1877, the only real "prison doctors" were those posted to the convict prisons.[4]

Yet the appointment of prison medical officers to the country's convict prisons does not in itself explain why several of their number embarked on detailed empirical research on the mental and physical characteristics of the prisoners in their charge, nor why such work emerged in the particular context of the 1860s. Stephen Watson has argued convincingly that such research grew out of the highly particular nature of the medical officer's function in the British penal regime as it developed in the 1850s and '60s. The prison doctor was under a statutory duty to distinguish on a daily basis between those prisoners "fit" for labour or punishment, and those "unfit" for physical or mental reasons. It was in this context that prison doctors began to diagnose a mental condition which, while short of certifiable insanity, nonetheless rendered certain prisoners "unfit for discipline". This was the context in which the label "weakminded" began to be used; not so much a description of a clearly-defined psychiatric condition as a pragmatic way for prison medical officers to segregate those inmates considered incapable of bearing the rigours of the prison regime.[5]

This triage was made all the more difficult by *malingering*, a problem regarded by doctors working inside the prison system as a major and highly specific burden placed on their shoulders.[6] An article from *The Lancet* in July 1877 summed up the difficulties involved here, seen from the point of view of the prison doctor:

> The medical officers of these prisons have to deal with malingering of every shape and form. The art, in fact, is practiced among convicts with a refinement that baffles description, and seems attainable only by cunning thieves and lazy wretches, who prefer preying on society to earning an honest livelihood, and who for the most part occupy our prisons. All this adds considerably to the difficulties of their work, and if errors of diagnosis are made occasionally, they are generally in the prisoners' favour.[7]

Indeed, according to Charles Pennell Measor, one-time deputy governor at Chatham Prison,

> The position of the medical officer over convicts is not at all an enviable one and it requires strongly to be upheld and shielded by the discipline authorities of a prison. … The Surgeon has enough to do to guard the door of his infirmary against malingers; and to do this effectually

> requires great firmness and determination. … There is no officer—not excepting the Governor, who exercises the power of punishment—who runs greater personal risks.[8]

The following testimony by Dartmoor's medical officer (contained in his annual report to his superiors for the year 1878–9) sets the problem of malingering in the context of the prison doctor's other responsibilities:

> Another year of anxious work has passed, how anxious, none but a prison surgeon can fully comprehend. Unlike his confrères in the public hospitals he bears an undivided responsibility, together with professional work of the most varied character. Disease in the most anomalous form comes under his treatment, complicated at all times with the possibility of malingering, and also with the possibility of genuine disease being treated as unreal, so clever are some imposters; thus entailing the greatest caution, and guiding the surgeon to err, if at all, on the safe side. In addition to his hospital work, he has in his charge everything relating to health in the prison, so that ventilation, dietary, clothing, work, [and] punishments are all guided by him, the latter especially gives him much thought and anxiety; careful as he must be to make the convicts' health his first charge, and yet, at the same time, not screen the offender, or seem to interfere with the duties and prerogatives of the discipline authority.[9]

It is not surprising perhaps in such circumstances that prison medical officers should sometimes have been assaulted by their would-be patients. A Pentonville prisoner in the 1850s "savagely" attacked the prison's medical officer, stabbing him with a weapon he had fashioned for the purpose. The avowed motive was that "a request to be allowed some indulgences in addition to his diet" had been turned down. Two warders who came to the doctor's rescue were also injured. The prisoner later "regretted that he had not 'killed the doctor' as he had intended, alleging that for some time past his food had been 'powdered' or poisoned by the medical officer's orders."[10] Such a level of violence was rare, but prisoners frequently took out their frustrations on prison property—tearing clothes, smashing windows and destroying bedding—or on each other. Such behaviour was likely to lead to demotion to the prison's "penal class", described by Dr C. Lawrence Bradley, Pentonville's medical officer in 1862 as containing "the refuse and scum of the convict population; the failures of the various schemes of prison discipline." Such men were, Bradley went on,

> Of lower physical status than ordinary convicts, with peculiarly perverse and uncontrollable tempers; damaged somewhat in health, and rendered still more irritable in mind by accumulated prison punishments, they may naturally be expected to increase the amount of disease and mortality in the prison.[11]

The kind of "accumulated punishments" to which Dr Bradley was referring included solitary confinement in a "dark cell" on a diet of bread of water, perhaps accompanied by the use of handcuffs, a body belt or straitjacket. In cases of repeated disruptive behaviour, a sentence of flogging might be ordered, though this was unusual.[12]

There is no evidence that prison doctors had any fundamental ethical difficulty in accommodating the humanitarian with the punitive aspects of their calling; a stance which has been condemned as callous by some historians[13], but which, as Martin Wiener points out, is perfectly consistent with the moral universe in which mid-Victorian doctors, like other prison officials, moved; one which sought to balance what he calls the "two faces of Benthamism": lenity and severity.[14] That being said, there seems little doubt that what Portland's medical officer called in 1870 "the unpleasant topic of malingering"[15] did make it all the more difficult to arrive at reliable diagnoses, something which added to the workload—and no doubt to the stress level—associated with the job.[16]

There was clearly room for disagreement with other members of the prison hierarchy on the issue of prisoners' "fitness" for a particular form of labour, diet or punishment, something which posed an additional headache for prison medical officers.[17] Convict prisons director Captain James Gambier referred in passing to such tensions in his evidence to the 1863 Royal Commission on Penal Servitude. He describes "invalids" as "the most troublesome men of all troublesome men to manage; one hardly knows how to deal with them; you cannot punish them, *the medical officer will not allow you to do it* ..."[18] Gambier went on to observe, seemingly with regret, that as many as 1360 out of 8000 inmates in Britain's convict prisons had been ruled "unfit for transportation" by prison medical officers.[19]

An incident at Parkhurst Prison in 1875 illustrates the difficulties which could arise in such cases. The prison had since 1869 been catering mainly for short-stay, mentally unstable and physically handicapped "invalid" inmates[20], and it was over the appropriate form of labour to be assigned to one such prisoner that medical officer Dr Henry Roome found himself at loggerheads with the prison governor. Roome argued that it was his job, and his alone, to assess "how men should be employed, taking peculiarities of mind and body into consideration". The Governor demurred, and evidently took his grievance to the top, for Chairman of the Directors of Convict Prisons, Edmund Du Cane, arrived in person at Parkhurst in October 1875 to sort out the problem. Dr Roome found himself on the receiving end of an official reprimand: Du Cane reminded him that it was the Governor's role, and *not* the doctor's, "to prescribe the exact employment of an invalid".[21] Roome clearly had some difficulty coping with these and other pressures single-handedly. In a letter of 1871, he lamented that his work was "greater than one man can perform"; and that while he had "endeavoured to discharge ... [his] daily increasing duties with a will", he had found himself "sorely pressed". The appointment of an assistant-surgeon was, he argued, an urgent necessity. His calls evidently fell on deaf ears, for his successor was still petitioning for an extra pair of hands in the early 1880s.[22]

It was clearly important to establish objective criteria for deciding just who was "fit" for labour and punishment and who was not, not just as an aid to rapid and accurate diagnosis, but also to pre-empt any challenge to that diagnosis from any other quarter. Here was an eminently practical reason for prison medical officers to reflect on the precise nature and extent of physical and mental disabilities among prison inmates.

The first example of such reflection dates from the beginning of the 1860s. Shortly before his death in 1863, Sir Joshua Jebb, the then head of the Home Office's Directorate of Convict Prisons, commissioned a "census" of the prisoners under his jurisdiction, some 7600 in all.[23] Of these, slightly over 20% were being held in separate confinement, mostly at Millbank and Pentonville, a similar number at one of the country's "invalid depots" at Dartmoor and Woking; 500 or so "juveniles" at Parkhurst; and the remaining 50% were engaged in public works at Portland, Portsmouth, and Chatham.[24]

The job of coordinating the survey was given to the medical superintendent at Millbank. The post of Medical Superintendent at the former General Penitentiary had come to be seen as the senior appointment in the service, its occupant filling the role of unofficial advisor to the Home Office on prison medical matters.[25] The doctor charged with carrying out Jebb's census was Dr William Augustus Guy (1810–1885), who has been described as "perhaps the foremost prison medical officer of the mid-Victorian period".[26] However, his career was untypical; unlike most prison doctors, he came into the convict service late in life (he was 49), and had already held senior posts at King's College London as Dean of the medical faculty and Professor of Forensic Medicine before taking up the post at Millbank in 1859. Indeed, he would leave the job just six years later to return to King's as Professor of Hygiene in 1865. Alongside his other interests, Guy campaigned energetically for sanitary reform, and was also a keen amateur statistician: he edited the *Journal of the Statistical Society* between 1852 and 1856 and would go on to become President of the Statistical Society in the 1870s.[27]

The status of Millbank at this period as a sorting house for convicts meant that Dr Guy was permanently having to make the kind of choices referred to earlier; to distinguish between those prisoners in his charge considered "fit" for transportation or assignment to one of the public works prisons, and those whose physical or mental disabilities necessitated internment in one of the country's two "invalid depots". There is also evidence that his diagnostic skills were called upon by other convict and local prisons when there was some doubt as to the mental or physical health of a particular prisoner.[28]

Guy had evidently been keeping statistical records on the prisoners coming through his doors from the moment of his appointment. His findings for 1859 revealed that of the 505 convicts he had examined, 28.7% were suffering from either "mental or bodily defects"; the former category being for the most part composed of the "weak-minded", with smaller numbers labelled as "insane" or suffering from "fits". The remaining 71% were declared "free from the above mental or bodily defects".[29] Guy extrapolated from these figures that "... in no class or section of the population would there be found so considerable a proportion affected with the mental bodily infirmities specified in the table."[30]

Three years later, Dr Guy extended his survey to the whole of Britain's convict population, aided by the medical officers of four other government-run prisons. In March 1862, 5952 men and 1218 women were examined. Dr Guy calculated the proportion of male and female convicts free of any infirmity or defect at 60% and 75% respectively. In spite of his observation that only 47.7% of male convicts were "able-bodied and robust", his overall conclusion was noticeably more optimistic than that of 1859: "the male convict population is at least as healthy as any other population with which it can be justly compared ..."[31]

It is interesting that Guy should have shifted ground on this issue, despite the fact that the results of the census were broadly similar to the figures he had collected three years earlier at Millbank. However, his revised position is in keeping with the stance he took in his evidence before the Carnarvon Commission of 1863, where he wholeheartedly backed demands for a renewed insistence on penal labour, and adamantly refuted the suggestion made by other medical witnesses that the prison regime contributed directly to prisoners' ill-health. Indeed, he lobbied for a *reduction* in the quantities hitherto prescribed by the prison dietary. Such a change, would, he argued with classic Benthamite logic, give the prison regime a more thoroughly punitive character, without having any adverse effects on prisoners' health, while saving taxpayers' money into the bargain.[32]

This was all grist to Lord Carnarvon's punitive mill of course, and while the committee declared itself unqualified to lay down guidelines for a modified prison dietary, it did announce the setting up of a "Committee of Scientific Inquiry" to look into the question further. The new committee, composed of three prison medical officers—including Guy himself[33]—would reach conclusions almost identical to those set out by the Millbank doctor in his evidence to the Carnarvon Committee, a fact which suggests to Anne Hardy that "he played a decisive part in formulating the [inquiry's] recommendations."[34]

In a paper read to the National Association for the Promotion of Social Science the same year, Guy expanded on his penal philosophy:

> The prisoner not only undergoes no punishment beyond that which the law awards him, or which his own perverse conduct in prison may bring upon him, ... but his health is carefully protected against every cause of injury not inseparable from the state of imprisonment and his own wilful conduct when in prison. ... It ought not to be forgotten, that the objects of all this watchful solicitude are not the mixed groups of debtors and criminals of very degree, on whose behalf John Howard exerted himself, but the most depraved, the most reckless, the most violent, the most brutal of mankind.[35]

In a later article, he again cautioned against inappropriately lenient treatment for criminals:

> I have always felt more sympathy with the victims, than with the perpetrators of crime; I do not shrink from the thought of the pain inflicted by corporal punishment when it falls on cruel and brutal offenders against the law, or on those who add serious breaches of the law to the crimes which led to their incarceration; nor have I have I found any reason to prefer any other punishment for murder to death upon the scaffold.[36]

Such comments were in perfect accord with a vocal section of public opinion, incensed that convicts in Jebb's regime apparently enjoyed better food than honest labourers on the outside. A caricature in *Punch* which appeared in December 1862 depicted Jebb's "Pen of Pet Lambs" feasting on the copious prison fare.[37] The "Committee of Scientific Inquiry", for its part, concluded that the weekly allowance of solid food could be safely cut by 15% in the public works prisons, and by 7% elsewhere.[38] Although both Guy and fellow committee member Dr Vans Clarke (who had previously collaborated on the 1862 census) extolled the virtues of the new slimmed-down dietary in their subsequent annual reports to the Convict Prison Commissioners, other prison doctors remained unconvinced, as was the medical profession more generally.[39] In 1868, *The Lancet* reminded its readers that the criminal constitution being "deteriorated by vice and privation", it was necessary for the prisoner's physique "to be raised rather than lowered". While making it clear that it did not advocate "the coddling of criminals", the journal added that "on the score of economy as well as humanity, it is wise to diminish the list of medical comforts by increasing the supply of butcher's meat."[40]

William Guy stood firm in the face of such pressure. In 1873, he repeated his prison census, confident, no doubt, that the results would silence his critics once and for all. A comparison of the results of the two national censuses was published by Her Majesty's Stationery Office in 1875.[41] As might have been expected, Guy found no evidence to support the contention that "male prisoners have degenerated and become less fit for labour since the date of the first census."[42] In fact, the tables, compiled by Guy with the help of the same four prison doctors as in 1862[43], revealed little evidence of change in the overall health of the prisoners between the two censuses. As far as their fitness for labour was concerned, 77% of the prisoners were now considered "able-bodied" or "healthy, as against 72% in 1862. The figures on the physical and mental health of the convict population revealed a similar picture: 63% were considered free of infirmities and defects in 1873, compared with 60% in 1862[44].

Indeed, Guy congratulated himself that at Millbank, "...very little, if anything, remained to be done to promote the health and well-being of the prisoners". "Our convicts", he added, "were the subject of constant solicitude in matters relating to their bodily health, their intellectual improvement, and their spiritual welfare."[45] Edmund Du Cane, Chairman of the Directors of Convict Prisons, lent his own considerable weight to the Millbank doctor's optimistic conclusion. In a preface to Guy's 1875 book, he wrote that "the medical opinion so generally expressed by medical officers and others that the male convicts are less physically able-bodied than in former years, is not all borne out by these statistics."[46]

One of those carping "medical officers" to whom Du Cane referred was undoubtedly Dr James Bruce Thomson of Perth General Prison. In an 1866 article for the *Journal of Mental Science*, the Scottish doctor had emphasised the "danger to the mental condition from the separate system of prison discipline" and warned of the dire consequences of a deficient dietary on "systems [already ...] deteriorated by hereditary and habitual vices."[47] By the end of the 1860s, however, as C. H. S. Jayewardine has pointed out[48], Thomson's focus had shifted. He did not abandon his conviction that "long and frequent imprisonments" had a debilitating effect on the criminal constitution[49], but his later work concentrated on the physical and mental traits which set the Criminal apart from the rest of humanity.

In his 1866 article, Thomson had already stated—echoing Mayhew—that

> The thief appears to me as completely marked off from honest working people as black-faced sheep are from other breeds … Their physique is coarse and repulsive; their complexion dingy, almost atrabilious; their face, figure and mien, disagreeable … In fact, there is a stamp upon them in form and expression which seems to me to be the heritage of the class.[50]

He expanded on these points in the first of his 1870 articles, emphasising the incorrigibility of this "born devil on whose nature, nurture could never stick":

> There is a criminal class distinct from other civilized and criminal men … marked by peculiar physical and mental characteristics. [Moreover, …] the hereditary nature of crime is shewn by the *family* histories of criminals [and …] the *incurable* nature of crime in the criminal class goes to prove its hereditary nature.[51]

Thomson's remarks on criminal physiognomy echoed those of his 1866 article: "a low type of men and women [with] a set of coarse, angular, clumsy, stupid set of features and dirty complexion. … all have a sinister and repulsive expression in look and mien."[52] This time, however, he supplemented such general descriptions with more specific observations drawn from his own clinical experience. Noting that ill-health and insanity were on the increase among prisoners, he also stressed the poor physical and mental condition of the prisoners he had examined:

> In all my experience, I have never seen such an accumulation of morbid appearances as I witness in the post mortem examinations of the prisoners who die here. Scarcely one of them can be said to die of one disease, for almost every organ of the body is more or less diseased; and the wonder to me is that life could have been supported in such a diseased frame.[53]

Mental and moral depravity were a direct result of this physical degeneration, Thomson argued, and according to his reckoning, 12% of the prison population were "mentally weak".[54]

The question of the psychology of the Criminal was further explored in a second, longer article for the *Journal of Mental Science*, published later in the same year. The first part of his paper was devoted to a discussion of the work of French alienist, Prosper Despine, one of several French practitioners who had sought to apply the concept of "moral insanity" to the study of crime.[55] The term had first been coined by the British physician and ethnologist James C. Prichard in 1835, though in fact the concept was even older.[56] Like the phrenologists, Prichard distinguished between the intellectual, cognitive, knowing aspects of man's mental life, and the feeling, conative, emotional part. A disorder of the former he termed "intellectual insanity", and of the latter "moral insanity". In his book *Treatise on Insanity* (1835), Prichard had provided the following definition:

> … madness consisting in morbid perversion of the natural feelings, affections, inclinations, temper, habits, moral dispositions, and natural impulses, without any remarkable disorder or defect of the intellect or knowing and reasoning faculties, and particularly without any insane illusion or hallucination … the moral and active principles of the mind are strangely perverted and depraved; the power of self-government is lost or greatly impaired; and the individual is found to be incapable, … of conducting himself with decency and propriety in the business of life.[57]

Despine's work, drawing on that of Prichard and Pinel, described a type of person whose behaviour was violent, cruel or avaricious, but who showed no signs of mental confusion. Such people were, in his view, natural anomalies, mental monstrosities. Thomson applied this concept to Britain's prison population, declaring that "violent and habitual criminals are, as a class, moral imbeciles"; a description, he suggests, proven by their "frequent re-committals" and "apparent absence of remorse". Other common behavioural characteristics confirmed this diagnosis: "want of control", "lying" and imperviousness to any kind of "moral treatment".[58] If, as he suggested, crime was "intractable in the highest degree and must be so because it is hereditary", it was no wonder that "all modes of criminal treatment, severe or mild, have failed in giving anything like satisfactory results." There was then little alternative but "life-confinement" for such "intractable" cases. Long sentences and transportation would break up the "*caste* and community of the [criminal] class"; a solution "at once economical to the country and a mercy to the criminal."[59] Thomson admitted that his views might be considered extreme; however, he insisted that his observations were but an accurate reflection of twelve years' practical experience with criminals as prison medical officer at Perth.[60]

Shortly before the first of Bruce Thomson's articles, Dr George Wilson, assistant surgeon at Woking Convict Prison, had read a paper before the British Association for the Advancement of Science, entitled "On Moral Imbecility of Habitual Criminals as exemplified by Cranial Measurement".[61] Unfortunately, the original paper has not survived, and all we have to go on is a later summary of Wilson's research, made in 1890 by Havelock

Ellis.[62] We learn that Wilson had measured the heads of 464 convicts, and reached the conclusion that 40% of his sample turned out to be "invalids" (i.e. weak-minded), with a concentration in the "professional thief class". Such habitual thieves presented, according to Dr Wilson's research, "well-marked signs of insufficient cranial development, particularly anteriorly". There were also physical abnormalities: "bullet heads, low brows, projecting ears, weasel eyes" and a "morbid condition of the brain or other organs in the shape of tumours, cancers, ulcerations or irritating secretions which have fully accounted for mental or moral defects." It is unclear whether Wilson provided any quantitative corroboration for these comments.[63]

Four years after George Wilson revealed his findings to the British Association, a prison medical officer from Portsmouth Prison went into print with his own reflections on convict physiognomy and psychology.[64] Like James Thomson, fellow Scot Dr David Nicolson (1844–1932) was at pains to distinguish the "accidental" from the "habitual and thorough criminal". His description of the latter, evocative of phrenological and physiognomic terminology, was also couched in terms similar to Thomson's: "… an unmistakable *physique* with rough and irregular outline and massiveness in the seats of an expression. His physiognomy is distinctive and seems to be a very embodiment of grossness and unworthiness."[65] As the title of Nicolson's articles suggests, he pays particular attention to the mental state of the prisoners in his charge. "Weak-mindedness" is considered to be essentially a "congenital defect"; and its manifestations to include a "lying propensity", a "persistency of malevolence", and "emotional outbursts". Such "criminal-mindedness", as Nicolson also terms it, is "supported by an appearance of motive and self-interest just sufficient to prevent it falling within the range of insanity."

In his 1874 article, Nicolson returned to the question of the physical appearance of these "prisoners of the congenitally weak stamp". Their "congenital defect" is often visible, he notes, in their "small and mis-shapen head [which] … renders impossible any considerable development of mental power." He goes on to point out that such criminals "carry their defects with them in their face; their gait and their expression at once tell those who come into contact with them what they are or are not to expect from them."[66] To illustrate his point, Nicolson included a page of photographic portraits, "sufficiently well-marked to form typical illustrations of the physiognomy of weak-minded criminals". One of the photographs, of an Irish pig-driver convicted of rape and manslaughter, was singled out for particular comment as follows: "Remarkable baboon-like expression—a veritable missing link".[67]

Page of Photographs of "Weak-Minded" Criminals, 1875

David Nicolson, "The Morbid Psychology of Criminals", *Journal of Mental Science*, vol. 21, 1875.

In some respects, these articles by Thomson and Nicolson can be seen as the direct descendants of the phrenological and physiognomic analyses discussed in the previous chapter. The conviction that, in Nicolson's words, criminals "carry their defects with them in their face", and that head shape and size provide a clue to intelligence, are both ideas that hark back to phrenological and physiognomic theories of the early and mid-Victorian periods.[68] Indeed, they point to a crucial point of contact between professional and educated lay opinion on the subject. Thomson's and Nicolson's research is couched in the language of the medical practitioner, but its assumptions are identical in their essentials to those of newspaper reviewers of Frith's painting *The Railway Station* discussed in the previous chapter.

For all its emphasis on the importance of empirical observation—"we neither deny nor affirm any thing", wrote Spurzheim, "which cannot be verified by experiment"[69]—phrenology had proved itself incapable of reproducing its results on a large scale.[70] Both Thomson and Nicolson, in contrast, were practised analysts of statistical data: Thomson had published an article in 1861 based on a quantitative study of the mental and physical ailments of prisoners, and in 1872 Nicolson had considered the question of mortality statistics.[71] This reflected the growing prestige of the new science of statistics, symbolised by the setting up of the Statistical Department of the Board of Trade in 1832 and the Statistical Society of London in 1834. By the 1840s, the manipulation of series of statistical data was a commonplace of government reports, whether on Britain's economic performance, conditions in its factories or the state of the country's provision of public health.[72]

An examination of the work of these three doctors, all of whom based their conclusions on direct clinical experience of the convict population, reveals, then, a certain continuity with earlier naturalistic approaches to criminal behaviour, but it could be argued that the latter were re-interpreted in the particular intellectual climate of the late 1860s and early 1870s. A useful way of tapping into that intellectual climate is to study the early works of alienist Henry Maudsley (1835–1918), the most influential practitioner of this period, well-known in France, Germany and Italy as well as in England.[73] Indeed, he was one of a select group of European alienists chosen in 1867 to pronounce on the mental state of the Habsburg Archduchess Charlotte, Empress of Mexico.[74]

Maudsley's best-known work was published between 1867 and 1874[75], precisely that period when Drs Thomson, Nicolson and Wilson were publishing their researches. In those years, Maudsley was in private practice in London, a physician in mental diseases at the West London Hospital and, from 1869, professor of medical jurisprudence at University College, London. He also found time to jointly edit the *Journal of Mental Science*.[76] His work is interesting not so much for the author's originality of thought, as for the opportunity it provides to examine a popular synthesis of several currents of contemporary opinion. As Daniel Pick has pointed out[77], his ideas contain a confluence of three elements, elements also present, if implicitly, in the work of Thomson and the other prison doctors.

Firstly, we see a determinist view of criminal inheritance. "Multitudes of individuals", he wrote in typically arresting style in *Body and Mind* (1870), "come into this world weighed with a destiny against which they have neither the will, nor the power to contend; they are the step-children of nature and groan under the worst of all tyrannies—the tyranny of a bad organisation."[78] Later in the book, he puts it even more bluntly: "in consequence of evil ancestral influences, individuals are born with such a flaw or warp in their nature that all the care in the world will not prevent them from being vicious or criminal, or insane." Returning to his term "the tyranny of organisation", he reminds his readers in no uncertain terms that "no one can elude the destiny that is innate in him, and which unconsciously and irresistibly shapes his ends, even when he believes that he is determining them with consummate foresight and skill."[79] In a later work, Maudsley put the same point rather differently, but no less alarmingly. Every individual can be sure, he wrote, "that he is living his forefathers essentially over again ... and furthermore suspect that the vicious or virtuous ancestral quality, imbued as silent memory in his nature may leap to light on the occasion of its fit stimulus."[80]

In this way the sins of the fathers would necessarily be visited on their children, the latter unaware of this "silent memory", implanted in their constitutions before their birth. Maudsley demonstrates here his belief in the Lamarckian doctrine that mental processes and habits acquired through experience could be transmitted to the next generation.[81] In theory at least, Lamarck's doctrine, born as it was in the French Enlightenment, held out the possibility that, given the right stimuli, the human will could intervene and modify such anti-social habits.[82] However, Maudsley emphasised instead the inevitability of criminal heredity; for him, like for Marx, the tradition of dead generations did indeed weigh like a nightmare on the brains of the living.[83] In *Responsibility in Mental Disease* (1874), Maudsley put it in his characteristic highly-charged language:

> No wonder that the criminal *psychosis*, which is the mental side of the *neurosis*, is for the most part an intractable malady, punishment being of no avail to produce permanent reformation. The dog returns to its vomit and the sow to its wallowing in the mire. A true reformation would be the *re*-forming of the individual nature; and how can that which has been forming through generations be *re*-formed within the term of a single life? Can the Ethiopian change his skin or the leopard his spots?[84]

The second element in Maudsley's conception is that the criminal-type represents "a degenerate or morbid variety of mankind", congenitally sick or diseased, both physically and mentally. Quoting the research of Dr Bruce Thomson, Maudsley observes:

> All persons who have made criminals their study recognise a distinct criminal class of beings, who herd together in our large cities in a thieves' quarter, giving themselves up to intemperance, rioting in debauchery, without regard to marriage ties or the bars of consanguinity, and propagating a criminal population of degenerate beings. For it is furthermore a matter of observation that this criminal class constitutes a degenerate or morbid variety of mankind, marked by peculiar low physical and mental characteristics ... so that an experienced detective officer or prison official could pick them out from any promiscuous assembly at church or market.[85]

Again, Maudsley was not particularly original here, combining a commonplace portrait of the moral bankruptcy and physiognomic specificity of the criminal classes with newer fashionable notions of "degeneration". The term, French in origin (*dégénérescence*), is associated particularly with the work of the alienist Dr Bénédict-Augustin Morel (1809–73) in the 1850s[86], but since the beginning of the '60s, there had been a lively debate on the topic in the pages of Britain's medical journals.[87]

American criminologist Nicole Hahn Rafter notes that in the nineteenth century, the term degeneration was

> ... roughly synonymous with *bad heredity* and conceived as an invisible attribute of the 'germ plasm' or 'blood', ... a tendency to devolve to a lower, simpler, less civilised state. Nineteenth-century theorists taught that the downward spiral into degeneracy could be brought on by immorality (e.g., drinking, gluttony, or sexual excess) and that, if sustained, it could damage the germ plasm. Thus future generations could inherit the degenerative tendency.[88]

A good example of such reasoning can be found in a paper by Thomas Beggs, read to the National Association for the Promotion of Social Science in 1868, entitled "Repression and Prevention of Crime."[89] In it we can see clearly the Lamarckian emphasis on the inheritance of acquired characteristics:

> Paupers and criminals are a degenerated class; their condition arises from defects of organisation; that is, the men, women, and children who comprise the dangerous classes have weak or diseased brains, and are physically stunted, scrofulous, or feeble. They are constitutionally incapacitated, or indisposed to learn or follow any fixed or settled pursuit. This is often the result of hereditary transmission, to which is added neglect in infancy and bad training, sometimes from insufficient or precarious supplies of food, or food of improper quality, of early indulgence in unnatural and vicious habits; and again, from living in fever nests, breathing a vitiated atmosphere, and drinking large quantities of intoxicating drinks.[90]

As Maudsley's remarks suggest, the *locus classicus* of such "degeneracy" was the "low neighbourhoods" of Britain's industrial towns and cities. Indeed, the whole degeneracy debate was closely linked to worries about the effects of urbanisation. An article in *The Lancet* in June 1866 expressed concern about the country's cities provoking "an overtaxing of the physical and mental energies of national life-blood." Though originating in the "vicious" criminal classes of the Victorian metropolis, it was feared that such processes of degeneration were "not confined in their consequences to the guilty sufferers, but are passed on to the offspring, and thus become year by year more generally diffused among the great mass of the people."[91]

A Dr Morgan, addressing the *National Association for the Promotion of Social Science* in 1865, described the effects of such diffusion, citing the case of the lower classes of Manchester:

> Few are men of that calibre from which we might expect either vigorous and healthy offspring, or arduous and sustained labour. Cases of deformity accompanied by actual distortion, are not uncommon, while minor physical defects, denoting constitutional ailments are deplorably frequent.

Dr Druitt, President of the Association of Medical Officers of Health for London, set out the wider context in 1870: "There is a general lowering of health, a degradation, as it were, of the whole system and character from overcrowding … There is general deterioration of the stock, if I may so call it, of the human plant."[92] One conclusion to draw from this gloomy prognosis was that there was an urgent need to control the reproduction of "degenerates", as Dr Bruce Thomson's comment, quoted at the head of this chapter, makes clear. Like many others, Thomson would see such a priority as a logical inference to be drawn from "the laws of natural selection so well set forth by Mr. Darwin."[93]

On the Origin of Species by Means of Natural Selection, or the Preservation of Favoured Races in the Struggle for Life, written by Charles Darwin (1809–82), had first appeared in 1859. In fact his theory of natural selection had been ready in embryonic form nearly twenty years earlier, but publication had been continually put off, perhaps in an effort to avoid political and theological controversy (Darwin had wrestled with his conscience on the subject, at considerable cost to his mental and physical health).[94] Even when *Origin* was finally published, Darwin deliberately chose to omit any discussion of his theory with reference to human affairs.[95] Though admitting in a letter of 1857 that the subject was "the highest and most interesting problem for the naturalist", it was, he lamented, "so surrounded with prejudices".[96]

However, even shorn of its direct reference to humankind, the wider relevance of the Darwinian model was not lost on contemporaries. Darwin had demonstrated the mechanism by which the "struggle for existence", in other words, "the doctrine of Malthus applied with manifold force to the whole animal and vegetable kingdoms", meant that cut-throat competition benefited each species through the survival of improved stock:

> New and improved varieties will inevitably supplant and exterminate the older, less improved and intermediate varieties; and thus species are rendered to a large extent defined and distinct objects. Dominant species belonging to the larger groups tend to give birth to new and dominant forms; so that each large group tends to become still larger, and at the same time more divergent in character. But as all groups cannot thus succeed in increasing in size, for the world would not hold them, the more dominant groups beat the less dominant.[97]

When it came to human reproduction, some contemporaries failed to see Darwin's "self-improving workshop"[98] at work in the uncontrolled growth of Maudsley's "degenerate or morbid variety of mankind". As Daniel Pick points out:

> The *laissez-faire* of child-birth which in Darwin might seem beneficial, could also appear fearsome given the pathogenic conditions of the city. This view did not mean a return to Malthus, with the bleak assurance of death as nature's response to over-population, but rather a vision of lingering degeneration in the individual, the procreation of a stunted race. Heredity was thus perceived as an unresolved problem which demanded drastic social action. Moral exhortation or illumination alone … was thus deemed incapable of resolving a crisis which was now evolving across generations.[99]

The relationship between Darwin's own theories, elaborated in greater detail in his second great work, *The Descent of Man, and Selection in Relation to Sex* (1871) and the Social Darwinism of the late nineteenth century is a highly complex one. Recent scholarship has tended to emphasise that "Social Darwinism … reasserted many of the traditional ways in which survival of the fittest and population pressure had been used before Darwin."[100] Moreover, the very term most closely identified with Social Darwinism, "the survival of the fittest" was not of Darwin's own invention, but was coined by English philosopher and sociologist, Herbert Spencer, in 1865.[101]

The latter had no difficulty seeing the relevance of the theory of natural selection to competitive, individualistic industrial society, where those with the requisite skills would prosper and those without those skills would adapt or perish. Such a struggle, Spencer believed, was a necessary part of Man's confrontation with his environment. Tinkering with this natural process—for example by welfare measures—would serve only to hinder social evolution by removing the incentive of each individual to adapt himself fully to his social environment (like Malthus, Spencer had vigorously opposed the New Poor Law[102]). The consequences of such reckless intervention for future generations would be catastrophic:

> Fostering the good-for-nothing at the expense of the good, is an extreme cruelty: It is a deliberate storing-up of miseries for future generations. There is no greater curse to prosperity than that of bequeathing them an increasing population of imbeciles and idlers and criminals. To aid the bad in multiplying is, in effect, the same as maliciously providing for our descendants a multitude of enemies. … Refusing to consider the remote influences of his incontinent generosity, the thoughtless giver stands but a degree above the drunkard who thinks only of today's pleasure and ignores tomorrow's pain, or the spendthrift who seeks immediate delights at the cost of ultimate poverty.[103]

Darwin's own position was more nuanced. *The Descent of Man* made it clear that strong and weak creatures of the same type were capable of co-operation, and that as far as Man was concerned, the effect of education and religion upon the "moral qualities" should not be discounted.[104]

Maudsley appears to have shared Spencer's view that human intervention in the process of *natural* selection was not necessary. He was more optimistic than Thomson about the polluting effects of "degenerates" on the rest of society, describing them in typically Social Darwinist fashion as "the waste thrown up by the silent but strong current of progress." The "weakest must suffer", he added, "and some of them break down into madness."[105]

His optimism derived, perhaps, from a reassuring theory (borrowed from Morel), that within a few generations, the degenerate were destined to become infertile and were thus doomed to extinction.

Others did not share the Spencerian vision of natural selection as a benevolent gardener, functioning unaided to weed out Thomson's "rogue plants". Chief among such pessimists was Darwin's cousin, Francis Galton (1822–1911). The year before Thomson's first article for the *Journal of Mental Science*, Galton published *Hereditary Genius: An Inquiry into its Laws and Consequences*, which argued that Man's abilities are chiefly inherited, and that by selective breeding it would be possible to produce a race of highly gifted men.[106] Galton was not, at this stage, particularly interested in the "criminal-type" as such, but as Thomson's remarks quoted above indicate, there was ripe potential for applying the theory of natural selection in this area. Later in the century, as we shall see, the science of "eugenics" would claim to provide the answers to society's ills with just such a programme of controlled reproduction.

To return to Henry Maudsley, the third element in his vision of the criminal was also strongly influenced by Darwin: the theory of evolutionary regression or "recapitulation" as it is sometimes known. Described by Stephen Jay Gould as "among the most influential ideas of late nineteenth-century science"[107], this theory, devised by the German zoologist Ernst Haeckel, held that an individual, as it grows, passes through a series of stages which represent *adult* ancestral forms in their correct order; as Gould puts it, the growing individual "climbs its own family tree."[108]

As far as the *social* sciences were concerned, recapitulation was important in that it gave the stamp of scientific respectability to what every Victorian anthropologist, psychologist and sociologist already knew, namely that the adult white male was at the pinnacle of evolutionary progress.[109] "Inferior" groups—races, sexes, and classes—were thus, like children, living representatives of earlier stages in that evolution. E. D. Cope, an influential American palaeontologist came up with four such "inferior" groups in a widely-read book of 1887: non-white races, all women, southern as opposed to northern European whites, and lower classes within superior races.[110] Similarly, a book of photographs by German ethnographers C. and F. W. Dammann, *Ethnological Photographic Gallery of the Various Races of Man* (1876) presented the world's races in order of their position in the racial hierarchy. His book opened with the "Germanic & Teutonic type", illustrated with a photograph of the celebrated Scottish explorer Dr David Livingstone, and ended with the Australian aborigines, widely considered by Victorian anthropology to be at the lowest stage of human evolution.[111]

In Henry Maudsley's book, *Body and Mind*, first published in 1870, the theory of recapitulation provides the implicit conceptual background to his description of the "degenerate" criminal:

> [There is] truly a brute brain within the man's; and when the latter stops short of its characteristic development as human—when it remains at or below the level of an orang's brain, it may be presumed that it will manifest its most primitive functions ... some very strong arguments in support of Mr Darwin's views may be drawn from the field of morbid psychology. We may, without much difficulty, trace savagery in civilisation, as we can trace animalism in savagery.[112]

Darwin repaid the compliment the following year when his *Descent of Man* quoted Maudsley with approval[113]; the book also recorded the zoologist's support for the recapitulation theory in the following terms:

> With mankind, some of the worst dispositions which occasionally, without any assignable cause make their appearance in families, may be reversions to a savage state from which we are not removed by very many generations. This view seems indeed recognised in the common expression that such men are the black sheep of the family.[114]

These three themes present in Maudsley's work—a determinist view of the weight of heredity in human behaviour, of the criminal as "degenerate", and the criminal as atavistic throwback to an earlier stage of evolution, a kind of walking museum piece—were common enough in medical circles in England and elsewhere in the first half of the 1870s. A good example of such views can be seen in a 1873 article from *The Lancet*:

> If among any body of the community hereditary transmission of physical and moral attributes is conspicuous, it is among the population which fills our gaols. Look at its general physique. Imperfect cranial development, with its concomitant of feeble cerebration, amounting almost to a retrogression in the direction of the brutes, is apparent in the mass of its members. Intellectually and morally they are imbeciles, intelligence being replaced by cunning and the will reduced to its elementary form of desire. In the struggle for existence, they herd together, deriving constant accessions from the degenerate of the classes immediately above them, and perpetuating themselves amid conditions most favourable to the reproduction of their like. [115]

Such views evidently shared by the Chairman of the Directors of Convict Prisons, ex-Royal Engineer Edmund Du Cane (1830–1903). In a speech given in 1875 to the *National Association for the Promotion of Social Science* entitled "Address on the Repression of Crime", he quoted favourably the work of Dr Bruce Thomson, estimating at a third the proportion of convicts with "decidedly diseased constitutions".[116] Such a favourable account of Dr Thomson's work may appear surprising given what Du Cane had to say about his ideas in the preface to Dr Guy's book on the convict census, published the same year. However, the general assertion that many of the weak-minded were habitual criminals and vice versa was a position shared by Guy and Thomson, despite their long-standing differences on the question of the prison dietary. In fact, William Guy, as former unofficial Home Office consultant on prison medical matters and a recognised academic authority on public health questions, was in a strong position to influence official policy on the matter.[117] Du Cane's observation that "in many knaves there is also a large spice of the fool"[118] shows official approval for Guy's position at the very top of the penal regime.

Like the ex-Millbank doctor and—as we have seen—Dr Bruce Thomson, Du Cane was of the opinion that there was little to be done with incorrigible offenders (which he defined as those who having reached the age of 35 were still committing crimes) save to lock them up for long periods. This was not, Du Cane reminded his audience, that in so doing such offenders might be reformed or deterred, but simply to protect the wider community against their depredations. This might appear an expensive solution, he added, but was much less so than letting such criminals at liberty.[119]

The Chairman of the Directors of Convict Prisons purported to keep an open mind on the question of whether the criminal disposition was hereditary or not (noting "differences of opinion" on the subject), but despite such caveats, he seemed drawn towards the biological explanation, for he went on:

> If a criminal disposition is hereditary and transmissible, and the race of criminals is kept up by breeding in-and-in, as is asserted, so that criminals form a distinct caste or type, it might be expected that some common physical peculiarity might be common to the criminal class.[120]

His own observation of prisoners did indeed confirm that "among a large number of criminals, there are sure to be found a considerable proportion who have certain physical characteristics in common ... which denote with certainty the habitual criminal." Du Cane noted the plausibility of the theory, put to him by Dr Robert Gover (William Guy's successor at Millbank), that habitual criminals represented an "ancestral type", an atavistic reminder of an earlier stage in Human evolution:

> The characteristics of this class are entirely those of the inferior races of mankind—wandering habits, utter laziness, absence of forethought or provision, want of moral sense, cunning, dirt, and instances may

Printed by the Heliotype process, at the School of Military Engineering, Chatham.

"Close to Type": Portrait Photograph of an Habitual Criminal, 1875

Edmund Du Cane, "Address on the Repression of Crime", *National Association for the Promotion of Social Science Transactions*, 1875, pp. 302–3. The original published caption read: "One man, now a prisoner, seems actually to have got back very close to that type [of 'our arboreal ancestors'], as is illustrated by his likeness, which bears an extraordinary resemblance to that class of animal."

> be found in which their physical characteristics approach those of the lower animals so that they seem to be going back to the type of what Professor Darwin calls 'our arboreal ancestors'.

Indeed, like Dr David Nicolson, Du Cane chose to use photography to illustrate his point: "One man, now a prisoner, seems actually to have got back very close to that type, as is illustrated by his likeness, which bears an extraordinary resemblance to that class of animal."[121]

What we have in Du Cane's paper, in the writings of Henry Maudsley and the research focus of Drs Thomson, Guy, Wilson and Nicolson is a coherent body of work, all of which emphasises the particularly intractable nature of habitual crime, its perpetrators living specimens of degeneracy and/or arrested evolutionary development, and as such largely impervious to traditional penal remedies. It is this specific class of offenders that would increasingly bear the brunt both of public anxiety (and fascination) and official intervention from the late 1860s onwards. Indeed, with the Habitual Offender cast as public enemy number one, more generalised concerns about the "criminal class" began to fade from view.[122]

Does all this make Maudsley and prison doctors like Thomson, Wilson and Nicolson Britain's first "criminologists"? David Garland clearly does not think so:

> … [T]o describe Maudsley and Thomson as criminologists before the fact was misleading. Maudsley was engaged in a distinctly psychiatric endeavour (the development and application of typologies dealing with various mental disorders and pathologies) and Thomson's concern was to assess the impact of prison discipline upon the bodies and minds of prisoners. … Neither of them for a moment imagined that there was any justification for a distinctive scientific specialism centred upon the criminal.[123]

I argued in the previous chapter, that unlike early nineteenth-century psychiatrists like Prichard and Pinel, and unlike the physiognomists and phrenologists, the work carried out by Thomson, Wilson and the others in the late 1860s and early 1870s *could* (*pace* Garland) legitimately be termed "criminological" because it met two key conditions: it was characterised by the self-conscious application of scientific principles to the study of crime and criminals, and for its authors it constituted a *central* and not merely peripheral aspect of their overall research priorities. Garland *is* right to point out that neither Maudsley nor Thomson conceived of their research as slotting into a distinctive scientific discipline devoted exclusively to the study of the criminal. In that sense, to label such researchers "precursors of Lombroso" is misleading.[124] However, the fact that Maudsley and Thomson approached their chosen subject of inquiry with specific psychiatric or medical concerns does not in itself make the use of the adjective *criminological* anachronistic. Indeed, the eclectic nature of research on criminal topics in the 1870s resembles in many ways Garland's description of the modern discipline of criminology:

> Modern criminology is a composite, eclectic, multidisciplinary enterprise [which ...] draw[s] upon a variety of other disciplines, most notably sociology, psychology, psychiatry, law, history and anthropology ... The list of 'central' topics is long and diverse, and each topic breaks down further into numerous sub-topics and specialisms ... [M]odern criminology is highly differentiated in its theoretical, methodological and empirical concerns.[125]

There was of course no formal scientific *discipline* in Britain devoted to the study of crime in the 1870s, still less any institutional arrangements for research and teaching (that would not come until the late 1890s and the 1930s respectively[126]), but there was already in existence a well-defined, if relatively circumscribed, body of officially-approved scientific *expertise* on the question of criminal causality, what Garland terms "a distinctive, indigenous tradition of applied medico-legal science ... sponsored by the penal and psychiatric establishments."[127] It was precisely this body of expertise which Du Cane sought to tap for his 1875 talk to the Social Science Association; what, in the sense defined here, may be termed *criminological* expertise.

A concrete manifestation of the concerns which inspired Du Cane's paper was the 1869 Habitual Criminals Bill, introduced in Parliament by the Liberal government, elected into office earlier that year. The new Bill followed on from a number of other laws passed in the 1860s, which as we saw earlier, had aimed at making prison conditions more severe and more uniform, imposing more stringent conditions for the early release of convicts and fixing minimum sentences for repeat offenders (prompted by public concern following the "ticket of leave men" scare), and authorising police supervision of convicts released before the expiration of their sentences.

The 1869 law tightened this regulatory machinery still further. Certain categories of recidivists were to be placed under police surveillance for seven years *after they had served their sentences*, and not only, as formerly, if they were released early. Both categories could now be imprisoned summarily by magistrates at any point during this period if they were found to be acting "suspiciously" or if they were unable to prove that they were not earning a living by dishonest means. The latter provision represented a significant shift in the burden of proof from accuser to accused.[128] In addition the government proposed to enshrine in British law for the first time a minimum seven-year sentence for a felon convicted of a third offence. As the government spokesman in the House of Lords put it, "Men who by repeated crimes have shown that they set the laws of society at defiance should be placed under a different code" from other men. These were the 40% of the criminal population described by Home Secretary Henry Bruce as "hopelessly irreclaimable".[129]

The final act was not quite the unalloyed crusade against habitual crime that the government had originally planned. The clause concerning cumulative sentencing was dropped when it was suggested that juries might prefer to acquit rather than apply a law considered by many too draconian. As the Liberal lawyer, Sir Thomas Chambers, put it in the Commons, "A boy, for instance, stole a bun; some years afterwards he stole a red herring; and finally, two years later, he stole a piece of cheese. Could it be seriously proposed that for this third offence he was to suffer seven years penal servitude?"[130] Similarly, the system of police supervision envisaged for released convicts, had to be scaled down when the enormity of the surveillance task became clear (a contemporary estimate put the final number of those who would need to be kept under supervision at 25 000).[131] Nevertheless, despite a certain amount of sail trimming, "the act contained enough enhancements of criminal liability and police power … to break significant new ground in the extension and intensification of state power."[132]

There remained the thorny problem of how policemen and magistrates were to recognise an "habitual criminal" when they saw one, since there was evidence that many recidivists represented themselves as first offenders, and were dealt with as such in summary courts.[133] Historian Simon A. Cole puts this issue in context:

> Changes in ideas about the causes of crime, the nature of criminals, and the purpose of punishment created a new demand for criminal identification. If habitual criminals were born, and not made, and destined inevitably to repeat their crimes, then it was an urgent necessity to link convicts to their past crimes in order to identify which of them were, indeed, habitual criminals or recidivists. The shift from classical to reformist jurisprudence [in the mid-nineteenth century] demanded technologies of criminal identification.[134]

As noted in the previous chapter, there had been talk in the early 1860s of bringing back branding to identify habitual criminals, but despite the support of influential figures like Sir Joshua Jebb and London Commissioner of Police, Sir Richard Mayne, the plan had come to nothing. The

1869 Act opted for a less controversial means of identifying recidivists, putting in place an annual register of those convicted of felony and certain misdemeanours. However, with offenders listed alphabetically, it remained impossible to trace the previous record of a suspect who had used an alias.

Following legislation in 1871, a photographic portrait was added to each register entry. Some local police forces had been using photographic portraits to help identify criminals since the early 1850s (Birmingham Police may have been the first in 1850), but the idea of *systematically* photographing both convicts and inmates of local gaols only began to be seriously mooted in the following decade. The earliest known instance of the medium being used in a British gaol are the experiments of Bristol prison governor James Anthony Gardner in 1852. Derby Gaol took a similar step four years later.[135] Gardner would later explain to the 1863 Carnarvon Committee how he used a stereoscopic device "in order to have a better opportunity of seeing the man … standing in relief".[136] In his evidence to the same committee, Superintendent of Irish Prisons, Sir Walter Crofton, confidently predicted that once implemented, criminal photography would "have a very great effect in reducing crime because it will lead at once to a man being suspended and identified."[137]

Others were less optimistic. An article of 1873 on the subject listed the following objections to photographing the occupants of the country's prisons: that a "most portentous bulk" of information would thereby be generated; that it was unfair to photograph someone against his or her will; that "an ingenious rogue might so effectively distort his features as to render identification difficult if not impossible"; and finally, and interestingly in the light of the themes addressed in this book, that criminal identification would be rendered difficult by the physiognomic resemblance between different offenders:

> Of what use will the photographs be? Criminal faces are all almost of one type. There is but little individuality about them; and the various photographic portraits which will compose the new criminal gallery, will have so unusually strong a family likeness as to be of little or no practical value in establishing the identity of a prisoner.[138]

Even the Home Office would later admit that "there is a great similarity between one convict [photograph] and another".[139]

Prisons inspector Major Arthur Griffiths was similarly unimpressed by the capacity of the photograph to reliably identify criminals. In his 1904 book of memoirs *Fifty Years of Public Service*, he observed:

Photographs of Prisoners, Wormwood Scrubs, c. 1880

> As a matter of fact, it is never easy to recognise the likeness in a photograph; there may be a general impression conveyed, but to swear an oath to a person's face as given by the camera is often most difficult. … It has been greatly obscured, moreover, by the not strange reluctance of the 'subject', the 'sitter', to 'give himself away', inclining him to twist or caricature his features, or even to refuse politely to be taken. Stratagem has then to be applied, and I have within my experience one case where the trick was done by fixing the camera at a cell window, but carefully concealed from the yard outside, in which the prisoner was exercising …, and when he crossed a particular spot, prearranged as exactly opposite the apparatus, he was 'caught' by the lens.[140]

A recognition of the imperfect character of the photographic likeness may explain why official regulations specifically required that convicts be photographed with a mirror placed at a 45° angle behind the subject to give simultaneously a full-face and profile image; and—surprisingly— that the individual's hands be clearly visible in the frame. Photographer H. Baden Pritchard, in a published account of the photographic studio at Pentonville Prison, explains the reasoning behind the latter rule: "The hands are pressed close against the breast—for a picture of the hands is deemed as requisite … as one of the face, from the fact they are so much an indication of a man's calling."[141]

In the event, growing confidence in the accuracy and objectivity of the camera lens proved sufficient to overcome any scruples that remained.[142] Once introduced, systematic criminal portraiture did make it easier to track down a particular individual, but a time-consuming trawl through the registers at Scotland Yard was still necessary in order to find a match, a task rendered more and more difficult as the data base expanded. By 1875, it was calculated that while 150 000 names and faces were now on file, only 1000 individuals arrested by local police forces had in fact been successfully identified as a result of an appeal for information to Scotland Yard. In 1877 these gargantuan registers were replaced by more manageable *Alphabetical Registers of Habitual Criminals* ("only" 22 000 names listed). The new registers were printed each year by inmates at Brixton Convict Prison (an irony that would not have been lost on Du Cane, who suggested the idea), and subsequently distributed to police forces and prisons. They were supplemented by an annual *Register of Distinctive Marks*, which sought to use such readily-visible stigmata as scars, tattoos and moles to reveal the identity of criminals. The register was based on a division of the body into nine areas[143]; each area would then be sub-divided by type of mark. Simon A. Cole explains the procedure:

> For example, if a prisoner was found to have a prominent and seemingly permanent burn scar on the inside of his right arm, the clerk would refer to the Distinctive Marks Register, look under the heading 'right arm', then consult the subheading 'scars from wounds or burns', and then the sub-subheading inside. There he would find a list of names of convicts with prominent burns on the insides of their right arms. He would then refer to the Alphabetical Register, look up each of these names, and study the complete physical descriptions found there to see if any of them matched the prisoner before him.[144]

This novel system, "the earliest attempt to ... use the criminal body itself as an index to a set of criminal records"[145], would prove to be just as cumbersome as the more orthodox lists of names, and of course would be useless for tracking those criminals devoid of any distinctive marks. In any case, the absence of any way of cross-referencing the data from the various annual registers considerably limited their usefulness, as did the delay between compilation and publication.[146]

Criminal photographic portraits suffered from the same drawbacks. "Ironically", observes historian of photography Jennifer Green-Lewis,

> as photography grew rapidly, the usefulness of criminal photographs — their portability, their two-dimensional reduction of unwieldy humanity—was equally rapidly undermined for practical purposes by the sheer enormity of the collections.[147]

Given these logistical problems, it is not surprising that regional police forces were loathe to use the Scotland Yard registers, preferring to rely on their own—local—sources of information. An official report of 1872 noted that "from Liverpool, Manchester, Birmingham, Sheffield, and Bristol, in which places ... it is presumed that the criminal classes abound, not one application has been received."[148]

The existing systems of registration and identification were clearly inadequate. They also posed problems for Edmund Du Cane in his own back yard. He became concerned that the procedure whereby prison warders formally identified habitual criminals was open to widespread abuse. Identification in court was rewarded by a finder's fee paid by the Home Office (officially to cover expenses resulting from a court appearance). Du Cane suspected his staff of collusion with police officers. The latter would get the credit for arresting an habitual offender, the warder would garner the identification fee. (Du Cane would later note sardonically that the ability of "identifying warders [to] recognise and profess to know the names of so many" was "somewhat of a mystery requiring explanation").[149]

Promoted to the chairmanship of the newly-created Prison Commission in 1877, Du Cane (now *Sir* Edmund) was thus only too aware of the deficiencies of the existing system for identifying habitual criminals. But what if there was an alternative to the time-consuming and ultimately ineffective trawl through the registers? What if it were to prove possible, as he put it, to "track it [crime] out to its source and see if we cannot check it there instead of waiting till it has developed and then striking at it"?[150] This would mean in effect identifying future habitual criminals *before they had committed any crimes*, or at least before they had become repeat offenders, which meant, according to Du Cane, before they reached the age of 35.[151] Given existing received wisdom about physiognomic characteristics of the habitual criminal, wisdom with which, as we have seen, Sir Edmund himself concurred, a *prima facie* case could be established for the existence of a generic *criminal-type*, one to which all habitual criminals could be expected to conform. It seems that Du Cane was the victim of what Simon A. Cole calls the "irresistible temptation" to extend the use of photography beyond that of recording the identities of known criminals to "something much more ambitious: to home in on the common physiognomic attributes of known criminals in order to have a picture of what criminals in a general might look like and thus to identify criminals *prospectively*, even before they committed crimes."[152]

Such reasoning may help explain Du Cane's otherwise puzzling decision to involve amateur statistician and anthropologist Francis Galton in an ambitious project aimed at identifying a visual "criminal-type" through the study of hundreds of photographic portraits of convicts.[153] The two men, who, surprisingly perhaps given their contrasting backgrounds, found they shared many of the same views[154], may have been in contact as early as 1865, but it was only after Du Cane's appointment to the Chair of the Prison Commission in 1877 that their collaboration took a practical form.[155] As Galton later explained in his autobiography, Du Cane asked him "… to examine the photographs of criminals, in order to discover and to define the types of features, if there be any, that are associated with different kinds of criminality. The popular ideas were known to be very inaccurate, and he thought the subject worthy of scientific study."[156]

Du Cane may have become interested in this question of the link between particular kinds of crime and the typical features of their perpetrators during his collaboration with Dr William Guy on the 1873 convict census and the latter's subsequent book. Certainly it was a subject which had found its way into Guy's statistical analysis. As part of his analysis of the 1862 census, Guy had divided crimes into five categories (violent, fraudulent, sexual, arson and miscellaneous) and tabulated their frequency against four groups of male offenders, classified according to mental and bodily condition.[157] The main conclusion to emerge from this study, according to Guy's later commentary, was that criminals suffering from mental disorders were particularly involved in sexual offences, arson and acts of violence and not often in crimes involving "a maximum of forethought and contrivance".[158]

Whatever the source of Du Cane's views, he had clearly come to believe in the existence of a link between particular crimes and a distinct criminal-type or sub-type. In an 1880 letter addressed to Francis Galton, he wrote, "Special forms of crime have a typical characteristic face; ... crimes of violence and crimes of lust certainly have."[159] Thanks to some "cordial and ready assistance" from Du Cane, Galton was able "to examine the many thousand photographs of criminals that are preserved for purposes of identification at the Home Office, to visit prisons and to confer with the authorities, and lastly to procure for my own statistical inquiries a large number of copies of photographs of heinous criminals."[160] Thus in the Spring of 1877, some 600 photographs of convicts from Pentonville and Millbank were provided for Galton by the Home Office, accompanied by personal details of the lives and criminal careers of the offenders in question.[161]

Galton had been fascinated with the idea of quantifying the physical attributes of different "races" ever since his travels in South Africa in the 1850s, and since 1875, he had been playing a leading role in the British Association's "Anthropometric and Racial Committee".[162] Galton's interest in anthropological measurement and his preoccupation with racial degeneration came together in his decision to begin measuring what he considered a self-evidently mentally homogenous group of men: the inmates of Britain's convict prisons. After all, was it not a fact that "the convict class includes a large number of consummate scoundrels"? Thus "we are entitled to expect ... in any large body of convicts a prevalence of the truly criminal characteristics, whatever these may be."[163]

In enumerating these "characteristics", Galton was following in the well-worn grooves of mid-Victorian thinking on the "criminal classes" described in the last chapter; it probably also reflects his close familiarity with the work of Thomson, Maudsley and other specialists on criminal anthropology and psychology.[164] Galton described the "ideal criminal" as follows:

> The ideal criminal has three peculiarities of character; his conscience is almost deficient, his instincts are vicious, and his power of self-control is very weak. As a consequence of all this, he usually detests continuous

> labour. This statement applies to the criminal classes generally, the special conditions that determine the description of crime being the character of the instincts; and the fact of the absence of self-control being due to ungovernable temper, or to passion, or to mere imbecility. [As for the] ... deficiency of conscience of criminals, as shown by the absence of remorse for their guilt, [it] appears to astonish all who first become familiar with the details of prison life.[165]

He also drew a parallel between the psychology of criminals and that of the "lower races", revealing the evolutionary assumptions which dominated Victorian social science. Thus:

> A man who is counted an atrocious criminal in England, and is punished as such by English law in self-defence, may nevertheless have acted in strict accordance with instincts that are laudable in less civilised societies. The ideal criminal is, unhappily for him, deficient in qualities that are capable of restraining his unkindly or inconvenient instincts; he has neither sympathy for others nor the sense of duty, both of which lie at the base of conscience ... He cannot be preserved from criminal misadventure, either by altruistic sentiments or by intelligently altruistic ones.[166]

Indeed, as James Ryan has pointed out, this vision of "deficient" humanity, unfettered by the conventional moral constraints of his age, recalls Galton's own perception of the "innately inferior" African peoples he met during his travels in that Continent in the 1850s.[167] In *Hereditary Genius*, Galton wrote: "It is seldom that we hear of a white traveller meeting with a black chief whom he feels to be the better man." He goes on to note that his own travels in Africa had left him with the strong impression of "negroes" as "... so childish, stupid and simpleton-like, as frequently to make me ashamed of my own species".[168] In the published account of his African travels, *Narrative of an Explorer in Tropical South Africa ... in 1851*, Galton noted how a group of Hottentots around him exhibited:

> ... that peculiar set of features which is so characteristic of bad characters in England, and so general among prisoners that it is usually, I believe, known by the name of the 'felon face', I mean they have the prominent cheek bones, bullet shaped head[s] covering but restless eyes, and heavy sensual lips, and added to this a shackling dress and manner.[169]

As I have shown elsewhere[170], there were a number of different avenues Galton could have pursued in his endeavours to establish precise scientific measurements for his convict group. Perhaps the most obvious was what anthropologists called "anthropometry", a technique already well-established by the 1870s. French anthropologist and founder of the Paris Société d'Anthropologie (1859), Paul Broca (1824–1880) had played a leading role in the development of this number-crunching science of bodily measurement, intended primarily to permit the differentiation of the various human "races" (in ascending order up to white European males of course). The skull was considered of special significance in this respect, and there were long and erudite debates on the "craniometrical" merits of such measures as the volume of the brain cavity, the relative size of the frontal and occipital regions of the brain, the facial angle (the extent to which the face and jaws jut forward), the size of the lower jaw and the cranial index.[171]

Why did Galton decide against pursuing this method of measuring his "consummate scoundrels"? It was certainly not because he had doubts about the veracity of the results obtained by anthropometry. As we have seen, he was an active member of the British Association's Anthropometric and Racial Committee (1875–1883)[172], and he would go on to establish an anthropometric laboratory (fitted out at his own expense) for the International Health Exhibition of 1884.[173] In *Inquiry into Human Faculty*, Galton explained his reasons: "The physiognomical difference between different men being so numerous and small, it is impossible to measure and compare them each to each, and to discover by ordinary statistical methods the true physiognomy of a race." Could photography be of assistance in the search for racial types? "The usual way", Galton goes on, "is to select individuals who are judged to be representatives of the prevalent type, and to photograph them".[174] Such indeed had been the practice since the 1860s among physical anthropologists. Thomas Huxley was an early advocate of such anthropometrically precise "ethnological photographs". He contacted the Colonial Office in 1869 with a detailed proposal to establish "a systematic series of photographs of the various races of men comprehended within the British Empire". He made it clear that while photographs had already been taken in large numbers by ethnographers,

> … they lose much of their value from not being taken upon a uniform and well considered plan. The result is that they are rarely either measurable or comparable with one another and … they fail to give that precise information respecting the proportions and the conformation of the body, which … [is of paramount] worth to the ethnologist.[175]

There was also, as we have seen, some precedent for the use of conventional convict portraits in research by prison doctors, and photography was also coming to be seen as a therapeutic tool of increasing importance among alienists, eager to find an "objective" means of classifying mental ailments into physically observable "types" of mania. As Dr Hugh Welch Diamond (1809–86), superintendent of the Surrey County Lunatic Asylum, and a founding member of the Royal Photographic Society, put it, the photographer

> ...catches in a moment the permanent cloud or the passing storm or the sunshine of the soul, and thus enables the metaphysician to witness and trace out the connection between the visible and the invisible in one important branch of his researches into the philosophy of the mind.[176]

The photographer, Diamond goes on, does not need to speak to the subject in front of him, "but prefers to listen, with the picture before him, to the silent but telling language of nature."[177]

Dr Diamond himself had begun photographing female patients at the Surrey Asylum since 1851, intent on using the resulting calotypes not just as a diagnostic tool, but as part of the treatment process. Diamond provided the photographs, which, as lithographs, featured in an influential series of articles in the *Medical Times and Gazette* in 1858–1859, written by fellow alienist, John Conolly (1794–1866). In France at about the same time, Morel's widely-read *Traité des dégénérescences* (1857) was also illustrated with a number of photographic lithographs. By the time Charles Darwin's *The Expression of the Emotions in Man and Animals* was published in 1872, photographs could be printed without being converted into line drawings, and by including a number of photographs of psychiatric patients sent to him by alienist and amateur photographer Dr James Crichton-Browne (1835–1938), the naturalist was following in what was now a well-established tradition.[178]

There was thus ample precedent for such a procedure. However, once again, Galton hesitated. As he wrote in *Inquiries into Human Faculty*, selecting individuals considered to be representative of a "racial"—or in this case, *criminal*—"type" was a procedure fraught with difficulties: "... this method is not trustworthy, because the judgement itself is fallacious. It is swayed by exceptional and grotesque features more than by ordinary ones, and the portraits supposed to be typical are likely to be caricatures."[179] Indeed, while observing Londoners walk through Kensington gardens, Galton found himself unable to pick out even one face which was that of "a typical John Bull".[180]

What was the solution to this conundrum? According to Galton's own account, the idea had come to him while flicking through the convict mug-shots provided for him by Sir Edmund Du Cane.[181] The anonymous photographs had been divided into groups according to the nature of the crime (murder, manslaughter and burglary; felony and forgery; and sexual crimes). Subsequently, Galton began sorting them "in tentative ways", after which "certain natural classes began to appear, some of them exceedingly well-marked."[182] This is when Galton hit upon the idea of superimposing several convict portraits to make a single "composite" photograph. In a paper read to the *Anthropological Institute* in 1878, Galton explained that he had tried copying the outlines of a series of photographic portraits onto tracing paper and then attaching them together. Then he had the idea of taking this process one step further by "throw[ing] faint images of the several portraits, in succession, upon the same sensitised photographic plate." Thus each portrait would be *re*-photographed for a fraction of the usual exposure time on the same photographic plate.[183]

Galton explains what results from this procedure:

> It is a composite of … component portraits. Those of its outlines are sharpest and darkest that are common to the largest number of the components; the purely individual peculiarities leave little or no visible trace. The latter being necessarily disposed equally on both sides of the average, the outline of the composite is the average of all the components.[184]

Galton goes on:

> It is a band and not a fine line, because the outlines of the components are seldom exactly superimposed. The band will be darkest in its middle whenever the component portraits have the same general type of features, and its breadth, or blur, will measure the tendency of the components to deviate from the common type.[185]

Thus, the composite photograph is perceived as a statistical distribution with the most common—and clearly-visible—features in the middle, and the unusual features only a blur on the edges of the image. This is what Galton meant when he later referred to his composites as "pictorial statistics".[186] In other words, in Allan Sekula's telling phrase, "the symmetrical bell curve now wore a human face." He adds: "Galton conveniently exiled blurring to the *edges* of the composite, when in fact blurring would occur over the entire surface of the image, although less perceptibly." It was only because he *wanted* to observe a visual representation of the standard bell curve distribution that he found "the type at the centre and the idiosyncratic at the periphery."[187]

Francis Galton's Composite Photographs of Criminals, c.1877

Karl Pearson, *The Life, Letters and Labours of Francis Galton*, 3 vols., Cambridge, Cambridge University Press, 1914–1930, vol. 2 (1924), plate 28.

These "pictorial statistics" should not be expected to resemble any one individual, but rather "an imaginary figure possessing the average features of any group of men"; in short, "the portrait of a type and not of an individual."[188] Thus, as Ronald A.Thomas observes:

> Galton uses the rhetoric of the 'type', the 'ideal' and the 'generic' to suggest the higher reality of an abstract yet authentic human norm, compared to which individuals are reduced to ghostly traces, existing literally as mere shadows of the more substantial type. ... Galton's composite photograph is able to achieve a level of reality and truth superior to what its individual subjects could by revealing through the machine what the natural eye cannot see.[189]

Galton's endeavours to photographically "fix" a racial type in this way need to be seen in the context of a drive which had been gathering steam among physical anthropologists since the 1850s to find ever more precise ways of picturing the anthropometric data they were collecting. It is no accident that the Anthropological Institute's famous guide for anthropological fieldwork, *Notes and Queries on Anthropology, for the Use of Travellers and Residents in Uncivilised Lands* (1874), contained an embossed gold ruler on the cover.[190]

Interestingly, it was Herbert Spencer who had originally suggested to Galton the use of tracing paper to superimpose outline drawings of heads. The former had even conceived a machine for the purpose in the 1840s, called the "Cephalograph", able to mechanically trace longitudinal, transverse and horizontal sections of heads onto paper.[191] This may have been similar to the device, christened the "Stereograph", invented by Paul Broca in 1868.[192] Both were part of a concerted drive to take the data produced by the human senses and translate it into the unerring movement of a mechanical instrument.[193] As French psychiatrist, Etienne Jules Marey, put it in 1885:

> Not only are these instruments sometimes destined to replace the observer, and in such circumstances to carry out their role with an incontestable superiority, but they also have their own domain where nothing can replace them. When the eye ceases to see, the ear to hear, touch to feel, or indeed when our senses give deceptive appearances, these instruments are like new senses of astonishing precision.[194]

Photography offered new possibilities in this area. The year after Broca revealed his "stereoscope" to the world, Jones H. Lamprey, Assistant-Secretary of the Ethnological Society of London (of which Galton was also a member), devised a measuring screen for ethnological purposes, whereby the human subject—naked to facilitate precise measurement—would be photographed against a grid of two-inch squares. The grid, based on the well-established drawing aid used by artists, was explicitly intended to provide a framework for categorising and comparing distinct racial types.[195]

Photographic experiments in the mid-1870s conducted by Dr William Matthews may also have left their mark on Galton. Matthews had sought to use a form of composite photography in an attempt to prove beyond all doubt the identity of the man claiming to be the long lost heir of the Tichborne estate. The family was split down the middle on the question, and the sceptics brought a legal suit against the man they considered an impostor in 1871. The so-called "Tichborne Claimant" case, which attracted widespread publicity during the three-year trial, hinged therefore on the veritable identity of the man claiming to be Sir Roger Tichborne (who, it had been thought, had died at sea twelve years previously). Mathews "blended" photographs of Sir Roger taken before his disappearance with a likeness of the claimant to form what he termed a "phototype". The doctor used a primitive anthropometric technique, based on the geometric proportions of the face, to argue that Sir Roger and the claimant were indeed one and the same person.[196] Although Galton made no direct reference to the Matthews' "phototypes", he was clearly aware of their existence for examples have survived amongst his personal papers.[197]

But did Galton's convict composites provide the incontrovertible evidence of a distinct *criminal*-type hoped for by their creator? He was forced to answer in the negative. In a paper read to the Anthropological Institute in 1878, he explained what had gone wrong:

> The first set of portraits are those of criminals convicted of murder, manslaughter, or robbery with violence. It will be observed that the features of the composites are much better looking than those of the components. The special villainous irregularities in the latter have disappeared and the common humanity that underlies them has prevailed. They represent, not the criminal, but the man who is liable to fall into crime. All composites are better looking than their components, because the averaged portrait of the many persons is free from the irregularities that variously blemish the looks of each of them. [198]

In an article for the journal *Nineteenth Century*, Galton developed this point:

> They [criminal-types] are instructive as showing the type of face that is apt to accompany criminal tendencies, *before* (if I may be allowed the expression) the features have become brutalised by crime. The brands of Cain are varied; therefore the special expressions of different criminals

> do not reinforce one another in the composite, but disappear. What remain are types of faces on which some one of the many brands of Cain is frequently destined to be set.[199]

In *Inquiries into Human Faculty and its Development* (1883), Galton revisited his experiments, now five years behind him:

> I have made numerous composites of various groups of convicts which are *interesting negatively rather than positively*. They produce faces of a mean description, with no villainy written on them. The individual faces are villainous enough, but they are villainous in different ways, and when they are combined, the individual peculiarities disappear, and the common humanity of a low type is all that is left.[200]

In other words, as Sekula argues, Galton "seems to have dissolved the boundary between the criminal and the working-class poor, the residuum that so haunted the political imagination of the late Victorian bourgeoisie. Given Galton's eugenic stance, this meant that he merely included the criminal in the general poor of the 'unfit'."[201]

Galton's eugenic project will be considered in a later chapter.[202] However, it can be noted at this point that it is highly misleading to view his work with composite photography as "peripheral" to British thinking on crime[203]. Contemporary reaction to Galton's experiments with composite photography gives some measure of this. In some quarters there was unalloyed enthusiasm. An 1883 review of *Inquiries* in the *Pall Mall Gazette*, for example, described Galton's work on the criminal and the insane as "very luminous in character", adding:

> ... it is interesting to compare the grossness or low cunning of the criminal-types with the honest intelligence of the Royal Engineer ... The perception of such typical tendencies becomes [in Galton's hands] a matter of the very plainest and most measurable evidence.[204]

The Spectator also reacted positively to Galton's experiments with composite photography ("wonderfully distinct faces") as did the *Journal of Mental Science*, which stated sombrely that "Galton portrays the criminal in colours desperately black indeed, but we fear not overdrawn."[205] The British Association also praised Galton's work. A sub-committee of its Racial and Anthropometric Committee set up in 1878 "for the purpose of inquiring into and determining the typical forms of our race", referred to the "remarkable results" Galton had obtained from his research on the composite portraits of criminals.[206]

However, some evidently felt that the scientist had overstepped the mark. *The Manchester Guardian* was clearly worried what some sections of public opinion might make of Galton's research on "criminal-types", a recurring preoccupation of the period. "Mr Galton's book is not one which can be recommended to the immature mind", the paper warned. "The value of the book lies in Mr Galton's close observations rather than in his generalisations."[207]

There was clearly considerable, if not unanimous, support for the assumptions behind composite photography from influential sections of educated opinion—hardly a "peripheral" phenomenon then. Indeed, with the impetus for Galton's experiments coming directly from the head of Britain's prison regime, in one sense it is difficult to see how the project could have been *less* "peripheral". Already Chairman of the Board of Directors of Convict Prisoners (since 1869), in 1877 Du Cane took up his new job as Chairman of the Prison Commissioners, a new position created by the administrative merger of Britain's convict and local prisons which followed the Prison Act of 1877. Indeed, from this point until his retirement in 1895, Du Cane "held an unprecedented sway over English imprisonment—local and convict alike".[208] True, as Sean McConville points out, "this early interest of Du Cane's had no policy or administrative outcome"[209], but it could be argued that this observation misses the point. Du Cane's intentions reflect a key priority of the period; to establish a physiologically-based "criminal-type". As we have seen, prison medical officers were closely involved in this project; also characteristic of the 1860s and 1870s is the extent of the links between the emerging science of criminology (though the term itself would not be in common use until the 1890s) and that of anthropology, the latter increasingly suffused with the tenets of evolutionary biology.

Francis Galton's own case illustrates this cross-fertilisation clearly. Galton worked closely with Her Majesty's Chairman of the Prison Commissioners while sitting on the Anthropometric and Racial Committee of the British Association for the Advancement of Science (1875–1883).[210] Among the other members of the committee was John Beddoe, a future president of the Anthropological Institute, whose 1885 work, *The Races of Britain* was discussed in the last chapter.[211] Galton was also president of the Anthropological Institute (1885–1889), and played a key role in popularising the use of more sophisticated statistical methods in British anthropological research.[212] Galton's research on the prison population provided some useful raw data for the Anthropometric Committee, enabling it to conclude in its final report that criminals show a deficiency of stature of 2.06 inches and in weight of 17.81 pounds: "a deficiency of physical as well as mental stamina in both these unfortunate classes of society." Criminals were also found to have an excess of 10% of dark hair and eyes, compared to the general population.[213] Indeed, according to anthropological historian George W. Stocking Jnr., the physical anthropology of men like Galton and Beddoe, together with the archaeologists, with its "pervasive ethnocentric aura of racial and cultural hierarchy", continued to dominate British anthropology into the 1890s.[214]

Francis Galton's case was of course most unusual. However, even without such institutional links, the theoretical and methodological input from anthropology to thinking on causes of crime was strong. This was particularly clear in the craniometric emphasis of George Wilson's 1869 paper, but more generally the notion of a distinct, fixed "criminal-type" owed much to the anthropological search for "pure" racial types, to be established on the basis of both anatomical and physiological criteria, chiefly derived from measuring the head (over forty specialised instruments were developed for the purpose).[215]

What future was there for the composite photography of criminals? Galton himself seems to have abandoned research in this area well before the publication of *Inquiries into Human Faculty* in 1883. Perhaps he was relieved to abandon an area of research which was not only unrewarding scientifically, but irksome as well: "I did not adequately appreciate the degradation of their expressions for some time", he wrote in 1883; "... at last the sense of it took firmly hold of me, and I cannot now handle the portraits without overcoming by an effort the aversion they suggest."[216]

Karl Pearson, eugenicist and semi-official biographer of Francis Galton, agreed with his mentor that the composite photograph had failed to reveal a distinct physical criminal-type. Looking back from 1924, he suggested, however, that "...where composite photography is applied to physically differentiated races, e.g. the Jews, it does in a marked manner indicate a type. And therein, I think, its future usefulness lies."[217]

Pearson was wrong in his prediction concerning the longevity of composite photography—in fact it had largely died out by the end of the 1880s. Indeed, with the exception of Havelock Ellis and his 1890 book, *The Criminal*—more of which later—, Galton was the only British specialist to make use of specifically *criminal* composite portraits.[218] In anthropology too, the days of composite photography were numbered. As early as 1877, doubt had been expressed by some members of the BAAS Anthropometric and Racial Committee that Galton's composite portraiture could generate a criminal-type; and by 1882, there was general agreement on the committee that "photographic portraits do not, as a fact, assist materially in the definition of racial characteristics". Instead, racial types would be identified by a technique termed "comparative physiognomy", with individuals classified according to type of forehead, cheeks, chin etc.[219]

There remains the question of what exactly Sir Edmund Du Cane hoped to gain from Galton's experiments. He provides the following account of his collaboration with Galton:

> In considering how best to deal with and repress crime, it occurred to me that we ought to try and track it out to its source and see if we cannot check it there instead of waiting till it has developed and then striking at it. To track crime to its source we must follow up the history of those who practice it, and specially in such lines as are likely (as has been alleged) to contain the true clue to their criminal career. Among these subjects for observation that of the hereditary disposition is one of the most important, and to disentangle the effect of this from the effect of bringing up. … Mr Galton's process would help to establish this point …[220]

There is no record of how Du Cane intended to proceed if Galton had indeed come up with the hoped-for visual criminal-type. Was he expecting to distribute to local police forces a photographic image of the potential "murderer", "rapist", "thief", etc., similar to flyers of "notorious criminals" that would be circulated from the beginning of the 1880s?[221] Might we even go further and suggest that the Chairman of the Prison Commissioners envisaged the creation of some kind of Victorian "department of Precrime", such as that featured in the science-fiction short story and subsequent Spielberg film, *Minority Report*?[222]

Unfortunately, Du Cane has left no record of his plans in this area. However, on the face of it, it seems unlikely that he would have involved himself in the project simply to satisfy himself as to the relative importance of nature and nurture in explaining criminal behaviour, and his reference to wanting to "check" crime at its source does seem to imply some kind of concrete intervention. That Du Cane had a long-standing interest in the subject is a matter of record. In a speech to the International Penitentiary Conference in July 1875, he had noted the importance of "ascertain[ing] the sources from which crime springs" in order to successfully prevent crime, and in his paper to the National Association for the Promotion of Social Science the same year, he referred in passing to having made "inquiries" on the question of the hereditary element in criminal causation.[223]

We may close this chapter with a consideration of the work of Dr Vans Clarke, medical officer of Pentonville prison, whose approach to the study of the Criminal admirably reflects the range of influences discussed above. An early interest in quantification, already seen in his participation in the controversial official inquiry into prison dietaries in 1863 and in Dr William Guy's two prison censuses, apparently stayed with him. Early in his career, he had extolled the virtues of compiling complete medical histories of the convicts in his charge, "based on a careful examination of each prisoner".[224] Ten years later, his "examination" of Pentonville inmates clearly involved much more than conventional medical record keeping. Between August 1877 and May 1878, Clarke traced the outlines of the heads of 145 criminals in his care, providing next to each brief details of the individual's age, bodily measurements, crime and sentence, plus some general observations on his appearance. In several cases, Dr Clarke pasted in newspaper cuttings concerning the criminal in question, and on one occasion, even provided a profile sketch of one of the inmates.[225]

The source of inspiration for this endeavour was apparently Francis Galton, for Clarke wrote to him in November 1879, from Millbank Prison (to where he had been transferred) describing how he had effected the profiles "in pursuance of your suggestion during our conversation, some time ago, at Pentonville, on the subject of craniometry". Clarke goes on to explain how he had fashioned strips of lead which were "applied from the root of the nose over the cranial vault down to the root of the hair on the nape. The finger was then pressed repeatedly along the band in order to get an exact mould." The lead strip was then "carefully lifted off, and so taken as to retain the form, it was laid and secured on the paper while the pencil was carried round the edge." Apologising for his "rough work", particularly with respect to the accompanying notes, the Millbank doctor concludes with an offer to explain his comments further, should it prove necessary.[226]

The scribbled notes which accompanied the cranial profiles in this remarkable collection (which survives among the Galton papers at University College London) provide individual examples of the kind of general principles enounced in the pages of the *Journal of Mental Science*. Taken together they leave little doubt that Dr Clarke considered Pentonville's inmates to represent a distinct criminal-type, diseased, weak-minded and atavistic. His descriptions of the individual criminals in his charge speak for themselves: "heart much diseased", "bad expression", "low type", "very heavy lids and low forehead", "very small head and superciliary ridges", "half sharp", "spare and weak, unsound lungs", "eyes very closely set", "prominent occipital", "low type -stupid—looks 18 or 19 [in fact 26]", "very large ears, stupid hang dog look", "feeble mind", "villainous expression", "very large ears", "skull looks like a cocoa nut", "much misshapen head, very long and compressed laterally", "monkey faced", "receding forehead and bad expression", and so on.

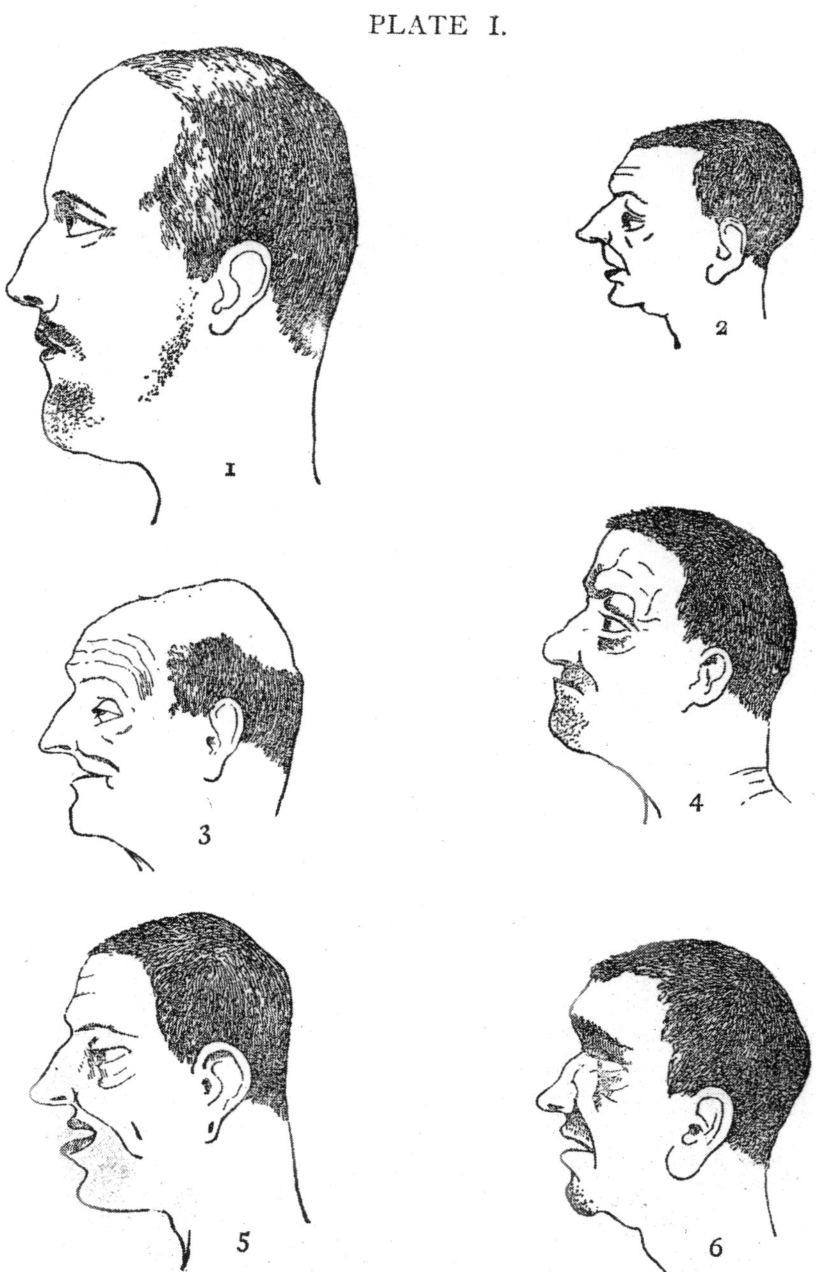

Dr Vans Clarke's Profile Sketches of Inmates at Pentonville, c.1877–1878
Havelock Ellis, *The Criminal*, London, Walter Scott, 1890, Plate I, p. 55.

One of Dr Clarke's cranial silhouettes, we noted, is accompanied by a sketch of the prisoner in question, seen in profile. A larger selection of such sketches of convict heads, thirty-six in all, were published in 1890 in Havelock Ellis's *The Criminal*.[227] In the explanatory notes at the end of the Ellis's book, there are captions accompanying each of the portraits, presumably supplied by Dr Clarke. Similar epithets are applied to those quoted earlier: "massive forehead", "weak-minded", "very low type", "eyes very close to the nose", "second and third toes webbed", "small eyes nearly concealed by upper lid", "strong villainous expression", and so on.[228]

The Pentonville doctor, subsequently promoted to the post of governor of Woking Prison, explained the origins of these sketches thus:

> My sketches were taken at the 'model prison' of Pentonville, where the duty of filling up the medical history-sheet of every convict on his arrival devolved on me, and I was prompted to use my sketch-book during the physical examination, on the observation of remarkable peculiarities in many of the heads and faces of criminals. The portraits were necessarily taken in haste, but they were true, and considered to be successful as likenesses. ... In a less marked degree the instances of misshapen heads and repulsive facial characteristics were very common.[229]

What is missing in Dr Clarke's work is a *systematic* theory linking the kinds of anatomical and physiognomic traits he describes to an explanation of criminal behaviour. The year before Dr Clarke began his sketches in Pentonville prison, an Italian doctor had published a book laying out the principles of just such a theory, and it is to this that we shall now turn.

Notes

1 J. Bruce Thomson, "The Psychology of Criminals", *Journal of Mental Science*, vol. 16, 1870, p. 331.

2 Anne Hardy, "Development of the Prison Medical Service, 1774–1895", in Richard Creese *et al.* (ed.), *The Health of Prisoners: Historical Essays*, Amsterdam, Rodopi, 1995, p. 60; McConville, *History of English Prison Administration*, pp. 215–17.

3 Hardy, *op. cit.*, pp. 60–62; Richard Smith, "History of the Prison Medical Services", *British Medical Journal*, vol. 287, 10 December 1983, p. 786.

4 Sim, *Medical Power in Prisons*, p. 41.

5 Stephen Watson, "'Malingers', the 'Weakminded' and the 'Moral Imbecile'; How the English Prison Medical Officer Became an Expert in Mental Deficiency", in Michael Clark and Catherine Crawford (eds.), *Legal Medicine in History*, Cambridge, Cambridge University Press, 1994, pp. 223–41.

6 Hardy, *op. cit.*, pp. 75–76; Sim, *op. cit.*, pp. 56–59.

7 *The Lancet*, 7 July 1877, p. 18.

8 Charles Pennell Measor, *Criminal Correction*, London, 1864, quoted in McConville, *History of English Prison Administration*, p. 451 (n. 92).

9 "Reports of the Directors of Convict Prisons", *Parliamentary Papers*, 1878–1879, vol. 35, p. 177. See also the remarks by Dr Vans Clarke to the 1879 Kimberley Commission: "The pressure is very great, and some of the duty must be almost omitted" (quoted in McConville, *op. cit.*, p. 450).

10 "Report of the Directors of Convict Prisons for the Year 1857", quoted in Sim, *op. cit.*, pp. 38–9.

11 "Report of the Directors of Convict Prisons for the Year 1861", *Parliamentary Papers*, 1862, vol. 25, p. 373.

12 Sim, *op. cit.*, p. 39; Priestley, *Victorian Prison Lives*, ch. 9; Radzinowicz and Hood, *Emergence of Penal Policy*, pp. 552–57. The latter estimate the proportion of prisoners flogged at "just over 1 per cent. of the daily average population." This amounted to about 85 floggings a year in the early 1880s and 39 in the mid-1890s. Although the numbers fell, this was a reflection, they note, not of changing policy, but of the shrinking prison population. Handcuffs as a form of punishment were made illegal from 1876, though until 1893 other forms of bodily restraint could still be used for this purpose (*ibid.*, p. 560).

13 For example, Sim, *op. cit.*, ch. 3 and Priestley, *Victorian Prison Lives*, ch. 8.

14 Martin J. Wiener, "The Health of Prisoners and the Two Faces of Benthamism", in Creese *et al.* (eds.), *op. cit.*, p. 52 and *passim*.

15 Quoted in Wiener, *Reconstructing the Criminal*, p. 125.

16 Hardy, *op. cit.*, p. 76.

17 McConville, *History of English Prison Administration*, pp. 451–52.

18 "Report of the Royal Commission on Transportation and Penal Servitude", p. 330 [my emphasis]. Captain Gambier was responsible for inspecting the prisons of Portland, Portsmouth, Chatham, Dartmoor and Woking.

19 *Ibid.*, p. 333.

20 Brian Manser, *Behind the Small Wooden Door: The Inside Story of Parkhurst Prison*, Freshwater, Isle of Wight, Coach House Publications, 2000, p. 44. Before 1869, Parkhurst had been first a juvenile prison, and from 1863–1869 was chiefly a women's prison (*ibid.*, pp. 25–6).

21 *Parkhurst Prison Archives: Bound Volume of Correspondence, Prison Medical Officers*, 1838–1883, under dates 16/19 October 1875. It may well be significant that in his official report for the year 1875, Roome insists on the fact that "a knowledge of each individual history and a nice discrimination [is] requisite in dealing with them [i.e. mentally deficient prisoners] ("Reports of the Directors of Convict Prisons", *Parliamentary Papers*, 1875, vol. 34, p. 404).

22 *Parkhurst Prison Archives, loc. cit.*, under dates 18 October 1871 and 27 August 1882.

23 "Report to the Convict Prison Commissioners", *Parliamentary Papers*, 1863, vol. 24, pp. 15–17.

24 These proportions are based on the returns for 1860: "Establishments at Home for Male and Female Convicts", *Parliamentary Papers*, 1861, vol. 30, pp. 239–40. The precise numbers for the male convict population at that date are: separate confinement (1685); public works (3640); juveniles (549); and invalid depots (1654). A third (524) of those undergoing separate confinement were being held in cells

rented in local prisons at Wakefield and Leicester. The 1371 female convicts were held at Millbank, Brixton and Fulham Prisons.

25 Following a recommendation of the 1879 Kimberley Commission, this position was given the formal title of "Superintending Medical Officer of Convict Prisons", and appointment was accompanied by an automatic place on the Board of Directors. Its first occupant, appointed in 1879, was Dr Robert Gover, who had been the senior medical officer at Millbank since 1865 (Hardy, *op. cit.*, pp. 61–62, 69).

26 Wiener, "The Health of Prisoners", p. 51.

27 *Ibid.*; Hardy, *op. cit.*, p. 62.

28 *Ibid.*, p. 72.

29 "Report to the Convict Prison Commissioners", *Parliamentary Papers*, 1862, vol. 25, pp. 418–9. "Bodily defects" were sub-divided as follows: scrofula; deformity, congenital; deformity, from accident; deformity, from disease; loss of arm; loss of leg; ruptured; vision defective.

30 *Ibid.*

31 "Report to the Convict Prison Commissioners", *Parliamentary Papers*, 1863, vol. 24, pp. 15–17.

32 Hardy, "Development of the Prison Medical Service", pp. 64–65; McConville, *English Local Prisons*, p. 115.

33 The two other members of the committee were Dr Vans Clarke of Dartmoor Prison and Dr Maitland of Gosport Military Prison (Hardy, *op. cit.*, p. 64).

34 *Ibid.*, p. 65.

35 William A. Guy, "On Some Results of a Recent Census of the Populations of the Convict Prisons of England and Wales", *Transactions of the National Association for the Promotion of Social Science*, 1863, quoted in Wiener, "The Health of Prisoners", pp. 54, 58 (n. 41).

36 William A. Guy, "On Insanity and Crime, and on the Plea of Insanity in Criminal Cases", *Journal of the Statistical Society of London*, vol. 32, no. 2, June 1869, p. 160.

37 Radzinowicz and Hood, *Emergence of Penal Policy*, pp. 507–9. The article from *Punch* was in the issue of December 13, 1862 (vol. 43, pp. 240–46).

38 "Report to the Convict Prison Commissioners", *Parliamentary Papers*, 1864, vol. 26, p. 217.

39 Hardy, *op. cit.*, pp. 65–67; Sim, *Medical Power in Prisons*, pp. 35–38.

40 Quoted in Hardy, *op. cit.*, p. 67. See also Sim, *op. cit.*, pp. 36–37. Cf. Sean McConville's point: "Prisoners were generally drawn from the lowest sections of society. Many came off the streets – starving, drunken, demented, filthy, lousy, and tubercular, suffering from mental and physical illnesses associated with long-term malnutrition and dissipation. … Many of the drunks, beggars, tramps, prostitutes, nuisances and petty thieves who populated the local prisons were habitual offenders. They would go to prison for a week or two on minimum diet, debilitating labour, and depressing conditions, would come out for a day or two of free-range starvation and sleeping rough on the streets, and would go back inside for another dose of the same, scientifically administered" (McConville, "The Victorian Prison", p. 133).

41 William A. Guy, *Results of the Census of the Population of the Convict Prisons in England, Taken in 1862 and 1873*, London, HMSO, 1875.

42 *Ibid.*, p. 12.

43 Namely Dr Burns of Chatham, Dr Rendle of Brixton, Mr Gover of Millbank and Dr Clarke, "now of Pentonville" *(ibid.*, p. 8).
44 *Ibid.*, Tables 7–8, pp. 12–13.
45 *Ibid.*, pp. 25–26.
46 *Ibid.*, p. 4.
47 J. Bruce Thomson, "The Effects of the Present System of Prison Discipline on the Body and Mind", *Journal of Mental Science*, vol. 12, 1866, pp. 343–44. See also *British Medical Journal*, 14 July 1866, p. 45.
48 Jayewardine, "English Precursors of Lombroso", p. 166.
49 See his official reports to his superiors for 1871 and 1872: "Report to the General Board of Directors of Prisons in Scotland", *Parliamentary Papers*, 1871, vol. 30, p. 664; 1872, vol. 32, p. 669.
50 Thomson, "Effects of the Present System", p. 341.
51 Thomson, "Hereditary Nature of Crime", p. 488.
52 Quoted in Jayewardine, *op. cit.*, pp. 165–66. See also Thomson, "Effects of the Present System", p. 341. On stereotypes of "criminal woman" at this period, see Zedner, *Women, Crime and Custody*, pp. 77–79.
53 Thomson, "Hereditary Nature", p. 492.
54 *Ibid.*, p. 491.
55 Prosper Despine, *La psychologie naturelle (Etude sur les facultés intellectuelles et morales dans leur état naturel et dans leurs manifestations anormales chez les aliénés et les criminels)*, 3 vols., Paris, 1868.
56 The French alienist and asylum physician, Philippe Pinel had used the term "la manie sans delire" at the beginning of the century (*Traité médico-philosophique sur l'aliénation mentale*, Paris, 1809).
57 James C. Prichard, *Treatise on Insanity*, 1835, quoted in Radzinowicz and Hood, *Emergence of Penal Policy*, pp. 9–10.
58 Thomson, "The Psychology of Criminals", pp. 321, 337. See Nicole Hahn Rafter, *Creating Born Criminals*, Urbana, University of Illinois, 1997 pp. 75–76.
59 *Ibid.*, p. 343; Thomson, "Hereditary Nature of Crime", pp. 496–98.
60 Thomson, "The Psychology of Criminals", p. 350
61 Jayewardine, *op. cit.*, pp. 167–68. Little is known about Dr George Wilson, save that he was assistant surgeon at Woking between 1865–70, where he worked under Dr John Campbell. In 1870 he became chief medical officer at the new Woking Female Prison; apparently a short-lived appointment, for he is listed as the medical surgeon at Portsmouth Convict Prison in the reports of the Directors of Convict Prisons for 1871. There is no subsequent record of his career. In his report for the latter year, Wilson observes: "... it cannot be denied that convicts as a body are less healthy than the civil population, because of their moral degradation is accompanied, if not caused, by a corresponding physical degeneration" (*Parliamentary Papers*, 1871, vol. 31, p. 265). It is possible that this was the same George Wilson who published a book on public hygiene in 1873: *A Handbook of Hygiene*, London, 1873 (I am grateful to Lesley A. Hall of the Wellcome Library for the History and Understanding of Medicine, London, for this suggestion).
62 Havelock Ellis, "The Study of the Criminal", *Journal of Mental Science*, vol. 36, p. 6.
63 Quoted in Jayewardine, *op. cit.*, p. 167–68.

64 David Nicolson, "The Morbid Psychology of Criminals", *Journal of Mental Science*, vol. 19, 1873, pp. 222–32, 398–409; vol. 20, 1874, pp. 20–37, 167–85, 527–51; vol. 21, 1875, pp. 18–31, 225–50.
65 Nicolson, *op. cit.*, vol. 19, pp. 222–24.
66 *Ibid.*, p. 547.
67 Nicholson, *op. cit.*, vol. 21, facing p. 250. Cf. The well-known comments of novelist Charles Kingsley (1819–75) while travelling in Ireland in 1860. In a letter to his wife, he wrote of being "haunted by the human chimpanzees I saw along that hundred miles of horrible country. ... [T]o see white chimpanzees is dreadful; if they were black, one would not feel it so much ..." (Frances Kingsley (ed.), *Charles Kingsley: His Letters and Memories of His Life*, 2 vols., London, 1877, vol. 1, p. 107). See L. Perry Curtis, *Apes and Angels: The Irishman in Victorian Caricature*, Newton Abbot, David and Charles, 1971.
68 For the same view, see "The Bodies of Executed Criminals", *The Lancet*, 10 March 1866, pp. 265–67.
69 Spurzheim, *Physionomical System*, p. 250.
70 Rafter, "The Murderous Dutch Fiddler", p. 87.
71 Jayewardine, "English Precursors of Lombroso", pp. 165, 168.
72 Theodore Porter, *The Rise of Statistical Thinking 1820–1900*, Princeton, Princeton University Press, 1986.
73 Radzinowicz and Hood, *op. cit.*, p. 10; Wiener, *Reconstructing the Criminal*, pp. 168–69; Daniel Pick, *Faces of Degeneration: A European Disorder, c. 1848–1918*, Cambridge, Cambridge University Press, 1989, p. 205.
74 Trevor Turner, "Henry Maudsley: Psychiatrist, Philosopher and Entrepreneur", *in* W. F. Bynum *et al.* (eds.), *The Anatomy of Madness: Essays in the History of Psychiatry*, vol. 3, London, Routledge, 1988, p. 151.
75 Henry Maudsley, *The Physiology and Pathology of the Mind*, London, 1867; *idem.*, *Body and Mind*, London, 1870; *Responsibility in Mental Disease*, London, 1874.
76 Pick, *op. cit.*, p. 206.
77 *Ibid.*, p. 203.
78 Maudsley, *Body and Mind*, p. 43.
79 *Ibid.*, p. 76.
80 Henry Maudsley, *Organic to Human, Psychological and Sociological*, London, 1916, p. 267.
81 Pick, *Faces of Degeneration*, p. 208.
82 Mike Hawkins, *Social Darwinism in European and American Thought: Nature as Model and Nature as Threat*, Cambridge, Cambridge University Press, 1997, pp. 39–44.
83 Cf. Karl Marx, *The 18th Brumaire of Louis Bonaparte*: "Men make their own history, but they do not make it just as they please; they do not make it under circumstances chosen by themselves, but under circumstances directly found, given and transmitted from the past. The tradition of all the dead generations weighs like a nightmare on the brain of the living." (repr. in David McClellan (ed.), *Karl Marx: Selected Writings*, Oxford, Oxford University Press, 1977, p. 300).
84 Henry Maudsley, *Responsibility in Mental Disease*, New York, c. 1900 [1874] p. 35.
85 *Ibid.*, pp. 31–32.
86 B. A. Morel, *Traité des dégénérescences physiques, intellectuelles et morales de l'espèce humaine*, 2 vols., Paris, 1857.

87 Gareth Stedman-Jones, *Outcast London: A Study in the Relationship Between Classes in Victorian Society*, Oxford, Clarendon Press, 1971, ch. 6.
88 Rafter, *Creating Born Criminals*, p. 36. See also Rafter, "Seeing is Believing", pp. 79–86.
89 The paper was reprinted as a pamphlet: Thomas Beggs, *Repression and Prevention of Crime*, London, 1868.
90 *Ibid.*, pp. 7–8.
91 "The Deterioration of Race", *The Lancet*, 1 June 1866, quoted in Pick *op. cit.*, pp. 190–91.
92 Both quotations are from Henry W. Rumsey, "On a Progressive Physical Degeneracy of Race in the Town Populations", *Transactions of the National Association for the Promotion of Social Science*, 1870, pp. 470–71.
93 Thompson, "The Psychology of Criminals", p. 331.
94 Adrian Desmond and James Moore, *Darwin: The Life of a Tormented Evolutionist*, New York, Warner Books, 1992.
95 Patrick Tort, *Darwin et la science de l'évolution*, Paris, Gallimard, 2000, p. 77; Pick, *op. cit.*, pp. 192–93 and n. 52 (p. 193).
96 Frederick Burkhardt (ed.), *Charles Darwin's Letters: A Selection*, Cambridge, Cambridge University Press, 1996, p. 185: C. Darwin to A. R. Wallace, 22 December 1857. For other similar views expressed in Darwin's notebooks, see Pick, *op. cit.*, p. 193, n. 52.
97 Charles Darwin, *On the Origin of Species by Means of Natural Selection or the Preservation of Favoured Races in the Struggle for Life*, London, 1859, pp. 63, 470–1.
98 Adrian Desmond, *The Politics of Evolution, Morphology, Medicine and Reform in Radical London*, Chicago, Chicago University Press, 1989, p. 406.
99 Pick, *op. cit.*, p. 195.
100 Greta Jones, *Social Darwinism and English Thought*, Brighton, Harvester, 1980, p. 8.
101 See Hawkins, *Social Darwinism*, ch. 4.
102 J. D. Y. Peel, *Herbert Spencer: the Evolution of a Sociologist*, London, Heinemann, 1971, n.63, p. 296.
103 Herbert Spencer, *The Study of Sociology*, London, 1873, p. 344.
104 Tort, *Darwin*, pp. 77–78, 93–96, 107–11.
105 Henry Maudsley, *Pathology of Mind* (1869), p. 202, quoted in Pick, *op. cit.*, p. 208.
106 Francis Galton, *Hereditary Genius: An Inquiry into its Laws and Consequences*, London, 1869.
107 Gould, *Mismeasure of Man*, p. 143.
108 *Ibid.*
109 Christine Bolt, *Victorian Attitudes to Race*, London, Routledge, 1971, p. 208; Hawkins, *Social Darwinism*, p. 81; Douglas A. Lorimer, "Theoretical racism in Late-Victorian Anthropology, 1870–1900", *Victorian Studies*, vol. 31, no. 3, Spring 1988, pp. 405–30; *idem.*, "Race, Science and Culture: historical Continuities and Discontinuities, 1850–1914", in Shearer West (ed.), *The Victorians and Race*, Aldershot, Scholar Press, 1996, pp. 12–33.
110 E. D. Cope, *The Origin of the Fittest*, New York, Macmillan, 1887, quoted in Gould, *op. cit.*, p. 144.

111 Roslyn Poignant, "Surveying the Field of View: The Making of the RAI Photographic Collection", in Elizabeth Edwards (ed.), *Anthropology and Photography 1860–1920*, New Haven, Yale University Press, 1992, p. 55.
112 Quoted in Pick, *Faces of Degeneration*, p. 208.
113 *Ibid.*, p. 205.
114 Charles Darwin, *Descent of Man, and Selection in Relation to Sex*, 2nd edition, London, 1882, p. 137.
115 Untitled, *The Lancet*, 18 January 1873, pp. 101–2.
116 Edmund Du Cane, "Address on the Repression of Crime", *NAPSS Transactions*, 1875, p. 300.
117 Saunders, "Quarantining the Weak-Minded", pp. 275–78.
118 Du Cane, *op. cit.*, p. 300.
119 *Ibid.*, p. 278.
120 *Ibid.*, p. 302.
121 *Ibid.*, pp. 302–3.
122 Wiener, *Reconstructing the Criminal*, p. 300 and n. 158.
123 Garland, "Of Crimes and Criminals", p. 30.
124 See my entry on "Criminology" in Pendergast and Pendergast, *Grolier Encyclopaedia* (forthcoming) for a recognition of this point.
125 Garland, "Of Crimes and Criminals", p. 15.
126 See Garland, "British Criminology before 1935", pp. 4–5.
127 *Ibid.*, p. 2.
128 Radzinowicz and Hood, *Emergence of Penal Policy*, p. 224.
129 Wiener, *op. cit.*, pp. 254–55.
130 Quoted in *ibid.*, p. 245
131 *Ibid.*, p. 256. The Prevention of Crimes Act (1871) was intended to reduce demands on police resources in this area by giving courts the discretion to rule on which ex-prisoners needed to be placed under surveillance. By the 1890s, with few court surveillance orders and even fewer prosecutions for "living dishonestly", it was admitted in official circles that this part of the 1869–1871 legislation was a dead letter. Supervision of ex-convicts was finally abolished in 1910 (Radzinowicz and Hood, *op. cit.*, pp. 257–58, 261).
132 Wiener, *op. cit.*, p. 149.
133 Radzinowicz and Hood, *op. cit.*, p. 251.
134 Simon A. Cole, *Suspect Identities: A History of Fingerprinting and Criminal Identification*, Cambridge, Mass., Harvard University Press, 2001, p. 15.
135 Helmut Gernsheim, *The History of Photography*, 2nd edition, London, Thames and Hudson, 1969, pp. 514–15; McConville, *English Local Prisons*, p. 128, n. 135.
136 "Carnarvon Committee", pp. 336–37.
137 "Carnarvon Committee", p. 304. See also Lord Brougham, "Opening Address", *Transactions of the National Association for the Promotion of Social Science*, Edinburgh, 1863, p. 11. The use of photography "as an aid to tracing second offenders" was recommended in the 1864 Penal Servitude Act (M. H. Tomlinson, "Penal Servitude 1846–1865: A System in Evolution", in Victor Bailey (ed.), *Policing and Punishment in Nineteenth Century Britain*, London, Croom Helm, 1981, p. 141). On Sir Richard Mayne's recommendation, the Home Office approved the photographing of "notable" prisoners at Scotland Yard from 1868 (Philip Thurmond

Smith, *Policing Victorian London: Political Policing, Public Order and the London Metropolitan Police*, London, Greenwood Press, 1985, p. 121).

138 "Criminal Photography", *All the Year Round*, New Ser., vol. 11, no. 257, 1 November 1873, p. 10.

139 Home Office memo (1888), quoted in McConville, *English Local Prisons*, p. 395.

140 Griffiths, *Fifty Years of Public Service*, p. 348.

141 H. Baden Pritchard, "At Pentonville Penitentiary", in *idem.*, *The Photographic Studios of Europe*, London, 1882, p. 122.

142 Jennifer Green-Lewis, *Framing the Victorians: Photography and the Culture of Realism*, Ithaca, Cornell University Press, 1996, p. 194.

143 Head and face; throat and neck; chest; belly and groin; back and loins; arms; hands and fingers; thighs and legs; feet and ankles.

144 Cole, *op. cit.*, p. 29.

145 *Ibid.*, p. 27.

146 The registers printed in October contained the returns for the previous year, so were already ten months out of date as they rolled off the presses (Radzinowicz and Hood, *op. cit.*, pp. 261–63; McConville, *op. cit.*, pp. 393–95). Arthur Griffiths described the logistical difficulties involved in their use in the early 1890s. At that time, he noted, there were fourteen albums, each containing 5000 photographic portraits. In addition, there was "a reference library of ninety volumes, dating back to 1864, each containing five hundred photographs, with complete descriptions. The contents of these albums were classified and indexed to assist search, which was, nevertheless, exceedingly tedious, and often most disappointing—a search would be repeated again and again for days together" (Griffiths, *op. cit.*, pp. 349–50).

147 Green-Lewis, *op. cit.*, p. 218. Cf. Cole, *op. cit.*, pp. 28–29.

148 Quoted in Radzinowicz and Hood, *op. cit.*, p. 262 and n. 2.

149 This paragraph is based on McConville, *op. cit.*, pp. 397–99.

150 Sir Edmund Du Cane, quoted in Francis Galton, "Composite Portraits", *Journal of the Anthropological Institute*, vol. 8, 1879, pp. 142–43. Du Cane was present at Galton's talk and contributed to the subsequent discussion.

151 Du Cane, "Address", p. 278.

152 Cole, *op. cit.*, p. 26 [my emphasis].

153 For the details of this technique, see Francis Galton, *Inquiries into Human Faculty and its Development*, London, Dent, 1907, Appendix 1 (pp. 221–41). For the context, see Peter Hamilton and Roger Hargreaves, *The Beautiful and the Damned: the Creation of Identity in Nineteenth Century Photography*, London, Lund Humphries/ National Portrait Gallery, 2001, ch. 3; David Green, "Veins of Resemblance: Photography and Eugenics", *Oxford Art Journal*, vol. 7, no. 2, 1985, pp. 3–16; Allan Sekula, "The Body and the Archive", *October*, no. 39, 1986, pp. 3–64; Neil Davie, "'Une des défigurations les plus tristes de la civilisation moderne': Francis Galton et le criminel composite", in Michel Prum (ed.), *Les malvenus: race et sexe dans le monde anglophone*, Paris, L'Harmattan, 2003, pp. 191–220.

154 Galton later described Du Cane as "an extremely accomplished man, with high and humane views, and [someone who] sympathised with not a few of the subjects on which I have been engaged" (*Memories of My Life*, London, Methuen, 1908, p. 261).

155 McConville, *English Local Prisons*, pp. 177–78.
156 Galton, *op. cit.*, p. 259.
157 The different mental and physical categories were as follows: affections of the mind and nervous system; scrofula and chronic diseases of the lungs and heart; congenital or acquired deformities and defects; not suffering from any deformities or defects. Guy, *Results of the Census*, Tables XXII–XXIII, pp. 27–8; "Reports of the Directors of Convict Prisons", *Parliamentary Papers*, 1863, vol. 24, p. 16.
158 Guy, "On Insanity", p. 171.
159 Sir Edmund Du Cane to Francis Galton, 12 February 1880 (?), University College London Archives (*Galton Papers*, 152/6A).
160 Francis Galton, "Address to the Department of Anthropology of the British Association", *Nature*, vol. 16, 23 August 1877, p. 346.
161 The Home Office to Francis Galton, 18 April/22 May 1877, University College Library, London (*Galton Papers*, 158/1B); Galton, "Composite Portraits", p. 143.
162 See Chapter Three.
163 Galton, *op. cit.*, p. 346.
164 In the archives of University College, London are preserved Galton's notes on works by Maudsley, Thomson, Benedikt and Despine, probably made in the late 1870s (University College Library, London, Galton Papers, 1529/A–B).
165 *Ibid.*, p. 346. Galton repeats this description of the Criminal, word for word, in *Inquiries into Human Faculty and its Development*, p. 42.
166 *Ibid.*, p. 43.
167 Ryan, *Picturing the Empire*, p. 173.
168 Galton, *Hereditary Genius*, p. 339.
169 Quoted in Ryan, *op. cit.*, p. 173.
170 Davie, "Une des défigurations", p. 201.
171 See Gould, *The Mismeasure of Man*, ch. 3.
172 Ryan, *op. cit.*, p. 151; James Urry, *Before Social Anthropology: Essays in the History of British Anthropology*, Chur, Switzerland, Harwood, 1993, ch. 4. The final report of this commission was presented to the British Association in 1883: Anthropometric Committee of the British Association for the Advancement of Science, "Final Report", *BAAS Transactions,* 1883, pp. 253–306.
173 D. W. Forrest, *Francis Galton: the Life and Work of a Victorian Genius*, New York, Tapling, 1974, pp. 181–183; Nicholas W. Gillham, *A Life of Sir Francis Galton: From African Explorer to the Birth of Eugenics*, Oxford, Oxford University Press, 2001, pp. 210–214. From 1885 until 1894, Galton's anthropometric laboratory was housed in the South Kensington Museum (now the Victoria and Albert Museum). By the time the laboratory closed its doors, the measurements of nearly 10 000 people had been taken.
174 Galton, *Inquiries into Human Faculty*, p. 4.
175 Ryan, *op. cit.*, ch. 5; Frank Spencer, "Some Notes on the Attempt to Apply Photography to Anthropometry during the Second Half of the Nineteenth Century", in Edwards (ed.), *Anthropology and Photography 1860*, pp. 99–107.
176 Dr Hugh Welch Diamond, "On the Application of Photography to the Physiognomic and Mental Phenomena of Insanity" (1856), quoted in John Tagg, *The Burden of Representation: Essays on Photography and Histories*, London, Macmillan, 1988, p. 78.
177 *Ibid.*

178 Janet Brown, "Darwin and the Face of Madness", in, W. F. Bynum *et al.* (eds.), *The Anatomy of Madness: Essays in the History of Psychiatry*, vol.1, London, Routledge, 1985, pp. 151–165; Hamilton and Hargreaves, *The Beautiful and the Damned*, pp. 79–81; Michel Frizot, "Body of Evidence: The Ethnophotography of Difference", in *idem.* (ed.), *A New History of Photography*, Cologne, Könemann, 1998, pp. 266–67. Extracts from one of Conolly's essays, "The Physiognomy of Insanity" (*Medical Times and Gazette*, 16 New Ser, January 1858) are reprinted in Bourne Taylor and Shuttleworth, *Embodied Selves*, pp. 18–22.

179 Galton, *op. cit.*, p. 4.

180 *Ibid.*

181 Galton, "Composite Portraits", p. 135.

182 Galton, "Address", p. 346.

183 For example, if there are seven portraits to be included in the composite, each is exposed to the photographic plate for *one seventh* of the usual exposure time.

184 Galton, "Composite Portraits", p. 134.

185 *Ibid.*

186 Francis Galton, "Generic Images", *Nineteenth Century*, vol. 6, 1879, p. 162. He writes: "Composite portraits are … *much more than averages*, because they include the features of every individual of whom they are composed. They are the pictorial equivalent of those elaborate statistical tables out of which averages are deduced. There cannot be a more perfect example … of what the metaphysicians mean by generalisations …" (*Ibid.*, p. 163 [my emphasis]).

187 Sekula, "The Body and the Archive", p. 48.

188 Galton, "Composite Portraits", p. 133.

189 Ronald A. Thomas, *Detective Fiction and the Rise of Forensic Science*, Cambridge, Cambridge University Press, 1999, pp. 125–126.

190 Ryan, *op. cit.*, pp. 148–49.

191 Galton, "Composite Portraits", p. 132. On this point, see Sekula, *op. cit.*, pp. 46–47.

192 Spencer, *op. cit.*, p. 106 et plate 65, p. 105.

193 David G. Horn, *The Criminal Body: Lombroso and the Anatomy of Deviance*, London, Routledge, 2003, pp. 78–86.

194 Quoted in *ibid.*, p. 85. Marey invented a mechanical cardiograph, which when strapped to the patient's wrist, transformed the pulse into a visual graph. It was now possible, enthused contemporaries, for the heart to "trace itself on paper each of its contractions with their slightest variations, and we can say, without metaphor, that we read in the human heart" (experimental physiologist Claude Bernard, 1866, quoted in *ibid.*, p. 86).

195 Ryan, *op. cit.*, p. 149; Spencer, *op. cit.*, pp. 102–3.

196 Jennifer Tucker, "Photography as Witness, Detective and Impostor: Visual Representation in Victorian Science", in Lightman (ed.), *Victorian Science*, pp. 397–98. Dr Matthews wrote about his technique in: *Identity Demonstrated Geometrically with Phototype Illustrations*, Bristol, 1876. Tucker describes Matthews as "a rival of Francis Galton" (*op. cit.*, p. 397). It is unclear whether the two men were in contact on the subject. The claimant, whom the prosecution claimed was in fact an Australian butcher called Arthur Orton, was subsequently found guilty of perjury (Cole, *Suspect Identities*, p. 13). Cole notes that the Tichborne case would be frequently cited later in the century by advocates of fingerprinting as an illustration of the need for a reliable system of identification.

197 University College Library, London: Galton papers, 58/2MJ. See Tucker, *op. cit.*, Fig. 18.7, p. 398.
198 Galton, "Composite Portraits", p. 135.
199 Galton, "Generic Images", pp. 161–62.
200 Galton, *Inquiries into Human Faculty*, p. 11 [my italics].
201 Sekula, *op. cit.*, p. 50
202 See chapter 5.
203 Sekula, *op. cit.*, p. 18.
204 *Pall Mall Gazette*, 18 June 1883.
205 *The Spectator*, 11 August 1883; *Journal of Mental Science*, vol. 29, 1884, p. 566.
206 *Transactions of the British Association for the Advancement of Science*, London, 1878, p. 156.
207 *The Manchester Guardian*, 6 August 1883. Cf. the review in *The Saint James Gazette* (12 June 1883). Composite photography is described as "a very curious and interesting discovery", but its inventor is taken to task for being "a little too much in a hurry to apply his statistical treatment where it is not altogether suitable."
208 McConville, "The Victorian Prison", pp. 127–38, quotation at p. 138. See also Forsythe, *Reform of Prisoners*, pp. 193–99; Radzinowicz and Hood, *Emergence of Penal Policy*, pp. 526–31.
209 McConville, *English Local Prisons*, p. 178.
210 Ryan, *Picturing Empire*, p. 151; Urry, *Before Social Anthropology*, ch. 4.
211 Poignant, "Surveying the Field of View", pp. 57–61; Stepan, *The Idea of Race*, p. 89.
212 Lorimer, "Theoretical Racism", pp. 422–424.
213 Anthropometric Committee of the British Association for the Advancement of Science, "Final Report", *BAAS Transactions*, 1883, p. 273.
214 Stocking, *Victorian Anthropology*, p. 262.
215 Stepan, *op. cit.*, ch. 4.
216 Galton, *Inquiries into Human Faculty*, pp. 12–13. Galton did not give up composite photography entirely, however, at least not yet. He issued a circular letter in 1882 to amateur photographers, requesting that they sent him individual portraits of as many family members as possible—full-face and profile. Galton would get to keep the original photographs, which would form part of his investigations into "the condition of the race"; the family would receive a composite photograph of the "family likeness" (Hamilton and Hargreaves, *op. cit.*, p. 98). Galton was forced to concede, however, that "the persons whose portraits are blended together seldom seem to care much for the result, except as a curiosity." His subjects seemed "to object to being mixed up indiscriminately with others" (Galton, *Inquiries into Human Faculty*, p. 9). In parallel, Galton's eugenic concern with "racial degeneration" led him to create composites of various groups considered mentally and physically deficient. He wrote a paper in 1882 with Dr Mahomed of Guy's Hospital, London on the physiognomy of consumptive patients ("An Inquiry into the Physiognomy of Phthisis by the Method of Composite Portraiture", *St Guy's Hospital Reports*, 25 Feb. 1882). Three years later, in what was his only direct application of composite photography to "racial" types, Galton published a series of portraits of "the Jewish type", in the April 1885 issue of *The Photographic News* ("Photographic Composites", *Photographic News*, vol. 29, 24 April 1885, no. 1390, pp. 234–245). Galton's anti-Semitism is clearly visible in the following description of a Jewish

quarter in London: "The feature that struck me most, as I drove through the ... Jewish quarter, was the cold, scanning gaze of man, woman and child ... I felt, rightly or wrongly, that every one of them was coolly appraising me at market" (quoted in Sekula, "The Body and the Archive", p. 52, n. 80).

217 Karl Pearson, *The Life, Letters and Labours of Francis Galton*, 3 vols., Cambridge, Cambridge University Press, 1914–1930, vol. 2, p. 286. Pearson goes on to state that Galton's "Jewish Type" was a "landmark" in the history of composite photography (*ibid.*, p. 293).

218 There were sporadic references to the technique from criminologists elsewhere in Europe, notably from Cesare Lombroso. A Galtonian "composite skull" was featured in the 1896–1897 Italian edition of his *Criminal Man* (Sekula, *op. cit.*, p. 43). See also Cesare Lombroso, *L'Anthropologie criminelle et ses récents progrès*, Paris, 1890, p. 11; Gabriel Tarde, *La Criminalité comparée*, Paris, 1924 [2nd edition, 1890], p. 53.

219 Poignant, "Surveying the Field of View", pp. 60–61. There did remain though some residual support for applying composite photography to anthropological research. At a BAAS meeting in Montreal in 1884, leading anthropologist E. B. Tylor called for "a thorough trial" of Galton's technique, suggesting that a "galtonised" set of composites of American Indian races be produced. Perhaps as a result of this initiative Dr John Billings of Washington's Army Medical Museum published a number of articles in the mid-1880s featuring composite skulls of, among others, the Ponca Indians and the Sandwich Islanders (J. S. Billings, *On Composite Photography Applied to Craniology*, Washington, Government Printing Office, 1886. See Spencer, *op. cit.*, p. 106 and plates 66i–ii, p. 105). French photographer Arthur Batut (1846–1918) also used Galton's technique in his attempts to uncover the various physical "types" in the area near his home in Toulouse (*L'Application de la photographie à la production du type d'une famille, d'une tribu ou d'une race*, Paris, 1887). Leading French anthropologist Paul Topinard encouraged Batut to exhibit his work at the Paris Exposition Internationale of 1889, keen to demonstrate that "we in France can do composite photography as well as *Monsieur* Galton in England" (Hamilton and Hargreaves, *The Beautiful and the Damned*, pp. 98–99). However, despite such experiments, anthropological use of composite photography seems to have been the exception rather than the rule in this period (Ryan, *Picturing Empire*, p. 172), though there is evidence of its use in the USA in other domains up to the end of the 1880s (e.g. Walter Rogers Furness, *Composite Photography Applied to the Portraits of Shakespeare*, Philadelphia, 1885; Perisfor Frazer, *The Application of Composite Photography to Hand-Writing and Especially to Signatures*, Philadelphia, 1886). It is misleading, therefore, to suggest that "Galton's composite process enjoyed a wide prestige until about 1915" (Sekula, *op. cit.*, p. 52), though mention should be made of Lewis Hine's well-known series of composites taken in US cotton mills in the 1910s (*ibid.*, pp. 52–53).

220 Galton, "Composite Portraits", pp. 142–43.

221 Public Record Office HO45/9518/22208C/6 (8 March 1883). An example of such a circular has survived: PRO HO45/9518/22208C/5.

222 The intriguing similarity between the Galton/Du Cane project and the assumptions behind science-fiction writer Philip K. Dick's *Minority Report*, recently brought to the screen by Stephen Spielberg, is the subject of my article for *Le Monde Diplomatique:* "Identifier les tueurs-nés", *Le Monde Diplomatique*, December 2002, p. 31.

223 *Commission Internationale Pénale et Pénitentiaire, Prisons and Reformatories at Home and Abroad, being the Transactions of the International Penitentiary Congress, held in London*, July 3–13, 1872, ed. Edwin Pears, Maidstone, H. M. Prison, 1912 [1872], p. 336; Du Cane, "Address", p. 301.

224 "Report to the Convict Prison Commissioners", *Parliamentary Papers*, 1865, vol. 25, p. 212.

225 University College London Archives (Galton Papers, p. 159).

226 Dr V.C. Clarke to Francis Galton, 27 November 1879, University College London Archives (*loc. cit.*). In a second letter to Galton (*loc. cit.*, 2 December 1879), Clarke thanks his mentor for having sent a copy of his article "Generic Images" from *Nineteenth Century* (see bibliography). In a speech to the British Association, Galton described Dr Clarke as "accomplished and zealous" (Galton, "Address", p. 346).

227 Havelock Ellis, *The Criminal*, London, 1890, repr. New York, AMS Press, 1972, pp. 55–60.

228 *Ibid.*, Appendix, pp. 303–5. In an 1892 book published in French, Cesare Lombroso noted that "in 25 of the 36 [sketches by Dr Clarke], we may observe the combination of 5 or 6 degenerative anomalies" (Cesare Lombroso, *Nouvelles recherches de psychiatrie et d'anthropologie criminelles*, Paris, 1892, pp. 48–51: my translation). 12 of Clarke's sketches are reproduced in Lombroso's book (Plates 1–11, pp. 49–50).

229 Ellis, *op. cit.*, pp. 53–54.

Chapter Three

The Triumph of Common Sense? Cesare Lombroso's "Born Criminal-Type" and its British Critics

> *The world will probably remain very much where it was before the evolution of the criminal type. The fact is interesting, but it cannot be imported into criminal methods with either fairness or safety.... Criminal anthropology rests at present on too insecure grounds, on too many suppositions and probabilities to be entitled to the name of a science. It has been deduced from too incomplete premises, too hasty inquiries to give substantial results.*
>
> Major Arthur Griffiths, HM Prisons Inspector, 1894[1]

> *The new phrenology differs from the old in respect that it changes its terms and insists on more exactness of measurement. Like the old, it may be fairly successful in judging men after they have shown their qualities.*
>
> Dr James Devon, Medical Officer, Glasgow Prison, 1912[2]

In 1890, a young Havelock Ellis began canvassing opinion among Britain's prison authorities as part of the research for his forthcoming book, *The Criminal*. The latter would be published later the same year as part of a popular science series Ellis was himself editing for the Walter Scott Publishing Company. Ellis was keen to learn what the country's criminal justice professionals had to say on the subject of "criminal anthropology", and on its instigator and leading proponent, Cesare Lombroso (1835–1909); subjects which, according to Ellis's own account, he had stumbled upon while perusing a copy of *La Criminalité comparée*, a recent book by French jurist and criminologist, Gabriel Tarde (1843–1904).[3] Although a number of prison doctors and psychiatrists agreed to provide information for *The Criminal* (among them Vans Clarke)[4], Ellis was disappointed by the overall response. "Some of my correspondents, I fear," he later wrote, "had not so much as heard whether there be a criminal anthropology." He was forced to reach the unwelcome conclusion that "Criminal anthropology, as an exact science is yet unknown in England."[5]

Ellis was aware of the importance of the work of British pioneers Thomson, Wilson, Nicolson, and Maudsley, but had concluded that this line of research, for all its promise, had petered out in the mid-1870s; at precisely the point when Cesare Lombroso was formulating his own—in many ways similar—theories in Turin. One can almost sense Havelock Ellis scratching his head at this conundrum; puzzled that a country which had "in the past been a home of studies connected with the condition of the criminal" should now "lag so far behind the rest of the civilised world".[6] Despite his hopes that *The Criminal* would remedy this regrettable situation, Ellis found few signs of improvement in the years that followed. In an 1895 article for the *Journal of Mental Science*, he wrote: "We do not yet possess a single centre at which elementary instruction may be obtained in anthropology and anthropometry and in precise psychological methods, such as should be possessed by everyone who expects to be in charge of the criminal and the insane."[7]

Ellis's version of events would become historiographical orthodoxy. In their influential survey of "English Reactions to Positivism" (first published in 1986 in volume 5 of the authoritative *A History of English Criminal Law from 1750*), Leon Radzinowicz and Roger Hood provide a rapid tour of what they call the "British avant-garde", active in the late 1860s and early 1870s—Thomson, Nicolson, Wilson and Maudsley among them—before concluding that "those early inquiries and expressions of view all came to a standstill by the mid-1870s, at the very time when the positivist school erupted and produced an unprecedented ferment on the Continent of Europe."[8] The authors imply that the issue simply disappeared from view in British medical and penological circles until "rediscovered" by Havelock Ellis in 1890.[9] Other historians have fallen in line behind this account.[10]

It will be argued here, that to infer from the relative paucity of published work in Britain on the causes of crime in these years that there was a fifteen-year "standstill" in research on the subject, is seriously misleading. Radzinowicz and Hood's account tends to imply, moreover, that this standstill represents a *hiatus*; in other words that the work of the British avant-garde was a conceptual dead-end. By the time British criminology reopened for business in the 1890s, they suggest, it had taken on a radically different form. It is true that the work of Thomson, Maudsley and the others from the late 1860s and '70s largely disappeared from view, at least in mainstream discourse. The theories advocated in that earlier period, in particular that there existed a criminal-type capable of defining with precision the physical and mental traits of the country's habitual criminals, were redefined, *rebranded* as it were, as a conception entirely alien to the "practical" or "inductive" approach favoured within these shores. The avant-garde was in effect frogmarched into the enemy camp, making "Criminal-type theory" and "British practice" into mutually exclusive categories. *Real* criminology in this country, it was argued, could only be based on intimate knowledge of the circumstances—social and psychiatric—surrounding each individual case of criminal behaviour. What was needed then was a individualised therapeutic diagnosis for every offender, not some catch-all "criminal-type", capable of generating a check-list of physical and mental traits. By implication, such expertise was considered the prerogative of those prison doctors, criminal psychiatrists and Home Office officials whose hands-on experience of flesh and blood offenders gave them a unique insight into the workings of the deviant brain. This was the conception of criminological practice described by David Garland in an influential article of 1988:

> ... a therapeutically oriented discipline based on a classification system of psychiatric disorders which, like the disease model of nineteenth century medicine, discussed the condition separately from the individual in whom it might be manifested. Within that classification system of morbid psychology, there was a variety of conditions which criminals were typically said to exhibit—insanity, moral insanity, degeneracy, feeble-mindedness, etc. But generally speaking, *the criminal was not conceived as a psychological type.*[11]

There are two problems with this account. Firstly, there is clear evidence that the kinds of theories promulgated by Thomson, Nicolson and Maudsley and the rest did *not* in fact peter out in the mid-1870s, but survived into the latter part of that decade and into the 1880s. Indeed, as late as 1892, published work can be found—from *within* the medico-penal Establishment—which reveals an approach to the study of the Criminal which is to all intents and purposes identical to that advocated by Perth Prison's resident surgeon twenty-two years previously. This is not to suggest that the whole story of that decade can be rewritten as one of continuity. There did indeed emerge in the 1890s, as we shall see in this chapter, a new vituperatively anti-Lombrosian criminological discourse, but the critical point is—and this brings us to the second problem with Radzinowicz and Hood's account, and indeed with Garland's—that it was not the *tabula rasa* that its practitioners claimed.

It is no doubt tempting to take British criminology of this period at its own word with its repeated emphasis on novelty and the diametrical opposition between its position and that of Lombrosian criminal anthropology; particularly since today the latter is often condemned as, at best, "an incongruous amalgamate of hypotheses, comparisons, generalisations and illogical conclusions"[12]; at worst, as having contributed to a medico-racist discourse which would seek to justify some of the darkest episodes of twentieth-century history.[13]

Laudable though such sentiments are, they fail to take account of the full complexity of the historical record. As David G. Horn has recently pointed out, the first generation of historians and criminologists to address themselves to the serious study of Lombrosian criminal anthropology tended to limit the latter to

> … a supporting role in a cautionary tale about deviant or spurious science; it has been invoked either to make visible the differences between pure and impure ways of knowing, or else to reassure us of the ability of real science to police borders or to straighten the path to truth.[14]

Horn goes on to refer to a simplistic "binary" opposition in such accounts, which, in classic Whig fashion, tend to portray the victory of "subtle French sociologists, attentive to milieu and environment" over "the crude and reductive Italian anthropologists, obsessively and excessively focussed on the deviant bodies of criminals."[15]

The apparent diametrical opposition we have noted between British criminological practice after 1890 and Lombrosian criminal anthropology is just as reductionist. In reality, the discipline as it developed in this country between 1890 and 1918 was an eclectic hybrid, grafting key epistemological and heuristic assumptions from the mid-Victorian period onto the new therapeutic stem. Some of these assumptions, in fact, would turn out to be remarkably similar to those marshalled by Cesare Lombroso in his book, *L'Uomo delinquente*, and this despite a barrage of white-coated criticism directed at the Italian school.[16] The claim made in Lombroso's 1899 book, *Crime: Its Causes and Remedies*, that the British had adopted an approach which had much in common with his own theory of the "born criminal-type", was thus not so wide of the mark after all. Lombroso wrote:

> While the less advanced peoples are lingering over the utopias of the old jurists and, believing that reform is possible for all criminals, [and] are taking no measures against the continually rising tide of crime, the English, more provident, have recognised that although they have been able by their efforts to eliminate the accidental criminal almost entirely, the born criminal still persists. *They are the only nation to admit the existence of criminals who resist all cure, the 'professional criminals' as they call them, and the 'criminal classes'.*[17]

The author is of course no dispassionate observer on this issue, and his summary of the British position conveniently glosses over the many areas of divergence with his own. But however self-interested his conclusions, they *do* reveal a critical point of convergence between his theories and those which informed British practice in the 1890s and after. That convergence will be the subject of the next chapter.

For the moment, however, let us return to Lombroso and his "born criminal-type". His own theories were first formulated in the 1870s. At the beginning of that decade, some ten years after qualifying with a degree in medicine, a thirty-five year old army doctor from Verona was engaged in research "upon cadavers and living persons" in the prisons and asylums of Pavia, in the Lombardy region of northern Italy. His goal was "to determine upon substantial differences between the insane and criminals" and, by his own admission, his researches were not proving very successful. The man was Cesare Lombroso.[18] Looking back on events some thirty-five years later, he recounts what happened next:

> At last I found in the skull of a brigand a very long series of atavistic anomalies, above all an enormous middle occipital fossa and a hypertrophy of the vermis analogous to those found in inferior vertebrates. At the sight of these strange anomalies the problem of the nature and of the origin of the criminal seemed to me resolved; the characteristics of primitive men and of inferior animals must be reproduced in our times.[19]

Seven years later, in 1876, Lombroso, now holding a post in forensic medicine and public hygiene at Turin University, shared his new theory with the Italian reading public. The 225-page book, published in Milan, bore the simple but arresting title, *L'Uomo delinquente*. "Criminal Man" was born.[20] The first edition of the book was not a great success, but its publication is widely considered to mark a defining moment in the emergence of the modern science of "criminology".[21] What set Lombroso's approach apart from writers of the Classical School like Beccaria and Bentham was his insistence on the need to seek explanations for crime through the systematic scientific scrutiny of *individual* criminals, rather than exploring the moral significance of different criminal acts.[22]

If the origins of the criminal act were to be found in a detailed study of the offender him- or herself, it followed that punishment needed to be tailored to the demands of each case. Perhaps *treatment* would be a better word than punishment in this context, for the criminal behaviour in question was considered to emanate from constitutional urges or environmental pressures—or both—beyond the control of individual volition. Each prisoner thus required an *individualised* penal regime. Not for Lombroso and his followers, then, the "quest for uniformity" which characterised the English prison regime of the Du Cane years.[23] Whatever their differences on other matters, the various "positivist" schools of criminology that emerged in this period—Italian, French, British—would all come to share these fundamental premises.[24]

Whether Lombroso's substitute for "the insecurity of the ancient criminological scaffolding" was the "more solid edifice" he claimed,[25] remained to be seen, but it was certainly constructed at impressive speed. Within ten years of the first edition of *L'Uomo delinquente*, the Italian *Scuola Positiva* or Positivist School had generated several important theoretical works and an academic journal. In addition, from 1885, its ideas were the driving force behind a series of international congresses of "criminal anthropology", as the new science came to be known, bringing together an illustrious cross-section of European lawyers, doctors, academics, and government officials. The first congress took place in Rome in August 1885; subsequent venues included Paris (1889), Brussels (1892) and Geneva (1896).[26] During this period, *L'Uomo delinquente* went through five Italian editions (the last totalling nearly 2,000 pages), was translated into French and German—but not English—and for some twenty-five years, Cesare Lombroso was either eulogised or vilified in legal and penal circles, but rarely ignored.[27] As Belgian psychiatrist and anthropologist Dr Jules Dallemagne—no friend of Lombrosian criminology[28]—put it, looking back from 1896:

> The question of the criminal-type [formulated by Lombroso] ... revolutionised our thinking and stimulated excitement and healthy competition everywhere. For twenty years, his ideas fed our discussions; the Italian master was at the centre of every debate; indeed his thoughts were events in themselves. There was everywhere an extraordinary level of intellectual animation.[29]

Cesare Lombroso's *Criminal Man* was based on two breathtakingly simple premises: that up to 70% of criminals were, as it were, programmed from birth to commit crime;[30] and that this "born criminal-type" (*delinquente-nato*) could be identified by the trained observer in the form of outward anatomical and physiological signs or "stigmata".[31] If Lombroso's later account of events is to be believed—and there is some doubt concerning the precise sequence of events[32]—the foundation of his future theories was laid when he examined the skull of that "notorious"[33] Italian brigand, Villella, on a dull December morning in 1870. At that precise moment, it became clear to him that Criminal Man was an atavistic throwback to an earlier stage in human evolution:

> This was not merely an idea but a revelation. At the sight of that skull, I seemed to see all of a sudden, lighted up as a vast plain under a flaming sky, the problem of the nature of the criminal—an atavistic being who reproduces in his person the ferocious instincts of primitive humanity and the inferior animals. Thus were explained anatomically the enormous jaws, high cheek bones, prominent superciliary arches, solitary lines in the palms, extreme size of orbits, handle-shaped ears found in criminals, savages and apes, insensibility to pain, extremely acute sight, tattooing, excessive idleness, love of orgies, and the irresponsible craving of evil for its own sake, the desire not only to extinguish life in the victim, but to mutilate the corpse, tear its flesh and drink its blood.[34]

Lombroso was clearly moving in the same intellectual universe as Henry Maudsley. Indeed, in the same year as Lombroso was rooting around for skulls in the prisons and asylums of Pavia, the English alienist was, as we have seen, writing of the "brute brain within the man's" and that it was possible "without much difficulty [to] trace savagery in civilisation, as we can trace animalism in savagery." The extent to which Maudsley himself influenced Lombroso is difficult to determine, though his works are quoted in the various editions of *L'Uomo delinquente*.[35] What *is* clear, however, is that Lombroso, like Maudsley, was well-read in the French literature of mental illness and degeneracy. Dr Bénédict-Augustin Morel's *Traité des dégénérescence physiques, intellectuelles et morales de l'espèce humaine* (1858) with its notion of distinct degenerate "types", "recognisable by external and internal signs" was particularly influential.[36]

> The insane type [wrote Morel] can be found all over the world, with the same combination of intellectual, physical and moral symptoms which are characteristic of all pathological states. When the acts and urges of the insane are examined, when a comparative study is made of their deliria, when their illness is followed from its beginning, through its mature phase to its terminal stages, and when one examines their facial expressions and even the forms of their heads, one is struck by the fact that they all suffer from the same degenerative causes running rife everywhere, and always in the same manner.[37]

Lombroso was equally well versed in the emerging evolutionary theories of biology and palaeontology, associated with Darwin, Haeckel, and Virchow, the positivist sociology of Comte and Spencer, the "moral statistics" of Quetelet as well as the pioneering work of British prison doctors Bruce Thomson and George Wilson.[38]

> What set Lombroso apart from his contemporaries was not his dictum that the it was important to study the criminal not the crime[39], nor even the originality of his theory of the inheritance of criminal tendencies,

> but rather his ability to link generalisations about the atavistic nature of the criminal constitution to the anthropological analysis of *individual* criminals.[40] Just like Schaafflhausen's "barbarous and savage" Neanderthal Man or the orthognathous face believed by Paul Broca to characterise "the highest groups in the human series", Lombroso's "born criminal" was a matter not for philosophical musings, but for hard-nosed measurement. As Broca had put it in a 1864 book of instructions for researchers in physical anthropology, "All too often, personal fancy, imagination, and preconceived ideas lead to unintended error. Such methods should have no place in research of this kind, which is the only way of establishing *all* the physical characteristics of a race."[41] Thus, a similarly thoroughgoing scientific criminology, based on the proven techniques of anthropometric, and in particular *cranio*metric, measurement, seemed to represent the way forward.[42] Whereas Broca had famously defined anthropology as "the natural history of Man", Lombroso and his followers would define their new discipline, "Criminal Anthropology", as "the natural history of *Criminal* Man."[43]

Like the "inferior" races and Man's prehistoric ancestors, Lombroso's born criminal-type was believed to possess a number of atavistic, ape-like characteristics. Thus for the second part of *Criminal Man*, 380 criminal skulls were subjected to a barrage of craniometric tests, beginning with cranial capacity, the anthropological gold-standard when it came to classifying different races in an evolutionary hierarchy.[44] After comparing the brain cavities of criminals with those of 328 "honest men" (a procedure which involved filling each with sand, and calculating the volume), Lombroso concluded that there was a concentration of small brains among the criminal skulls, but also a disproportionate number of very large ones. The latter fact might be thought to contradict the conventional criminal = small brain hypothesis, but Lombroso suggests that a very large brain is itself an anomaly (he notes that assassins tend to have large brains).[45] Perhaps, as Paul Topinard would later suggest, "a certain proportion of criminals are pushed to depart from present social conditions by an exuberance of cerebral activity and consequently, by the fact of a large or heavy brain."[46]

Lombroso then takes us through the standard anthropometric tests one by one, ranging from the question of the relative size of the frontal and occipital regions of the brain, the facial angle (the extent to which the face and jaws jut forward), the size of the lower jaw[47] and the cranial index. Similar tests were also performed on nearly 4000 living criminals; or rather Lombroso combined the results of his own researches on the Italian prison population with the published work of a number of other criminologists, including Enrico Ferri and the Frenchman Alexandre Lacassagne.[48]

His results proved once again to his satisfaction the atavistic nature of Criminal Man:

> Those who have followed us so far have seen that many of the characteristics presented by savage races are very often found among born criminals. Such, for example, are: the slight development of the pilar system; low cranial capacity; retreating forehead; highly developed frontal sinuses; greater frequency of Wormian bones; early closing of the cranial sutures; the simplicity of the sutures; the thickness of the bones of the skull; enormous development of the maximillaries and the zygomata; prognathism; obliquity of the orbits ...[49]

And so on. However, the list does not restrict itself to anatomical anomalies, but extends to distinctive physiological features associated with the born criminal-type:

> [T]hough they do not always have an unprepossessing and frightening physiognomy, they all have a distinctive face, and often one specific to a particular kind of crime. ... In general, many criminals have jug ears and a full head of hair; are rarely bearded; have heavy jaws and frontal sinuses; a square and jutting chin; and prominent cheekbones. Gesticulation is also frequent. In short, we have here a type closely resembling that of the Mongol or the Negro.[50]

Lombrosian criminologists viewed portrait photography as a valuable short-cut to the observation of such outwardly-visible stigmata, much as doctors and psychiatrists would subsequently make use of the new medium in their efforts to "scientifically" define "feeble-mindedness".[51] The photographic portrait was perfectly suited to the positivist idiom of the Italian School, ostensibly providing an unmediated reflection of empirical reality. The Italian professor saw in the 219 criminal portraits he studied for *Criminal Man* incontrovertible evidence of an atavistic criminal type, just as alienists and anthropologists catalogued external physical signs to classify—respectively—types of mania and racial differences. Indeed, Lombroso's observations reveal his faith in the power of photography not only to catalogue such anatomical and physiognomic stigmata, but also in Diamond's terms, to provide a window on the criminal's inner soul. Thus, he notes that 39% had a "prominent jaw" and 21% had "thick hair", but also makes the imaginative jump to psychological inference with his quantification of those with a "sinister and shifty look" (23%). The corresponding figures for the control group of "honest men" were 7%, 1% and 1% respectively.[52] On the basis of this comparison, Lombroso was able to conclude—"an easy task", he added, "when one has photographs at hand"—that "among criminals, what stands out is the marked prominence of the jaw, the rarity of the beard, the harshness of the look, and the abundance of hair. To a lesser extent, one also finds jug ears, a retreating forehead, strabismus and a deformed nose."[53]

However, it is when Lombroso draws together the anthropometric and photographic inferences from the data on anatomical and physiognomical stigmata and provides the reader with apparently scientifically-generated thumbnail sketches of "typical" criminals that we may observe what it was about Lombroso's born criminal-type which caught the imagination of specialists and public alike. His portraits have all the striking visual clarity of a photographic plate. Here, for example, is the "common murderer":

> [They] … have a glassy look, cold and immobile, but sometimes bloodthirsty and bloodshot. The nose is prominent, often aquiline or hooked, like one finds on a bird of prey. The jaw is robust; the ears long; the cheekbones wide; and the hair is frizzy, abundant and dark. Quite often there is no beard, the canine teeth are highly developed and the lips thin.[54]

Forgers and swindlers are also singled out for the Lombroso treatment:

> A great many forgers and swindlers that I have studied have a distinctive physiognomy and display a certain bonhomie, something almost clerical which in their pitiful criminal careers tends to inspire trust. I have seen individuals of this type with a pale face, haggard or very small eyes, a twisted nose, and in some cases early hair loss and a face resembling that of an old woman. Indeed, often the parents of such subjects are old.[55]

But Lombroso's argument does not rely purely on the observation of such visual stigmata of criminality. To prove that Criminal Man is indeed an atavistic throwback to earlier stages of evolution, a kind of walking museum piece, it needs to be demonstrated that those earlier stages in human development were indeed marked by physical and mental traits which can justifiably be labelled "criminal". With this objective in mind, Lombroso devotes considerable attention to the question of crime amongst children and "inferior races", but to open his book, Lombroso chooses to climb even higher up Man's family tree, and devotes the first chapter to the subject of "Crime among Lower Organisms"; an enterprise described by historian of science, S. J. Gould, as "the most ludicrous excursion into anthropomorphism ever published".[56]

The theory of recapitulation demanded not only that men—or some men—should carry the atavistic stigmata of savages and cavemen, but that, as we noted in the last chapter, the individual as it grows, should pass through a number of stages equivalent to the stages in Man's evolutionary past. From this point of view, the child is considered analogous to an ancestral adult.[57] Lombroso believed that, in most cases, an appropriate education was sufficient to achieve what he called a "normal metamorphosis" of children—considered inherently deviant—into law-abiding adults (though members of "savage races" were significantly excluded from this generalisation).[58] For those who had not achieved this transformation, he claimed to have identified certain behavioural traits, equally atavistic in nature. The frequent use of a professional *argot* among criminals was likened to the language of savages and children. Tattooing on the other hand, not only resembled the customs of primitive races; it also reflected, it was argued, the criminal's "relative insensitivity to pain".[59]

Other social attributes of the criminal resembled closely the dominant mid-Victorian stereotypes of the "criminal classes" we have met on a number of occasions in this book. Lombroso thus provides the following list of mental attributes associated with criminals:

> ... blunted affections, precocity as to sensual pleasures; greater resemblance between the sexes; greater incorrigibility of the woman (Spencer); laziness; absence of remorse; impulsiveness; physiopsychic excitability; and especially improvidence, which sometimes appears as courage and a gain as recklessness changing to cowardice. Besides these there is a great vanity; a passion for gambling and alcoholic drinks; violent but fleeting passions; superstition; extraordinary sensitiveness with regard to one's own personality; and a special conception of God's morality.[60]

It should be emphasised, however, that the Italian school did not (despite the charges consistently laid at its door by the French, and later by the British) propose an explanation of criminal behaviour based *solely* on the theory of the atavistic born criminal. As early as the second Italian edition of *Criminal Man*, published in 1878 (at 740 pages, nearly three times longer than its predecessor), exogenous factors make their appearance in the explanation of criminal behaviour: factors like poverty and alcoholism rub shoulders with inherited atavism.[61] The influence of Enrico Ferri may have been important here. In an 1878 article reviewing *L'Uomo delinquente*, Ferri argued that the results of criminal anthropology had shown that only about a third of criminals had an "extraordinary number" of organic and psychic abnormalities, with a further 50 to 60% manifesting a small number of such defects.[62] Indeed, in his 1895 book, *Criminal Sociology*, Ferri stated that the psychological, rather than the anthropometric, aspect of criminal anthropology was "by far the more important".[63] By the end of the 1890s, Lombroso had come round to Ferri's way of thinking. The last Italian edition of *L'Uomo delinquente*, published in 1897, put the proportion of born criminals at 40%, and in *Crime: Its Causes and Remedies* (1899), Lombroso pared the number still further, this time to about to a third.[64]

The Italian seems to have been somewhat exasperated by what looked like a wilful refusal on the part of his critics to recognise the modification of his initial position. Chided by Alexandre Lacassagne at the Rome congress of 1885 for his underestimation of the role of the *milieu social*, Lombroso riposted by reminding his critic that on "almost every page" of his intervention at the congress, he had spoken of "occasional criminals", and of the "influence of the family, society, the State, etc.", in other words, of social factors. He even managed a swipe at the Lyons professor concerning the latter's theory of the *criminel occipital*.[65] Such a notion reflected, Lombroso concluded, "an exaggerated belief in the importance of purely craniological influences" ...[66]

The world turned upside down? Not exactly. It *is* true that Lombroso was increasingly prepared, like Ferri, to grant a role to socio-economic and even climactic factors in the explanation of some "occasional" crime. However, the largest group of occasional criminals, whom he termed "criminaloids", were considered to "differ, from born criminals in degree, not in kind." Many, he notes, go on to become habitual criminals, "thanks to a long sojourn in prison"; at which point, "they can no longer be distinguished from born criminals except by the slighter character of their physical marks of criminality."[67]

Despite the modifications made to his theory, Lombroso never abandoned his initial premise that the most dangerous category of criminals was determined by defective biology to commit crime.[68] New strings were added to Lombroso's explanatory bow when it became clear that many of the anomalies he had found in the criminal could not be explained by atavism alone. Thus, later editions of *Criminal Man* together with *Crime: Its Causes and Remedies*, contain a more diffuse, but also more inclusive, version of his original thesis.[69] Atavism remained the primary biological cause of criminal behaviour, but a range of congenital illnesses and forms of *dégénérescence* were mobilised in order to shore up the Lombrosian theoretical edifice. Criminal man was now not only a "savage man", Lombroso wrote in the first French edition of his book, but is "at the same time, a sick man."[70] Thus criminality became increasingly bound up in his mind with both insanity and epilepsy. *Crime: Its Causes and Remedies*, his last major work on crime, went as far as suggesting that almost all born criminals suffered to some extent from epilepsy.[71]

Lombroso and his fellow members of the Italian *Scuola Positiva* believed that these new (or not so new) ideas would sweep away the intellectual cobwebs, replacing the abstract, philosophical discussion of crime which had characterised the period since the Enlightenment with an entirely new "positive" empirical science based on the observation of individual criminals. Criminal anthropology was never conceived as a purely academic discipline, but as a technique that would take criminal trials out of the dark ages by bringing to court proceedings a new level of scientific objectivity. The Lombrosian project must also, as Daniel Pick has argued, be situated in the context of post-independence Italy's efforts to free itself of cultural and racial "backwardness" and politically instability:

> The criminal class was … an obsolete freight carried by the State. Unified Italy, he [Lombroso] argued, would have to streamline evolution, eliminate the unproductive. The point of the positivist study of the criminal was to produce a science of social defence against atavism and anarchy. … Enemies were without and within, dispersed everywhere. Lombroso's criminal anthropology sought to help to contain this threat: to comprehend it scientifically and hence exclude it politically.[72]

In this respect, the criminal anthropologists saw themselves as progressives, not reactionaries, dragging their often unwilling compatriots into an enlightened era of scientific progress and liberal political institutions, a fact confirmed, as Stephen Jay Gould has noted, by their frequent support for progressive causes.[73] Enrico Ferri, for example, one of Lombroso's closest collaborators, edited the left-wing journal *Avanti* and was a well-known writer on socialist topics.[74] The only way forward, in his view, was to ditch the anachronistic obsession with the moral significance of the crime and direct attention to what was the main point of the exercise: "a physio-psychological examination of the accused".[75]

> [T]he whole process of a criminal trial consists in the assemblage of facts, the discussion and the decision upon the evidence. … A criminal trial ought to retrace the path of the crime itself, passing backwards from the criminal action (a violation of the law), in order to discover the criminal, and in the psychological domain, to establish the determining motives and the anthropological type.[76]

Ferri outlines the way in which "the data of criminal biology, psychology and psycho-pathology" would permit "an anthropological classification, certain and speedy, of every convicted person … by the character of the accused and of his action … whether he is a born criminal, or mad, or an habitual or occasional criminal, or a criminal of passion."[77]

No more then would criminal trials be "those combats of craft, manipulations, declamations and legal devices, which makes every criminal trial a game of chance, destroying public confidence in the administration of justice, a sort of spider's web which catches the flies and lets the wasps escape."[78] Instead, Ferri offers us a brave new world of scientific investigation in which the role of the judge and litigants is reduced to calling for explanations from the experts. The advantages for all concerned are presented in the following glowing terms:

> A study of the anthropological factors of crime provides the guardians and administrators of the law with new and more certain methods in the detection of the guilty. Tattooing, anthropometry, physiognomy, physical and mental conditions, records of sensibility, reflex activity, vaso-motor reactions, the range of sight, the data of criminal statistics, [all of these] facilitate and complete the amassing of evidence, personal identification, and hints as to the capacity [of an individual] to commit any particular crime ... [Such evidence] will frequently suffice to give police agents and examining magistrates a scientific guidance in their inquiries, which now depend entirely on their individual acuteness and mental sagacity.[79]

Such "scientific guidance" from benighted criminal anthropologists (attached as a matter of course to every criminal court) would mean, Ferri believed, that the professionals of the crime detection and the legal process would no longer be blundering around intuitively in the semi-darkness, illuminated only by the flickering candle of classical jurisprudence. Instead, criminal anthropology offered the pure, bright light of objective scientific knowledge.

With the criminal "the true and living subject of the trial"[80], it followed as a matter of course for Lombroso, Ferri, and their associates that the traditional framework of more or less standardised punishments for particular crimes was out of the question. Thus, Lombroso explains:

> ... in cases of assault it is absurd to establish, as the codes do, a great differentiation according to the seriousness and duration of the effects, especially since antiseptic methods now hasten the cure; for the murderer does not measure his blows, and it is only purely by chance if they are not mortal. On the contrary, in crimes of this kind we must observe carefully to see whether the guilty person is a respectable man and whether he had serious provocation.[81]

In the last case, Lombroso goes on, we would be dealing with a "criminal of passion", which would demand a very different sentence to that to be meted out on a born criminal. Thus Lombroso, echoing the views of

Ferri and Garofalo, comes to the conclusion that "the penalty should be *indeterminate*." As Ferri put it,

> For every crime which is committed, the problem of punishment ought no longer to consist in administering a particular dose, as being proportionate to the moral culpability of the criminal; but it should be limited to the question whether by the actual conditions (breach of the law or infliction of injury) and by the personal conditions (the anthropological type of the criminal) it is necessary to separate the offender from his social environment for ever, for a longer or shorter period, according as he is or is not regarded as capable of being restored to society.[82]

The appropriate moment for release would be determined by a commission, equivalent to a parole board, a decision in which criminal anthropologists would again play a key role. Ferri adds, however, that such a procedure would not be available to "mad and born criminals who are guilty of great crimes."[83]

There would be different penal institutions for different categories of offender. Those requiring long-term or indefinite confinement would be incarcerated in "special establishments", criminal asylums or specialised prisons, while "occasional" criminals would be sent to a "penal agricultural colony". In the latter, "air, light, movement, field labour … are the only physical and moral disinfectants possible for prisoners not entirely degenerate, or likely to prevent at least the absolute brutalisation of the incorrigible, by giving them healthy and more remunerative work."[84]

For hardened yet physically fit criminals, those "less capable of restoration to social life", there was the option of transportation overseas, perhaps to a penal colony on the English model in Italy's new African colony, Abyssinia. Alternatively, there was the option of "internal deportation", setting criminals to work in malaria-infested fields or in the mines. There were of course considerable health risks posed by malaria or fire-damp, but was it not "much better that these should kill off criminals than honest workmen"? Incarceration was not a panacea, however. Both Lombroso and Ferri stress that for minor offences, corporal punishment, probation or a fine would be sufficient.[85]

As for those criminals who, "in spite of the prison, transportation, and hard labour … repeat their sanguinary crimes and threaten the lives of honest men for the third or fourth time", there remained no option but what Lombroso describes as "the last selection, painful but sure—the death penalty." In this way society is protected. "Shall we hesitate", he asks, "when it is a question of suppressing some few criminal individuals, a hundred times more dangerous and fatal than a foreign enemy, in whose ranks a chance bullet may strike a Darwin or a Gladstone?" At the same time the criminal him or herself is offered a humane alternative to lifelong imprisonment.[86]

Both Lombroso and Ferri anticipated the conventional moral and religious arguments against capital punishment, arguing that society had the right to protect itself from such dangerous elements as born criminals, "organically fitted for evil, atavistic reproductions not simply of savage men but even of the fiercest animals."[87] And was not the taking of life not also Nature's way? For Lombroso, "the very process of the organic world is entirely based on the struggle for existence". Ferri spelt out the Social Darwinist message even more explicitly:

> The universal law of evolution shows us that vital progress of every kind is due to continual selection, by the death of the least fit in the struggle for life. Now this selection, in humanity as with lower animals, may be natural or artificial. It would therefore be in agreement with natural laws that human society should make an artificial selection, by the elimination of anti-social and incongruous elements.[88]

Let us now return to contemporary developments in Britain. Lombroso's theories would not be widely disseminated there for another decade yet; it has been suggested that it was ready availability of French and German translations of *Criminal Man* from the late 1880s which played a key role in bringing his born criminal-type to an international audience, including that in Britain.[89] The evidence we examined in chapter two from Maudsley's *Responsibility in Mental Disease* (1874), from Du Cane's 1875 talk to the Social Science Association, from Francis Galton's 1877 experiments with composite photography, and from Dr Vans Clarke's medical records from Pentonville (1877–1878), all point to a coherent mind-set which held sway in the mid-1870s, well before Lombroso's ideas reached the English-speaking world. Like *Criminal Man*, this mind-set emphasised that habitual criminals were at once atavistic and degenerate, and as such were largely immune to conventional prison regimes. Sir Edmund Du Cane summed up this view in his remarks following Francis Galton's 1878 talk on "Composite Portraits". It was probable, he observed, that

> … certain personal peculiarities distinguish those who commit certain classes of crime; the tendency to crime is in those persons born or bred in them, and either they are incurable or the tendency can only be checked by taking them in hand at the earliest periods of life. … I should anticipate that a great number of those who commit certain classes of crime would be found to show an entirely inferior mental and bodily organisation …[90]

Radzinowicz and Hood suggest such views were a temporary aberration; the penal administrator with his "Royal Engineers' training and straightforward approach" momentarily "bewildered" by all this talk of atavism and degeneration.[91] Later, they suggest, Du Cane's views became "more and more sceptical" concerning the ideas of the Italian school.[92] Listening with approval to a 1895 speech criticising Lombrosian criminology, Du Cane declared that

> … too much is made of the idea that criminality is a special quality of the mind. It has nothing to do with it. A person may be very wise and yet be a criminal; he may be a great fool and yet be a criminal. There are many specimens of both sorts in our prisons.[93]

He accused the criminal anthropologists of "leading the public astray" when they "put forward those doctrines try[ing] to prove that people are criminals because they are born criminals".[94]

Yet the picture is not complete. In the same year as he was applauding this withering attack on criminal anthropology, Du Cane gave evidence to a government committee to the effect that, in his opinion, "the class from which criminals are drawn is a class mentally, physically and morally below the average of the population."[95] Elsewhere in his writings there is, according to William James Forsythe, ample evidence from the 1880s and 1890s that "Du Cane considered that many prisoners were of a 'type' unlikely in fact to be altered by any discipline".[96] As Du Cane himself put it in his 1885 book, *The Punishment and Prevention of Crime*:

> Many of them [criminals] do not, and some possibly cannot, comprehend their own position or realise their true self-interest as social and responsible beings, and their actions are but too frequently prompted by what appears to them the expediency of the moment … Speaking proverbially, they form a class of fools whom even experience fails to teach.[97]

Du Cane's position would seem to be a good example of the phenomenon noted with perspicacity by Daniel Pick, namely that "Views perceived as foreign and 'hysterical' were often refuted only in the name of a more refined version of the same language."[98]

That Du Cane's views were not exceptional is confirmed by the testimony collected by the "Royal Commission into the Working of the Penal Servitude Acts" in 1879, better-known under the name of its chairman, the Earl of Kimberley.[99] The published report came to the conclusion that "weak-minded or imbecile" convicts represented "a large proportion of the habitual criminal class" and that such prisoners were the source of "constant annoyance and perplexity" to all prison officers. It was recommended that they be separated completely from other convicts and placed in their own wing or ward of the prison.[100] Lord Kimberley and his colleagues were no doubt influenced in this area by the sole medical specialist on the Commission, none other than Dr William Augustus Guy.[101] However, a close scrutiny of the oral testimony given before the Commission reveals that such views were widespread. Many witnesses emphasised that criminals were a degenerate group of individuals, with outwardly visible physical signs of their inferior status. Dr Henry Askham, principal surgeon at Portland Convict Prison, noted that "the criminal class altogether are greatly deteriorating. They are not nearly the vigorous set that they were when I first joined the service nineteen years ago." When asked the reasons for this change, he replied:

> I do not know, except that it is from the degeneration of the race of the criminal class, that it descends from parent to child, and they gradually dwindle away. They are smaller in stature, and you will find a great deal of scrofula amongst them which goes down from parent to child.[102]

Askham was one of several witnesses[103] to emphasise the greater *urban* component in the contemporary criminal class. William Fagan, a director of convict prisons (responsible for the establishments at Millbank, Wormwood Scrubs, Brixton and Portsmouth) noting that felons "have materially fallen off in strength and robustness most certainly", suggests that "… we get the waste of all the large towns and of London particularly". Asked whether he would describe such men as a lower class of men, physically and morally, he replies in the affirmative, calling them (in terms reminiscent of David Nicolson) "an inferior stamp of men".[104]

It could be argued that such evidence belongs to the tail-end of the 1870s, only a couple of years after Radzinowicz and Hood's alleged "standstill" in British theorising on crime. What about the subsequent period? The general criminological perspective of the years from the 1880s to the First World War is the subject of the next chapter, so will not be considered in detail here. However, we will make a brief foray into that period to suggest that prison doctors were still prepared to take seriously the evidence for an anatomical and physiognomic criminal-type into the 1880s and '90s.

We shall look firstly at the memoirs of Dr John Campbell, *Thirty Years' Experience of a Medical Officer in the English Convict Service*, published in 1884. In his book, Campbell makes remarks about the habitual criminal which leave no doubt that he subscribed to the notion of a physical and mental criminal-type:

> The physiognomy, as well as the confirmation of the skull, is often remarkable; and the result of many *post-mortem* examinations has proved that the brains of prisoners weigh less than the average, and that a large brain is an exception.[105]

As far as mental traits are concerned, he observes:

> Mental deficiency is by no means uncommon among habitual criminals, and prevails in many different forms. Some display a marked degree of dullness or stupor; others sharpness or cunning more allied to the tricks of monkeys than the acts of reasonable men.[106]

Campbell, former medical officer at Woking Invalid Prison, goes on to describe such mentally-weak prisoners as "the most insubordinate inmates of our convict prisons", echoing his evidence to the 1863 Royal Commission on Penal Servitude, in which he had complained of the disruptive behaviour of this category of prisoners "upsetting the whole establishment".[107] Such "troublesome creatures", he wrote in his memoirs, "are often the children of debased and drunken parents, generally of the habitual criminal class; so that the inherent hereditary predisposition, as well as the bad example set them at home, renders removal from such baneful influences the surest safeguard."[108]

Campbell advocated indeterminate seclusion for such incorrigible cases, involving their transfer, on discharge, to a "refuge". Such a solution—"a more humane procedure than to allow these people to return to their haunts of vice and misery and to resume their pilfering habits"—would represent what he calls "imprisonment in a modified form", with "increased comforts and an improved dietary, with due encouragement to industry". Like the Italian positivists, Campbell clearly regarded this class of habitual criminals as beyond the reach of conventional prison regimes: "The indifference shown by some of the habitual or frequently convicted prisoners, on their return to prison, is a sad spectacle enough, as is the fact that prisons are less dreaded by the older criminals than the workhouses ..."[109]

Secondly, we may refer to an article published in the *Journal of Mental Science* eight years after Dr Campbell's memoirs, by Dr John Baker, like David Nicolson before him, medical officer at Portsmouth Convict Prison.[110] There is nothing startlingly original in the article, "Some Points connected with Criminals", but it is significant that nearly twenty years after Radzinowicz and Hood's supposed hiatus in British biological theories of crime, members of the prison medical service were clearly still examining criminal heads for signs of the physical stigmata of crime. Baker's analysis of twenty-five male specimens of what he calls (following Maudsley[111]) "essential criminals"—many of them "weak-minded" and "degenerate physically"—revealed that in a majority of cases, the forehead was "generally low", the frontal sinuses and zygoma "prominent", the lower jaw generally "weak" (except in four cases of epileptic prisoners with "massive and square" jaws), and most remarkable of all, he notes, the prisoners' palates were "frequently" abnormal. Indeed, Dr Baker found that only six of the twenty-five prisoners examined were "normal" in this respect.[112]

Scattered evidence from the beginning of the 1890s suggests that Baker was not the only prison doctor carrying out such research. Havelock Ellis's inquiries in 1890 had thrown up a few examples of anthropometric measurement in the prison medical service—though frustratingly, few of his correspondents are quoted by name in *The Criminal*.[113] We also learn in 1896 that Dr James Scott of London's Holloway Prison, the only British prison doctor to attend one of the international congresses on criminal anthropology, had reached the conclusion that criminals had a higher than average incidence of "abnormality of palate".[114]

Given the existence of such views as these in the 1880s and 1890s, how, then, are we to account for the virulent hostility to Lombrosian criminology on record in Britain at precisely this period? Were Drs Campbell and Baker simply beyond the criminological fringe, dinosaurs in a rapidly-changing discipline? One way towards an answer to this question is provided by an article from the respected *British Medical Journal*, published in September 1889. Interestingly, the article, entitled "The Physiognomy of Murderers", provides a commentary on Cesare Lombroso's description of the murderer in *Criminal Man* a year before Havelock Ellis claimed to have "discovered" criminal anthropology. The *British Medical Journal*'s remarks on Lombroso's theories are a revealing foretaste of the subsequent British reaction to the new science:

> We are prepared to admit that habitual crime is a constitutional disease, which is often inherited and, like other diatheses, has its outward physiognomical expression. [... Lombroso's] may possibly be an accurate portrait of the wretch whose butcheries have for so long made a reign of terror in Whitechapel, but it would hardly be safe for a detective to arrest the possessor of such physical attractions on the strength of his murderous countenance. Many habitual homicides [...] have been of particularly attractive appearance. The 'high *a priori* method' is as unsatisfactory in criminal physiognomy as in other branches of science, and might lead to highly inconvenient results in practice.[115]

These comments indicate, first of all, that rejecting the approach of Cesare Lombroso and his followers did not mean ruling out a role for hereditary factors in the generation of criminal behaviour, nor their manifestation in outward physiognomic stigmata. On the contrary, habitual crime is quite explicitly described as both "a constitutional disease … which is often inherited", and one which has its "outward physiological expression". The objection to criminal anthropology is *not* to the Italian's depiction of the "born criminal" murderer as such ("[it] may possibly be an *accurate portrait* of the wretch …"), but to its capacity to predict the external stigmata of *all* criminals. (The author appears unaware of the fact that by the end of the 1880s, Lombroso had revised downward his initial estimate of the numerical significance of the "born criminal" in the wider delinquent population.) The *British Medical Journal* author thus gives the argument, also noted by Du Cane[116], that "many" murderers "have been of particularly attractive appearance"; an observation which could be taken to undermine the notion of the criminal-type or alternatively to suggest the possibility of multiple criminal-*types*.

There are other articles, both from the BMJ and its sister journal, *The Lancet*, published between 1891 and 1896 which in their different ways evidence an equally equivocal reaction to criminal anthropology. The various authors clearly felt the need to tread carefully and hedge their comments with qualifications and nods to the anti-Lombrosian position. However, reading between the lines, it is possible to detect at least qualified support for some of the theories of the *Scuola Positiva*.

In a July 1891 issue of *British Medical Journal*, for example, while there is concern that criminal anthropology with its "hasty conclusions and immature classifications, which seem to gain vogue merely because they are startling" will feed "the morbid love of notoriety" already too widely spread in the population, it is "doubtless true that the degenerated classes have certain deficiencies of structure which show a hereditary weakness of constitution". Indeed, the British Medical Journal freely accedes the "usefulness" of studying "the degenerated classes to which habitual criminals, lunatics and imbeciles often belong". It is just there are more reliable ways than Lombrosian criminology of achieving this. The "distinguished professor" is castigated for "getting looser and looser in his methods" … The same equivocation can be detected in an article from the same journal, published in February 1894. Criminal anthropologists are mocked as "criminological Zadigs", always on the lookout for " 'atypical confluence' of the fissures of the brain". However, the *BMJ* adds: "That there is a solid basis of truth in the teachings of Lombroso and his followers no physiologist would deny …".[117]

The first of *The Lancet* articles in this series, published in August 1892—probably to coincide with the Brussels international congress on criminal anthropology which had opened the previous week—is, if anything, more sympathetic to Lombroso and his works than the *BMJ*. The article refers to the work of Drs Bruce Thomson, David Nicolson and William [*sic*] Wilson, as well as that of the Italian school. The author notes the sceptical attitude of British jurists towards Lombroso's theories, before adding that "Between the cautious attitude of the British law and the confident procedure of the Italian there is surely a *via media*."[118] After all, was it not true that "Criminals … generally come far short of a high or ideal standard of brain, body and mind"? The article concluded that more research was needed before firm conclusions could be reached.

The following autumn, *The Lancet* returned to the subject of the born criminal, noting that while of course there was no such thing as a criminal constitution, "there is such a thing as a degenerate physical type, capable, indeed of improvement under wholesome conditions of life, but which without these becomes the fruitful soil of moral weed growths."[119] In February 1894, the journal discussed the appropriate punishment for these "physiologically incapacitated members of society". Commending the view of the Lombrosians that such criminals from this class did not belong in prison, the article concludes: "… civil governments will one day find their account in giving better heed to criminal anthropology—even with its occasional exaggerations—than they have hitherto shown a disposition to bestow."[120]

That call would remain largely unanswered, and the subsequent British response to Lombroso's *Criminal Man* would remain silent on the points shared with the Italian *Scuola Positiva*. Instead, British practitioners, like their colleagues of the *Milieu Social* School across the Channel, would choose to emphasise the differences—or perceived differences—between the two traditions. In this sense the articles from the *British Medical Journal* and *The Lancet* are unusual in conceding a certain amount of common ground between the two approaches; perhaps at this early stage in the Anglo-Italian exchanges, positions had not become entrenched to the degree they would subsequently. Or was it, as Radzinowicz and Hood suggest, that Havelock Ellis's book "instead of converting the English, … alienated them because of its extreme and unsophisticated endorsement of the Italian doctrine"?[121]

Whatever the reasons, by the late-1890s, a consensus had emerged among British criminal justice professionals that the theories of criminal anthropology were of little relevance to their own practice. It was certainly the overall impression gleaned by Major Arthur Griffiths, visibly a fish out of water among the "abstract and rather threadbare themes"[122] of the 1896

Geneva Congress on Criminal Anthropology. By this time, *The Lancet* had fallen in line behind this new consensus. Commenting on the agenda paper at Geneva, the journal pronounced itself "very doubtful" that the criminal could

> … ever be reduced to anything like an exclusive or distinctive type by any grouping of physical characteristics in individual cases. It is all very well to make selections from among the inmates of a prison and discover 'criminal' resemblances, forgetful that similar resemblances are to be found among those upon whom prison gates have never been shut and who are not criminal.[123]

Just four years after advocating a *via media* between criminal anthropology and British jurisprudence, the journal was extolling the virtues of traditional explanations of crime, and "the influence of circumstance and motive in leading up to the commission of criminal acts." *The Lancet* concluded by warning its readers "not to allow themselves to wander away from the regions of common sense and everyday experience."[124]

The British Medical Journal, however, was not yet quite ready to give up its crypto-Lombrosianism. In a 1896 review of a book by German criminal anthropologist Dr Eugen Bleuler, the journal accepted that the Italian School had gone beyond the evidence in their reliance on anatomical and physiological stigmata, but nevertheless made the following comment:

> It may be that lawyers pay too little regard to such stigmata, but detectives all recognise that habitual criminals generally have a physiognomy of their own. This is partly due to the effect of a course of crime upon the facial expression, but most of the lower class of criminals have some varying deformities or ugliness, the result of a faulty or incomplete development.[125]

In fact, the 1896 Geneva congress on criminal anthropology was intended to mark Cesare Lombroso's triumphant return to the international stage. The Italian delegation had stayed away from the previous congress at Brussels in 1892, upset by the stinging criticism of the delegates at the previous conference in Paris (and hoping, perhaps, that in the absence of Lombroso, the meeting would be a failure). Lombroso was not ready to hang up his gloves just yet however, and at Geneva he came out of his corner fighting, more determined than ever to defend "his" theory of the born criminal type.[126] His rearguard action was witnessed by Major Griffiths, Britain's sole official representative at the conference. Indeed, Griffiths' presence there was the only example of official involvement in *any* of the ten or so international congresses on criminal anthropology which took place during the period 1885–1914.[127] When rousec by hostility", Griffiths later recalled, Lombroso had cried,

> 'They say I am dead and buried. Do I look like it? … They say that the edifice I have built up is tottering to its fall. I admit nothing of the kind. I am raising it higher and higher, daily adding stone to stone. At least, I believe in my own theories, and care not one jot what others say.'"[128]

As S. J. Gould has observed, Lombroso "retreated like a military master" in the face of sustained criticism of his theory and methods.[129] He thus permitted his opponents some non-essential territorial gains in the matter of occasional crime, but refused to concede any ground when it came to his theoretical heartland, that of the atavistic born criminal. Indeed, like any good general, he sought to shore up his position: additional data (such as the analysis of control groups of "honest men") were called up, as were some new causal elements (*dégénérescence*, moral insanity, epilepsy, etc.). David G. Horn has noted that later editions of *Criminal Man* are notable above all for the "simple accretion" of data, rather than any modification of their author's initial premises. The final volumes, published in 1896–1897, contained anthropometric data on a total of 689 criminal crania (up from 55 in the first edition), as well as 6,608 living offenders.[130] "It is striking", Horn adds,

> to see how little Lombroso revises. The result is a heterogeneous text, full of contradictions, inconsistencies and errors. The work is at once organised by an ambition to build a totalizing science of criminal man, animated by an insatiable hunger to know (to measure, to collect, to probe, to categorize) and held together by a naïve hope that knowledge is additive or cumulative.[131]

Nicole Hahn Rafter and Mary Gibson have detected a similar process at work in Lombroso's *Criminal Woman, the Prostitute and the Normal Woman*, written with his son-in-law Guglielmo Ferrero (1871–1942) and first published in 1893.[132] Rafter and Gibson note that in one sense, the structure of the work reflects Lombroso's "willingness to take criticism to heart", notably in its inclusion of a long section on "normal women" to serve as a control group. They conclude, however, that while "he acknowledges earlier errors, … [he] does so with such caveats, contradictions, and contortions that the final impression is one of responsibility evaded." [133]

In fact, it is difficult to avoid the conclusion suggested by the words of the Lombroso himself in another work, published in French the previous year. In *Nouvelles recherches de psychiatrie et d'anthropologie criminelles*, he admitted that "as far as my fundamental conclusions are concerned, I would not wish to budge one iota." He added petulantly that if his theories were no longer of interest to anthropologists, he could always return to his first love, medicine.[134] Despite such a spirited defence, the general feeling at Geneva four years later was that Lombroso's opponents had won a decisive victory. Congresses continued to be held up to the First World War, but with criminal anthropology's ageing founding father increasingly isolated, there was an inevitable sense of anti-climax about future gatherings: the innovation and enthusiasm of Rome, Paris and Geneva had gone, never to return.[135]

Within four years of Geneva, the last mainstream British authority prepared to give qualified support to criminal anthropology had joined the ranks of the critics. In an article called "The Fallacy of the Criminal-type", the BMJ dismissed the "science of criminal physiognomics" as irrelevant. "Living illustrations of the type", noted its author, "appear to be more often found among law-abiding citizens than among thieves and murderers."[136] Such appeals to Anglo-Saxon common sense from the BMJ and *The Lancet* were echoed in the language of Major Griffiths' report, written for his Home Office superiors after the Geneva congress:

> Criminal anthropology ... has never seriously taken root in this country, the seeming extravagance of its momentous deductions and from such imperfect premises has tabooed it among men of real science, and its consideration has been left exclusively to those little qualified or competent to deal with it. [137]

Indeed, a common thread running through British responses to Lombrosian criminology in this period is an emphasis on the self-evident professional (i.e. medical) competence of home-grown criminologists, in contrast to the dubious scientific credentials of the (generally foreign) practitioners of criminal anthropology. While the latter might "make the vulgar stare", a leading psychiatric critic pointed out huffily in an article of 1895, "they make the judicious grieve."[138]

This point was spelled out clearly by Britain's first Medical Commissioner of Prisons, Sir Bryan Donkin, in a 1917 article in the *Journal of Mental Science.* He made a distinction between the work of "real" criminologists, namely "persons concerned in some way with the prison authorities who strive to discover just principles on which to base their work", and that of "theoretical" criminologists whose ideas concerning the "causation of crime" were based on "preconceived assumptions regardless of fact."[139] Donkin would no doubt have seen the wisdom in Marshal de Saxe's admonition for architects to learn the stonemason's trade.[140]

Unwilling to sully their hands with stone dust, the Continental theoreticians were, it was argued, unable to assess the validity of the arguments they were advancing. These were Charles Mercier's "grave professors", whose "eager gullibility" meant that they would swallow doctrines "without any attempt to examine them critically".[141] This was not simply harmless fun, Donkin pointed out in a 1908 speech on "The Feeble-Minded Criminal", for peddling theories of the "born criminal" served to tar all criminologists with the Lombrosian brush, making it difficult for any scientific study of criminal behaviour to be taken seriously.[142]

Lombroso's British critics were clearly concerned that the notion of the criminal-type had wormed its way into the public consciousness. We quoted earlier the *British Medical Journal*'s concern that the "morbid love of notoriety fostered by the cheap newspapers" was responsible for more crime and posed a greater threat to society than the anatomical stigmata dear to criminal anthropologists. The eugenicist Karl Pearson made a similar point, noting that Lombrosian criminology was "dead as a science", but "as a superstition it is not dead". He went on:

> There is some quality in it which has appealed to the imagination of the unscientific public, whose impressions of the criminal have been gained from hasty newspaper sketches, from the romantic literature of picturesque criminals, from popular pseudo-scientific treatises where accuracy is subordinated to piquancy, and from the galleries of Madame Tussaud.[143]

According to such a view, the dissemination of the kinds of crude stereotypes contained in Lombroso's *Criminal Man* could only make matters worse. As Sir Evelyn Ruggles-Brise, Du Cane's successor as Chairman of the Prison Commissioners, put it in a book of memoirs published to mark his retirement in 1921:

> Like all sensational dogmas, based on untested observation, it [Lombroso's born criminal-type] affected the public imagination prone to believe that the criminal is a sort of 'bogey-man'—the stealthy enemy of peaceful persons, ever ready to leap in the dark. This uneasy feeling encouraged the idea that the criminal was a class by himself—an abnormal being, the child of darkness, without pity and without shame, and with the predatory instincts of a wild beast. Thus gradually the common belief has taken root that there is a criminal-type, and that it is persons of this particular brand or species who commit crime, and go to prison.[144]

This well-worn image of the criminal as a stalking beast, ever-ready to prey on unwitting members of the general public, can be seen in striking form in a book of memoirs published by prison visitor Francis Scougal in 1889.[145] Clearly intended for the same kind of middle-class readership which would have bought Henry Mayhew's *London Labour and the London Poor* thirty years earlier, the book demonstrates how Darwinian evolutionary biology dovetailed seamlessly with early Victorian stereotypes of the brutish "predatory classes". Indeed, as Mary Cowling points out, the latter were given a new lease of life by the scientific "proof" afforded by Darwin's theory for the link between mankind and the brute creation.[146]

Scougal recounts the story of a prisoner whom he calls Ted Brown, who had murdered his wife, and then, according to the author's account, "composedly lay down by the side of the corpse and slept till morning".[147] Brown is described as being

> ... not only absolutely illiterate, but of so low an order of intelligence that he was very happily characterised by one of the prison officials as the missing link which Darwinism seeks to find between our race and the ascidians. It may really be doubted, however, whether any respectable gorilla would have demeaned himself to Ted Brown's level.[148]

Scougal goes on to portray Brown's 10- or 11-year-old daughter in the same simian terms:

> ... in her resemblance to the gorilla tribe [she] was quite as strongly marked as her father. In all her ways and movements, she was exactly like a monkey, with the one exception that she could speak with a human tongue in the lowest dialect of her native country.[149]

Du Cane's "arboreal ancestors" of the mid-1870s were apparently alive and well and still committing serious crimes. However, the insidious influence of criminal anthropology was considered to go beyond its contribution to unwholesome public fears of a brachiating criminal "bogey-man". By painting the criminal as the passive victim of defective heredity, it was argued, the doctrine of an individual's legal responsibility for his actions could be called into question, thereby undermining the whole philosophical basis of traditional criminal jurisprudence.[150] In the following parody of Lombrosian reasoning, psychiatrist Charles Mercier expresses the point flippantly, but his argument is no less serious for all that:

> You are a criminal, it is true, but the fault is not yours. It is not in the habit you have formed of yielding to your passions. It is not in your self-indulgence; your laziness; your slavery to impulse; your selfishness; your cultivated lack of control. No! It is impressed on you by your inheritance. You, poor fellow, are visited with the sins of your father and grandfather. ... In a word, you are a degenerate; and since your crimes are no fault of yours, you shall not be punished for them.[151]

In the same way, there was a concern that if the criminal was not responsible for his actions, the public perception of the perpetrators of crime would become less censorious as a result. Thus Hargrave Adam, in his 1911 *Police Encyclopaedia*, notes that the public frequently had an "erroneous image" of habitual offenders due to their ability to "put their own case in the most sympathetic light".[152]

An 1895 speech by the newly-elected president of the prestigious Medico-Psychological Society illustrates the range of criticisms to which criminal anthropology was subjected at this period. It also provides evidence for an intriguing aspect of the British anti-Lombrosian camp: that their number included several former paid-up members of Radzinowicz and Hood's "avant-garde" from the 1860s and '70s, for the new president of the Medico-Psychological Society was none other than Dr David Nicolson.

In his presidential address to the Society, Nicolson poured scorn on the very idea of looking for the physical characteristics of criminals. If the term "criminology" could be given to such an enterprise, he suggested, "the terms doctorology, parsonology, [and] shoe-maker anthropology could be applied to similar studies on other groups of men who follow special occupations in life." Nicolson also questioned the value of the statistical apparatus accompanying published work in criminal anthropology. The number of cases examined was small, and there was a tendency to rash generalisation: "The whole picture is by some writers exaggerated to distortion as regards even the few, and it is in its main features so spurious and unfair as regards the many that it becomes impossible to regard its conclusions or assumptions to be either authentic or authoritative." Criminologists in the Lombrosian mould, he added, "explore the anatomical, physiological, intellectual and moral and evil obliquities in the structure and personality of the criminal: they find them and tabulate them; they do not look for good [ones]; they neither find them nor tabulate them."[153] Nicolson concluded his address with a warning:

> [I]t is not for us to stamp 'criminals' as lunatics or quasi-lunatics, or to place them on a special morbid platform of mental existence, merely because they prefer thieving, with all its concomitant risk, to more respectable, if more laborious, modes of maintaining themselves. … I hope the day will never come when, in our official examination into the medical condition of suspected persons, or persons lying in prison upon a criminal charge, we as medical men will be expected to produce our craniometer for the head measurements, and to place reliance upon statistical information as to the colour, size, or shape of any organ.[154]

Mercier too criticised the methodology of the Italian school, echoing the attacks on criminal anthropology made by Frenchmen Paul Topinard and Léonce Manouvrier in the 1880s and '90s.[155] Mercier pointed out that Lombroso and his supporters defined their "criminal-type" in terms of its departure from the standard of the average or normal man, without defining the latter: "… no human being was safe from having criminal 'stigmata' attributed to him … It was easy to pick out in every criminal some character or other that appeared exaggerated or defective to a prejudiced eye and to declare that this character is a 'stigma' of criminality."[156]

Arthur Griffiths, writing in his memoirs published in 1894, expresses his sympathy for those

> unfortunate people [who] display some of the criminal characteristics and yet avoid crime. Their case would be a hard one if they were made responsible for the size of their heads, their large ears and beardless chins, and not for what they chose to do. A man is surely only accountable for his acts, not for his looks.[157]

In similar fashion, Hargrave Adam points out that a man

> … may have a twisted eye, a short leg, and a humped back, and yet be an honest, peaceable citizen; he may have a peculiarly-formed frontal bone, an abnormally-developed jaw, a malformed nasal organ, or his brain may be deficient in 'grey matter', and yet never commits a crime as long as he lives.… In fact many criminals have been examined and found to be almost normal in physical conformation.[158]

The 1900 article from the *British Medical Journal* referred to earlier was similarly disparaging: "The mildest and most blameless curate may be branded by the world as a sleeping volcano of criminal tendencies by the mere fact of his possessing a Mongolian cast of feature, large lobed ears or a misshapen skull." The author goes on to recount a recent experiment in which 500 prison photographs were placed before a "learned panel of experts", composed of a lawyer, a doctor, a criminal judge and a university professor. When asked to group the criminal portraits in categories according to the crime committed, the panel admitted defeat. What is more, the article notes wryly, the scientist conducting the experiment found "more anomalies of organisation in these distinguished citizens than were to be found in the criminals."[159]

Even Henry Maudsley recanted some of his former opinions and threw in his lot with the critics, much to the chagrin of Havelock Ellis.[160] He was able to state in the 1888 article quoted in the introduction that "there is no general criminal constitution predisposing to and, as it were, excusing crime." Like the 1889 article from the *British Medical Journal*, he did not seek to deny the importance of hereditary factors. In language reminiscent of the oft-quoted aphorism attributed to the French professor of forensic medicine, Alexandre Lacassagne (1843–1924) to the effect that "The social milieu is the culture medium of criminal behaviour; the microbe is the criminal, an element which only becomes active when it finds the medium which makes it ferment"[161], Maudsley states that "a criminal outcome … never could have been without its evil germ in the line of hereditary descent." He reminds his readers, however, that the combination of "internal factors of the individual nature" and "external factors of his circumstances" will be different in each case. He adds that the latter may be sufficiently powerful to push individuals "not constitutionally below the average level of human virtue" into crime. This reluctance to generalise—which implicitly rejects any notion of a criminal-type—leads Maudsley to the following conclusion: "In all departments of psychology, healthy, morbid and criminal, we must abandon empty generalities and phrases, and apply ourselves to the laborious observation of *particulars* if we wish to gather practical fruit."[162]

In the 1895 edition of his *Pathology of Mind*, he returns to the question of the role of heredity in criminal behaviour. He does not name Lombroso specifically, but he no doubt has the Italian school in mind when he issues the following salutary warning:

> It is easy to make too much of criminal instincts or dispositions and tempting to be content with them as a sufficient explanation of crime. But no criminal is really explicable except by an exact study of his circumstances as well as his nature; when there is a struggle in him between social habits and savage instincts it will depend much on the surroundings which shall gain and keep the upper hand.[163]

Indeed, Maudsley emphasises the almost *accidental* nature of the outcome of this "struggle":

> On the one hand, there are thousands who are not criminals because they are not at all, or not opportunely, or not strongly, tempted by the circumstances of their lives to do amiss; on the other hand, there are thousands of criminals who are so only because time and chance has been unpropitious to them by exposing them unprepared to the sudden and urgent temptation, or gradually to the slow sap of insidious temptation, or untowardly to a conjugation of circumstances suited to put a great strain on the weak fibres of their natures. How many persons are there in a large city who are moral, nay, how many do not commit robbery or other crime, simply because of the strong ally which gaslight is to morality? … Many men therefore have good reason to bless, not only

> the prevenient grace of their genitives, but also the special providence which ordained the special circumstances of their lives. [164]

What was at issue here then was not simply the perceived incompetence of Lombroso and his followers in their handling of statistical analysis. There was a more profound epistemological gulf separating the two approaches. Among British criminologists, there was a pronounced reluctance to impose the straightjacket of a "criminal-type" on the complexity of clinical case histories, each of which was considered to present unique characteristics. "Even *correct* generalisations … concerning convicted criminals in the mass", opined Sir Bryan Donkin in a 1919 article, "are not likely to be of much positive value in the treatment of individuals …"[165]

Indeed, by the latter part of the Edwardian period, the late gentleman of Verona had become something of a joke among British criminologists. In 1914 Hargrave Adam was able to wonder "how such a fallacy ever came to be taken seriously"[166] while in 1918 Charles Mercier, in similar vein, asked himself how was it that "in an age in which scientific methods were extending rapidly into ever new fields of research and endeavour, such stuff as this should ever have been accepted, and should have attained the extraordinary vogue that it did"?[167]

James Devon, medical officer of Glasgow Prison, brought his own brand of dry wit to bear on the subject:

> We have been reproached in this country with a failure to make a scientific study of the criminal, and the works of foreign writers have been translated for our example and emulation. They contain a certain amount of useful information, but its value is not to be measured by the difficulty of understanding it. Big and strange words may as easily mask an absence of useful knowledge as convey a fruitful idea … The criminal is a man or woman like the rest of us, and information about his head or heels, while it may have a special value in relation to his case should not be confounded with knowledge of himself. He is something more than a brain or a stomach.[168]

Concerning the resort to photography characteristic of the Lombrosians, Devon echoed a point made by Paul Topinard at the 1896 Geneva Congress: "Anyone who glances at the illustrated papers will see for himself as many villainous-looking faces among notable people, even among able people, as he will find in prison."[169] As for Galton's "composite photographs", a technique embraced with enthusiasm by the criminal anthropologists, Devon dismisses them as "photograph[s] of nothing at all".[170]

There were exceptions of course to this barrage of scornful criticism. Undoubtedly the most influential was Havelock Ellis's book, *The Criminal*.[171]

Ellis freely admitted that his "little book" offered no original theory of criminal behaviour, but simply sought to place before a British audience the principal findings of criminal anthropology, this "young and rapidly growing science", in order to "arouse interest in problems which are of personal concern to every citizen, problems which are indeed the concerns of every person who cares about the reasonable organisation of social life."[172]

In the main, Ellis does not exceed his brief, and restricts himself largely to what one observer has termed the "collecting [of] notes and references from various published works and connecting them by a thread of discussion, but avoiding any empirical investigations of his own and omitting any rigorous logical analysis or systematic discussion of the reliability of the findings he reported."[173] Given the lack of a clear theoretical position on the part of the author, the result inevitably lacks coherence. Ellis seems to have adhered to a modified version of the theory expounded in Lombroso's *Criminal Man*, but this is never made explicit. He does acknowledge some of the charges laid at the door of the *Scuola Positiva*; as for example, when he cites the Italian professor's "abrupt" style, "impetuous" methods, and over-hasty conclusions which tend to be "lacking in critical faculty and in balance".[174] He also suggests that Lombroso was over-dependant on the "atavistic key" in the early editions of *Criminal Man* (though does not explain how this "abuse" manifested itself); advocates caution when it comes to the role of heredity in the study of criminal physiognomy ("not a very exact science") and similarly has little time for the idea of inherent criminality among the "lower races", and among animals and plants: "If the *Dionea Muscipula* that eats an insect is a criminal, much more must the European man who eats beef or mutton be a criminal."[175]

There are limits, however, to Ellis's questioning of the Lombrosian model. Lacassagne's dictums about the microbe and the culture jar and to the effect that society has the criminals it deserves are quoted with approval[176], but the biological model of crime is not rejected as such (not even in the limited sense associated with the French *Milieu Social* School), nor is Lombroso's notion of the "born criminal-type". Indeed, at times, Ellis seems to forget his own strictures regarding the role of atavism and the imprecision of external stigmata. The following passage, which contains his portrait of what he calls the "instinctive criminal" (a "more simple term", he suggests than Lombroso's "born criminal"[177]) is remarkable above all for its similarity to the atavistic offender of *L'Uomo delinquente*:

> By some accident of development, by some defect of birth or training, he [the Criminal] belongs as it were to a lower and older social state

> than that in which he is actually living. It thus happens that our own criminals frequently resemble in physical and psychical characters the normal individuals of a lower race. This is that 'atavism' which has so been so frequently observed in criminals and so much discussed.[178]

Ellis goes on:

> To admit, therefore, in the criminal a certain psychical and even physical element belonging to a more primitive age is simple and perfectly reasonable … That this resemblance is not merely superficial, but that some arrest of development sometimes produces an individual inapt to our civilisation, but apt to a lower civilisation which we have outgrown, and which we call criminal we have had occasion to observe repeatedly in our brief summary of the facts of criminal anthropology.[179]

It follows from this that the criminal manifests both "physical" and "psychical" stigmata of his "primitive" status. On the first point, Ellis is no doubt that:

> … criminals present a far larger proportion of anatomical abnormalities than the ordinary European population. Now this is precisely the characteristic of the anatomy of the lower human races: they present a far larger proportion of anatomical abnormalities than the ordinary European population … the evidence as far as it goes is absolutely clear.

Criminal Man's "psychical" character is similarly familiar from the work of Lombroso and his colleagues:

> The instinctive criminal, in his fully developed form, is a moral monster. In him the absence of guiding or inhibiting social instincts is accompanied by unusual development of the sensual or self-seeking impulses. … Our survey of the psychical character of criminals showed that they constantly reproduce the features of savage character—want of forethought, inaptitude for sustained labour, love of orgy, etc. … The criminal is an individual who, to some extent, remains a child his life long—a child of larger growth and with greater capacity for evil.[180]

Like Lombroso and Ferri, Ellis considered the prison to be an inappropriate way of dealing with his "instinctive criminal". "We cannot punish a monstrosity", Ellis wrote, "for acting according to its monstrous nature."[181] He did not go as far as the criminal anthropologists and advocate the death penalty in such cases[182], but he clearly considered the prison, "with its monotonous routine of solitary confinement, varied by bad company" to be "fruitful of nothing but disaster to the prisoner and to the society on which he is set loose."[183] Like Dr John Campbell, Ellis adds that for "the confirmed recidivist", the prison is "simply a welcome and comfortable home", preferred to the workhouse.[184] Such disillusion with conventional punishment regimes leads Ellis to advocate indefinite sentences and the abolition of cellular confinement (to be replaced with "intelligent and energetic treatment" and "intercourse with selected persons of the outside world"). For "occasional" criminals, he argues, carceral sentences should be scrapped altogether.[185]

It is significant that unlike in the United States where *The Criminal* served as "the well into which many Americans dipped for data on born criminals",[186] and in Continental Europe where it was welcomed by the criminal anthropologists[187], it did not receive public backing from any of Britain's prison-based psychiatrists and medical officers. Indeed, one hostile review pronounced it a credit to national sanity that the book's author was alone in championing the Lombrosian cause.[188] There seems to have been a general consensus, at least in professional circles, that as a *Times* leader of 1900 put it, "we do no not wish to see craniology mixed up with criminology."[189]

There was thus no British equivalent of US prison chaplain, August Drähms, whose 1900 book, *The Criminal: His Personnel and Environment*—boasting a laudatory introduction by Lombroso himself—sought to apply the methods of criminal anthropology to the study of several thousand American prisoners.[190] However, there *is* one example of support—albeit qualified—for Lombroso's ideas from within the prison system in the person of William Douglas Morrison (1852–1943). Like Drähms, Morrison was a prison chaplain, occupying the cure at Wandsworth Prison between 1883 and 1898. As W. J. Forsythe observes, this was a function which placed its occupant at once within the system and slightly aloof from it.[191]

Unlike his American colleague of the cloth, however, the Reverend Morrison had some doubts about the reliability of the findings generated by the Italian school. His 1891 book, *Crime and its Causes* echoes the medico-psychiatric consensus of his day in referring to the craniometric data on the born criminal-type as "untrustworthy", and notes that the "laborious investigations" of the criminal anthropologists "have so far led to few solid conclusions."[192] He goes on to suggest that while there is no evidence of a distinct born criminal-type—either anatomical or morphological—criminals as a group do exhibit a higher proportion of "physical abnormalities" and "physical degeneracy" than the rest of the community.[193] It is the frequency of such "inherited disorders" among prisoners, he argues, "which largely account[s] for the high rate of mortality among them when in prison."[194]

Morrison does not, however, rule out the notion of a criminal-type *per se*: "it is not born with a man, but originates either in prison ... or in criminal habits of life", he suggests. Echoing the theory of the "professional type" elaborated by Gabriel Tarde[195], Morrison argues that criminals acquire what he terms a "prison look"—a distinctive "caste of features"—as a result of unconscious imitation arising from prolonged contact with other malefactors over a prolonged period; "the acquired expression frequently tending to obliterate family resemblances." A similar phenomenon, he notes, can be observed among other professional groups, in the Army for example, or the Church.[196] Perhaps Dr Nicolson's "parsonology" was not so far-fetched after all. Morrison does concede, however, that the "practical utility [of the criminal-type] is impaired by the fact that certain of its features are sometimes visible in men who have never been convicted of crime."[197]

Like Lombroso, the Wandsworth chaplain emphasises too the blunted feelings and what he calls the "boundless egoism" of the criminal, "which so completely overpowers both his sense of duty and his fear of punishment that it demands gratification at whatever cost." He acknowledges that "defective early training" helps to account for the generally low intelligence of the prison population, but maintains that "a certain number of criminals are almost incapable of acquiring instruction."[198] As far as Morrison is concerned, habitual criminals clearly fall into this category. "Unfit to take a part in working the modern industrial machine", he writes, all that can be done is "to seclude them in such a way that they will no longer be able to injure those who can work it."[199]

In an 1889 article for the *Journal of Mental Science*, Morrison acknowledged Maudsley's point from the previous year that "a minute and comprehensive" examination is required in order to unravel the relative weight of hereditary and environmental factors in a particular case of criminal behaviour.[200] He provides an example of how such an examination might proceed, citing the case of a murderer, sentenced to death for the killing of his son. After an examination of the background to the crime, of the mental state and physical characteristics of the prisoner, Morrison reached the following conclusion: "Stated in general terms, this case of murder is the result of adverse social circumstances [i.e. unemployment] acting on a criminally-constituted organism, and the crime would not have been committed unless both these factors had been present."[201] He provides further detail of the criminal's defective "organism", grouped under three heads: hereditary factors, pathological factors and physical traits. In the first category, Morrison places "descent from a consumptive parent and membership of a family with a predisposition to neurosis"; in the second, "drunken habits, and the after effects of enteric fever"; and in the third, an "abnormal shortness of stature, an abnormal length of arms, a huge under jaw, and a Mongolian type of face."[202]

Morrison believed, unlike the statisticians of the Home Office, that the crime problem was getting worse. In an article for the review *Nineteenth Century*, he outlined what he considered to be the reasons for this phenomenon. "It is almost entirely to be attributed", he argued, "to the growing tendency of the community to become concentrated in large cities." Such a concentration not only afforded increased opportunities for inter-personal conflict, it also provided more temptation for potential criminal behaviour. In addition, an increasingly complex society necessitated a "huge network of laws", thereby widening the scope for the intervention of law enforcement agencies. Finally, he attributed to burgeoning towns "the creation of a large degenerate caste".[203]

The Reverend Douglas Morrison was an important figure in the dissemination of the theories of the criminal anthropologists in Britain. It was thanks to a collection called "The Criminology Series", he edited for publishers Fisher Unwin that translations of works by Lombroso (*The Female Offender*, co-authored with Guglielmo Ferrero) and Ferri (*Criminal Sociology*) became available to British readers for the first time in 1895.[204] Indeed, *The Female Offender*, for all its faults[205], was the *only* English translation of Lombroso's criminological work undertaken during the author's lifetime. *Crime: Its Causes and Remedies* would follow two years after his death, in 1911.[206] Morrison published a second book of his own in the Criminology series, *Juvenile Offenders* in 1896.[207]

As we have seen, however, the big guns of the medical and psychiatric professions along with government officials appear to have been little moved by such arguments. Traditional historical accounts have tended to concur with the contemporary assessment of the mainstream British response to Lombroso in terms of a straightforward victory of white-coated British "common sense" over incoherent Continental "dogma".[208] We would take issue with this interpretation, and concur with an alternative view, which offers a more nuanced picture of the English response. Firstly, it is important to recognise, as David Garland has pointed out[209], that while the arguments put forward in Havelock Ellis's *The Criminal* were rejected out of hand by the bulk of the medico-psychiatric Establishment, the book was clearly a success with the wider reading public, going through four editions by 1910.[210] It was also welcomed by a number of lay reviewers, including, significantly, leading Scottish psychiatrist T. S. Clouston in the *Journal of the Anthropological Institute* ("...that fascinating work. Few who begin to read it will lay it down again till it is finished")[211] and Francis Galton. In an article for *Nature* in May 1990, Galton wrote:

> The hope of the criminal anthropologist is to increase the power of discriminating between the natural and accidental criminal. He aims at being able to say with well-founded confidence of certain men that it is impossible to make them safe members of a free society by any reasonable amount of discipline, instruction, and watchfulness, and that they must be locked up wholly out of the way. Also, to say of some others that it would be both cruel and unwise to treat them as ordinary criminals because they have been the victims of exceptional circumstances: they are not naturally unfit, and therefore still admit of being turned into useful members of society.[212]

"Abundant evidence of all this", he added, "is to be found in Mr Ellis's book, and there seems to be a consensus among experts as to its trustworthiness."[213]

Dr Samuel Strahan, assistant medical officer at Northampton County Asylum, would no doubt have concurred with Galton's positive appraisal of Ellis's work. In a 1891 paper read to the British Association, entitled "Instinctive Criminality, Its True Character and Rational Treatment", Strahan argued that a full two-thirds of the prison population were "instinctive criminals". The latter, he suggests, are "... drawn to such a course by an instinct which is born in them, which is too strong to be resisted by their weak volitional power had they the desire to resist, which they have not." In a passage that could have come straight out of *The Criminal* or *L'Uomo delinquente*, Strahan gives the following description of the physical traits of the instinctive criminal. They include:

> ... such grossly degenerate characters as a small, overlarge and ill-shapen head; paralysis; squint; asymmetrical features; deformities; a shrunken, ill-developed body; abnormal conditions of the genital organs; liability to tubercular disease; premature decay of the tissues; large, heavy misshapen jaws, outstanding ears, and a restless, animal-like or brutal expression. The instinctive criminal lacks the moral sense, as the idiot lacks the intellectual, and in both we find more or less deep degeneration affecting the whole economy, physical, moral and intellectual.[214]

Drawing parallels with his own psychiatric experience (in 1888, Northampton had been the first provincial asylum to build a separate block for idiots and imbeciles[215]), Dr Strahan adds:

> [All of these traits ...] are common ... amongst the inmates of our idiot and imbecile asylums; and as there is no beauty to be found among

> the inmates of such asylums, neither is there to be discovered in our prisons, proving how well-founded is that instinctive repulsion excited by the sight of the ill-favoured and deformed.[216]

Strahan points out, in a classic piece of degenerationist argument, that crime is interchangeable with other inherited conditions like idiocy, epilepsy, insanity, prostitution and drunkenness. In a passage which recalls Richard Dugdale's influential 1877 study of the endemically-criminal "Jukes" family[217], Strahan notes that in a degenerate family, crime will appear in some of its members, while insanity, idiocy or prostitution appears in others. Any exposure to what Strahan calls "deteriorating influences" (he mentions drunkenness, tuberculosis, and senility or immaturity in parents) is likely to lead to degenerate offspring.[218]

Ironically, Strahan's degenerationist discourse has much in common with the apparently environmentalist theories of criminal causation associated with the French *Milieu Social* School. The overall approach of the French School was summed up at the 1892 congress on criminal anthropology at Brussels, where Alexandre Lacassagne told the assembled delegates, "there are two factors which explain crime: an individual factor, which I do not consider very important, and a social factor which I consider very important."[219] Throughout his career, he would continue to repeat the same principle in different words. Thus in 1908, in the preface to a work by one of his former students, he wrote: "Man acts, but society leads him, that is to say pushes him, guides him, steers him in this or that direction."[220]

Yet things are not quite what they seem. A number of historians of criminology have recently called into question the clear-cut division which appears at first sight to have split the European criminological fraternity along national as well as theoretical lines.[221] Firstly, it is important to point out that while Lacassagne and his colleagues differed from Lombroso on some important points, they did *not* rule out of hand the role of biological heredity in the explanation of crime, far from it. According to French criminologist Marc Renneville, the kind of statement made by Lacassagne to the 1892 congress, along with his afore-mentioned aphorisms, have to be seen as part of a concerted strategy on the part of the Lyons professor to differentiate his own approach, and that of his colleagues, from that of the *Scuola Positiva*.[222]

In reality, Lacassagne did not consider the *milieu social* to be the *sole* cause of crime; rather it served as a trigger, activating a dormant "criminal nature", *a nature entirely predetermined by heredity.* He was in no doubt that there was a class of criminals whose deficient heredity predisposed them to crime. All that was needed then was the right combination of conditions to spark off criminal behaviour, hence the talk of the "microbe" and the "culture medium". This is in its essentials the same theory advanced by Henry Maudsley in his mature writings.

Those most vulnerable to the nefarious effects of the social milieu, those whom he termed, in language reminiscent of Maudsley, "the slaves of fatal organic predispositions", a group he referred to as "occipitals".[223] This idea derived from an anthropological theory, popularised by Paul Broca, which sought to classify the human race into three categories, according to their skull shape: *races frontales*, *races pariétales*, and *races occipitales* (with Whites in the first, Mongolians in the second, and Blacks in the third).[224] Lacassagne applied this taxonomy to contemporary French society, dovetailing the three anthropological groupings into a conventional three-way division of the social hierarchy (upper, middle, and lower classes). Unsurprisingly, the "occipitals", whose brains functioned mainly by instinct, were to be found among the members of the lower classes. To each of these "racial" categories belonged a specific kind of crime: the *races frontales* were associated with cerebral crime ("the truly insane"); the *races pariétales* with "occasional" crime or *le crime passionel*, and the *races occipitales* with instinctive crime; its perpetrators, the "real criminals, the incorrigibles".[225]

What we have here is something clearly very different from modern psychological or sociological explanations of criminal behaviour. Does that make Lacassagne a closet Lombrosian? Well, not exactly. As Renneville points out, Lacassagne's insistence on the role of the *milieu social* was perfectly compatible with his remarks about the existence of an organic substratum of "defective individuals".[226] Firstly, he admitted that there was a concentration of anatomical and physiological defects among the criminal population. This was particularly true of the "occipital" criminal, whom he described as "sometimes a product of teratogeny, a monster, something resembling a malign tumour or a parasite."[227] Lacassagne sought to explain this correlation not in terms of *atavism*, but, after Dr Morel, in terms of long-term *dégénérescence*:

> The signs of physical and moral degeneration that can be observed are not some kind of miraculous resurrection of atavism, but are in fact a real deviation from normal Man, in the way shown by Morel. They are the result of a corrupting social milieu: bad eating habits and drink which harms the functions of the nervous system, together with diseases like tuberculosis, syphilis, etc., the microbes of which teem like lice in the houses of the Poor.[228]

In Lacassagne's view, then,—like Samuel Strahan's—inimical social conditions could directly affect the brain, and these acquired defects could then, according to the Lamarckian theory of evolutionary heredity shared by Henry Maudsley and Herbert Spencer, be passed on to succeeding generations. In short, over several generations, "bad" social conditions worked on "bad" heredity to produce crime, piling on additional moral and physical defects in the process. As Lacassagne put it in 1889, "poverty leaves its imprint and creates those anomalies and anatomical particularities so well observed by Lombroso."[229]

There was thus in Lacassagne's conception a constant fluidity in the relations between heredity and environment. At least in theory, if you improved the social conditions, you could—in the long term—reverse the trend of *dégénérescence*, though it might be too late for the poor souls with "fatal organic predispositions".[230] With slight differences of emphasis, other French criminologists like Manouvrier, Topinard and Tarde shared this neo-Lamarckian outlook. Indeed, such an approach—often implicit—may be considered as the intellectual foundation of the French school as a whole.[231] The French School's decision to emphasise the "social" over the "hereditary" component of degeneration was thus, in part at least, a strategic one. The result is a rather less fatalistic theory of criminal causation than Strahan's, but in essence Lacassagne's *criminel occipital* is the precise equivalent of the Englishman's "instinctive criminal".

T. S. Clouston's article for the *Anthropological Institute*, published in its journal in 1894, comes to similar conclusions, though puts greater emphasis on the role of atavism rather than degeneration. Thomas (later Sir Thomas) Clouston (1840–1915) was, like Dr Strahan, an asylum-based psychiatrist: he had been medical superintendent of the Royal Edinburgh Asylum since 1873 and lectured in mental diseases at nearby Edinburgh University. Commenting favourably on the new science of "criminal anthropology" ("I think the time is very near when some knowledge of it will be required by all medical men, and especially of all lawyers and the higher officials of our prisons"[232]), he notes the "anatomical, physiological and psychological resemblances" between criminals and a "man or a woman who is only slightly imbecile in mind." He follows Lombroso in explaining such hereditary defects among criminals in terms of atavism or arrested development. Indeed, he marshals evidence to show that such a "not fully evolved man" is more likely to have a "neurotic" or "deformed" palate (78%, against 59.5% in the population as a whole).[233] Such atavism means that the criminal is unable to adapt to modern, industrialised society:

> He is not technically imbecile, but such arrested brains, being subjected to the highly organised modern city life, cannot exhibit qualities that they do not possess. Their owners become to a large extent the professional criminals and prostitutes of our large cities, and the tramps, idlers, paupers and stupid unenergetic denizens of our country places.[234]

Interestingly, Dr Clouston was also present at the afore-mentioned paper read by Dr David Nicolson to the Medico-Psychological Society in 1895. At the end of the address given by the Society's new president, Clouston made the following comment, which is worth quoting in full:

> I am certain that most of us will scarcely agree with you in your optimistic view of criminology and its psychological relations. No doubt most of us who have looked through the books of Lombroso and Havelock Ellis and others are inclined to admit that it is a little overdone by some of our continental brethren, but to say that the mass of criminals in this country are merely criminals by want of opportunity of doing good, by want of education, and not by their organisation, is absolutely contrary to the results of psychological investigation for the last fifty years. I once had the occasion to carefully examine the inmates of the Edinburgh prison, and if there were one thing that impressed itself upon me it was that I had to do with a degenerate aggregation of human beings.[235]

That most of the British "experts" referred to by Francis Galton in his review of *The Criminal* would have begged to differ with such sentiments should by now be clear. Rather than reading off the criminal personality from a generalised criminal-type (whether inherited or acquired), they argued, the role of the psychiatrist or prison doctor was to examine each case individually—or as Nicolson put it, judge it "on its own merits"[236]—in order to tease out the relative significance of the various causes of criminal behaviour. James Devon explains this pragmatic approach further:

> It is impossible to discriminate between the part played by inherited tendencies and social pressure, in the production of certain acts. ... There is only one way of finding out why people commit crimes and that is by making a patient enquiry in each case. The causes in many cases may be similar, but the part they play may be different.[237]

It was this approach to crime and the criminal which, David Garland has suggested, had become accepted practice among the country's medico-psychiatric establishment by the 1890s.[238]

We shall see in the following chapter that in fact many British "experts" agreed with Francis Galton that it was possible—indeed an urgent necessity—to distinguish between those criminals who could be "turned into useful members of society" and others for whom the only solution was to lock them up "wholly out of the way". Where British criminologists parted company from Ellis and the criminal anthropologists was over the latter's view that a criminal-type based on external anatomical and physiological stigmata could be used with scientific accuracy to predict deviant behaviour.

This is not to say that criminals displaying a range of psychiatric disorders could not typically exhibit a variety of "abnormal" outward physical defects and that the latter could, in part, be inherited. This may appear to be splitting hairs, but for British criminal justice professionals, the difference was a crucial one. It was a question of scientific method. The criminal anthropologists (at least as the British typically understood them) posited an unchanging anatomical and physiognomical template of "Criminal Man", against which "real" criminals could be measured to see if there was a perfect match. If the "stigmata" were there, a whole raft of behavioural anomalies could be inferred. This was a classic example, it was argued, of *deductive* reasoning, and went against the whole *inductive* ethos of Victorian science which assumed facts to be "out there"; facts which could be approached unproblematically by the disinterested observer. As Henry Maudsley put it, it was only after the "patient interrogation of nature" that "natural laws" could be elaborated. There was, he added, "no study to which the inductive method of research is not applicable." This was *real* science, not "the invention of theories by invoking our own minds to utter oracles to us".[239] Maudsley would no doubt have approved of the motto adopted by French criminologist Armand Corre: "*Honni soit qui mal y voit*".[240]

Thus eschewing the kind of Delphic theories they associated with the criminal anthropologists, British prison doctors and psychiatrists favoured at most tentative generalisations after lengthy clinical experience with individual criminals. This was the basis of their scornful rejection of the scientific credentials of the Lombrosians. Where was the evidence of the latter's clinical experience? Where were their case-notes? Was skill with the callipers a substitute for a lifetime's experience in the doctor's surgery or the psychiatrist's consulting rooms? Of course not. If their own case-histories revealed physical as well as mental abnormalities, then that needed explaining, but Lombroso's cardboard cut-out criminal-type was a pitifully inadequate tool for the purpose. It was a bit like expecting to understand the complexities of bridge construction with a child's set of wooden building blocks.

David Nicolson spelt out this point in replying to T. S. Clouston's comments at the close of his 1895 speech. Clouston had, he said, misrepresented his views. He (Nicolson) was *not* suggesting that there was no truth in criminal anthropology. "What I object to", he went on, "is that a description—honest, true, verbose if you like—applicable to the few should be held up to the world as being applicable to the whole criminal class."[241] To back up his arguments, Nicolson reminded his audience of what he had written twenty years previously in the pages of the *Journal of Mental Science*, namely that some 5–10% of the prison population were "weak-minded". It was to this small minority of offenders, he insisted, *and to them alone*, that the descriptions of the criminal anthropologists may be applied.[242]

Thus, as David Garland points out[243], British criminologists did not reject positivism *per se* as Radzinowicz and Hood imply, but instead rejected one version of positivism in favour of another. The British variety of the species acknowledged both environmental and biological determinism, and as we shall see in the following chapter, criminologists combined and re-combined elements of both in varying quantities, producing an almost infinite variety of permutations. We shall see that classical voluntarist conceptions of human agency were not entirely absent from the resulting mix, but on the whole they played second fiddle to a vision of criminal behaviour which emphasised the relative impunity of the individual offender in the face of biological and environmental forces beyond his control. As Dr David Nicolson's revealing off-the-cuff remarks suggest, inherited physical defects, visible in the form of external physical stigmata, came to be associated with a particular criminal sub-group, known variously as "weak-minded" or "feeble-minded". As we shall see, this group would come to play a central role in discussions of crime and crime prevention among criminologists and policy-makers in late-Victorian and Edwardian Britain.

Notes

1 Major Arthur Griffiths, *Secrets of the Prison House*, 2 vols., London, 1894, vol. 1, pp. 19, 38.

2 James Devon, *The Criminal and the Community*, London, John Lane/Bodley Head, 1912, pp. 15–6.

3 Gabriel Tarde, *La Criminalité comparée*, Paris, 1886.

4 See Ellis, *The Criminal*, pp. 47–48, 66, 88–89, 94, 103.

5 *Ibid.*, pp. 47–48. See also *idem.*, "The Study of the Criminal", *Journal of Mental Science*, vol. 36, 1890, p. 14.

6 Ellis, *The Criminal*, p. 48.

7 Havelock Ellis, "Retrospect of Criminal Anthropology", *Journal of Mental Science*, vol. 49, 1895, pp. 367–68.
8 Radzinowicz & Hood, *The Emergence of Penal Policy*, pp. 6–11.
9 *Ibid.*, p. 11.
10 For example, Wiener, *Reconstructing the Criminal*, p. 233.
11 Garland, "British Criminology", p. 3 (my emphasis). See also *idem.*, "Of Crimes and Criminals", pp. 7–50.
12 Radzinowicz & Hood, *Emergence of Penal Policy*, p. 5. We shall return to this quotation in the conclusion.
13 Pick, *Faces of Degeneration*, pp. 27–33.
14 David G. Horn, *The Criminal Body: Lombroso and the Anatomy of Deviance*, London, Routledge, 2003, p. 2.
15 *Ibid.*, p. 3.
16 Again, Horn (*ibid.*, p. 4) makes a similar point with regard to Italian and French approaches.
17 Lombroso, *Crime: Its Causes and Remedies*, p. 432 [my emphasis]. The date of 1899 given here refers to the original French edition (*Crime, causes et remèdes*, Paris, 1899).
18 Quoted in Lombroso, *op. cit.*, "Introduction to the English Edition", p. xiv. This account first appeared in the Lyons-based journal *Archives d'anthropologie criminelle* in June 1906.
19 *Ibid.*
20 Cesare Lombroso, *L'Uomo delinquente*, 1st ed., Milan, Hoepli, 1876. On the book's publication history, see Marvin E. Wolfgang, "Cesare Lombroso", in Mannheim, *Pioneers in Criminology*, p. 249.
21 Wolfgang, "Cesare Lombroso", *passim*.
22 Garland, "British Criminology", pp. 1–2.
23 McConville, "The Victorian Prison", p. 130.
24 Laurent Mucchielli, "Hérédité et milieu social: le faux-antagonisme franco-italien", *in idem.* (ed.), *Histoire de la criminologie française*, Paris, L'Harmattan, 1994, pp. 189–214; Marie-Christine Leps, *Apprehending the Criminal: The Production of Deviance in Nineteenth-Century Discourse*, Durham & London, Duke University Press, 1992, ch. 2; Victor Bailey, "English Prisons, Penal Culture and the Abatement of Imprisonment, 1895–1922", *Journal of British Studies*, vol. 36, no. 3, July 1997, p. 290.
25 Lombroso, *Crime: Its Causes and Remedies*, p. 365.
26 Leps, *op. cit.*, pp. 32–33, 41.
27 On the French and German reactions to Lombrosian theory, see Renneville, *op. cit.*; Robert Nye, *Crime, Madness and Politics in Modern France*, Princeton, Princeton University Press, 1984; Richard F. Wetzell, *Inventing the Criminal: A History of German Criminology, 1880–1945*, Chapel Hill & London, University of North Carolina Press, 2000.
28 See his remarks on criminal anthropology in his book, *Les Stigmates anatomiques de la criminalité*, Paris, 1894, pp. 6–7. Major Arthur Griffiths, British delegate at Geneva, observed: "The Belgian Professor, Dr d'Allemagne [*sic*], with great nicety of touch, analyses and dissects [Lombroso's] arguments till they seem to lose all their vitality" (Griffiths, *Fifty Years of Public Service*, p. 383).
29 *Congrès international de l'anthropologie criminelle: travaux du IVe session … Genève, 1896*, Geneva, 1897, p. 201 [my translation].

30 In later editions of *L'Uomo delinquente*, Lombroso modified this figure. By the late 1890s, with the publication of *Crime, causes et remèdes*, he had reached the conclusion that "only" 33% of criminals should be placed in the "born-criminal" category.

31 Perhaps the best descriptions of Lombroso's ideas are contained in David Horn, *The Criminal Body: Lombroso and the Anatomy of Deviance*, London, Routledge, 2003 and Mary Gibson, *Born to Crime: Cesare Lombroso and the Origins of Modern Criminology*, Praeger, Westport, Conn., 1992. The late Stephen Jay Gould's discussion (*Mismeasure of Man*, pp. 151–72) is also stimulating, if more cursory.

32 Horn, *op. cit.*, pp. 30–1.

33 In reality Villella was a 69-year old peasant, convicted for theft and arson. His "notoriety" seems to have been largely a figment of Lombroso's own imagination (*ibid.*).

34 Quoted in Pick, *Faces of Degeneration*, p. 122.

35 For example, Cesare Lombroso, *L'homme criminel—criminel né, fou moral, épileptique*, Paris, 1887, p. 393.

36 Morel, *Traité des dégénérescences*, vol. 1, p. 685 [my translation]. On Morel, see Elof Axel Carlson, *The Unfit: A History of a Bad Idea*, Cold Spring Harbour N.Y., Cold Spring Harbour Laboratory Press, 2001, ch. 4; Christian Debuyst *et al.* (eds.), *Histoire des savoirs sur le crime et la peine*, vol. 2: *La rationnalité pénale et la naissance de la criminologie*, Paris, De Boeck Université, 1998, ch. 8.

37 Morel, *op. cit.*, vol. 1, Preface, p. vii [my translation].

38 Wolfgang, *op. cit.*, pp. 241–6.

39 See for example, Charles Lucas, *Du système pénal et du système répressif en général de la peine de mort en particulier*, Paris, 1827.

40 Gould, *Mismeasure of Man*, p. 153; Leps, *Apprehending the Criminal*, p. 35.

41 Paul Broca, *Instructions générales pour les recherches anthropologiques à faire sur le vivant*, Paris, Masson, 1879 [1st edition, 1864], p. 27 [my translation].

42 Stepan, *The Idea of Race*, ch. 4; Gould, *op. cit.*, ch. 3.

43 Enrico Ferri, *Criminal Sociology*, New York, 1899, p. 4 [my emphasis]. Anthropologists took umbrage in fact at the term "criminal anthropology". Paul Topinard (1830–1911), a discipline of Broca, and president of the *Société d'anthropologie française*, dismissed criminology as an *applied* science, in contrast to the *pure* nature of his own discipline. He castigated criminology for its habit of borrowing selectively from other disciplines such as anthropology and medicine for "practical" ends, which meant that the demands of scientific rigour inevitably took second place (Debuyst, "L'Ecole française", pp. 349–50). In an article of 1887, Topinard condemned the deductive reasoning behind Lombroso's method: "He did not say: here is a fact which suggests an induction to me, let's see if I'm mistaken, let's proceed rigorously, let us collect other facts … The conclusion is fashioned in advance; he seeks proof, he defends his thesis like an advocate who ends up persuading himself" (quoted in Gould, *op. cit.*, pp. 162–64).

44 Gould, *op. cit.*, pp. 114–28.

45 Lombroso, *op. cit.*, pp. 142–49.

46 Paul Topinard (1888), quoted in Gould, *op. cit.*, p. 127.

47 A prominent lower jaw was a phenomenon well-known known to anthropologists by the name of "prognathism" and widely seen as an indicator of atavistic tendencies. Cf. the observation of anthropologist Robert Dunn: "… whenever and wherever

ignorance and brutality, destitution and squalor have for a long time existed, this prognathous type invariably prevails" (quoted in Bolt, *Victorian Attitudes to Race*, p. 16). For a similar point from Broca, see Gould, *The Mismeasure of Man*, pp. 115–16. Lombroso observes that the jaws of criminals are on average wider and heavier (by 4 grams) than those of "honest" people (Lombroso, *op. cit.*, p. 158).

48 Lombroso, *op. cit.*, Part 2, ch. 1.

49 Lombroso, *Crime: Its Causes and Remedies*, p. 365.

50 Lombroso, *L'Homme criminel*, pp. 224–25 [my translation].

51 Mark Jackson, *The Borderland of Imbecility: Medicine, Society and the Fabrication of the Feeble Mind in Later Victorian and Edwardian England*, Manchester, Manchester University Press, 2000, ch. 4.

52 Lombroso, *L'Homme criminel*, p. 232 [my translation].

53 *Ibid.*, p. 233 [my translation].

54 *Ibid.*, pp. 225–26 [my translation].

55 *Ibid.*, p. 226 [my translation].

56 Gould, *op. cit.*, p. 154. See also Horn, *The Criminal Body*, pp. 38–51.

57 In the Appendix to the French edition of *Crime: Its Causes and Remedies*, Lombroso includes a brief description of the Dinka people of the Sudan. He notes that they "resemble big children" (Cesare Lombroso, *Le crime, ses causes et remèdes*, Paris, 1899, p. 572). This appendix did not appear in the English edition of 1911.

58 Lombroso, *L'Homme criminel*, p. 137.

59 Lombroso, *Crime: Its Causes and Remedies*, Part 3, ch. 1.

60 *Ibid.*, pp. 365–6. See also Leps, *Apprehending the Criminal*, pp. 55–58.

61 Renneville, "La réception de Lombroso", p. 110.

62 Quoted in Wolfgang, "Cesare Lombroso", p. 268.

63 Ferri, *Criminal Sociology*, p. 9.

64 Wolfgang, *op. cit.*, pp. 257, 268.

65 See below, p. 173.

66 Renneville, *op. cit.*, p. 116.

67 Lombroso, *Crime: Its Causes and Remedies*, p. 374.

68 Gould, *Mismeasure of Man*, p. 164; Pick, *Faces of Degeneration*, p. 121.

69 Gould, *op. cit.*, p. 164.

70 Lombroso, *L'Homme criminel*, p. 651.

71 Lombroso, *Crime: Its Causes and Remedies*, Part 3, ch. 1.

72 Pick, *Faces of Degeneration*, pp. 113–32. Quotation at p. 126.

73 Gould, *Mismeasure*, p. 170.

74 On Enrico Ferri, see Françoise Digneffe, "L'Ecole positive italienne et le mouvement de la défense sociale", in Debuyst, *Histoire des savoirs*, pp. 244–46, 257–61; Pick, *op. cit.*, pp. 145–48.

75 Ferri, *Criminal Anthropology*, p. 176.

76 *Ibid.*, p. 165.

77 *Ibid.*, pp. 164, 170.

78 *Ibid.*, p. 164.

79 *Ibid.*, p. 166.

80 *Ibid.*, p. 165.

81 Lombroso, *Crime: Its Causes and Remedies*, pp. 385–86.

82 Ferri, *op. cit.*, p. 207.

83 Lombroso, *op. cit.*, p. 387; Ferri, *op. cit.*, p. 216.

84 *Ibid.*, p. 265.
85 Ferri, *op. cit.*, pp. 236, 248–50, 265; Lombroso, *op. cit.*, pp. 387–93.
86 *Ibid.*, pp. 426–26.
87 *Ibid.*, p. 520.
88 Ferri, *op. cit.*, p. 240.
89 Wolfgang, "Cesare Lombroso", p. 249. Both French and German translations of *L'Uomo delinquente* appeared in 1887.
90 Sir Edmund Du Cane in Galton, "Composite Portraits", p. 143.
91 Radzinowicz & Hood, *Emergence of Penal Policy*, pp. 9, 529.
92 *Ibid.*, p. 14, note n° 30.
93 David Nicolson, "Presidential Address", *Journal of Mental Science*, vol. 49, 1895, p. 588.
94 *Ibid.*
95 "Report from the Departmental Committee on Prisons", *Parliamentary Papers*, 1895, vol. 56, p. 372.
96 Forsythe, *Reform of Prisoners*, p. 197. See also *idem.*, W. J. Forsythe, *Penal Discipline, Reformatory Projects and the English Prison Commission 1895–1939*, Exeter, University of Exeter Press, 1991, pp. 19–21.
97 Sir Edmund Du Cane, *The Punishment and Prevention of Crime*, London, 1885, pp. 2–3.
98 Pick, *Faces of Degeneration*, p. 185.
99 "Report of the Royal Commission into the Working of the Penal Servitude Acts", 2 vols., *Parliamentary Papers*, 1878–1879, vol. 37–38.
100 *Ibid.*, p. xliii.
101 Saunders, "Quarantining the Weak-Minded", p. 279.
102 "Report of the Royal Commission", vol. 2, p. 739.
103 See also the testimony of George Clifton, governor of Portland Prison (*ibid.*, vol. 1, p. 177), of Sarah Gibson, the Lady Superintendent of Woking Female Prison, of Eliza Pumphrey, head of Winchester Refuge (vol. 1, p. 607) and of Captain John Barlow, Director of Irish Prisons (vol. 2, p. 822).
104 *Ibid.*, vol. 2, p. 718.
105 John Campbell, *Thirty Years Experience of a Medical Officer in the English Convict Service*, London, 1884, p. 74. Campbell had made a similar point in his evidence to the Kimberley Commission in 1878 (vol. 1, p. 574). In his official report to his superiors for 1871, Campbell wrote: "Some of the habitual criminals appear closely allied to the imbecile class both in appearance and behaviour.... There is generally something in the countenance of these men expressive of their sullen dispositions ..." ("Reports of the Directors of Convict Prisons", *Parliamentary Papers*, 1871, vol. 31, p. 480).
106 *Ibid.*, p. 73.
107 "Royal Commission on Penal Servitude", p. 331.
108 Campbell, *Thirty Years Experience*, p. 105.
109 *Ibid.*, pp. 52, 132. For other similar examples from this period, see Sim, *Medical Power in Prisons*, pp. 27, 49.
110 John Baker, "Some Points Connected with Criminals", *Journal of Mental Science*, vol. 38, 1892, pp. 364–69.
111 Henry Maudsley, "Remarks on Crime and Criminals", *Journal of Mental Science*, vol. 34, 1888, pp. 159–67.

112 *Ibid.*, pp. 368–69.
113 The only two prison doctors quoted by name are Dr Vans Clarke and Dr Greaves, medical officer of Derby Prison (Ellis, *The Criminal*, pp. 66, 103).
114 Major Arthur Griffiths, *Report to the Secretary of State for the Home Department on the Proceedings of the Fourth Congress of Criminal Anthropology, Held at Geneva in 1896*, London, 1896, p. 8.
115 "The Physiognomy of Murderers", *British Medical Journal*, 14 September 1889, p. 612.
116 "... a very large number of criminals are rather superior in intelligence ... In fact, it is often misplaced and unbalanced cleverness that leads to the attempt to commit crime, and this characteristic might very probably be found in the features of criminals of this class" (Sir Edmund Du Cane, in Galton, "Composite Portraits", p. 143).
117 "Criminals, Anarchists and Lunatics", *British Medical Journal*, 4 July 1891, pp. 19–20; "Criminals and Criminal Anthropology", *British Medical Journal*, 24 February 1894, p. 427.
118 (Untitled), *The Lancet*, 13 August 1892, pp. 370–71.
119 "Crime and its Treatment", *The Lancet*, 14 October 1893, p. 940.
120 (Untitled), *The Lancet*, 24 February 1894.
121 Radzinowicz & Hood, *Emergence of Penal Policy*, p. 13. Cf. Garland, "British Criminology", p. 6, where the author suggests that Ellis's "... introduction into English of the term 'criminology' in 1890 had the effect of firmly associating that name with the 'criminal-type' doctrines of Lombroso, thereby making it the subject of considerable scepticism, even where the Lombrosian legacy was actually negligible."
122 Griffiths, *Fifty Years of Public Service*, p. 385.
123 Editorial Article, *The Lancet*, 31 October 1896, p. 1243.
124 *Ibid.* Despite such views, an article written a month earlier by *The Lancet*'s "special correspondent", at Geneva, had given a much more positive image of criminal anthropology, describing it as a science which was "... year by year ... justifying its activity by ever-multiplying proofs of its value as an agent in healthy evolution ..." (*The Lancet*, 29 September 1896, p. 628).
125 Review of Eugen Bleuler, *Der Geborene Verbrecher: Eine Kritische Studie, British Medical Journal*, 7 November 1896, p. 1389. Historian of German criminology Richard F. Wetzell describes Bleuler as "one of the most prominent psychiatrists in German-speaking Europe" at this period (*Inventing the Criminal*, p. 56).
126 Pierre Darmon, *Médecins et assassins à la Belle Epoque: la médicalisation du crime*, Paris, Seuil, 1989, pp. 87, 106.
127 Other Britons attended the various international Congresses on Criminal Anthropology in a personal capacity, among them Havelock Ellis, Francis Galton and W. Douglas Morrison (Pick, *Faces of Degeneration*, p. 179, n. 3).
128 Griffiths, *Report to the Secretary of State* pp. 12–13; *idem.*, *Fifty Years of Public Service*, pp. 382–83.
129 Gould, *Mismeasure of Man*, p. 164.
130 Horn, *Criminal Body*, pp. 13–14.
131 *Ibid.*, pp. 4–5. On the epistemological assumptions underlying the work of early criminologists, including Lombroso, see Leps, *Apprehending the Criminal*, ch. 3.
132 Cesare Lombroso and Guglielmo Ferrero, *La donna delinquente, la prostitute e la donna normale*, Turin, 1893.

133 Lombroso and Ferrero, *Criminal Woman*, ed. Rafter & Gibson, "Editors' Introduction", pp. 12, 20.
134 Lombroso, *Nouvelles recherches*, pp. 4–5 [my translation].
135 Darmon, *op. cit.*, p. 109.
136 "The Fallacy of the Criminal-type", *British Medical Journal*, 21 April 1900, p. 980.
137 Griffiths, *Report to the Secretary of State*, p. 12.
138 Henry Maudsley (1895), quoted in Garland, "British Criminology", p. 4, n. 9.
139 Sir H. Bryan Donkin, "Notes on Mental defect in Criminals", *Journal of Mental Science*, vol. 63, 1917, p. 17, quoted in Garland, *op. cit.*, p. 6.
140 See chapter 4.
141 Charles Mercier, *Crime and Criminals: Being the Jurisprudence of Crime Medical, Biological and Psychological*, London, University of London Press, 1918, p. 40.
142 "The Feeble-Minded Criminal", *The Lancet*, 15 February 1908, p. 511. See also Sir Bryan Donkin, "The State Punishment of Crime", *British Medical Journal*, 2 August 1913, pp. 234–36.
143 University College Library, University College London: *Pearson Papers*, 366: "Report upon the aims, methods, progress and results of a statistical investigation now being conducted for the prison commissioners at the Biometric Laboratory, University College", [?1909], p. 6.
144 Evelyn Ruggles-Brise, *The English Prison System*, London, Macmillan, 1921, pp. 199–200.
145 Francis Scougal, *Scenes from a Silent World or Prisons and their Inmates*, Edinburgh, 1889.
146 Cowling, *The Artist as Anthropologist*, p. 312.
147 Scougal, *op. cit.*, p. 10.
148 *Ibid.*, p. 5.
149 *Ibid.*, pp. 8–9. Cf. the words of French philosopher Hippolyte Taine, quoted with approval by Lombroso (*Crime: Its Causes and Remedies*, p. 428): "You have shown us fierce and lubricious orang-utans with human faces. It is evident that as such they cannot act otherwise. If they ravish, steal and kill, it is by virtue of their own nature and their past, but there is all the more reason for destroying them when it has been proved that they will always remain orang-utans."
150 Cf. Radzinowicz and Hood, *Emergence of Penal Policy*, pp. 16–19.
151 Mercier, *op. cit.*, p. 210.
152 Hargrave L. Adam, *The Police Encyclopaedia*, 8 vols., London, Waverley, 1911, vol. 7, p. 164.
153 Nicolson, "Presidential Address", pp. 579–81.
154 *Ibid.*, p. 580.
155 Debuyst, "L'Ecole française", pp. 350–53.
156 Mercier, *op. cit.*, pp. 208–209. See also his comments in *The Lancet*, 1 October 1904, p. 861 & 15 October 1904, p. 957, quoted in Forsythe, *Penal Discipline*, p. 13.
157 Griffiths, *Secrets of the Prison House*, vol. 1, p. 19.
158 Adam, *op. cit.*, vol. 5, p. 5.
159 "The Fallacy of the Criminal-type", *British Medical Journal*, 21 April 1900, p. 980.
160 In "The Study of the Criminal", 1890, p. 6, Ellis writes: "In recent utterances Dr Maudsley seems to ignore, or to treat with indifference, the results of criminal anthropology. These results are, however, but the legitimate outcome of the ideas of which it is his chief distinction to have been the champion."

161 Quoted in Debuyst, "L'Ecole francaise", pp. 344–45: my translation. The other aphorism associated with Lacassagne is "Societies have the criminals they deserve" (quoted in *ibid.*).
162 Maudsley, "Remarks on Crime", pp. 164–67.
163 Henry Maudsley, *The Pathology of Mind*, London, 1895, p. 82.
164 *Ibid.*, p. 81.
165 Quoted in Garland, *op. cit.*, p. 11 [emphasis added]. Cf. Sir Bryan Donkin, "The State Punishment of Crime", *British Medical Journal*, 2 August 1913, pp. 234–36.
166 Hargrave Adam, *Women and Crime*, London, Warner Laurie, 1914, p. 23.
167 Mercier, *op. cit.*, p. 210.
168 Devon, *The Criminal and the Community*, p. 13.
169 *Ibid.*, p. 13. Topinard had said that Lombroso's portraits were similar to those of himself and his friends, recorded in his own photographic album (Griffiths, *Report to the Secretary of State*, pp. 7–8).
170 Devon, *op. cit.*, p. 14.
171 Havelock Ellis, *The Criminal*, London, Walter Scott, 1890, repr. New York, AMS Press, 1972.
172 Ellis, *The Criminal*, "Preface", pp. vii–viii.
173 Sydney G. Norris, "Preface to the AMS Reprint Edition", in *ibid.*, p.ix.
174 Ellis, *op. cit.*, p. 39.
175 *Ibid.*, pp. 38, 85–87, 203–4, 205–7.
176 *Ibid.*, p. 24.
177 *Ibid.*, p. 17. He notes "The term 'instinctive criminal' seems to be safer, as it is not always possible to estimate the congenital element." (p. 17, n. 2).
178 *Ibid.*, pp. 206–7.
179 *Ibid.*, p. 208.
180 *Ibid.*, pp. 17, 209, 214. The respect between Ellis and Lombroso was clearly mutual, for the latter appointed Ellis Honorary Secretary of the Psychiatric Section at the 1894 Rome Congress on Criminal Anthropology (Radzinowicz & Hood, *Emergence of Penal Policy*, p. 12, n. 21).
181 Ellis, *op. cit.*, p. 233.
182 *Ibid.*, pp. 236–39.
183 Ellis, *op. cit.*, p. 251.
184 *Ibid.*, p. 251.
185 *Ibid.* pp. 257–82.
186 Rafter, *Creating Born Criminals*, p. 115.
187 For example, Cesare Lombroso, *Nouvelles recherches*, pp. 48–51.
188 Quoted in Radzinowicz & Hood, *op. cit.*, p. 15.
189 Leading Article, *The Times*, 25 May 1900.
190 August Drähms, *The Criminal: His Personnel and Environment*, New York, Macmillan, 1900. On Drähms' influence in the USA, see Rafter, *Creating Born Criminals*, pp. 121–122; Fink, *Causes of Crime*, pp. 118–19.
191 Forsythe, *Reform of Prisoners*, pp. 202–3.
192 W. D. Morrison, *Crime and its Causes*, London, 1891, p. 198. See also *idem.*, "Reflections on the Theories of Criminality", *Journal of Mental Science*, vol. 35, 1889, p. 16.
193 See also W. Douglas Morrison, "The Interpretation of Criminal Statistics", *Journal of the Royal Statistical Society*, vol. 60, no. 1, March 1897, p. 17. The anti-Lombrosian

French School of criminologists shared this point of view. See for example, Dallemagne, *Les stigmates anatomiques*, pp. 167–68.

194 Morrison, *Crime and its Causes*, pp. 192–93.

195 On Tarde's "professional type", see Davie, *Visages de la criminalité*, pp. 113–4.

196 Morrison, *op. cit.*, pp. 185–88. Interestingly, in later editions of *Criminal Man*, Lombroso acknowledged this "behavioural" explanation of criminal physiognomy—up to a point. For example, the frequency of wrinkles on the faces of criminals was attributed to their habit of cynical laughter, and thin lips—also a common feature—apparently derived from repeated expressions of hatred. See Horn, *Criminal Body*, pp. 14–15.

197 Morrison, *op. cit.*, pp. 188–89.

198 *Ibid.*, p. 195.

199 *Ibid.*, pp. 226–27.

200 Morrison, "Reflections", p. 16.

201 *Ibid.*, p. 22.

202 *Ibid.*, p. 21.

203 W. D. Morrison, "The Increase of Crime", *Nineteenth Century*, vol. 31, June 1892, pp. 950–57. Morrison's article provoked a reply from Sir Edmund Du Cane ("The Decrease of Crime", *Nineteenth Century*, vol. 33, March 1893, pp. 480–92).

204 Cesare Lombroso & Guglielmo Ferrero, *The Female Offender*, London, 1895, Enrico Ferri, *Criminal Sociology*, London, 1895.

205 Only one of the Italian's edition original four parts was fully translated (together with bits of another). The authors' discussion of female criminals' alleged sexual traits, for example, was omitted, and some of the book's more explicit language was toned down, often misleadingly so (Lombroso & Ferrero, *Criminal Woman*, "Editors' Introduction", pp. 4–5).

206 Cesare Lombroso, *Crime: Its Causes and Remedies*, Boston, Little Brown & Co., 1911.

207 W. D. Morrison, *Juvenile Offenders*, London, 1896.

208 Radzinowicz & Hood, *Emergence of Penal Policy*, pp. 15, 16. The title of a 1912 article by Arthur St John sums up this contrast neatly: "Common Sense and Criminal Anthropology" (*Sociological Review*, vol. 5, 1912, pp. 65–67).

209 Garland, "British Criminology Before 1935", pp. 5–6.

210 Norris, "Introduction", in Ellis, *The Criminal*, p. 11.

211 T. S. Clouston, "The Developmental Aspects of Criminal Anthropology", *Journal of the Royal Anthropological Institute of Great Britain and Ireland*, vol. 23, 1894, p. 217.

212 Francis Galton, "Criminal Anthropology", *Nature*, vol. 42, 1890, p. 76. Galton noted elsewhere that "It is unhappily a fact that fairly distinct types of criminals breeding true to their kind have become established, and are one of the saddest disfigurements of civilisation" (Galton, *Inquiries into Human Faculty* pp. 10–11).

213 *Ibid.*, p. 75.

214 S[amuel]. A. K. Strahan, "Instinctive Criminality: Its True Character and National Treatment", *Report of the British Association for the Advancement of Science*, London, 1891, pp. 811–13. Dr Strahan published the same year *Marriage and Disease: A Study of Heredity and the More Important Family Degenerations* (London, 1892). *The Lancet* published a very critical article on Strahan's paper (*The Lancet*, 13 February 1892, pp. 368–70). According to the anonymous author, the proportion

of "instinctive criminals" was not "two thirds" (as Strahan alleged), but only 5% (p. 369).

215 Jackson, *Borderland of Imbecility*, p. 36.

216 Strahan, quoted in *The Lancet*, *op. cit.*, p. 370.

217 Richard L. Dugdale, *"The Jukes": A Study in Crime, Pauperism, Disease and Heredity*, New York, 1877. Nicole Hahn Rafter describes Dugdale as "by far the most influential American degenerationist" (see Rafter, *Creating Born Criminals*, pp. 38–39).

218 Strahan, "Instinctive Criminality", p. 812.

219 Quoted in Mucchielli, *op. cit.*, p. 191.

220 Alexandre Lacassagne, "Préface", in Emile Laurent, *Le Criminel aux points de vue anthropologique, psychologique et social*, Paris, Vigot Frères, 1908, p. xi.

221 Laurent Mucchielli, "Hérédité et 'milieu social', le faux-antagonisme franco-italien, la place de l'école de Lacassagne dans l'histoire de la criminologie", in *idem.* (ed.), *Histoire de la criminologie française*, Paris, L'Harmattan, 1994, pp. 189–214; Renneville, "La réception de Lombroso en France", *in* Muchielli, *op. cit.*, pp. 107–35; Philippe Artières (ed.), *Le livre de vies coupables: autobiographies de criminels (1896–1909)*, Paris, Albin Michel, 2000; Leps, *Apprehending the Criminal*, ch. 1–3. For a more "traditional" analysis of the French School, see Robert Badinter *La Prison républicaine 1871–1914*, Paris, Fayard, 1992, pp. 199–212.

222 Renneville, *op. cit.*, p. 115.

223 *Ibid.*, p. 113.

224 Gould, *Mismeasure of Man*, p. 129. The first category had brains with highly-developed frontal or anterior lobes; the second with large parietal or mid lobes, and the third with prominent back or occipital lobes. For Broca's opinion on this point, see Broca, *Instructions générales pour les recherches anthropologiques*, p. 146.

225 Renneville, *op. cit.*, pp. 112–13; Debuyst, *op. cit.*, pp. 347–49; Mucchielli, *op. cit.*, pp. 190–91.

226 *Ibid.*, p. 113.

227 Lacassagne, *op. cit.*, p. xi.

228 *Ibid.*

229 Quoted in Renneville, *op. cit.*, pp. 113–17.

230 Pick, *op. cit.*, p. 140; Renneville, *op. cit.*, p. 114.

231 Mucchielli, *op. cit.*, pp. 113–14. Claude Blanckaert, "Des sauvages en pays civilisé: l'anthropologie des criminels (1850–1900)", in Mucchielli, *Histoire de la criminologie française.*, pp. 55–88.

232 He did however acknowledge that up to that point, the discipline had been in the hands of "enthusiasts" who "... have seen perhaps both more and less than the men of cooler judgement who will follow them." (Clouston, *op. cit.*, p. 219). See also T.S. Clouston, "Some Developmental and Evolutional Aspects of Criminal Anthropology", *Report of the British Association for the Advancement of Science*, London, 1892, pp. 904–5.

233 Clouston, "Developmental Aspects", pp. 222–25.

234 *Ibid.*, p. 222.

235 Nicolson, "Presidential Address", discussion, p. 589.

236 *Ibid.*, p. 580.

237 Devon, *The Criminal and the Community*, pp. 21, 23.

238 Garland, "British Criminology", p. 5.

239 Maudsley, *Responsibility in Mental Disease*, pp. 36–37.

240 Armand Corre, *Les Criminels: caractères physiques et psychologiques*, Paris, 1889, p. ii.

241 This point recalls the comment made by French criminologist Gabriel Tarde in the second edition of *La Criminalité comparée* (1890): "My criticisms of Lombroso only relate … to his *interpretation* of the physical and other traits so frequently observed in criminals. They are not intended in any way to question the existence of the criminal-type" (p. 50: my translation).

242 Nicolson, *op. cit.*, p. 590.

243 Garland, *op. cit.*, pp. 5–6.

Chapter Four

A Criminal-Type in all but Name? British Theories of Crime and the Criminal (c. 1885–1914)

> *There is no 'criminal type'; and all formulated doctrines of 'hereditary crime' are gravely misleading. A marked degree of mental defect, signalised otherwise than by commission of crime doubtless characterises a notable proportion of actual law-breakers; while on the other hand there are many persons who commit serious crime, but to whom the word 'criminal' in its popular and intellectual sense does not apply.*
>
> Sir Bryan Donkin, Medical Commissioner of Prisons, 1913[1]

> *When the higher faculties have dwindled, the lower, or merely animal, take command.*
>
> Mary Dendy, letter to Sir Francis Galton, 1909[2]

Martin Wiener rightly observes in the introduction to his 1990 book *Reconstructing the Criminal: Culture, Law and Policy in England, 1830–1914* that we are a long way from being able to write a complete history of Britain's criminal justice policy in the nineteenth and early twentieth century.[3] He is at pains to point out that his approach represents "a contribution from *one particular point of view* toward more complete histories of crime and punishment, and Establishment culture, in modern English history."[4] Interestingly, he declares his intention to focus "on a consensus within officialdom, rather than on conflict, on images and values that were widely held at a given moment within this social stratum, rather than those which were in intense dispute". Such "shared elements of middle- and upper-class culture" Wiener goes on, "have received short shrift in favour of those that were contested."[5]

His book explicitly positions itself in opposition to earlier contributions to the field, notably David Garland's *Punishment and Welfare: A History of Penal Strategies* (1985).[6] The latter in turn owes a considerable, though largely unacknowledged, intellectual debt to Michel Foucault, and his *Surveiller et punir*, published in English as *Discipline and Punish: The Birth of the Modern Prison* in 1977.[7] The first "Foucauldian" study of British penal history, Michael Ignatieff's *A Just Measure of Pain: The Penitentiary in the Industrial Revolution*, followed the following year.[8]

In *Discipline and Punish*, Foucault had postulated the emergence of an all-pervasive disciplinary ideology or *savoir*, an "eye of power"[9], bent on bringing every last member of the population, both inside the prison and outside its walls, within its unblinking gaze: "… not to punish less, but to punish better; … to insert the power to punish more deeply into the social body."[10] Its objective was the subjugation of the mind as much as the body; its methods, the inculcation of habits of obedience and deference through mind-numbing routine and back-breaking labour. In this sense the prison regime was seen as playing a key role in shoring up the political and economic dominance of the ruling elite, forcibly preventing a potentially threatening "criminal class" from contaminating the rest of the working class with its habits of idleness and non-respect for property and public order. In this way, Foucault argued, the punitive *savoir* (seen not just in prisons but also in other disciplinary institutions like the police, the school and the workhouse[11]) contributed to the creation of a population of what he termed "docile bodies", terrorised or indoctrinated so that each became an

> … obedient subject, … subjected to habits, rules, orders, an authority that is exercised continually around him and upon him, and which he must allow to function automatically in him. [… This involved] a meticulous assumption of responsibility for the body and the time of the convict, a regulation of his movements and behaviour by a system of authority and knowledge … The human body was entering a machinery of power that explores it, breaks it down and rearranges it.… This discipline produces subjected and practiced bodies, 'docile' bodies.[12]

Although in the case of Britain, Garland situates the key changes in a period significantly later than does Foucault (that is to say between 1895 and 1914 rather than 1775 and 1850), his approach is based on the same epistemological and heuristic foundations. Both authors posit the spread of a hegemonic punitive discourse, serving to legitimise and reinforce the power base of an omnipotent and omniscient ruling elite. Both look for "proof" of the existence of this discourse in the works of contemporary intellectuals, professionals and functionaries working within, or on the margins of, the criminal justice system; and both devote considerable space to describing the theories of the latter concerning the origins of criminal behaviour and their solutions for its eradication. These authorities are seen, as it were, as providing the blueprints of the new penal systems; the bricks and mortar of the new penitentiaries and the minutiae of the new prison regimes constitute the concrete embodiment of their thoughts and words.

In Garland's case, the spread of this carceral *savoir* in Britain is situated in the context of the emergence of a new medico-scientific discipline—criminology—at the turn of the nineteenth and twentieth centuries, itself influenced by Darwinian natural science, French theories of *dégénérescence* and the emerging agenda of the Eugenics movement. In varying combinations, this new positivist scientific discourse emphasised the force of environmental and biological determinism, portraying the criminal as a helpless victim at the mercy of social or hereditary pressures beyond his control. It is out of this heady mix of new theories—ably placed in a wider European context by Daniel Pick's 1989 book, *Faces of Degeneration*[13] —it is argued, that emerged the individualised, medicalised solutions to crime we have come to associate with this period. These included colonies for vagrants, sterilisation for the "unfit", preventative detention for "habituals", incarceration for the "feeble-minded" and inebriated, and so on.

In *Discipline and Punish*, Michel Foucault cites the words of Marshal de Saxe from 1756; words which can, in fact, be turned against his own method. "It is not enough to have a liking for architecture", wrote the Marshal, "one must also know stone-cutting."[14] It could be argued that while both Foucault and Garland are on excellent terms with the "architects" of penal reform—the intellectuals, criminologists and functionaries at the top of the system—their knowledge of what goes on at the sharp end of criminal justice, in the stonemason's workshop as it were, is much less satisfactory.[15] That is not to say that the architects' blueprints for reform are irrelevant—on the contrary. It is just that it should not be assumed that there is a seamless progression from theory to legislation, and from legislation to reality on the cell block or in the prison doctor's surgery. [16]

As Michael Ignatieff recognised in his perspicacious auto-critique published in 1983:

> It appears … that the revolution in punishment was not the generalised triumph of Weberian rationalisation which the revisionist account suggested. Foucault's work (and my own as well) remained captive of that Weberian equation of the *ancien régime* with the customary, the traditional and the particularistic, and of the modern with the rational, the disciplined, the impersonal and the bureaucratic.[17]

The historical record is more complex. A closer examination of the empirical—particularly local—history of punishment in England, the USA and France in the eighteenth and early nineteenth centuries led Ignatieff to doubt that "the history of the institution [of the prison] between 1780 and 1840 can be described as a passage from squalid neglect to hygienic order". He admitted in fact that "the revisionist account may have been taken in by the reformers' sources".[18]

In reality, at each stage of this process, penal policy was subject to debate—often heated—between competing points of view; while at lower levels of the system, reactions ranged from enthusiastic compliance to outright rejection.[19] It is essential therefore, as Stephen Watson has argued[20], to integrate macrosocial and microsocial levels of analysis. Only in this way is it possible to pay attention not only to the complex interplay of social forces, political groupings and professional interests in the genesis of legislation and policy directives, but also to the myriad ways in which that legislation and those directives were modified, or in some cases blocked, by the those charged with putting it into practice on the ground. As Ignatieff puts it, "Foucault's conception of the disciplinary … *savoir* effectively forecloses on the possibility that the *savoir* itself was a site of contradiction, argument and conflict."[21] Or as American anthropologist Marshall Sahlins puts it succinctly, "Hegemonizing is homogenizing".[22]

Martin Wiener makes a similar point when he argues that such revisionist penal history, with its "picture of an onward march of surveillance and control, embodies an unconvincingly gloomy photographic negative image of Whiggism. To replace humanitarian reform by social control is to offer one simplism in place of another."[23] Instead, Wiener seeks to offer a *cultural* history of Victorian and Edwardian penal policy, an attempt, as he puts it, to "locate the transformation of English thought and policy about crime within … changing mental constellations and affective structures related to (though not determined by) specific social developments", an approach already used with considerable success by US-based cultural anthropologists like Clifford Geertz and Victor Turner.

Such an approach leads Wiener to conclude that there was a "sea change" in constructions of human nature and agency in Britain the 1870s, and his remarks are worth quoting at length:

> [By the mid-1870s,] the giddy sense of unleashed powers that had excited, and frightened, middle class early Victorians was … nowhere to be seen; in its place was a less intense and essentially opposite concern about the dangers of organic enervation and insufficient natural energies ... Running through late Victorian and Edwardian social policymaking can be traced a mental thread of diminishing faith in rationality, freedom and the efficacy of the will power of the ordinary individual … The concepts of unfitness and social wreckage were ever

> more pervasive, *sometimes in environmental, sometimes in biological dress ... The criminal was no longer a wicked individual, but rather a product of his environment and heredity.*[24]

This insight represents a key contribution to the understanding of the criminological mind-frame of the late-Victorian and Edwardian periods. Seen from Wiener's perspective, the nature-nurture debate takes on a new significance. Rather than being diametrically opposed, as traditional accounts—and contemporary participants in the debate—have tended to imply, they are in reality two sides of the same determinist, or as Wiener calls it, "causalist" coin.[25]

This is not to say there was not a considerable variety of approaches on offer in the forty-year period from the mid-1870s up to the First World War. A useful way of bringing order to what can appear, at times, a bewilderingly complex reality is to distinguish, as Wiener suggests, between those who favoured active intervention (usually by the State) to modify criminal behaviour and those who took a less sanguine view of the possibilities of preventing crime.[26] In the former camp were those who believed that government social policy and/or humanitarian effort could transform the socio-economic environment that bred crime. Also in the "optimist" camp were those who believed that criminals were born not made, and argued for the preventative solution of sterilisation associated with the Eugenics movement. In the "pessimist" camp, it was felt that little could be done except to sit back and wait for the gradual extinction of the "degenerate classes" (within four generations according to one prediction of 1890[27]); or alternatively, the problem could be removed from the public sphere altogether by the application of policies of indefinite imprisonment or capital punishment.

What all of these viewpoints had in common, Wiener notes, whether optimistic or pessimistic, was their emphasis on the ineffectual and devitalised, almost pathetic nature of the criminal, buffeted by social and/or biological forces beyond his or her control.[28] He quotes the words of Thomas Holmes, secretary of the Howard Association, who in a book of reminiscences published in 1908 clearly regrets the passing of the time when, as it were, criminals were criminals:

> Prisoners generally have changed. I am not sure that the change is for the better. Time was when prisoners had grit, pluck and personality, but now these qualities are not often met with. ... [T]hey are devoid of strong personality, and the mass of people in many respects resembles a flock of sheep. They have no desire to do wrong, but they constantly go wrong; they have no wish to do evil, but they have little

> inclination for good. In a word, weakness, not wickedness, is their great characteristic.[29]

Elsewhere, Holmes confided in a letter that "I would prefer to have under my charge a hundred wicked, desperate men, rather than fifty of these poor weaklings."[30]

A certain number of caveats need to be taken into account concerning Wiener's persuasive account of the changing perception of the criminal population, from public enemy number one to psychological and physical detritus to be "treated" or even pitied. Firstly, the shift in opinion was an uneven one during the forty years after 1875, and could be vulnerable to temporary reverses associated with "moral panics", such as during the social and political unrest of the mid- and late-1880s vividly portrayed by Gareth Steadman-Jones.[31] Secondly, as W. J. Forsythe has pointed out, the writers on crime in this period were often self-contradictory, and hybrid combinations of old and new approaches and attitudes often co-existed at the same time and sometimes in the same individual.[32] Thirdly, and following on from the last point, it could be argued that in emphasising coherence and consensus, "shared" rather than "contested" elements in middle and upper-class culture, Wiener falls—ironically—into the same trap as the Foucault-Garland approach, leading him to underestimate Ignatieff's "contradiction, argument and conflict". Thus, while Wiener presents a convincing case for a "sea-change" in the assumptions and concerns of the central government's policymaking classes from the 1870s—a shift in the perception of the criminal personality, as he puts it, from "wilfulness to wreckage"[33]—it could be argued that he pays insufficient attention to those whose views did not match the new positivistic, "de-moralised" view of crime.

Thus Wiener, like Garland and Foucault before him, overestimates both the internal cohesion of the middle- and upper-class position on penal policy, and by restricting analysis to the movers and shakers in the criminal justice system, the extent of its penetration to every level of the criminal justice system. This in essence is the criticism made by Victor Bailey in a closely-argued article published in the *Journal of British Studies* in 1997.[34] It also provides the main thrust of Bill Forsythe's second book on Victorian and Edwardian penal policy, *Penal Discipline, Reformatory Projects and the English Prison Commission, 1895–1939* (1991), and his 1995 article in *The Howard Journal* on the Garland thesis.[35]

Both Bailey and Forsythe emphasise the gap between the aspirations of the new positivist criminology of the period 1895–1914 and the reality on the ground. "Classical" notions of personal moral responsibility for criminal acts were, they argue, much more resilient than either Garland or Wiener allow, a position which tends to lend grist to the mill of Leon Radzinowicz and Roger Hood's earlier account of penal reform, published as volume 5 of the *History of English Criminal Law and its Administration from 1750* (1986).[36] Bailey and Forsythe both point to the relative failure of those laws which were inspired by the positivists—the Inebriates Act (1898), the Prevention of Crime Act (1908) and the Mental Deficiency Act (1913)—and question the extent of support for their theories among criminal justice professionals.[37]

Just as Michael Ignatieff had recognised that in reality the penitentiaries were a far cry from the idealised images of the reformers' tracts (a fact confirmed by local research), so Bailey and Forsythe emphasise the continuing attachment to classical notions of moral culpability, both among the members of the legal profession, and in the lower echelons of the prison service. "While top penal administrators were willing to accept that criminality might have a physical basis in 'degeneracy' ", writes Bailey, "particularly in 'feeblemindedness', *at the level of the prison medical officer, continuity prevailed*."[38] Forsythe, for his part, argues that "... *old fashioned early Victorian moralism was more important than the new positivistic science* in formulating discourse about prisoner reformation at the end of the [nineteenth] century."[39]

Does this mean that Radzinowicz and Hood had got it right when they concluded:

> The English critics could not accept the positivism in the determinist doctrine, according to which certain individuals had no choice but to commit crime. They accepted the idea of extenuating circumstances mitigating the individual's guilt, but nevertheless they regarded all criminals except the insane, as agents with free-will who were to be held responsible for their criminal acts. They held that to depart from this position would injure public respect for the law and weaken its effectiveness.[40]?

This would seem to me to be pushing the argument for continuity too far. It is true, as we saw in the last chapter, that the English medico-penal establishment of prison doctors, psychiatrists and Home Office officials rejected the *locus classicus* of continental positivist criminology, Cesare Lombroso's model of the "born criminal-type" with its check-list of anatomical and physiological "stigmata". Indeed, as David Garland has pointed out, there is a certain irony in the fact that British criminology "came to be recognised as an accredited scientific specialism only when it began to rid itself of the notion of a distinct 'criminal-type'—the very entity that had originally grounded the claim that a special science of the criminal was justified."[41] This did not mean, however, *pace* Radzinowicz and Hood, that English medico-penal establishment systematically took refuge in "classical" notions of personal responsibility—far from it.

Here Marshal de Saxe's image of the architect and the stone-cutter may be less appropriate. It is not—as Bailey implies—that support for positivist criminology was confined to some central government policy-makers and found little echo in the lower reaches of the criminal justice system; nor, as Forsythe suggests, that "the new positivist mental sciences were *additional extras* grafted onto a general set of moralistic assumptions about personal guilt and responsibility".[42] Rather, throughout the prison regime, *different kinds of criminality were widely held to dictate different penal solutions*. An increasing emphasis in late-Victorian theorising on crime in Britain—by now beginning to be given the name of "criminology"—was placed on what distinguished different kinds of offender, rather than what they shared as members of an homogenous "criminal class".

Differentiation and *individualisation* were thus the watchwords of this new science.[43] A paper read before a meeting of the psychology section of the British Medical Association in 1892 called for the creation of a prison "medico-psychological service" in order to explore in more depth the mental state of individual convicts, particularly "recidivists" and all the "great criminals". Such a service would bring the following benefits:

> *It would allow us to class ... delinquents, and subsequently to begin an individual treatment*, so far as their cerebral power allows it. It would allow us ... to make known the undisciplined and those who would simulate mental disease; it would allow us to take the necessary measures to repress their conduct.[44]

Similarly, an influential government inquiry on the prison regime, conducted in 1895, came to the conclusion that "... the system should be made elastic, more capable of being adopted [sic] to the special cases of individual prisoners".[45]

To each criminal then—or rather to *each sub-class of criminal*[46]—his or her own tailor-made penal solutions, both in terms of sentencing and subsequent treatment. More and more categories of prisoner—juveniles, women, politicals, "gentlemen" prisoners and the physically and mentally disabled—were seen to require specific treatment by the courts and the prison regime.[47]

Thus penal policy with regard to juvenile and occasional offenders was dominated by a combination of "classical" notions of free-will and a recognition of the sociological force of environmental pressure (the latter particularly in the case of the young). It was here that the kind of moralistic Christian, humanitarian, Idealist and socialist emphasis on the reformability of the Criminal highlighted by Bailey and Forsythe was increasingly influential as the century drew to a close.[48] However, as far as the *habitual* offender concerned, he or she was much more likely to be viewed as the passive victim of a defective heredity, and thus largely impervious to traditional penal remedies. In short, the dominant mind-set during the forty year period before the First World War may be characterised in bi-polar terms: "optimism" for juvenile and occasional crime and "pessimism" for the habitual offender.[49] This observation helps account for the otherwise puzzling fact that politicians and senior government officials—Du Cane's successor as Chairman of the Prison Commissioners, Sir Evelyn Ruggles-Brise, is a good example—drew on both classical and positivist explanations of criminal behaviour, according to the category of offenders concerned.

A superficial reading of the literature might suggest that British criminology in the period 1890–1910 did indeed reject biological explanations of crime out of hand in the way Radzinowicz and Hood suggest. Thus apparently at the opposite end of the spectrum from Dr Strahan, popular crime writer Hargrave Adam declared in 1911 that there was "not the slightest doubt that the majority of them [criminals] are 'made', moulded by environment and circumstance."[50] *The Lancet* made a similar point in two articles published between October 1983 and February 1894. Neither denied the reality of a degenerate physical type associated with crime, but insisted that given "wholesome conditions of life" as the earlier of the two articles put it, or what was termed "an early and well-inspired beginning" in the later one, incipient criminal behaviour could be nipped in the bud.[51] Dr Robert Gover, writing in the same journal the following year concurred that "there can be no doubt that the criminal elements in society may be largely reduced by such social reforms as the prevention of overcrowding, by attention to the details of sanitation, by judicious education and by such training as will tend to eradicate habits of idleness."[52] A majority of the medical specialists brought together in December 1907 to discuss "The Psychology of Crime" came to similar conclusions.[53]

Yet Adam had clearly considered the problem raised by Enrico Ferri in response to the sociological theories of the French school: if the crime-generating pressures of a particular social milieu act indiscriminately on all those who live within its orbit, why is it that some individuals succumb to its baneful influence, while others escape unscathed?[54] Adam gives the answer to this conundrum on the page after his unequivocal statement about criminals being "made" not "born". Crucially, he concedes that crime is the result of a *combination* of "unfortunate or undesirable circumstances" operating over time, and "*a mind that may, nay, doubtless had, its weaknesses at the outset*."[55]

In similar fashion, Dr Charles Mercier begins his 1918 book *Crime and Criminals* with a withering condemnation of both Lombrosian criminology and its environmentalist antithesis, urging in its place an approach based on "common sense".[56] The theory of crime which emerges from these reflections is based on the notion of "temptation":

> The difference between the criminal and the non-criminal is ... first the combination in varying degrees of qualities that both and all possess in common, and second that the criminal is subjected to temptation that, relatively to his combination of qualities, is excessive.

In a variation on the proverb *Every man has his price*, Mercier argues that every man has his own personal "breaking point". Thus, "But for the absence of sufficient temptation, every man is a criminal."[57]

Yet, like Adam, Mercier has conceded an important principle here to the biological theory of criminal behaviour. Habitual criminals, he suggests, are those with a "low breaking point", who succumb easily to temptation. (Those with a higher—but still insufficiently high—breaking point are described as "occasional criminals", another Lombrosian favourite). In this habitual category can be found a hard core of "instinctive criminals", possessed of uncontrollable propensities to commit crimes, often from an early age. Such an individual is, Mercier suggests, lacking in social instincts ("the instinct of forbearance and duty towards other members of the society"); "he is wholly selfish, and without scruple or hesitation will take all and give nothing in return. He is a truly instinctive criminal in that his criminality is due to the absence or imperfect development of an instinct that other people possess."[58] Rejecting ultimately the term "instinctive criminals" for its Lombrosian resonance, Mercier prefers to call such criminals "moral imbeciles". Although he concedes that some habitual criminals have "weak, but not entirely absent, social instincts"—generally when still young—his general conclusion on this class of criminal admits little hope of reform: "The habitual criminal ... cannot be reformed either by the ancient method of brutal severity or by the modern method of providing him with beer and skittles, with newspapers to read and Sophocles to listen to."[59]

So like Hargrave Adam, Mercier adopts a *de facto* bi-causal approach to the explanation of criminal behaviour: crime results from environmental pressures ("temptation") working on defective individuals (a low "breaking point"). For some lawbreakers, moreover, this breaking point is absent altogether: their social instincts are non-existent. Mercier may shy away from the term "instinctive criminal" because of its Lombrosian associations, but his gloomy prognosis concerning the incorrigible nature of most habitual criminals is strongly reminiscent of the Italian's reference to "a group of criminals born for evil, against whom all social cures break as against a rock"[60]; or indeed of Henry Maudsley's verbose prediction of 1873 that come what may, the dog will return "to its vomit and the sow to its wallowing in the mire."

An analysis of the position of Major Arthur Griffiths, whom we met earlier as Britain's sole official representative at the series of international congresses on criminal anthropology, reveals a similar conceptual framework to that of Adam and Mercier. In his report on the 1896 Geneva Congress on criminal anthropology, addressed to his superiors at the Home Office, Griffiths explained that he had been on the lookout for visible "criminal traits" since Lombroso's ideas had first been publicised, but declared that he had "almost invariably failed to find them."[61] While not ruling out the possibility of establishing a link between physical traits and crime, Griffiths saw environmental factors as primordial. In a metaphor strongly reminiscent of Alexandre Lacassagne, he writes of the "hotbed ... in which the germs of crime find congenial soil to take root, develop and exhibit a noxious vitality"; a better explanation of the origins of crime, he suggests, than "the somewhat far-fetched and inconclusive theories of anatomical criminology."[62]

However, Griffiths' role in Geneva was not solely that of an observer, for he read a paper to the congress on recidivism and the treatment of the habitual criminal. Unfortunately, the author's original English version has not survived. However, the French translation of the paper, read out on Griffiths' behalf on the final morning at Geneva is printed *in extenso* in the published *Travaux* of the congress.[63] Portraying himself as but a "modest practical administrator", he judiciously side-stepped the Franco-Italian quarrels on the causes of criminal behaviour, and concentrated instead on the search for what he called the "concrete" solutions to the problem of the habitual offender. Griffiths proceeds to argue, with the positivists, that incarceration had singularly failed to solve the problem of this "criminal residuum", an "army of wickedness, permanently at war against society, and against whom the Law fights with more or less vigour, but generally without success."[64] Although he puts on record his support for the principle that no criminal is beyond hope of reform, Griffiths seems to contradict himself later in his paper when he describes the habitual criminal as "an outcast incapable of reform". He reiterated the latter point in his report for the Home Office.[65] What was to be done with such "avowed evildoers"? Griffiths argues that the criminal justice system has the duty to protect society from habitual crime which "rears its ugly head, Hydra-like, with such persistent vigour and worrying vitality." Like Enrico Ferri, Griffiths advocates "indefinite detention", perhaps in agricultural or industrial colonies, as the only practical solution for such hardened criminals. He admits, however, that such a policy would create the thorny problem of determining the criteria to be taken into account when making a decision on whether an inmate was ready or not to be released into the community.[66]

In a book of memoirs published two years before the Geneva Congress, Arthur Griffiths described at greater length his views regarding the springs of criminal behaviour. While sceptical concerning the notion of an "actual anatomical physiognomy" among criminals—"I cannot admit the universal ugliness of the class"—Griffiths was prepared to concede that "most of them had a peculiar and generally displeasing expression ... the slow, outward and visible imprint of the evil passions within."[67] He agreed with Lombroso that criminals often display a "feline look", and

> ... with it a certain stealthy, loping walk like that of wild and wily animals. ... Nothing will more forcibly strike the unaccustomed visitor to a prison than the back-turned, watchful eye of the prisoner, the quick stealthy glance diverted directly it is detected.[68]

Like Gabriel Tarde and the Reverend Morrison, however, Griffiths ascribes this "gaol look" to the "artificial" environment of the prison, rather than to congenital factors.[69]

Griffiths also begged to differ with Lombroso on some of the other so-called criminal traits (frequency of gesticulation, ape-like agility, inability to blush, left-handedness, superiority of eyesight and inferiority of hearing), while accepting that prisoners are relatively insensitive to pain (a "fact" which Lombroso used as part of his explanation for the popularity of tattoos among criminals): "They bear pain with a more or less callous indifference and face 'without shrinking' situations that will certainly inflict it in a very acute form."[70] Griffiths was also—unlike Mercier—sceptical concerning the idea of moral insensibility among criminals, though was prepared to make an exception in cases of "mental aberration or degeneracy". Otherwise, his description of criminal psychology is little different from the Lombrosian model. The typical offender is described as astute rather than intellectual, reckless, cowardly, secretive, painstaking, self-indulgent, vain, intractable, and easily moved to anger. While "not insensible to kindness",

Griffiths concludes, the prison inmate is "at heart generally incorrigible and sometimes openly mutinous".[71]

Such a combination of environmental and hereditary factors in generating criminal behaviour is given more explicit form in Gordon Rylands' *Crime: Its Causes and Remedy*, published five years before Griffiths' book. As Rylands puts it, "Two influences which determine above all others the amount of crime … to one or the other of which indeed all others may be ultimately reduced … [are] Heredity and Environment."[72] As far as hereditary influences are concerned, Rylands argues that:

> Many unfortunate persons have bequeathed to them by their parents morbid affections of the brain which compel some to homicide, some to suicide, some to drunkenness, and its consequent vicious and degraded mode of life, reducing others to idiocy or raving madness. In this sad class of cases it is obvious enough to say that the criminal should be no less an object of our deep commiseration than the man who has been seized by a loathsome and painful disease.[73]

For the most hopeless cases, men of a "vicious and degraded …nature, …[those] literally on a level with the brutes …[who] combine the cunning of a fox with the ferocity of a tiger", no system of punishment would make good citizens of them. In such cases, Rylands suggests (echoing Lombroso and Ferri), "the words punishment and vengeance are tragically ludicrous". The only option remaining therefore is the death penalty; the most "merciful" solution in the circumstances.[74]

However, when Rylands turns to juvenile crime, he embraces environmental determinism. In an early variant of the sociological "labelling" theory of deviance, he describes how:

> Children of the very poor, playing in idleness about the slums will, out of natural childish mischief and thoughtlessness, do things which their more fortunate richer brother does almost daily with no more serious consequences than a slapping, and not always that, but which lodge the friendless gutter-child in prison, and on the way to a criminal career … Now it cannot be denied that these unfortunate boys were all the victims of circumstances; and that, so far from the acts which brought them into trouble being essentially immoral, in some cases a really generous disposition and loftiness of purpose was evinced, albeit obscured and misdirected by lack of training.[75]

On the basis of such opinions, it could be argued that Garland overplays the contrast between the approach of British criminologists and that of their Lombrosian colleagues. It is true that by the 1890s, the outwardly-visible simian "stigmata" dear to criminal anthropologists were now beyond the pale; talk of "brute brains" "arboreal ancestors" and "low, misshapen brows" was out, but the general principle of the habitual offender as someone both low in intelligence and largely intractable was most definitely *de rigueur* among Britain's criminologists and government officials. There were Rylands' and Maudsley's[76] vicious and degraded brutes, half-tiger, half-fox; Campbell's monkeys; Mercier's criminals impervious both to harsh discipline and to beer, sandwiches, newspapers and Sophocles; and Griffiths' outcasts incapable of reform. Indeed, on the basis of such evidence, it is difficult to resist the conclusion that habituals were conceived in terms of precisely the kind of "psychological type" which David Garland argued was *not* a feature of fin de siècle criminology in this country.

Moreover, British criminologists did not stop at *psychological* traits. As we saw with Major Arthur Griffiths, a Tardean belief in the *acquisition* rather than inheritance of physiognomic characteristics permitted the identification of a physical criminal-type (though not described as such) while steering well clear of Lombroso's *delinquento nato*. As we saw in Chapter Three, Drs Campbell and Baker went further than this in ascribing what was clearly a born criminal-type to certain classes of habitual criminal. David Nicolson too clearly believed the generalisations of the criminal anthropologists could be applied to at least certain categories of offenders.

Dr John Campbell, who retired from government service in 1880 after thirty years' work as a prison medical officer, is described by Wiener as belonging to the "post-Evangelical but pretherapeutic generation"[77], so it could be argued that by the late 1880s, his views about criminal "monkeys" had become an anachronism. Certainly his generalisations about the "conformation of the skull" and weight of prisoners' brains is strongly reminiscent of the work of Drs Thomson and Wilson in the late '60s and early 70s. What we shall suggest, however, is not that physical generalisations about prisoners ceased, or even that they became confined to the kind of pseudo-environmental explanations of the kind Major Griffiths borrowed from Gabriel Tarde. In reality, as the "problem" of the habitual criminal or "recidivist" became an increasing focus of criminological debate, a broad consensus emerged among both leading government officials and psychiatric and medical practitioners that habitual offenders were drawn disproportionately from a mentally *and physically* defective category of the population: a "criminal-type" in all but name.[78]

British concerns about recidivism in the late 1880s and early 1890s have to be seen in the context of rising middle-class fears about the dangers posed by the urban "residuum", particularly in London. As Gareth Steadman-Jones has shown, a combination of economic depression, a chronic shortage of working class housing and the emergence of socialist organisations, combined to create a social and political crisis, in which, it was feared, a radicalised "respectable" working class would throw in its lot with the casual poor of the residuum in a "sancullotic" insurrection.[79] Concerns about urban degeneration, which as we have seen were first voiced in the 1860s, now spread beyond the pages of specialised journals and "in the 1880s came to colour all social debate on the condition of the casual poor."[80]

The pressures of city existence were felt to be crushing the Poor both mentally and physically. Writing in 1886, Lord Brabazon articulated what was a common image of the "degenerate" urban poor:

> Let the reader walk through the wretched streets ... of the Eastern or Southern districts of London ... should he be of average height, he will find himself a head taller than those around him; he will see on all sides pale faces, stunted figures, debilitated forms, narrow chests, and all the outward signs of a low vital power.[81]

There were, moreover, sound reasons to believe the situation was getting worse. Was not the birth rate higher among the "criminal and pauperised classes with their low cerebral development", making them able to "renew their race more rapidly than those of higher nervous natures"?[82] And had not the agricultural depression of the 1870s led to a massive influx from the countryside into the towns, swelling the ranks of the urban poor in Britain's cities and thus exposing ever greater numbers to the debilitating effects of these "graves ... of our race"?[83]

Finally, a Darwinian twist was given to the situation by the belief that this burgeoning underclass was no longer feeling the socially beneficial effects of natural selection. Steadman-Jones explains:

> Darwinian laws of nature had weeded out the unfit products of urban life. But these laws had been increasingly violated. Medical science, sanitary improvement, and humanitarian legislation were now enabling an ever greater proportion of the 'unfit' to reach maturity and multiply their kind. As one popular pamphleteer put it: *It is monstrous that the weak should be destroyed by the strong. How much more repugnant is it to reason and to instinct that the strong should be overwhelmed by the feeble, ailing and unfit!*[84]

If only such "natural" laws could be left to get on with their work in peace, some argued, the problem of the residuum would take care of itself. Journalist Arnold White, writing in 1885 estimated that 40% of the Capital's unemployed was wholly degenerate, "physically, mentally and morally unfit." The nation could do nothing for such people, White concluded,

"… except to let them die out by leaving them alone."[85] H. M. Hyndman, leader of the Marxist-inspired Social Democratic Federation, approached the problem from a very different ideological perspective, but his conclusions were not very different from White's. There was, he wrote, "a certain percentage who are almost beyond hope of being reached at all. Crushed down into the gutter, physically and mentally by their surroundings, they can but die out, leaving, it is hoped, no progeny as a burden on a better state of things."[86]

Commentators like Arnold White, an early convert to the eugenics cause, were on the alarmist fringe of contemporary opinion[87]; a niche also occupied by writers like Eugene Talbot and Albert Wilson.[88] However, as Daniel Pick has persuasively argued, the language of degeneration permeated the whole of late-Victorian and Edwardian debate on social questions, reaching even as far as those who categorically rejected White's gloom-laden prophesies:

> Those who portrayed the social danger in … sensational terms were … often effectively marginalised, coded as scare-mongers. The more-pervasive worries, as expressed by more 'sober' commentators tended to qualify the alarmist picture; they tended to involve a slower, mediated process of decline in which a relative deterioration in the body of the city population in turn undermined the "imperial race" with ensuing disintegrative effects upon the nation and empire.[89]

Not only was the Metropolis held to accelerate the degeneration and thus the criminalisation of the Poor, there were fears that its anonymity was also casting a sinister veil of secrecy over new, or at least newly-*recognised*, kinds of white-collar crime. Essentially middle-class crimes like poisoning, embezzlement, fraud and blackmail were no less serious than their plebeian counterparts, but perhaps even more difficult to elucidate, ill-suited as they were to detection by traditional policing methods.[90] The Criminal was thus no longer necessarily recognisable on sight, confined in the working class rookeries of the country's big cities; he could be sitting next to you on the Clapham Omnibus, or smoking a cigar in the leather armchair next to yours at your West End club.[91] As Martin Wiener observes:

> Thus Jack the Ripper, the most celebrated criminal of the age, was often suggested to be not a denizen of the Jago but a medical doctor (implying a certain distrust, even fear, of the growing power of professionals and scientific experts). In this way, a double image of murderers—as both irresponsible brutes but also, at times, carefully premeditating and dissembling members of respectable society—came to flourish in the late Victorian era.[92]

In real life, one could not rely on Sherlock Holmes (who made his first appearance in *A Study in Scarlet* in 1887) being on hand to unmask such carefully-concealed crimes. Many feared that traditional policing methods—typified in the Holmes stories in the person of dogged but unimaginative Inspector Lestrade—were woefully inadequate when it came to apprehending this new (or apparently new) breed of criminal.

The development of the fingerprint as a reliable forensic tool in the early years of the twentieth century would help allay public suspicions that the police were largely impotent in the face of such white-collar crime.[93] However, as early as the 1890s, some were seeing an entirely different potential in this study of the human hand's combination of arches, loops and whorls. As Simon A. Cole has shown, there were those—Francis Galton among them—who saw in dactyloscopy the promise of isolating a tell-tale generic pattern of fingerprints common to *all* criminals.[94] Galton had first become acquainted with the technique in 1880 when his cousin Charles Darwin forwarded a letter he had received on the subject from a medical missionary in Japan. It was not until 1888, however, that Galton began to experiment with "finger marks" for himself. In a talk given to the Royal Institution in May that year, entitled "Personal Identification and Description", he introduced the subject that would occupy his energies for the next five years or so, "... perhaps the most beautiful and characteristic of all superficial marks, ... the small furrows with their intervening ridges and their pores that are disposed in a singularly complex yet even order on the under surfaces of the hands and the feet."[95] Other, more detailed, work would follow shortly after.[96]

Like Galton's earlier experiments with the composite portrait, here was a method which might provide the means of identifying not only known criminals, but *potential* wrongdoers as well.[97] With the history of fingerprinting conventionally written in terms of its growing status as a near-infallible method of identifying *individual* offenders, to discover such early attempts to isolate a kind of dactyloscopic criminal-type comes as something of a surprise. In fact, Cole suggests that such early experiments were deliberately written out of the history books in order to add weight to the "objectivity" of the fingerprinting method:

> Fingerprint examiners strengthened their authority by disassociating themselves from their colleagues who speculated about the predictive powers of fingerprints to tell, not only the past, but also the future. By turning the fingerprint into an empty signifier—a sign devoid of information about a body's race, ethnicity, heredity, character, or criminal propensity—fingerprint examiners made fingerprint examination seem

> less value-laden, more factual.... [A]ny correlation of fingerprint patterns with race, heredity or criminal propensity would have been dangerous to the credibility of forensic fingerprint identification.[98]

A number of French researchers, on the lookout for concrete markers of *dégénérescence*, claimed to have found a correlation between fingerprint patterns and crime in the 1890s—most famously Charles Féré, author of *Dégénérescence et criminalité* (1888).[99] There were also scattered examples elsewhere in this period of research based on similar hereditarian premises—in Ireland, the USA, and in Britain at the Biometric Laboratory, set up by Galton[100]—although by the early 1900s such work had become a scientific backwater, increasingly confined to dyed-in-the-wool eugenicists. There is no evidence, however, that such work had any echo in mainstream criminological work in this country.[101] In fact, by 1892, even Galton had been forced to concede, in an admission reminiscent of his 1878 *mea culpa* on composite portraiture, that there was no evidence that hereditary social or intellectual traits could be discerned from finger prints: "I have prints of eminent thinkers and of eminent statesmen that can be matched by those of congenital idiots. No indications of temperament, character, or ability are to be found in finger marks, so far as I have been able to discover."[102]

Dactyloscopy's day would come.[103] For the moment, however, criminal identification in Britain took a very different form. If Galton's composite portrait can be seen as the symbol of the old homogenising criminology, the new French system of anthropometric measurement, capable of pinpointing with apparently unerring accuracy the physical characteristics of tens of thousands of different criminals, symbolises the new *individualising* order.[104] Introduced at the Paris Prefecture de Police in 1883 at a time of acute public and political concern in that country concerning *le récidivisme*[105], "Bertillonage", named after its inventor Alphonse Bertillon (1853–1914), was officially adopted by Scotland Yard in 1895, following the recommendations of a government inquiry set up by the Home Secretary on the advice of Sir Edmund Du Cane.[106] The inquiry recognised that the existing system of annual Habitual Criminal Registers was "little used by the police" on account of the "extremely laborious" nature of any search for a particular criminal.[107] As part of the research for the report, committee members observed Bertillonage in action in Paris and at Pontoise Prison, and made inquiries on the methods of criminal identification adopted elsewhere in Europe and in India.[108]

Although the committee ended up rejecting the option of adopting a full-blown Bertillonage system in Britain—"It would not be consistent with

English ideas to entrust to the police an arbitrary power of measuring or photographing every person arrested without authority from a magistrate and without regard to the necessity for the purposes of justice of discovering his antecedents and character"— the 1894 report did recommend a scaled-down version of the Frenchman's anthropometric measurements, with fingerprints (which had the merit of being a home-grown invention) being used to define the smallest sub-groups.[109] Other countries adopted the French system at about the same time.[110]

An individual who was "Bertillonaged" was subjected to eleven different anthropometric measurements[111]—height, head length, arm span, right ear length, etc.—and the information collected recorded on a special "signaletic" card, invented for the purpose. There was also room on the card for a description of the individual (the ear was considered particularly informative: its profile might be "concave", "rectilinear", "intermediate" or "projecting" for example); for two photographic portraits, taken under the most stringent scientific conditions (one full face, one profile); and later, fingerprints.[112] However, it was the anthropometric measurements which were the key to the system, enabling the cards to be filed according to different statistical categories and sub-categories. In this way, in a few minutes it would be possible to check if a "new" set of measurements matched an existing criminal on file.[113] The recidivist could escape detection no longer, or so it seemed:

> No longer a name or a position in society, the individual became biological, defined simply, crudely as a unique body, distinguishable, in the eyes of science, from all others. No name change, no change in personality, could elude Bertillon's classification system, which ensnared the body in a textual net made of its own naked corporeality. The individual, perhaps for the first time, began and ended at its skin and bones. In short, Bertillon created a definition of the individual that the body could not escape.[114]

Ironically, this renewed focus on the identification and sentencing of habitual criminals came at a time when overall crime levels in Britain were visibly falling. Unsurprisingly, Police Forces around the country, as well as politicians of all political hues, were quick to take credit for the improved crime figures.[115] As Home Secretary Sir William Harcourt put in 1885, "it may ... be safely concluded that we have successfully tapped the fountains of crime, and that the labour and expense to which we have gone in the improvement of the social soil, has not been without its results."[116] Historians have confirmed the veracity of the trend. Indeed, indictable crime rates had been falling steadily since the late 1850s; by 1914 the reported larceny rate for example (per 100,000 of the population) had fallen by 35%, common assault by 71%, wounding by 20%, and homicide by 42%.[117] Victor Gatrell points out with reference to these figures that:

> ... other things being equal, many pressures should have pushed recorded crime *upwards* in these decades. Policing was expanding, more people were acquiescing in and co-operating with it, prosecution was becoming easier, sentences shorter and imprisoned offenders were released into society more rapidly.[118]

That recorded crime was in fact *falling* in this period would seem to indicate what Gatrell describes as "an era of rare success" for the criminal justice system.[119]

Official figures revealed that while the prison population as a whole was falling[120], the proportion of recidivists was on the rise. Whereas habitual criminals had only accounted for 55% of assize and quarter sessions convictions in 1893 (when Home Office statisticians first began to look into the problem in detail), the figure rose constantly thereafter, reaching a proportion of between 60 and 75% by the Edwardian period.[121] There was some comfort for Du Cane and his colleagues in the fact that proportionally more recidivists meant fewer first-time offenders, leading the Chairman of the Prison Commissioners to claim in 1895 that "the supply from which the habitual criminal is recruited is being cut off". His successor would concur, observing in 1900 that "an alarming roll of recidivism is quite consistent with a well-ordered and law-abiding community."[122] However, the reality of the problem of recidivism, of "BRITAIN'S BLOT", as the capitalised title of a 1908 book on the subject described it (complete with evocative black stain on the cover), could not be gainsaid.[123] Just like their neighbours across the Channel, British penologists and administrators at the turn of the century were "obsessed" with this apparently insoluble problem.[124]

Several historians have suggested that in fact there is a link between this growing "obsession" and the lower crime figures: as crime decreased overall, attention focused increasingly on a "hard core" of often persistent offenders whose deviant behaviour bucked the general downward trend.[125] With conventional jail terms—and the thirty-year-old Du Cane regime of harsh prison discipline which accompanied them—apparently unable to stem the tide of habitual criminal behaviour, there was an urgent need to find a solution to what a government report of 1895 called this" most important of all prison questions as well as the most difficult", this "growing stain on our civilisation".[126] In this context, Du Cane's claims that the supply of habitual criminals was being "cut off", were beginning to ring more and more hollow.

Indeed, by the early 1890s, this was but one of several fronts on which the Chairman of the Prison Commission was facing "mounting criticism".[127] The latter clearly had few friends inside the Home Office, where his autocratic management caused widespread resentment. As for Du Cane's fellow members of the Prison Commission, they frequently had the impression that their views were being ignored, and that meetings had become little more than an occasion to rubber stamp decisions already made by the Chairman.[128]

At the same time, there was a long-running campaign in the pages of *The Lancet* concerning "two main subjects of unfavourable criticism … the prevalence of insanity and the death rate". The combination of a scanty diet and punitive labour meant, it was alleged, that inmates were "reduced to such a state of weakness that it often happens they leave prison physically unfit for work."[129] Prisoners themselves lent grist to this particular mill in the form of a growing number of published memoirs openly critical of the Du Cane regime. Perhaps the best known were those written by Irish Nationalist MP Michael Davitt who had served a seven-year term of penal servitude between 1870–1877 for his activities in connection with the outlawed Land League. In his *Leaves from a Prison Diary* (1885), Davitt describes penal servitude as:

> … a huge punishing machine, destitute, through centralised control and responsibility of discrimination, feeling or sensitiveness; and its non-success as a deterrent from crime, and complete failure in reformative effect upon criminal character, are owing to its obvious essential tendency to deal with erring human beings—who are still men despite their crimes—in a manner which mechanically reduces them to a uniform level of disciplined brutes.[130]

From the other side of the prison bars, Major Arthur Griffiths provides a more positive picture of the Du Cane regime, recalling his time as deputy-governor at Chatham Public Works Prison in the 1870s, but it shares with Davitt's account the metaphor of an impersonal punishing machine:

> Everything worked with clock-like precision; the worst that could be said was that it was too mechanical, the inmates were treated too much en masse, with no attempt at distinguishing between them. They were as one in the eyes of authority, a single entity, ground under the hard and fast rules of the prison system. The wheels went on and on, round and round, with ceaseless, methodic movement, and everyone must conform, and either fall out or be crushed; the happiest were those who

> allowed themselves to be carried along without protest or hesitation, adapting themselves automatically to the monotonous movement.[131]

There were also voices raised from within the prison system. The Reverend W. D. Morrison, whom we met earlier as an advocate of Lombrosian criminology, was also an implacable critic of the Du Cane regime. All the existing system accomplished, he argued, was to further debilitate individuals already weakened by constitutional defects. Juvenile delinquents were thus made into hardened habitual offenders; while long-term prisoners were driven mad or reduced to unthinking automatons:

> Imprisonment so far from serving the purpose of protecting society adds considerably to its dangers. The casual offender is the person to whom crime is merely an isolated incident in an otherwise law-abiding life. The habitual criminal is a person to whom crime has become a trade; he is a person who makes his living preying on the community. The prison is the breeding ground of the habitual criminal. The habitual offender is the casual offender to begin with. But the prison deteriorates him, debases him mentally and morally, reduces him to a condition of apathy, unfits and indisposes him for the tasks and duties of life; and when liberated he is infinitely more dangerous to society than when he entered it. It is not sufficiently recognised that punishment may be of a character which defeats the ends of justice.[132]

A widely-read series of articles for the *Daily Chronicle* in 1894—probably penned by Morrison himself—hammered the message home. Letters from prison staff, prisoners and humanitarian groups sent in response to the articles provided corroborative evidence.[133]

With Du Cane on the defensive, the stage was set for a government investigation into the prison service, to be chaired by Liberal Home Office minister and future Home Secretary, Herbert Gladstone. Set up in June 1894, the "Departmental Committee on Prisons" produced its report the following year. A detailed examination of this influential report will permit us to gauge contemporary opinion on habitual crime, both in terms of the perception of the problem, and the solutions proposed. The published report was careful to avoid any direct attack on Du Cane himself (it praised his "strong and masterful action" in implementing the 1877 act), but was nevertheless highly critical of the tendency of the prison regime in place to treat prisoners "as a hopeless or worthless element of the community". Instead, it urged both more humane administration (with less hard labour and separate confinement and more emphasis on education and re-training) and more individualised treatment for juvenile and habitual offenders. It was hoped that as a result prisoners would be "prevent[ed...]

from feeling that the state merely chains them for a certain period and cares nothing about them beyond keeping them in safe custody and under iron discipline."[134]

Habitual crime or recidivism was regarded as a particularly thorny problem, but the Gladstone Committee failed to provide a clear-cut answer. As Leon Radzinowicz and Roger Hood point out, part of the problem lay in the committee's failure to elaborate a precise definition of what the habitual criminal actually *was*. The result was that they "got lost in a tortuous maze of definitions. They encountered great difficulties in distinguishing mere repetition of crime from 'professionalism' in crime."[135] The primary concern of the committee seems to have been with that "large class of habitual criminals who are not of the desperate order, who live by robbery and thieving and petty larceny, who run the risk of comparatively short sentences with comparative indifference." When caught and convicted, "they serve their time quietly with the full determination to revert to crime when they come out."[136] It was precisely the same category of offenders which had come under the legislative spotlight in France in 1885 with that country's decision to extend its policy of transportation to persistent petty offenders. By the end of the century, nearly 10 000 multi-recidivists were shipped out of France in this way.[137]

Elsewhere in the Gladstone committee report, those offenders "not of the desperate order" are described as "one of the most dangerous classes of offenders", but the sense in which they are more "dangerous" than those committing violent crimes is not specified. The latter were largely absent from the committee's concerns. In addition, applying the sobriquet "professional" to habitual petty criminals ("when an offender has been convicted a fourth time or more, he or she is pretty sure to have taken to crime as a profession") is confusing, since in the criminological literature and in the wider public debate on crime, the term *professional* was often used to describe "specialist skills, systematically applied, to a high standard of competence". All the evidence suggested that most habitual crime was opportunistic and its spoils meagre.[138]

The report also noted that "criminal anthropology as a science is in embryo stage … it would be a loss of time to search for a perfect system in learned but conflicting theories." Instead, committee members emphasised their intention—in language reminiscent of the medico-psychiatric and official sources quoted in the previous chapter—to rely on "the *plain fact* that the great majority of prisoners are ordinary men and women amenable, more or less, to all those influences which affect persons on the outside."[139]

Such sentiments would appear to confirm the point made in a recent survey of the period by Philip Rawlings that the Gladstone Committee "largely rejected the idea that criminals were born and were therefore essentially irredeemable."[140] Rawlings gives the following quotation from the report to back up his argument:

> There are but few prisoners, other than those who are in a hopeless state through physical or mental deficiencies, who are irreclaimable. Even in the case of habitual criminals there appears to come a time when repeated imprisonments or the gradual awakening of better feelings wean them away from habitual crime.[141]

However, as Daniel Pick has pointed out, despite the committee's championing of "plain facts" as opposed to the excesses of the continental theorists, "a great deal had already been conceded to the positivist theory of crime".[142] Pick quotes the authors of the report when they acknowledge that "It may be true that some criminals are irredeemable, just as some diseases are incurable and in such cases it is not unreasonable to acquiesce in the theory that criminality is a disease and the result of physical imperfection."[143]

Criminality is a disease. It is in this way that "irredeemable" or "irreclaimable" habitual offenders become more and more associated with the psychiatric categories of the "feeble-minded" and the "moral imbeciles".[144] Specialist opinion differed as to the size of this mentally deficient category in the prison population, but that such a sub-group existed and could be clinically identified was universally acknowledged. In April 1881, Dr Robert Gover, Superintending Medical Officer of Convict Prisons, had conducted a census among Britain's "Habitual Criminal Class", serving sentences of five years or more in the country's convict prisons, in order to "furnish statistical information in reference to certain mental and physical characteristics". He found about 25% of this group to be either "unfit for labour" or "only fit for light labour" The latter group, composing 21.5% of the total, included, he noted, "a large number" of those judged insane, weak-minded, epileptic or scrofulous.[145] In his concluding remarks, Gover noted sardonically that the census had revealed convict prisons to be "… establishments for maintaining some thousands of persons of the lowest moral type in the highest attainable degree of physical efficiency for preying on the public."[146]

As we have noted previously, prison medical officers had different professional priorities from their asylum-based colleagues; and for this reason it is not surprising perhaps that they tended to be more cautious in their assessment of the extent of the "weak-minded" problem. Thus Dr David

Nicolson told the Gladstone Committee that in his view, "a very large proportion" of criminals were sane, and could be considered responsible for their actions.[147] In similar spirit, Dr Gover, in a memorandum commenting on the recommendations of the committee, warned that "weak-mindedness" was an "exceeding vague term", and that it should not be used to enable "brutish and sensual men" to avoid punishment and hard labour.[148]

In the following decade, Dr W. C. Sullivan, medical officer at Holloway Prison would come to similar conclusions, quoting with approval the work of Dr Charles Mercier, and the latter's emphasis on the interplay of two variables, "structure" and "stress":[149]

> We cannot [wrote Sullivan,] speak of a special innate predisposition to crime except in connection with *a small minority of offenders*, and then only in a very loose sense as meaning that in certain cases of mental debility, impulsiveness and affective insensibility are so predominant and the power of inhibition so weak that the individuals are more prone to criminal conduct than are other weak-minded persons.[150]

Sullivan stressed that most criminals were "of average stock", and that "criminal conduct is usually the outcome of the action of the environment on an organisation of normal aptitudes."[151]

Compare the tenor of such remarks with those of psychiatrist Dr Bevan Lewis, medical superintendent at Wakefield Asylum, contained in his evidence to the Gladstone committee:

> The habitual criminal I regard as simply a degenerate offspring of a very degenerate stock; and if I may be allowed to express my opinion more freely, I would say that both insanity and crime are simply morbid branches of the same stock … on the borderline between insanity and crime *a very large proportion* of the criminal class stand.[152]

Significantly, in the their evidence to the Gladstone Committee, both Du Cane and his soon-to-be successor, Sir Evelyn Ruggles-Brise chose to emphasise the currency of the weak-minded offender in the prison population, rather than his or her relative scarcity, as Nicolson and Gover had done (and Sullivan would do). For Du Cane (who, in what seems to have been a piece of malingering worthy of the wiliest lag, repeatedly delayed appearing before the committee, pleading ill-health[153]), there were "a great number of prisoners" who were "below par mentally, [men who had become criminals] because they are not up to the level morally, mentally or physically." As for Ruggles-Brise, he told the committee that "the bulk of recidivists" were suffering from "moral imbecility", earning them the nickname "half-sharps".[154]

Such comments have to be interpreted with some caution. Neither Du Cane nor Ruggles-Brise would have disputed the point made by Nicolson and Gover that most criminals could be held responsible for their actions, and should be punished accordingly. As we shall see in the next chapter, Ruggles-Brise would cross swords with the eugenics movement over precisely this point in the Edwardian period. To a certain extent at least, the evidence of both Du Cane and Ruggles-Brise should be seen as part of a deliberate strategy on the part of government officials to forestall the argument advanced by critics like W. D. Morrison that the prison regime had a detrimental effect on the mental health of its inmates. In such circumstances, there was a strong incentive to emphasise that many criminals were *naturally* weak-minded.[155]

That being said, it is probably true to state, with Martin Wiener, that by the time of the Gladstone Committee hearings, it had become the received wisdom in official circles—among senior Home Office officials and among leading prison doctors and psychiatrists —that a significant minority of the prison population, and perhaps a majority of "habituals", was if not insane, at least irrevocably deficient mentally. In such cases, the only viable solution was an indeterminate period of imprisonment.[156] Dr Gover again, this time in his report to the Directors of Convict Prisons for 1893–1894:

> Many of the convicts are persons of low type who have never developed any degree of mental capacity. [Most] are of normal physical development and do not manifest any defect until they are subject to discipline, or are put to some kind of work requiring an average amount of intelligence for its proper performance. A proportion of these semi-imbeciles tend to degenerate and to become wholly irresponsible so as to necessitate their removal to an asylum.[157]

It was this view of the habitual criminal as an offender for whom conventional penal solutions were manifestly ill-suited that led to the Prevention of Crime Act (1908), a "dual track" regime, which gave statutory credence to the idea of "preventative detention".[158] The principle of long-term or indefinite detention for recidivists was not a new one; it was, we have seen, a staple of the Italian *Scuola Positiva*, and cumulative sentencing had been tried in the 1869 Habitual Criminals Act. By the 1890s, influential voices had come out in favour of a modified form of the indeterminate sentence, what was now being called "preventative confinement". Supported by former head of Scotland Yard, Sir Robert Anderson, and by new Chairman of the Prison Commissioners, Sir Evelyn Ruggles-Brise, the new scheme envisaged that habituals would serve out their statutory sentence like any other prisoner. At its end, however, they would be transferred to a penal colony with a more relaxed system of discipline, where they would serve out a supplementary sentence, or according to some versions of the plan, be confined until their behaviour merited release.

In a paper prepared for the 1900 International Penitentiary Conference in Brussels, Ruggles-Brise lamented:

> ... the powerlessness of existing methods to make any sensible impression on a solid, and compact, and resisting mass of offenders whose depredations on society are only alternated by long or short periods of internment in Prisons, which have lost their power of deterrence and become nothing else than costly shelter-houses, where the energies of a certain number of lawless bandits—for such these men are—may be recruited for new enterprises against the goods and chattels of defenceless and unoffending citizens.[159]

Given this bleak prognosis, Ruggles-Brise goes on:

> ... in the interest of *social defence*, it is justifiable where a prisoner is proved, by his antecedents and previous convictions, to have habitually preyed upon society, to sentence that prisoner, though the immediate offence may be trivial, to a long deprivation of his liberty, under conditions which, while they are less severe than those commonly associated with a formal sentence of imprisonment, are yet irksome enough to afford a very disagreeable contrast with the state of liberty.[160]

Sir Robert Anderson, an inveterate publicist for his own ideas, envisaged two different penal regimes: one for so-called "professional" criminals, the "aristocracy of crime in England", those "human beasts of prey ...now hold[ing] the community in a state of siege"; another for the "poor wretch who, born and bred in crime, has not the moral stamina to resist when opportunity for theft presents itself."[161] As far as the latter group is concerned, Anderson writes:

> Stern severity may be justifiable in our treatment of the wicked, but let the weak be placed in confinement in a state of social tutelage for the protection of society and for their own good.... Some among them are probably intractable and hopeless; but the great majority of such offenders might, in an asylum prison, be trained to lead not only useful lives, but brighter and happier lives than they can know in the vile slums which are their usual haunts.[162]

Ruggles-Brise made no such distinction between "professional" and weak-minded" criminals, considering that four or five previous convictions, or perhaps one previous sentence of penal servitude would suffice to label an offender "recidivist" and thus be subject to an extended period of imprisonment.[163]

The Gladstone committee of 1895 had recommended that a special "cumulative" sentence be created to incapacitate habitual criminals,

> ... by which these offenders might be segregated for long periods of detention during which they would not be treated with the severity of first-class hard-labour or penal servitude, but would be forced to work under less onerous conditions.[164]

After a long period of "prolific discussion"[165], and several false starts, these ideas were put in legislative form in Herbert Gladstone's 1908 Prevention of Crime Bill, which put forward a scheme of preventative confinement, writing, as it were the positivist principle of the incurable recidivist into British law, punishing criminals not just for what they had done, but for what they were.[166] Sir Robert Anderson's "professional criminals" were the intended target of the bill, those "men with an object, sound in mind—as far as a criminal could be sound in mind—and in body, competent, often highly skilled, and who deliberately, and with their eyes open, preferred a life of crime and knew all the tricks and turns and manoeuvres necessary for that life." Those criminals who were "criminals chiefly because of physical or mental deficiency", on the other hand, would be excluded from its provisions.[167] Indeterminate detention would be reserved for those with three previous convictions whose latest offence carried a minimum sentence of three years penal servitude. Following a jury conviction for "habitual criminality", the offender would be held at His Majesty's pleasure in a purpose-built detention prison. According to contemporary estimates, about 5 000 offenders would come within the remit of the Act.[168]

Some felt that in excluding Sir Robert Anderson's weak-minded petty criminals from its provisions, the Act did not go far enough; others, including influential voices on the Commons' Liberal and Irish Nationalist benches, poured scorn on what they called the "pseudo-scientists with broken-down reputations like Lombroso's"[169], and opposed the very principle of the indeterminate sentence. In the end, the government was forced to compromise, and when Gladstone's bill became law as the Prevention of Crime Act, the "indeterminate" element of the sentence was—much to the consternation of Sir Evelyn Ruggles-Brise—limited to a period of between five and ten years.

Even with this watered-down version of the scheme on the statute book, the legal profession remained profoundly suspicious of what it considered "double sentencing". This, coupled with the arrival in 1910 of a new Home Secretary, a thirty-six-year-old Winston Churchill, alarmed at what he considered a potentially reactionary measure, limited the impact of the new law. In the year following Churchill's appointment, the number of sentences of preventative detention fell by two-thirds.[170] By the autumn of 1920, the population at Camp Hill, the purpose-built detainment prison on the Isle of Wight, had fallen to seventy-one; in the first thirteen years of the Act's existence, it has been calculated, only 577 convictions were brought under the Act.[171]

The fate of the 1908 Prevention of Crime Act illustrates clearly the point raised earlier in the writings of Bill Forsythe and Victor Bailey: that there were limits to the penetration of the new ideas highlighted by Martin Wiener, of the criminals as human flotsam and jetsam, passive victims of environmental and hereditary forces beyond their control. However, we would not wish, as Victor Bailey does, to conclude from these events that positivism was only of minor importance in this period[172]; rather to emphasise that the main force of its impact was felt elsewhere.

A closer examination of Winston Churchill's position bears this out. The Home Secretary's chief anxiety about the Prevention of Crime Act was that despite its promoters' avowed intentions, the main criterion being applied by the courts for imposing preventative detention, was the *number*, rather than the gravity of the offences committed. Given that before the passage of the Act, sentences of penal servitude were already being handed out to persistent thieves who had committed petty offences, it was not surprising that a large number of merely nuisanceful recidivists came to be prosecuted under the terms of the Act.[173]

Yet as Radzinowicz and Hood point out, Churchill did not in fact reject the principle of preventative detention *per se*; rather he felt that the Act should, as he put it, be "applied without hesitation to dangerous and brutal criminals, whose passions of predatory violence render them a peril and an affront to civilised society." Moreover, the offender's criminal record "should show that he is a danger to society. Violence in crime would be an adverse factor here. His general mode of life should reflect hopelessness. Any spell of honest work would count favourably."[174] In short, Churchill advocated preventative detention for what he considered the truly incorrigible—or "hopeless"—serious, often violent, offender, not the opportunistic thief.

Churchill's views on the "feeble-minded" offender add further weight to our point that it is misleading to see him simply as a liberal defender of classical jurisprudence in the face of the positivist onslaught.[175] In December 1911, the Home Secretary circulated to the rest of the Cabinet a paper by Dr Alfred Tredgold, entitled "The Feeble-Minded: A Social Danger", which argued for a close blood relation between criminals and the feeble-minded, and more widely, pointed to the "serious reality of national degeneracy".[176]

The paper provided, Churchill noted, "a concise, and I am informed, not exaggerated statement of the serious problem to be faced."[177] Tredgold's closing remarks give a good idea of the tone of his article:

> Delay is dangerous, the disease has already spread to such an extent and the case has already become so urgent that we must not wait; but must, each one of us, as intelligent citizens of a great Empire, bestir ourselves to see that this great social evil is removed and that this tide of degeneracy is stemmed.[178]

Churchill was one of many politicians convinced by the alarming findings of the Royal Commission on the Care and Control of the Feeble-Minded which reported in 1908, after hearing 248 expert witnesses and amassing seven volumes of oral evidence.[179] The Commission, which had begun collecting evidence in 1904, came to the following conclusion:

> Of the gravity of the present state of things, there is no doubt. The mass of facts that we have collected, the statements of our witnesses, and our own personal visits and investigations compel the conclusion that there are numbers of mentally defective persons whose training is neglected, over whom no sufficient control is exercised, and whose wayward and irresponsible lives are productive of crime and misery, and of much injury and mischief to themselves and to others and of much continuous expenditure wasteful to the community and to individual families.[180]

Although the Commission acknowledged that there was disagreement among specialists as to relative importance of nature and nurture in the genesis of feeble-mindedness, it came down firmly on the side of the inheritance of mental deficiency: "There is", the report noted, "the highest degree of probability that 'feeble-mindedness' is usually spontaneous in origin—that is not due to influences acting on the parent—and tends strongly to be inherited."[181] According to Mark Jackson, who has made a detailed study of contemporary responses to the report, dissenting voices were rare indeed.[182] Indeed, according to José Harris,

> It was here, rather than upon the wider spectrum of Edwardian thought that one finds in concentrated form the link between Darwinian beliefs about biological inheritance and random mutation, and the spectre of social degeneration and national decay.[183]

Many penal specialists were now prepared to state confidently that habitual crime and feeble-mindedness were at the very least closely connected. Britain's most senior prison doctor, Medical Commissioner of Prisons Sir Bryan Donkin, argued in a 1908 speech that "a very large proportion" of convicts were "congenitally feeble-minded".[184] In similar fashion, Dr W. C. Sullivan, in his 1909 article on "Eugenics and Crime", referred to a category of "very dangerous delinquents ... who are congenitally defective and by reason of their mental inferiority are incapable of forming the higher and more complex associations which are involved in social conduct."[185] Quoting with approval Sir Bryan Donkin on this point, Sullivan refers to this group as "moral idiots", and points out that "in biological terms", they resemble the feeble-minded as a whole.[186]

In their evidence to the Commission on the Care and Control of the Feeble-Minded, Dr Parker Wilson of Pentonville prison and Dr Treadwell of Parkhurst put the proportion of mentally deficient prisoners at over 20% and at 25% respectively, similar figures in fact to those calculated by Dr Gover in 1881.[187] Treadwell characterised such prisoners as "incapable of organising their own occupations, of withstanding the stress of competition and the evil influences of criminal associates when free, and necessarily from this cause they relapse into crime."[188]

Special arrangements were made at Parkhurst for feeble-minded prisoners. They had their own exercise yard, part of the farmland was allocated uniquely to their use, as was a portion of the prison chapel (entrance to which was by a separate door to prevent mixing with "ordinary" convicts), and a team of warders was specifically allocated to this class of prisoners.[189] Apparently each of these warders was provided with a ten-inch stave or stick, hollowed-out and filled with lead, an indication perhaps of the continuing reputation of mentally weak convicts as being difficult to handle. It is unclear to what extent they were used in practice.[190]

The report of the Commission on the Care and Control of the Feeble-Minded conjured up an image of a dangerous, shiftless population of feeble-minded criminals, "wandering to and from prisons, workhouses, casual wards and shelters"[191], not dissimilar in its essentials to Henry Mayhew's parasitic "nomadic tribe" of "vagrants, beggars and pilferers" at large in the 1850s and '60s. In a chapter of the report entitled "Mental Defect and Crime", the views of Dr James Scott, medical officer of Brixton prison, were quoted at length. This was the same Dr Scott who had accompanied Major Arthur Griffiths to the 1896 International Congress on Criminal Anthropology in Geneva, and had conducted anthropometric research which had come to the conclusion that criminals had a higher than average incidence of "abnormality of palate".[192] Some twenty years later, Scott clearly remained convinced that heredity was an important factor in crime. For the "bulk of feeble-mindedness", he told the committee, "heredity has a very great influence indeed."[193] He provides the following portrait of the feeble-minded offender:

> Their moral sense is very defective, and they have little self-control or power to resist temptation when it comes their way. They are frequently in trouble for breaking the law, and it is difficult to know what to do with them ... Punishment has little effect on them. Reforming influences also fail with them usually. ... When they are at liberty, their friends do not usually welcome them, and they are quite unfit to compete with the better endowed individuals in the struggle for existence. It is not at all uncommon for them to break windows, or commit a petty theft, in order to get back to prison again. ... By their proneness to commit larceny, arson, indecent assaults on children, etc., they are a constant source of annoyance, expense and danger.[194]

Like the Commission, Scott concluded that "Many of them are quite unfit, if left to themselves to lead decent, inoffensive lives; they require care and discipline." He rejected the eugenicist solution of forced sterilisation[195], but did note that it was "... important to consider from the point of view of the improvement of the race, if any means can be taken to prevent these 'undesirables' from producing their like."[196] The previous year, Scott had already argued that those who "lived by crime", but were not lunatics, "should be restrained indefinitely". His strictures were presumably aimed chiefly at the feeble-minded offender.[197]

How was this "care and discipline" to be effected? In the first place, there was the problem of *identifying* "this wandering population of mentally defective persons, who are many of them dangerous, morally and physically, and criminal in their characteristics". As Mark Jackson has observed, according to contemporaries, "the covert nature of their defects and their apparent proximity to the normal population rendered the feeble-minded more dangerous than idiots and imbeciles."[198] The commission suggested that Galton's finger-print system (in use since 1901) could be useful in this context. Once identified, the feeble-minded needed to be *controlled*—or "contained" as the report puts it—both to protect the community and to avoid the proliferation of such "undesirables".[199]

Could the elaboration of an anatomical and physiognomic type of feeble-minded offender be useful for such "identification" and "containment"? Certainly, as Jackson has shown, "physical stigmata of deficiency" were an integral part of the medical conception of mental deficiency in the Edwardian period: "... the belief that mental defectives constituted a physically distinct sub-section of the population proved a popular refrain in medical writings on idiocy, imbecility and feeble-mindedness."[200] Indeed, with the help (again) of the photographic portrait, this previously hidden but deviant section of society could be unequivocally identified (given the right medical expertise of course), thereby facilitating subsequent surveillance and control.[201]

As far as mentally deficient habitual criminals are concerned, there is convincing evidence that many doctors and psychiatrists working within the prison system at the turn of the century continued to associate them with a range of anatomical and physiognomic abnormalities. Indeed, as late as the 1920s, a historian of the Prison Medical Service has detected "a residue of nineteenth-century Lombrosian theorising" among prison doctors.[202] In the early 1900s, it seems to have been much more than a "residue". Dr J. F. Sutherland, deputy commissioner in lunacy for Scotland, and a leading criminal psychiatrist, published in 1908 what was the most detailed study to date of habitual crime in Britain.[203] His research claimed to have uncovered "that elusive yet unmistakable physiognomy which recidivists present to the observer … as real as the facial types met with in asylums." He gives the following portrait of this "facial type":

> Coarseness, scars, and a *sui generis* expression tell their own tale. They are the hallmarks of alcoholism, debauchery, ruffianism, dishonesty, lying and unchastity; each criminal and delinquent, according to the vocation he has chosen and followed, presenting appearances which do not make it a matter of great difficulty to determine fairly correctly into which class he is to be relegated.[204]

Sutherland did follow the consensus of the period in noting the unreliability of Lombroso's physical stigmata. A few pages later, however, he announced some anthropometric results of his own, based on a study of 370 criminals (75% of whom were recidivists). Commenting that "in stature the criminals form a special class of the population", he explains that criminals convicted of murder or assault were found to have longer heads than those convicted of other crimes, and Scottish criminals had broader heads than their English counterparts.[205]

Sutherland seems to have followed the French Lamarckians in his description of the way in which facial characteristics acquired by criminals (a "functional and passing physiognomy") would, over time, lead to permanent changes to the brain, producing a "fixed physiognomy".[206] He also suggested, however, that in addition to such "functional" causes of criminal physiognomy, there was also an hereditary or "pathological" element found among congenital imbeciles and the feeble-minded. He associates such hereditary causes with petty thieves, prostitutes and vagrants.

Sutherland thus distinguishes between the "professional" criminal, characterised by *acquired* physical traits—"the furtive, restless eye, a look of boldness, cunning and determination"—and the "pathological" petty delinquent with his *inherited* "stolid apathy of helplessness, [and] the abject look of passivity."[207] "In a very large number of instances" he adds, one finds a combination of functional and pathological influences, producing a "... striking physiognomy of a *composite* character, the appearances [of which can be] directly traceable to the mode of life lived being interwoven with evidences of mental defect, or mental warp of the genetous or acquired type."[208] He concludes that "there need be no doubt that many of the rank and file of both types are physically weak and degenerate, feeble-minded, mentally-perverted and obsessed in various directions ..."[209]

Sutherland seems to have been unusual among British practitioners of this period in identifying a physical type *specific to criminals*. More widespread, it seems, was the view which simply considered mentally-deficient prisoners as one—relatively common—manifestation of feeble-mindedness in general. The most well-known contemporary exponent of this view was Dr Alfred Tredgold (1870–1952), the psychiatrist whose paper Churchill would circulate to the Cabinet in 1911. Tredgold has been described as "perhaps the most influential Edwardian medical commentator on the problem of the feeble-minded"[210], and his study of mental deficiency—or *amentia*—first published in 1908, became the standard text on the subject.[211]

According to Tredgold, incorrigible criminals were by definition mentally deficient. How did he deal with the frequently-voiced objection that there existed habitual criminals with no moral sense but high intelligence, men like Sherlock Holmes' Reichenbach adversary, Professor Moriaty? Indeed, this had long been one of the key British objections to a Lombrosian catch-all criminal-type. No problem, retorted Dr Tredgold. The fact that such cerebral criminals were utterly unable to control their evil propensities when they knew full well that punishment had in the past followed and must certainly follow again, implies, he reasoned, "a serious defect of either judgement or of volition". They could not, therefore, be considered "intelligent".[212]

In this way, Tredgold neatly extends his category of the "criminal ament" beyond the well-established one of the "weak-minded offender" or "moral imbecile" to include *all* incorrigible habitual criminals, an example perhaps of what Nicole Hahn Rafter has described as "professional self-legitimation": "To advance themselves", she notes, "individuals occasionally attempted a hostile take-over of an adjacent jurisdiction, claiming ... to be better at identifying born criminals than were the current authorities."[213] In the same spirit, other experts on the feeble-minded like Mary Dendy (secretary to the Lancashire and Cheshire Society for the Permanent Care of the Feeble-Minded) tended to play down the significance of the "moral imbecile" category, emphasising that the numbers of moral defectives were insignificant in comparison with the plethora of cases of feeble-mindedness.[214]

As far as the physical characteristics of "criminal aments" were concerned, Tredgold considered them as in large measure "identical" to those of the mentally deficient in general.[215] Interestingly, he quotes evidence from such authorities as Havelock Ellis, Bruce Thomson, David Nicolson and of course Cesare Lombroso, to support his view. Since both criminal aments and aments in general both come from the same "neuropathic stock", he argues, it should come as no surprise to discover that they tend to share the same physical characteristics.[216] Indeed, he terms the most common kind of criminal ament, with no moral sense, as "the morally perverse or habitual criminal type".[217]

The evidence presented by Dr Treadwell of Parkhurst Prison, to the Royal Commission on Feeble-Mindedness illustrates the kind of mental and physical traits commonly attributed to mental deficiency. Treadwell makes the following generalisations about the weak-minded prisoners in his care:

> An appearance of congenital imbecility with vacancy of expression, dull and listless manner, variability of mood, purposeless and meaningless amusement or mirth and exaggerated emotional outbursts; coupled perhaps with coarseness of features, physical malformations, easily-apparent asymmetry, abnormally-shaped heads, deformed palates, etc.[218]

Dr Treadwell proceeds to provide a series of case-histories to support his general points, of which the following may be taken as an example:

> G.C., aged 22. One conviction in 1903 for robbery with violence. Offence committed with and of two other persons unknown. A brother and a sister had fits—no other history of insanity, epilepsy, alcohol or crime obtained. Parents of labourer class; had a good home, but bad companions; educated at industrial school; education standard IV; occupation, labourer; is a drunkard.

After listing G. C.'s previous convictions (twelve are itemised, covering the period 1888–1902, mostly for theft, plus sixteen further un-named "summary" offences), and noting in passing that the subject's "prison conduct" was "insubordinate", Dr Treadwell goes on:

> Palate high and narrow; head asymmetrical, and bears evidence of head injury when a child; facial expression dull and unintelligent. Moods variable, sometimes emotional and tearful, at other times morose and quarrelsome; of low intelligence and poor memory; little, if any, moral

> perception of the rights of others. Suffers from genuine epileptic fits and also feigns them. Easily led astray and not likely to keep from a career of crime. Unfit to take care of himself and requires control. Defect dates from childhood or is congenital.[219]

Interestingly, a case-book of Dr Treadwell's, covering the years 1904–1911, has survived among the archives held at Parkhurst Prison.[220] For each mentally deficient prisoner in his care (which apparently included those judged "insane" as well as the "feeble-minded"), room was left in the ledger for information on each inmate's "habits", "diseases", "stigmata" and "condition of mind previous to conviction"; striking testimony to the physiognomic as well as mental preoccupations of Edwardian psychiatry. William Brake for example, admitted to Parkhurst in October 1905, was described as a man of "irregular and intemperate habits", with a "low narrow forehead [and] from all accounts somewhat refractory and very suspicious". It was concluded that Brake was "unfit for prison discipline". Another inmate was credited with a "high narrow palate".[221]

As W. J. Forsythe points out, prison medical officers like Dr Treadwell, were—unlike asylum-based practitioners like Alfred Tredgold—caught on the horns of a dilemma. As an integral cog in the machine of prison discipline, they had little sympathy for the view which absolved criminals from responsibility for their acts. As we noted earlier, prison medical officers saw a key aspect of their role as being the flushing out of often ingenious prison "malingers". There was thus no question of accepting as a general principle Havelock Ellis's dictum that "we cannot punish a monstrosity for acting according to its monstrous nature". The views of prison medical officer Dr R. F. Quinton, expressed in his autobiography *Crime and Criminals 1876–1910*, are typical of this mind-set. Noting that in his experience the daily sick list amounted to about 10 per cent of the prison population, of whom "not more than a dozen needed medical treatment of any kind", Quinton wrote:

> It is not unlikely that I may be called a stony-hearted official for taking a cold common-place view of the treatment that is most calculated to reclaim prisoners and to reduce crime, but I have at all events more than an arm-chair knowledge of the subject, and more than a nodding acquaintance with the material to be experimented on. These credentials must be my excuse for denouncing a pampering system as one that is likely to cause much more harm than good. Pampering, in fact, is just as unsound in principle, and just as futile in practice with a naughty man as it is with a naughty child. ... If ... our prisons offered such attractions as are here described, thousands would avail themselves forthwith of a rest-cure under conditions that would really mean to them Oriental splendour and luxury.[222]

And yet, despite such talk of "pampering" and "Oriental splendour", many prison doctors genuinely believed that there were large—and perhaps growing— numbers of vagrants, inebriates and feeble-minded offenders who had inherited constitutional defects or acquired them as a result of harmful environmental pressures, and that for such prisoners the most appropriate penal solution was long-term supervisory or medical control.[223]

In the context of Edwardian England, the question of just where to draw the line between a congenital "feeble-minded" minority and the morally as well as legally responsible majority of "ordinary" prisoners could no longer be seen as a purely administrative or theoretical question. Since the beginning of the century, the Eugenics movement had been ramming home the argument that urgent action was necessary to isolate the "deficient" group from the rest of the community and prevent it from propagating itself. Only in this way, it argued, could the future health of the British race be guaranteed. From 1907, the debate intensified with the creation of the pressure group, the Eugenics Education Society. Both it and the National Association for Promoting the Welfare of the Feeble-Minded were campaigning hard for legislation to put into practice the findings of the 1908 Royal Commission.[224] Prison medical staff were thus drawn into the debate about national efficiency and eugenics, eager to discover "the truth or otherwise of various parts of that discourse as far as prisoners were concerned."[225] Experiments by Dr William Norwood East, deputy medical officer at Portland Public Works Prison, the results of which were published in 1901, are a good example of such curiosity. Subjecting his sample group to a barrage of physical and psychological tests, Norwood East concluded that Britain's recidivists had weak moral and physical sensibility compared with non-criminals, and accidental or occasional offenders.[226]

The following year, a much more ambitious research programme would be launched in order to settle once and for all the question of what exactly it was which distinguished the criminal from the non-criminal. The aims of the project, backed by the country's most senior prison doctors and financed by the Home Office, were two-fold, the second dependent on the success of the first. There was, it was felt, an urgent need to "register the extinction" of the "superstitious" theories associated with Cesare Lombroso. Only once such a demolition job had been completed, and the ground cleared as it were, would it be possible to "lay the foundation of a science of the criminal, truly accurate and unbiased by prejudice."[227] It would be eleven years before this research saw the light of day, and when its findings were published in 1913, it would indeed provide the wherewithal to hole Lombrosian criminal anthropology below the water. Why then would its sponsors come to disown some of the report's key conclusions, together with the prison doctor who had overseen the statistical analysis on which they were based?

Notes

1 Sir Bryan Donkin, "The State Punishment of Crime", *British Medical Journal*, 2 August 1913 (emphasis in original).
2 Quoted in Jackson, *Borderland of Imbecility*, p. 146.
3 Wiener, *Reconstructing the Criminal*, p. 10.
4 *Ibid.* (my emphasis).
5 *Ibid.*, p. 10.
6 David Garland, *Punishment and Welfare: A History of Penal Strategies*, Aldershot, Gower, 1985. For a similar approach to Garland's, see V. A. C. Gatrell, "Crime, Authority and the Policeman State", *in* F. M. L. Thompson (ed.), *The Cambridge Social History of Britain 1750–1950*, 3 vols., vol. 3: *Social Agencies and Institutions*, Cambridge, Cambridge University Press, 1990, pp. 243–310.
7 Michel Foucault, *Discipline and Punish: The Birth of the Modern Prison*, London, Penguin, 1977.
8 Michael Ignatieff, *A Just Measure of Pain: The Penitentiary in the Industrial Revolution*, London, Macmillan, 1978.
9 Michel Foucault, "The Eye of Power", in Sylvère Lotringer (ed.), *Foucault Live: Collected Interviews, 1961–1984*, New York, Semiotext(e), 1996, pp. 226–40.
10 Foucault, *Discipline and Punish*, p. 82.
11 Garland, *Punishment and Welfare*, ch. 2.
12 Foucault, *op. cit.*, pp. 128–29, 130, 138.
13 Daniel Pick, *Faces of Degeneration: A European Disorder, c. 1848–1918*, Cambridge, Cambridge University Press, 1989.
14 Quoted in Foucault, *op. cit.*, p. 139.
15 Janet Semple, "Foucault & Bentham: A Defence of Panopticism", *Utilitas*, vol. 4, no. 1, May 1992, p. 111.
16 There is some recognition of this in Garland's 1992 article: "Criminological Knowledge and its Relation to Power", *British Journal of Criminology*, vol. 32, no. 4, Autumn 1992, pp. 403–22: "... the (partial) 'scientization' of criminal justice could only occur to the extent that it was allowed to do so by the established participants—lawyers, judges, penal authorities, even offenders themselves ..." (p. 418).
17 Michael Ignatieff, "State, Civil Society and Total Institutions: A Critique of Recent Social Histories of Punishment", in Stanley Cohen and Andrew Scull (eds.), *Social Control and the State*, Oxford, Robertson, 1983, p. 83.
18 *Ibid.*, p. 82.
19 A key conclusion of W. J. Forsythe, *The Reform of Prisoners 1830–1900*, London, Croom Helm, 1987.
20 Stephen Watson, "Applying Foucault: Some Problems Encountered in the Application of Foucault's Methods to the History of Medicine", in Colin Jones and Roy Porter (eds.), *Reassessing Foucault: Medicine and the Body*, London, Routledge, 1994, pp. 139, 148.
21 Ignatieff, *op. cit.*, p. 95.

22 Marshall Sahlins, *Waiting for Foucault, Still*, Chicago, Prickly Paradigm Press, 2002, p. 20. Sahlins is the author of an interesting work seeking to combine anthropology and history: *How "Natives" Think About Captain Cook, for Example*, London, University of Chicago Press, 1995.
23 Wiener, *Reconstructing the Criminal*, p. 8.
24 Wiener, *op. cit*, pp. 160, 240, 174, 186, 226 [my italics].
25 *Ibid.*, p. 338.
26 *Ibid.*, p. 228.
27 Stedman-Jones, *Outcast London*, p. 127.
28 Wiener, *op. cit.*, pp. 184, 217.
29 Thomas Holmes, *Known to the Police*, London, Arnold, 1908, pp. 10–11, quoted in Wiener, *op. cit.*, p. 346.
30 Quoted in *ibid.*, p. 351. For similar views, see *ibid.*, p. 345.
31 Stedman-Jones, *op. cit.*, ch. 16.
32 Forsythe, *The Reform of Prisoners*, p. 188.
33 Wiener, *op. cit.*, p. 10.
34 Bailey, "English Prisons, Penal Culture", pp. 285–324.
35 William J. Forsythe, *Penal Discipline, Reformatory Projects and the English Prison Commission*, Exeter, Exeter University Press, 1991; *idem.*, "The Garland Thesis and the Origins of Modern English Prison Discipline", *The Howard Journal*, vol. 34, no. 3, August 1995, pp. 259–73.
36 Leon Radzinowicz and Roger Hood, *The Emergence of Penal Policy in Victorian and Edwardian England*, Oxford, Clarendon Press, 1990 [first published as vol. 5 of *A History of English Criminal Law*, London, Stevens and Sons, 1986].
37 Bailey, *op. cit.*, pp. 302–3; Forsythe, "The Garland Thesis", pp. 268–70.
38 Bailey, *op. cit.*, pp. 312–13 [my emphasis].
39 Forsythe, "The Garland Thesis", p. 268 [my emphasis].
40 Radzinowicz and Hood, *The Emergence of Penal Policy*, pp. 16–17.
41 Garland, "Of Crimes and Criminals", p. 32.
42 Forsythe, "The Garland Thesis", p. 271 [my emphasis].
43 David Garland, "The Criminal and his Science", *British Journal of Criminology* vol. 25, no. 2, April 1985, p. 122.
44 J. Morel, "The Psychological Examination of Prisoners", *Journal of Mental Science*, vol. 39, 1892, pp. 13–14, quoted in Sim, *Medical Power in Prisons*, p. 60 [my emphasis].
45 "Report from the Departmental Committee on Prisons", *Parliamentary Papers*, 1895, vol. 56, p. 12.
46 Cf. Cole, *Suspect Identities*, pp. 56–57: "... penologists and criminologists were not able to follow through on the individualising project. Criminal anthropology, for all its supposed attention to individuals, could only shuffle individuals into a bestiary of deviant 'types': idiots, imbeciles, morons, lunatics, epileptics, moral imbeciles, degenerates, defective delinquents, born criminals, criminaloids, prostitutes and so on.... Thus they achieved 'individualised' treatment by sorting inmates back into general types."
47 Wiener, *Reconstructing the Criminal*, chs. 8–9.
48 It should be noted (*pace* Forsythe and Bailey) that the partial acceptance among the "moralists" of the role of environmental factors in generating criminal behaviour indicates a limited acceptance of the "positivist" agenda. In this sense, I

would agree with Bailey's point (*op. cit.*, p. 309), that "it is misleading ... to see humanitarianism as the antithesis of social science.... Rather the Edwardian years point to a more complex relationship between the two. A reinvigorated humanitarianism accompanied the rise of positivist criminology. As a result, humanitarians began to use more deterministic language, and to propose more 'scientific' remedies."

49 Cf. The subtle analysis of José Harris, *Private Lives: Public Spirit: Britain 1870–1914*, Harmondsworth, Penguin, 1994, pp. 244–45.

50 Adam, *Police Encyclopaedia*, vol. 5, p. 8.

51 "Crime and its Treatment", *The Lancet*, 14 October 1893, p. 940; [Untitled], *The Lancet*, 24 February 1894, p. 487.

52 *The Lancet*, 12 October 1895, p. 911, quoted in Sim, *Medical Power in Prisons*, p. 61.

53 "The Psychology of Crime", *The Lancet*, 7 December 1907, pp. 1613–14.

54 Ferri, *Criminal Sociology*, p. 56. See also Morrison, "Reflections", pp. 14–15 for a discussion of this point.

55 Adam, *op. cit.*, p. 9 [my emphasis]. Nicole Hahn Rafter and Mary Gibson have recently come to similar conclusions concerning Adam's later work on female crime, *Women and Crime* (London, Werner Laurie, 1914): "Adam begins by rejecting criminal anthropology out of hand, ... But he goes on to parrot Lombroso, ... Despite his mockery, Adam produces a book substantively close to [Lombroso's] *The Female Offender*" (Lombroso and Ferrero, *Criminal Woman*, trans. and ed. Rafter and Gibson, "Editors' Introduction", p. 24).

56 Mercier, *Crime and Criminals*, pp. 40, 227.

57 *Ibid.*, pp. 232–33.

58 *Ibid.*, p. 236.

59 *Ibid.*, p. 282. See also Charles Mercier, *British Medical Journal*, 1 October 1904, p. 861; C. Mercier, letter to *British Medical Journal*, 15 October 1904, quoted in Forsythe, *Penal Discipline*, p. 13.

60 Lombroso, *Crime, its Causes and Remedies*, p. 447.

61 Griffiths, *Proceedings of the Fourth Congress of Criminal Anthropology*, p. 8.

62 *Ibid.*, p. 14.

63 *Congrès international*, pp. 340–47; 364–74.

64 *Ibid.*, p. 342.

65 Griffiths, *Proceedings*, p. 20; *Congrès international*, p. 344. In his memoirs, published in 1894, Griffiths described criminals as "generally incorrigible". (*Secrets of the Prison House*, p. 40).

66 Griffiths, *Proceedings*, p. 20; *Congrès international*, pp. 344–47.

67 Griffiths, *Secrets of the Prison-House*, vol. 1, pp. 22–23.

68 *Ibid.*, p. 23.

69 *Ibid.*, pp. 23, 39.

70 *Ibid.*, pp. 24–25.

71 *Ibid.*, pp. 32–40.

72 L. Gordon Rylands, *Crime: Its Causes and Remedy*, London, Fisher Unwin, 1889, p. 29.

73 *Ibid.*, p. 35.

74 *Ibid.*, pp. 43, 35, 251–52.

75 Rylands, *op. cit.*, pp. 37, 42.

76 In 1889, Henry Maudsley described the essential criminal as someone capable of "some intellectual acuteness of a low order ... sharpened by continual exercise ... to a fine edge of low, fox-like cunning" ("Remarks on Crime", p. 163).
77 Wiener, *op. cit.*, p. 126.
78 *Ibid.*, p. 342.
79 Steadman-Jones, *Outcast London*, pp. 281–85, 295.
80 *Ibid.*, p. 286. See also Pick, *Faces of Degeneration*, pp. 180, 201–3; Harris, *Private Lives*, pp. 241–5; Richard A. Soloway, *Demography and Degeneration: Eugenics and the Declining Birthrate in Twentieth-Century Britain*, 2nd edition, London, University of North Carolina Press, 1995, pp. 39–41.
81 Lord Brabazon, *Social Arrows* (1886), quoted in Steadman-Jones, *op. cit.*, p. 308.
82 Arnold White, *Problems of a Great City* (1887), quoted in *ibid.*, p. 223.
83 Soloway, *op. cit.*, p. 39. The quotation is from F. W. Farrar (1888).
84 *Ibid.*, pp. 286–287.
85 Arnold White, "The Nomad Poor of London", *Contemporary Review*, vol. 47, May 1885, p. 715.
86 H.M. Hyndman, "English Workers as they are", *Contemporary Review*, vol. 52, July 1887, p. 129.
87 Daniel Pick, (*op. cit.*, p. 215) describes him as "one of the more extremist degenerationist scaremongers". See Arnold White, *The Problems of a Great City* (London, 1886). In later years, White would serve on the council of the Eugenics Education Society, and took the creed seriously enough to boycott his own son's wedding on the grounds that the latter's fiancée was "eugenically unsuitable" (Soloway, *op. cit.*, p. 54).
88 See Eugene S. Talbot, *Degeneracy: Its Causes, Signs and Results* (London, 1898) and Albert Wilson, *Unfinished Man: A Scientific Analysis of the Psychopath or Human Degenerate* (London, 1910). Talbot's book was published by The Walter Scott Publishing Company in the same "Contemporary Science" series as Havelock Ellis's *The Criminal* (1890).
89 Pick, *op. cit.*, p. 184.
90 Wiener, *op. cit.*, pp. 244–56.
91 David G. Horn notes that similar conclusions could be drawn from Lombroso's montage of German and American criminals reproduced in the "atlas" volume accompanying later editions of *Criminal Man*: "Far from reassuring, it appears to be a montage of the citizens of the modern European city; readers could reasonably be expected to bring the scrutiny of the criminologist to their encounters on the streets of Turin, Paris, London and New York. A generalised anxiety—that everyone was potentially dangerous, if not equally so—was only partially assuaged by the hope that the bodies of the truly dangerous would signal their difference" (*The Criminal Body*, p. 143).
92 *Ibid.*, pp. 245–46.
93 There is a certain irony in the fact that a technique which would come to be seen as a key weapon in the fight against the criminal Moriarties of this world was first developed in the 1870s and 1880s as a way of identifying those at the other extreme of the Victorian social hierarchy. In both the British colonies and in America, early advocates of "dactyloscopy", as it came to be known, saw fingerprinting above all as a way of identifying racial groups considered, from the white European standpoint, to be physiologically homogenous. In the context of immigration control

and colonial policing, fingerprinting provided a much-needed way of identifying racial "otherness" where written description or even photography were considered inadequate. On this point, see the fascinating account in Cole, *Suspect Identities*, chs. 3, 5.

94 *Ibid.*, pp. 100–7.

95 Francis Galton, "Personal Identification and Description", *Nature*, vol. 38, 1890, p. 201.

96 Francis Galton, "The Patterns in Thumb and Finger Marks", *Proceedings of the Royal Society*, vol. 48, 1890, pp. 455–7. A more popular version of the same paper appeared in the journal *Nineteenth Century*: "Identification by Finger-Tips", *Nineteenth Century*, vol. 30, 1891, pp. 303–11. His ideas were most fully developed in *Finger Prints*, London, 1892.

97 Cole, *op. cit.*, p. 107.

98 *Ibid.*, p. 100.

99 Charles Féré, *Dégénérescence et criminalité: essai physiologique*, Paris, 1888.

100 On this laboratory, set up in 1906, see Chapter Five.

101 Cole, *op. cit.*, pp. 106–11.

102 Quoted in Forrest, *Francis Galton*, p. 217.

103 Systematic fingerprinting of criminals became official policy in Britain following the recommendations of the Belper Committee (1901): "Report of a Committee Appointed by the Secretary of State to Inquire into the Method of Identification of Criminals by Measurements and Finger Prints", London, Wyman and Sons, 1901. On the context, see Cole, *op. cit.*, pp. 90–94.

104 Sekula, "The Body and the Archive", p. 55. Interestingly though, Bertillon did not reject composite photography as such. In his 1890 book, *La Photographie judiciaire*, he observed that "composite photography or typical facial profiles" could be used to establish "ethnic, professional or picturesque types" (quoted in Phéline, *L'Image Accusatrice*, p. 66: my translation). It may be significant in this context that Bertillon had previously tried (and failed) to sort police mug-shots Galton-style into categories on the basis of their offence (A. Bertillon, *L'Identité des récidivistes et la loi de relégation*, Paris, 1883, p. 11, quoted in Sekula, *op. cit.*, p. 27). On Bertillon and his method, Phéline and Sekula are particularly useful. See also Henry Taylor Fowkes Rhodes, *Alphonse Bertillon, Father of Scientific Detection*, London, Harrap, 1956.

105 See Robert A. Nye, *Crime, Madness and Politics in Modern France*, Princeton, Princeton University Press, 1984, pp. 49–96.

106 "Report of a Committee appointed by the Secretary of State to inquire into the best means available for identifying Habitual Criminals", *Parliamentary Papers*, 1893–94, vol. 72, pp. 209–291. The committee, set up in October 1893, was chaired by Home Office civil servant, Charles Edward Troup. The other members were Melville Macnaughton of Scotland Yard's Criminal Investigation Division and Major Arthur Griffiths. Its report was issued in February 1894.

107 *Ibid.*, p. 18.

108 *Ibid.*, p. 28; Public Record Office HO 144/190/A46508B: "Documents relating to the use of the anthropometric system, 1893–6". Inquiries were made between November 1893 and February 1894 in Belgium, Austro-Hungary, Italy and India. Arthur Griffiths gives a typically colourful account of the committee's visit to Bertillon's Paris offices in his book, *Fifty Years of Public Service*, pp. 364–66, 368–77.

109 "Report of a Committee", pp. 28–30 (quotation at p. 28). Cf. Public Record Office PCOM 7/57: Sir Evelyn Ruggles-Brise, *Proceedings of the Fifth International Penitentiary Congress, Held at Paris in 1895*, London, HMSO, 1895. Ruggles-Brise noted that Bertillonage was "at present the best system for the rapid identification of criminals" (p. 48). For the point of view of a British champion of Bertillonage from this period, see Edmund R. Spearman, "Known to the Police", *Nineteenth Century*, vol. 36, 1894, pp. 356–70. Compare this with the more sceptical tone of Francis Galton's *Finger Print Directories*, London, 1895. Committee member Arthur Griffiths later referred to finger prints as "a more certain means of identification than any other; quite superior to Bertillonage" (*Fifty Years of Public Service*, p. 367). Possibly, this assessment was with the benefit of hindsight, for by the time Griffiths was writing (1904), Bertillonage had been definitively abandoned in favour of dactyloscopy. Historian Ronald R. Thomas raises the intriguing possibility that the penchant for fingerprinting among US and British law enforcement agencies may have been stimulated by the prominence of the technique in early detective fiction, such as the work of Arthur Conan Doyle and Edgar Allan Poe (Thomas, *Detective Fiction*, p. 207).

110 Cole, *op. cit.*, p. 51.

111 In Britain's scaled-down version of Bertillonage, just five measurements were taken: length/breadth of head; length of left middle finger; length of left forearm and length of left foot ("Report of a Committee", p. 30).

112 Bertillon introduced fingerprints into his system in 1894, possibly as a result of a suggestion by Galton, who had written to the Frenchman on the subject three years earlier (Forrest, *Francis Galton*, p. 222).

113 Cole, *op. cit.*, pp. 33–49.

114 *Ibid.*, p. 53.

115 Emsley, *The English Police*, p. 71.

116 Quoted in Wiener, *Reconstructing the Criminal*, p. 282.

117 Gatrell, "Crime, Authority and the Policeman State", pp. 290–91 [my italics].

118 *Ibid.*, p. 292.

119 *Ibid.*

120 In the local prisons, the average daily population fell from 18,000 to 13,500 between 1880 and 1995. For the convict prisons, there was an equivalent drop of 10,000 to 4,000 during the period 1878–1894 (Forsythe, *Penal Discipline*, p. 19).

121 Wiener, *op. cit.*, p. 342 and n. 11.

122 Sir Edmund Du Cane, "The Prison Committee Report", *Nineteenth Century*, vol. 38, August 1895, p. 287; Sir Evelyn Ruggles-Brise (1900), quoted in Radzinowicz and Hood, *Emergence of penal Policy*, p. 120.

123 J. F. Sutherland, *Recidivism: Habitual Criminality and Habitual Petty Delinquency: A Problem in Sociology, Psycho-Pathology and Criminology*, Edinburgh, William Green, 1908.

124 Petit, *Histoire des galères, des bagnes et des prisons*, pp. 270–71.

125 Wiener, *op. cit.*, p. 300; Pick, *Faces of Degeneration*, p. 182; Gatrell, *op. cit.*, pp. 306–10.

126 "Report from the Departmental Committee on Prisons", *Parliamentary Papers*, 1895, vol. 56, p. 5.

127 Forsythe, *Penal Discipline*, p. 21. See also McConville, *English Local Prisons*, ch. 4, 13; Radzinowicz and Hood, *Emergence of Penal Policy*, pp. 571–76.

128 Forsythe, *op. cit.*, p. 21. For a vivid impression of Du Cane's character, see Griffiths, *Fifty Years of Public Service*, ch. 18. He was, Griffiths recalls, "as sharp as a needle, … his mastery of details was almost phenomenal, … and he could carry long arrays of figures in his head, and marshal elaborate facts with the utmost precision.… He was easily moved to wrath, … and there were many unpleasant quarters of an hour for his subordinates when summoned to his presence.… As a rule, however, Sir Edmund mostly vented his wrath on paper, when he let his pen run freely, having first dipped it in gall.… [H]e had no advisors, no coadjutors; he would brook no interference, but did everything so to speak, off his own bat, with the assistance of his own clerks" (pp. 256–59).

129 *The Lancet*, 9 March 1895, quoted in Sim, *Medical Power in Prisons*, p. 51.

130 Quoted in Wiener, *Reconstructing the Criminal*, p. 328. For a similar vision of prison life at this period, see the published account of American fraudster Austin Bidwell, who served nineteen years of a twenty year sentence of penal servitude in England between 1873 and 1892. "An English prison", Bidwell wrote in his memoirs of 1895, "is a vast machine in which man counts for just nothing at all. He is to the establishment what a bale of merchandise is to a merchant's warehouse. The prison does not look on him as a man at all. He is merely an object which must move in a certain rut and occupy a certain niche provided for it. There is no room for the smallest sentiment. The vast machine of which he is an item keeps undisturbed on its course. Move with it and all is well. Resist, and you will be crushed as inevitably as the man who plants himself on the railroad track when the express is coming. Without passion, without prejudice, but also without pity and without remorse, the machine crushes and passes on. The dead man is carried to his grave and in ten minutes is as much forgotten as though he never existed" (Austin Bidwell, *From Wall Street to Newgate*, Hartford, Conn., Bidwell Publishing Co., 1895, p. 460). Bidwell's brother George, also given a life sentence in the same trial, but released early owing to ill-health, similarly wrote a book about his experiences: George Bidwell, *Forging His Chains: The Autobiography of George Bidwell*, Hartford, Conn., S. S. Scranton, 1888. The Bidwells' experiences are quoted at length in Philip Priestley, *Victorian Prison Lives: English Prison Biography 1830–1914*, 2nd edn., London, Pimlico, 1999.

131 Griffiths, *Fifty Years of Public Service*, p. 166.

132 W. Douglas Morrison, "Prison Reform: Prisons and Prisoners", *Fortnightly Review*, vol. 69, May 1898, p. 782.

133 Forsythe, *op. cit.*, p. 23. Radzinowicz and Hood (*op. cit.*, p. 574) are less certain that Morrison was indeed the author of these articles, stating that he may have played the role of a "trusted confidential advisor" instead.

134 Bailey, *op. cit.*, pp. 288–89; Forsythe, *Penal Discipline*, p. 27.

135 Radzinowicz and Hood, *Emergence of Penal Policy*, p. 265.

136 "Report from the Departmental Committee on Prisons", p. 31.

137 Petit, *Histoire des galères, bagnes et prisons*, p. 271; Michelle Perrot, "Délinquance et système pénitentiaire en France au XIXe siècle", *in idem.*, *Les Ombres de l'histoire: crime et châtiment au XIXe siècle*, Paris, Flammarion, 2001, p. 185.

138 Radzinowicz and Hood, *op. cit.*, p. 268.

139 *Ibid.*, p. 8 (my emphasis).

140 Philip Rawlings, *Crime and Power: A History of Criminal Justice, 1688–1998*, London, Longman, 1999, p. 108. For similar views, see Wiener, *Reconstructing the Criminal*, p. 346.

141 "Report from the Departmental Committee", p. 13.
142 Pick, *Faces of Degeneration*, p. 184. See also Radzinowicz and Hood, *op. cit.*, p. 267.
143 "Report from the Departmental Committee", p. 8, quoted in Pick, *op. cit.*, p. 183.
144 The term "moral imbecile" was often used as a synonym for the mentally-deficient incorrigible criminal. Cf. Jackson, *Borderland of Imbecility*, p. 141 and n. 92.
145 "Reports of the Directors of Convict Prisons", *Parliamentary Papers*, 1881, vol. 34, pp. 37–43.
146 *Ibid.*, p. 43.
147 Minutes of Evidence, "Report from the Departmental Committee", p. 312. Cf. Garland, "British Criminology", pp. 4–5: "As far as most prison doctors and experienced psychiatrists were concerned, the majority of criminals were more or less normal individuals; only a minority required psychiatric treatment, and this usually involved removing them from the penal system and into institutions for the mentally ill or defective."
148 Quoted in Wiener, *op. cit.*, p. 353 (n. 58).
149 W.C. Sullivan, "Eugenics and Crime", *The Eugenics Review*, vol. 1, no. 2, July 1909, p. 112.
150 *Ibid.*, p. 117 [my emphasis].
151 *Ibid.*, pp. 113, 119–20.
152 Minutes of Evidence, "Report from the Departmental Committee", p. 303 [my emphasis].
153 McConville, "The Victorian Prison", p. 138.
154 Evidence of Sir Edmund Du Cane and Sir Evelyn Ruggles-Brise, "Report from the Departmental Committee", pp. 362, 372, 346. See also Ruggles-Brise, *The English Prison System*, p. 208.
155 In the case of Ruggles-Brise, interpretation is further complicated by the fact that as Du Cane's subordinate during the Gladstone Committee hearings, he was by no means free to speak his mind. His evidence may thus, as Radzinowicz and Hood argue, tell us more about Ruggles-Brise's "loyalty to his chief and his diplomatic skill" than his personal opinions (*Emergence of Penal Policy*, p. 596).
156 Wiener, *op. cit.*, p. 348, 354; Radzinowicz and Hood, *op. cit*, p. 268; Watson, "'Malingers', the 'Weakminded' and the 'Moral Imbecile' ", p. 232.
157 Quoted in Wiener, *op. cit.*, p. 352.
158 Radzinowicz and Hood, *op. cit.*, pp. 272–78.
159 Public Record Office, PCOM 7/286: "Measures to deal with habitual criminals, 1899–1904". The above quotation comes from a response to a question put at the congress: "Are there any categories of offenders to whom the 'indeterminate sentence' could be applied, and according to what fashion could this system be realised?"
160 *Ibid.*
161 Sir Robert Anderson, *Criminals and Crime: Some Facts and Suggestions*, London, James Nisbet, 1907, pp. 24–25. See also *idem.*, "Our Absurd System of Punishing Crime", *Nineteenth Century and After*, February 1901, pp. 268–84; *idem.*, "Professional Crime", *Blackwood's Magazine*, vol. 159, February 1896, pp. 294–307.
162 Robert Anderson, *Criminals and Crime*, pp. 105–6.
163 Radzinowicz and Hood, *op. cit*, pp. 270–71; Forsythe, *Penal Discipline*, pp. 78–83.
164 "Report from the Departmental Committee", pp. 31–34.
165 Forsythe, *op. cit.*, p. 80.

166 McConville, "The Victorian Prison", p. 140
167 Quoted in Radzinowicz and Hood, *op. cit*, p. 274.
168 *Ibid*., p. 275; Forsythe, *op. cit*., p. 84.
169 Hilaire Belloc, speaking in the in the Commons debate on the bill in December 1908. Belloc (1870–1953), a successful poet, novelist and essayist was also a Liberal MP between 1906 and 1910 (quoted in Radzinowicz and Hood, *op. cit*., pp. 276–77).
170 In 1910, 177 sentences of preventative detention were imposed; in 1911 the number was 53 (McConville, *op. cit*., p. 141).
171 Radzinowicz and Hood, *op. cit*., pp. 281–87; Forsythe, *op. cit*., p. 88; Bailey, *op. cit*., p. 302.
172 "... positivism was only one, and not the most important, framework of social and political thought in the Edwardian debate on prisons." (*Ibid*., p. 305, n. 82).
173 Radzinowicz and Hood, *op. cit*., p. 283; Forsythe, *op. cit*., p. 87.
174 Quoted in *ibid*., p. 285.
175 On Churchill's policies whilst Home Secretary and his relations with the Home Office, see Forsythe, *Penal Discipline*, pp. 38–39, 66–69, 72, 87–89.
176 Wiener, *Reconstructing the Criminal*, pp. 354–55.
177 Quoted in G.R. Searle, *Eugenics and Politics in Britain, 1900–1914*, Leyden, 1976, p. 107.
178 A. F. Tredgold, "The Feeble-Minded—A Social Danger", *The Eugenics Review*, vol. 1, no. 2, July 1909, p. 104.
179 Matthew Thomson, *The Problem of Mental Deficiency: Eugenics, Democracy and Social Policy in Britain, c. 1870–1959*, Oxford, Oxford University Press, 1998, pp. 33 (and n. 131), 25–6. Leon Radzinowicz and Roger Hood quote the diaries of Churchill's friend and confident William Scawen Blunt, published in 1920: "He [Churchill] told us that he had himself drafted the Bill [on the Care and Control of the Feeble-Minded] which is to give power of shutting up people of weak intellect and so to prevent their breeding. He thought it might be arranged to sterilise them ... He thought that if shut up with no prospect of release without it many would ask to be sterilised as a condition of having their liberty restored" (quoted in *Emergence of Penal Policy*, p. 333). The authors discount the suggestion that Churchill was responsible for drafting the bill for what would become the Mental Deficiency Act (1913).
180 "Royal Commission on the Care and Control of the Feeble-Minded", 2 vols., *Parliamentary Papers*, XXXIV–XXXV, 1908, vol. 1, p. 3.
181 *Ibid*., p. 185. A notable exception was Chief Inspector of special schools, Dr Alfred Eicholz. In a classic piece of Lamarckian reasoning, he told the Commission: "There is much reason for believing that the feeble-minded are largely recruited from the considerable portion of physical degenerates in the poor urban areas ... In fact drink, phthisis, depravity of living in the parent are much more frequently associated with feeble-mindedness in the child than direct or even indirect heredity.... We shall always have the feeble-minded with us as long as physical degeneracy exists" ("Report of the Royal Commission on the Care and Control of the Feeble-Minded", vol. 2: Minutes of Evidence, *Parliamentary Papers*, 1908, vol. 35, pp. 205–6). See also his article: "The Treatment of the Feeble-Minded", *British Medical Journal*, vol. 2, 1902, pp. 683–87. Eicholz had played an important role in convincing the 1904 Physical Deterioration Committee of the strength

of the environmental case (Harris, *Private Lives*, pp. 244–45). Harris adds that Eichholz's proposals for dealing with the feeble-minded were "considerably more draconian than those of many supporters of the eugenics school" (*ibid.*, p. 245). Dr Frederick Mott, Pathologist and director of the Pathological Laboratory of the London County Council came to similar conclusions to Eicholz. Feeble-mindedness, in his view, was above all the result of a harmful "social environment of the slum population", characterised by "… deficient and imperfect food, unhealthy criminal and vicious surroundings, the crowding of whole families into one-roomed tenements with no separation of the sexes, or children from the adults, inevitably leads to mental and moral degradation" ("Royal Commission", vol. 2, p. 454).

182 Jackson, *Borderland of Imbecility*, pp. 209–10. See also Thomson, *op. cit.*, pp. 23–33; Radzinowicz and Hood, *Emergence of Penal Policy*, p. 318.

183 Harris, *Private Lives*, p. 245.

184 "The Feeble-Minded Criminal", *The Lancet*, 15 February 1908, p. 511.

185 Sullivan, "Eugenics and Crime", p. 116.

186 *Ibid.*, pp. 116–17.

187 "Royal Commission", vol. 1, pp. 123, 125. There were also, the Commission suggested, significant numbers of feeble-minded prisoners in the country's local prisons. Statistical evidence based on the examination of inmates by medical inspectors had revealed that 10% were "mentally defective", a "much larger [proportion] than is generally supposed (*ibid.*, p. 171). In 1901, feeble-mindedness specialist Mary Dendy put the figure of mentally deficient prisoners considerably higher than this, at three-quarters (Jackson, *op. cit.*, p. 140).

188 "Royal Commission", vol. 1, p. 125.

189 *Ibid.*, p. 127. In 1907 the Home Secretary had ruled that "mentally deficient prisoners" be placed in the permanent care of "selected warders" (Sim, *Medical Power in Prisons*, p. 63).

190 Manser, *Behind the Small Wooden Door*, p. 46.

191 *Ibid.*, p. 133.

192 Griffiths, *Proceedings of the Fourth Congress of Criminal Anthropology*, p. 8.

193 "Royal Commission", vol. 2, p. 277.

194 *Ibid.*, vol. 1, p. 117.

195 See ch. 5.

196 "Royal Commission", vol. 2, p. 276, vol. 1, p. 117.

197 "Psychology of Crime", *The Lancet*, 7 December 1907, p. 1614.

198 Jackson, *Borderland of Imbecility*, pp. 95–96.

199 "Royal Commission", vol. 1, p. 133.

200 Jackson, *op. cit.*, pp. 89–90.

201 *Ibid.*, pp. 90–109. For the details of these stigmata, strongly evocative of Lombrosian criminology, see *ibid.*, pp. 102–105. Interestingly, Alfred Tredgold experimented with mirrors to provide a simultaneous full-face and profile portrait of feeble-minded subjects in the same way as in the convict portraits favoured by the Home Office in the 1880s, as described in chapter 2 (*ibid.*, pp. 105–6).

202 Sim, *Medical Power in Prisons*, p. 64. See Sir William Norwood East, *The Relation of the Skull and Brain to Crime*, Edinburgh, Oliver and Boyd, 1928, p. 17–18. Norwood East, Medical Inspector for HM Prisons, gives the following defence of Tarde's theory of the "gaol look": "… if we accept modern psychological teaching

that the instincts and their accompanying emotions form the basis of character and temperament, and thereby affect human conduct; and if we consider that the emotional reaction is reflected in part by an alteration of facial expression, we can believe the features will show characteristic engraining from a frequently repeated emotion, or its corresponding mood if long continued." In a book published the previous year, he had observed that "the measurement of the head circumference may be of value" (*Introduction to Forensic Psychiatry*, 1927, quoted in Sim, *op. cit.*, p. 64). Norwood East was a key figure in British criminology in this period. In the 1930s he would become Medical Director on the Prison Commission and President of the Medico-Legal Society. His books *Introduction to Forensic Psychiatry* (1927), *The Medical Aspects of Crime* (1936) and *Report on the Psychological Treatment of Crime* (1939, co-authored with Dr W. H. de B. Hubert) were highly influential (Garland, "British Criminology", p. 9).

203 J. F. Sutherland, *Recidivism: Habitual Criminality and Habitual Petty Delinquency: A Problem in Sociology, Psycho-Pathology and Criminology*, Edinburgh, William Green, 1908.

204 *Ibid.*, p. 44.

205 *Ibid.*, pp. 38–44.

206 *Ibid.*, pp. 44–45.

207 *Ibid.*, p. 45.

208 *Ibid.*

209 *Ibid.*, pp. 12–13.

210 Jackson, *Borderland of Imbecility*, p. 91.

211 A. F. Tredgold, *Mental Deficiency (Amentia)*, 2nd edition, London, Ballière, Tindall and Cox, 1914.

212 *Ibid.*, pp. 320–21.

213 Rafter, *Creating Born Criminals*, p. 89.

214 Jackson, *Borderland of Imbecility*, p. 141. Cf. Mary Dendy, *Feebleness of Mind, Pauperism and Crime*, Glasgow, Provincial Committee for the Permanent Care of the Feeble-Minded, 1901; *idem.*, "The Feeble-Minded and Crime", *The Lancet*, 24 May 1902, pp. 1460–63.

215 Cf. His evidence to the Royal Commission on the Care and Control of the Feeble-Minded ("Royal Commission", vol. 2, pp. 398–404).

216 Tredgold, *Mental Deficiency*, pp. 321–23.

217 *Ibid.*, pp. 326–27. See also Jackson, *Borderland of Imbecility*, p. 141.

218 "Royal Commission", vol. 2, p. 246. Treadwell subsequently gives statistical "proof" of physical abnormality among Parkhurst's weak-minded prisoners: 74.3%, he concludes, have "abnormal" palates (*ibid.*, p. 251). Compare this with similar comments about the feeble-minded *as a whole*, quoted in Jackson, *op. cit.*, p. 94.

219 "Royal Commission", vol. 2, p. 250. Dr Mott of the Pathological Laboratory of the London County Council Asylums gives several similar examples, "illustrative of the feeble-mindedness and criminality of young persons who are temporarily detained in asylums". One 16-year-old is described with the following epithet: "Mania: Moral Insanity. Defective. Criminal Type" (*ibid.*, pp. 118–119).

220 Parkhurst Prison Archives: Case Book no. 800, Parkhurst Lunatic Asylum, 1904–1911.

221 *Ibid.*, ff. 2–3, 1. Unfortunately for our purposes, in most cases, these headings were left blank. See also Manser, *op. cit.*, p. 49.

222 Quinton, *Crime and Criminals*, pp. 18–19, 225–27, quoted in Sim, *Medical Power in Prisons*, pp. 58–59. On the details of malingering, see Priestley, *Victorian Prison Lives*, pp. 173–80.

223 Forsythe, *Penal Discipline*, pp. 153–54.

224 Thomson, *Problem of Mental Deficiency*, pp. 19, 33; Jackson, *Borderland of Imbecility*, pp. 212–13; Zedner, *Women, Crime and Custody*, p. 289.

225 Forsythe, *op. cit.*, p. 154.

226 William Norwood East, "Physical and Moral Insensitivity in the Criminal", *Journal of Mental Science*, vol. 47, 1901, pp. 737–58.

227 University College Library, University College London: Pearson Papers, 366: "Report upon the aims, methods, progress and results of a statistical investigation now being conducted for the prison commissioners at the Biometric Laboratory, University College by K[arl] Pearson", [1909?], p. 6. For a similar point concerning the harmful impact of Lombroso on the development of British criminology, see "The Feeble-Minded Criminal", *The Lancet*, 15 February 1908, p. 511. It quotes the views of Sir Bryan Donkin, one of those involved in the project at the start in 1902.

Chapter Five

The English Convict *and the Challenge of Eugenics*

The physical and mental constitution of both criminal and law-abiding persons, of the same age, stature, class and intelligence, are identical. There is no such thing as an anthropological criminal type.
Charles Goring, *The English Convict*, 1913[1]

Goring is more Lombrosian than Lombroso.
Gina Lombroso-Ferrero, 1914[2]

The best minds of today have accepted the fact that if superior people are desired, they must be bred; and if imbeciles, criminals, paupers and [the] otherwise unfit are undesirable citizens, they must not be bred.
Victoria Woodhull, *The Rapid Multiplication of the Unfit*, 1891[3]

William Forsythe has argued that "... the essential basis of reformatory prison discipline was an address to the prisoner as at heart rational, responsible and culpable albeit weaker or more mentally fragile than the norm and this classical base remained easily the firmest intellectual foundation of prisoner reformation between 1895 and 1939."[4] We argued in the last chapter that while this generalisation is unobjectionable in many areas of penal policy (and indeed provides a useful corrective to the unstoppable "onward march of surveillance and control" emphasised by some previous accounts), classical-cum-environmental explanations of crime enjoyed no monopoly in this period: indeed, in the case of the habitual weak- or feeble-minded offender, explanations based on deficient heredity held sway. In this latter case, moreover, there was a substantial degree of continuity both with earlier British theories of the "criminal-type", first formulated in the 1860s and '70s, and with some the key tenets of Lombrosian criminal anthropology. The habitual criminal served, in this sense, as an—often unacknowledged—"bridge" between the theories of the Italian School and those of its vociferous British critics.

In this chapter it will be argued that such a conception of the habitual offender, which remained dominant in the Edwardian period, would also provide a bridge between mainstream criminological thinking and the Eugenics movement. This is not to suggest that Britain's medico-penal Establishment adhered to the agenda of the Eugenics movement in its entirety; as we shall see, many penal administrators and prison doctors remained consistently and publicly hostile to the Galtonian creed. Rather, it will be suggested that British criminologists shared with the eugenicists a commitment to the incarceration and medical surveillance of a criminal or proto-criminal residuum of mentally deficient men and women, defined in terms of hereditary deficiency or degeneration. A further area of common ground between the two apparently warring camps was the idea that the segregation of mental defectives would fulfil the double objective of protecting the community from their depredations and preventing them from transmitting their degenerate seed to future generations. In this respect it is possible to detect a leakage of eugenicist assumptions into mainstream criminology, despite the latter's insistence that it was hermetic to such influences. However, the episode of *The English Convict*, with which we open this chapter, shows that the bridge between the Eugenics movement and the key players in the penal regime was a precarious one—a rope bridge perhaps?—and if too heavily laden, was likely to collapse under the strain.

Charles Goring's *The English Convict* (1913)

As early as 1889, at the second Congress on Criminal Anthropology in Paris, Italian positivist Baron Raffaele Garofalo (1851–1934) had suggested that an international commission be set up to carry out a large-scale study comparing the anatomical and physiognomic characteristics of the criminal and non-criminal populations. The work of this seven-man commission, its composition a deliberate reflection of the diversity of contemporary criminological opinion would, it was hoped, provide definitive evidence to either confirm or refute Cesare Lombroso's theory of the "born-criminal" type.[5] In the event, the commission never got off the ground; anti-Lombrosian commission members like Frenchman Léonce Manouvrier (1850–1927), despite their initial enthusiasm for the project, subsequently withdrew their support. Indeed, Manouvrier told the next congress in Brussels (1892)—boycotted by Lombroso and his colleagues—that the very idea of such a comparative study was, in his view, fundamentally flawed.[6]

Manouvrier suggested first of all that the selection of both the "criminal" and the "honest" samples for comparative study was problematic. The "criminal" was a legal rather than a scientific entity; part of a sub-category of deviants whose wrong-doing had been detected and successfully proven in a court of law (as Paul Topinard pointed out, their "criminal" status could therefore hang on the thread of a single jury vote).[7] There was thus nothing to prevent the "honest" group containing *de facto* law-breakers whose deviancy had simply escaped the attention of the police, or whose offence had not resulted in a successful prosecution.

Manouvrier did not stop there, however. Even if the two study groups *could* be satisfactorily established, he argued, a search for anatomical and physiological "stigmata" would not and could not, prove or disprove anything, for who was to say which physical characteristics were *genuine criminal stigmata*? Thus a physical feature which is considered an "anomaly" among criminals, loses its significance when it occurs in "honest men". As Manouvrier put it, "it is no good calling something a *beam* when you find it in a criminal and *straw* when you find it in an honest man."[8] The *principal* causes of crime, Manouvrier concluded, were to be found elsewhere, in the particularities of the social milieu.

At the next congress, held in Geneva in 1896, the Italians were back in town, and the controversy showed no signs of abating. Britain's official delegate, Major Arthur Griffiths, frustrated at the inconclusive nature of the debates, recognised the need for "more medical experiments on the links between physical traits and crime", a state of affairs which prompted him to recommend to the Home Office that research should be undertaken so that a "decisive opinion" might be reached.[9] As Marc Renneville notes, not without a certain Gallic regret, Manouvrier had lost his chance; the honour of demolishing the Lombrosian edifice would now pass to the English.[10]

There were a number of prison doctors qualified for such work: Dr James Scott of Holloway Prison, accompanying Major Griffiths to Geneva, had clearly been carrying out anthropometric measurements on the prisoners in his charge, and both Dr John Baker of Portsmouth Prison and Dr William Norwood East of Portland had also published research in this field in the 1890s and early 1900s. In the event, however, the project was placed in the hands of a small team led by Dr G. B. Griffiths (no relation), deputy medical officer at Parkhurst convict prison. 3000 English prisoners, convicted of similar offences, would be subjected to Lombroso-style anthropometric measurement to see if they deviated from the non-criminal population.[11]

Work by Griffiths and his team began in 1901, and from 1902 Britain's two most senior prison medical officials, Sir Bryan Donkin and Sir Herbert Smalley, respectively medical commissioner and medical inspector of prisons, joined the project. Measurements began to be collected from inmates at Parkhurst, Portland, Dartmoor and Borstal prisons and in 1904 results from a preliminary sample were ready for publication. An article authored jointly by Griffiths and Donkin listed measurements for such anthropometric stalwarts as the antero-posterior curve, the height, length and breadth of the cranium and facial symmetry.[12] By this time, however, co-ordination of the project had passed to Griffiths' successor at Parkhurst, Dr Charles Goring (1870–1919).[13] Under his leadership, the size of the convict population under study was extended to nearly 4000 prisoners, each of whom would be analysed in terms of 96 different variables. The collection of the data was completed in 1908; its analysis would take a further four years.[14]

Charles Goring had studied at University College London where he had distinguished himself in philosophy as well as medicine, attracting the attention of mathematician and close collaborator of Francis Galton, Professor Karl Pearson (1857–1936). A committed socialist, at least initially[15], Pearson had, in early adulthood, moved in a circle of late-Victorian and Edwardian freethinkers, Marxists and Fabians, which included Havelock Ellis, leading socialists Beatrice and Sidney Webb, Karl Marx's daughter Eleanor, playwright George Bernard Shaw, and birth-control pioneer Annie Besant.[16]

Like Galton, Pearson was fascinated by the application of statistical methods to evolutionary questions, and with Galton and biologist W. R. Weldon, he founded the academic journal *Biometrika* in 1901 to explore these issues. A privately-funded Biometric Laboratory followed in 1906. Pearson was by this time a convinced eugenicist. In 1907 he became the director of the Francis Galton Laboratory for the Study of National Eugenics, set up, like the Biometric Laboratory within his Applied Statistics department at University College, and after Galton's death in 1911, he would become the university's first Professor of Eugenics.[17]

The two laboratories instructed students in biometrics, assisted the projects of visiting research scientists, and issued joint publications. It was here that between May 1909 and November 1911, Charles Goring, on leave of absence from Parkhurst, came to analyse his data and prepare it for publication. The two men clearly worked closely together, as the voluminous body of correspondence in the archives of University College attests.[18] Pearson later described Goring as a man with "remarkable powers of sympathy … width of interest and … facility of expression"[19], and Goring reciprocated the compliment by quoting widely from the work of his *cher maître*, as he referred to Pearson in a letter of 1912.[20]

Although Goring published some preliminary results in 1909 in a series of research papers published by the Biometric Laboratory, his final results were not ready until 1912.[21] Well before that date, however, Home Office officials were convinced that Goring's results would put the final nail in the coffin of Lombrosian criminal anthropology. As Evelyn Ruggles-Brise put it in 1910, "The Lombrosian theories of the criminal-né [sic] are exploded. Our own investigations now being conducted into the physiology of crime will, I think, fire the last shot at this deserted ship."[22]

Goring claimed to have embarked upon his study of the physical characteristics of the British convict population with an open mind.[23] Not wishing to pre-judge the issue as to the relative significance of hereditary and environmental factors in generating crime, he set about measuring the extent to which the propensity to commit crime, what he termed "the criminal diathesis", was "associated with environment, training, stock, and the physical attributes of the criminal."[24]

When asked by Karl Pearson how he would react if Lombroso's "criminal-type" was confirmed by his own analysis, he replied that he would "accept it, as the foundation of criminology, but none the less condemn Lombroso as a traitor to science."[25] Goring's intemperate comments reflect his poor opinion of the Italian's scientific method, a view he shared not only with Pearson[26] but also with the French *milieu social* school of criminology, though he seems to have been largely unaware of the common ground he shared with some of his continental colleagues. He also displayed what Piers Beirne has called a "perplexing ignorance" towards the modifications made over the years by Lombroso himself to his theory of the atavistic born criminal (a failing shared by most British commentators on criminal issues). The theory with which Goring takes issue in *The English Convict* is thus the unalloyed Lombrosianism of the first 1876 edition of *L'Uomo delinquente*, not the multi-causal explanation of crime found in the book's later editions or in *Crime: Its Causes and Remedies*.[27]

Thus following unwittingly in the footsteps of French critics from the 1880s and '90s, Goring argued that in conjuring up his atavistic *criminal man*, Lombroso had more in common with the astrologer or alchemist than the rigorous scientific researcher.[28] The Parkhurst doctor considered that the methodology used by criminal anthropologists rode a coach and horses through every basic rule of statistical method. Thus means were calculated without publishing the raw data from which they were derived; measures of the variability and margin of error for the statistical series quoted were missing; there was no effort to control for such factors as differences of age, stature and intelligence in the criminal populations under study; and finally, controlled comparisons between the criminal and non-criminal populations had been woefully neglected.[29]

Goring also charged Lombroso with a fundamental error regarding the epistemological status of the category "criminal". Like Léonce Manouvrier before him, he reminded his readers that the term "criminal" only designated the legal fact of an individual who had been imprisoned, it was not a scientific description of a category of individuals sharing certain *abnormal* characteristics. In an indirect attack on the notion of a "criminal-type", Goring berated the "unfortunate tendency to theorise as to the existence of *abnormal types* of human being".[30] Statistically unusual qualities were not necessarily *abnormal*: "criminologists, although they make frequent use of some standard [of what is normal], have consistently evaded its definition."[31]

Thus Goring could argue:

> The 'facts' of criminal anthropology, gathered by prejudiced observers employing unscientific methods, are inadmissible as evidence either for, or against, [Lombroso's born criminal] type. The criminal may be a real thing; but if so, it is despite of, not because of the spurious evidence of its supporters; its existence may be scientifically proved by future investigation.[32]

In fact, Goring's own analysis did *not* confirm that Lombroso's anatomical and physiognomic stigmata accurately defined the convict population; on the contrary. He investigated the connection between criminal behaviour and thirty-seven physical and mental traits commonly alluded to in Lombrosian criminology, including stature, distance between the eyes, head circumference, left-handedness, weight, hair colour and cephalic index.[33] He surmised that if these "stigmata" did exist, they would be most in evidence where the "criminal diathesis" was strongest, amongst habitual criminals convicted of serious crimes. He thus classified his 2,348 male convicts into groups according to length of sentence and gravity of offence and looked for statistical correlations with Lombroso's thirty-seven stigmata. He failed to find strong statistical relationships between particular crimes and physical and mental characteristics, and he was unable to identify a specifically "recidivist" type either. He concluded that

> ... *no evidence has emerged confirming the existence of a physical criminal-type, such as Lombroso and his disciples have described.* Our data shows that physical differences exist between different kinds of criminals: precisely as they exist between different kinds of law-abiding people. But, when allowance is made for a certain range of probable variation, and when they are reduced to a common standard of age, stature, intelligence and class, etc., these differences tend entirely to disappear.[34]

In short, the "anthropological monster", familiar from the work of the Italian School, had "no existence in fact".[35]

Goring provided some additional—and for our purposes striking—evidence to support his conclusions, by reproducing in the frontispiece to *The English Convict* thirty of the convict profiles sketched by Dr Vans Clarke (taken from Havelock Ellis's book, *The Criminal*) alongside thirty specially-commissioned line drawings, based on convict photographs. In both cases, Goring constructed a Galton-like composite portrait, combining thirty individual faces into one generic one. When the two composites were compared, the result could brook no argument. The uneven features of Clarke's so-called likenesses, still visible in the composite in the form of a low forehead and prominent jaw, were entirely absent from the equivalent image generated by the objective evidence of the camera lens.[36]

However, Goring did not leave matters there. His initial brief had been to establish "How and why, if at all, does a criminal differ physically and mentally, in health and disease, from law-abiding persons?"[37] In seeking to answer this question, he had found no statistical evidence for Lombroso's atavistic "stigmata", but that did not mean that his control group of "law-abiding persons" was necessarily identical to the "criminal" group. He thus needed to compare his convict sample with a control group of non-criminals. The latter was a motley assortment, chosen for convenience and ease of access.[38] It included a company of the Royal Engineers (already used by Galton as paragons of "health" in his *Inquiries into Human Faculty*), undergraduates from Oxford, Cambridge and Aberdeen, and nearer to home, staff from University College. Controlling for age, social class and the effects of imprisonment, he compared height, weight, arm span, general health, physical constitution, muscularity and obesity in the two target populations. The comparison yielded the following conclusion:

> [I]t appears to be an … indisputable fact that *there is a physical, mental, and moral type of normal person who tends to be convicted of crime*: that is to say, our evidence conclusively shows that, on the average, the criminal of English prisons is markedly differentiated by defective physique – as measured by stature and body weight; by defective mental capacity – as measured by general intelligence; and by anti-social proclivities – as measured apart from intelligence by length of sentence of imprisonment.[39]

As far as the physical characteristics of the typical convicted prisoner are concerned, Goring speculated "with some hesitation and little persuasiveness", as Piers Beirne puts it[40], that "physique selects crime". In other words, certain physical traits would come in useful for particular kinds of crime – a developed musculature for violent crime for example – and a generally inferior physique would make capture by the police more likely.[41] Goring's conclusion on this point began by emphasising that criminals were "selected" in this way, but significantly, did not rule out the possibility that these physical traits could become, as it were, "fixed" by heredity:

> … the inferior stature and weight of criminals is the result of selection, and is not an inbred criminal trait. A possibility, however, not to be lost sight of, is that this physical inferiority, although originating and fostered by selection, may tend with time to become an inbred characteristic of the criminal classes.[42]

For Goring, however, it was congenital "*mental* defectiveness", which constituted "the principle constitutional determinant of crime".[43] Karl Pearson reiterated this point in his introduction to the 1919 abridged edition of *The English Convict*, where he described criminality as "hereditary, … not crime as a legal offence, but that so-called 'high-class mental defectiveness', the social ineffectiveness, which, given the occasion or environment, leads almost certainly to the commission of crime." "In this sense", Pearson concluded, "I think we make take as a working hypothesis that crime is more largely a result of nature than of nurture." As he had put it in starker terms in a lecture given in 1900, "You cannot change the leopard's spots, and you cannot change bad stock into good."[44]

Pearson's conclusion needs to be seen in the context of a second, largely implicit, objective of Goring's research project.[45] In fact, *The English Convict* fired off a double broadside, its target not only Ruggles-Brise's "deserted ship" of criminal anthropology, but also an older vessel: the statistical tradition, born in France and Belgium, stressing the influence of environmental factors in explaining patterns of criminality.[46] This second objective of *The English Convict* needs to be placed in the context of the eugenicist agenda of the whole biometrics enterprise with which the Parkhurst doctor had become so closely involved. Goring's intellectual influences can be seen clearly in the authorities he cites in support of his attack on environmentalism, which are drawn almost exclusively from the works of Eugenicists like Pearson, Francis Galton or the populist literature of the Eugenics Education Society.[47]

Goring's conclusions on the impact of the environment on criminal behaviour were in a sense even more categorical than those of Lombroso himself (thus giving partial succour to the comment made by Lombroso's daughter and editor, Gina Lombroso-Ferrero, to the effect that Goring was "more Lombrosian than Lombroso"):

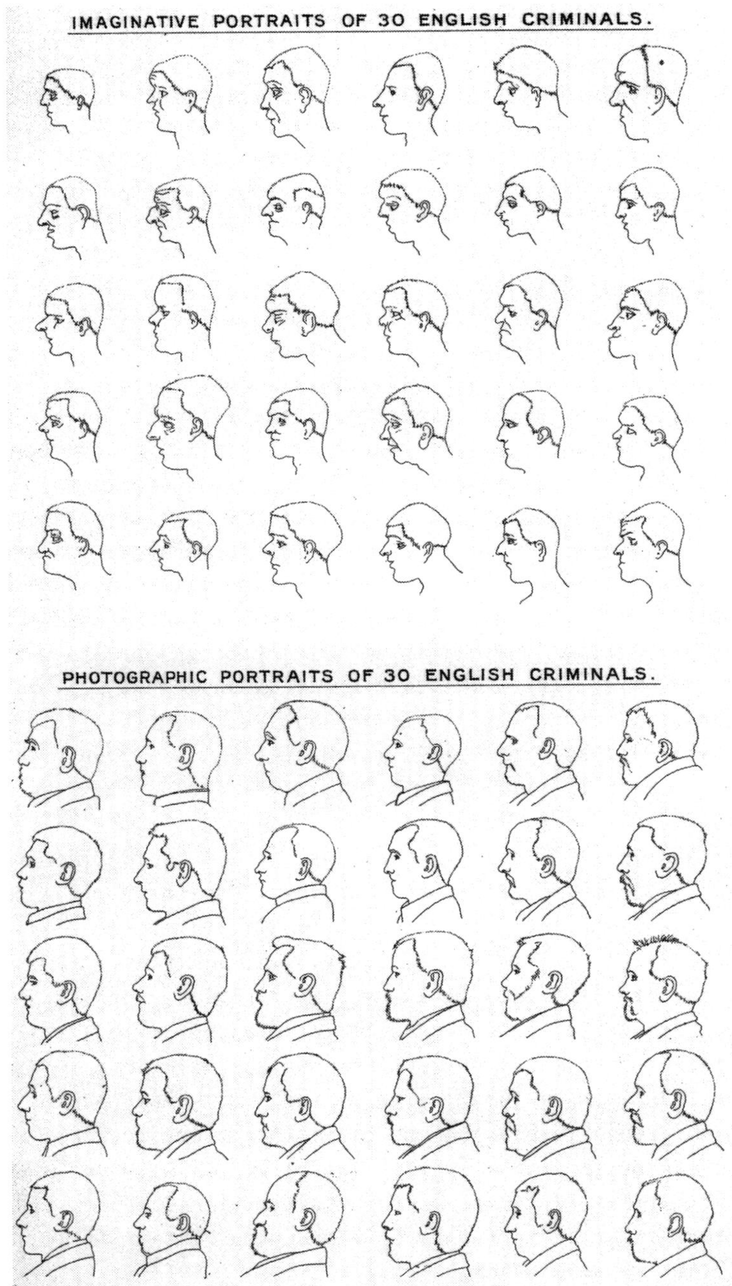

Imaginative and Photographic Portraits of 30 English Convicts Compared, 1913
Charles Goring, *The English Convict: A Statistical Study*, London, HMSO, 1913, frontispiece.

> [O]ur interim conclusion is that, relative to its origin in the constitution of the malefactor, and especially in his mentally defective constitution, crime in this country is only to a trifling extent (if to any) the product of social inequalities, of adverse environment, or of other manifestations of what may be comprehensively termed the force of circumstances.[48]

Goring shared the view taken as read among eugenicists that, as he put it, "the criminal diathesis, revealed by the tendency to be convicted and imprisoned for crime, is inherited at much the same rate as are other physical and mental qualities and pathological conditions in man."[49] He admitted the possibility that "appropriate educational measures" could "modify the inherited tendency to crime" (though he had largely ruled out the effect of "parental contagion" in explaining the genesis of criminal behaviour[50]). However, he concluded that education on its own was not sufficient to solve the crime problem. He proceeded to advocate what had by then become the familiar eugenicist policy of segregation and supervision of the "unfit", but did not stop there. It would be necessary, Going wrote, in order to attack "the evil at its root", "*to regulate the reproduction of those degrees of constitutional qualities – feeble-mindedness, inebriety, epilepsy, deficient social instinct, etc. – which conduces to the committing of crime.*"[51] In short, Goring had singled out a number of categories of offender for forced sterilisation, a controversial suggestion, as we shall see, even among convinced eugenicists.

Goring's *The English Convict* was the first large-scale statistical comparison of criminals and non-criminals, and its findings fast became a talking-point among criminologists everywhere. There was, in a sense, something for everyone in the book's conclusions. On the international stage, it was Goring's combat with Lombroso's "anthropological monster" that attracted the most attention. In Italy, where the book's impact has been described as a "bombshell"[52], it was welcomed by neo-classicists, while Enrico Ferri argued that Goring's reaffirmation of heredity in generating criminal behaviour was at least in part a vindication of Lombroso. Some American Lombrosians took a similar line[53], though more generally Goring's influence on the other side of the Atlantic has been described as "more decisive perhaps than any other factor in undermining belief in an anthropological criminal-type."[54] Among French and German criminologists, in contrast, the book was seen as providing conclusive evidence that they had been right all along in their vehement opposition to the Lombrosian project.[55]

In Britain, reactions were both more muted and more complex. Unsurprisingly, the book's conclusion that criminals constituted a mentally and physically deficient sub-category of the population was warmly welcomed by the Eugenics movement. Major Leonard Darwin, the second-youngest of Charles Darwin's five sons, expressed open support for Goring's findings in his presidential address to the Eugenics Education Society in July 1914. The fact that the habitual criminal had not turned out to be an "anthropological monster", was not sufficient reason, he argued, to conclude that the effects for posterity of letting such individuals breed freely could be ignored. Goring had found upwards of 100 000 criminals who had committed six or more crimes. Eugenics, observed Darwin, could at least do something about the worst of these cases: "... some relative increase in the powers of resistance of our nation in the future could be obtained even if only a proportion, small or great, of the criminal members of bad families were prevented from becoming parents."[56]

Karl Pearson, for his part, wrote a laudatory introduction for the abridged edition of *The English Convict*, published in 1919.[57] Pearson praised the Prison Commissioners for their "unusual boldness" (not exactly an unalloyed compliment) and went on to assure the members of that august body that "all future criminologists will be grateful for their courage." His most fulsome praise, however, was reserved for the author of *The English Convict*:

> He started with no theory, he took his facts and analysed them by the modern statistico-mathematical method. Until that was achieved, he neither knew what would come out of them, nor desired one result rather than another to be the culmination of his investigations. ... It is not too much to say that in the early chapters of Goring's work he clears out of the way for ever the tangled and exuberant growths of the Lombrosian school.[58]

Official reaction was more circumspect. The book was published by the Home Office, with a lengthy preface by President of the Prison Commission, Sir Evelyn Ruggles-Brise, apparently an official stamp of approval. There were mutterings in the Home Office, however, that Goring's notion of the "criminal diathesis" was, in its way, as deterministic as the theories of the Italian master himself, and would "appeal to the popular imagination ... [generating] a superstition as difficult to eradicate as was Lombroso's". There was also the view that great sums of public money did not need to be spent to confirm what every right-thinking Englishman already knew, namely that Lombroso was a charlatan. The style of Goring's work grated too: "... arguments ... so elaborate and so much disfigured by the excessive use of algebraical symbols" were appropriate, perhaps, for biometrics-obsessed "admirers of Dr Karl Pearson", but it was felt that people would not be queuing up to buy *The English Convict.*[59] As W. J. Forsythe concludes, "the Home Office was not only suspicious of policies based on mere intellectual theories, but were worried more generally about the effect of publication by employees of the Prison Commission on public opinion."[60]

Such concerns may explain why the Home Office seems to have hesitated before publishing *The English Convict.* In 1912, the government department had apparently not even deigned to reply to Goring's repeated "direct inquiries" addressed to Dr Smalley. The Parkhurst doctor confided his frustration in a letter to Karl Pearson written in April 1912, in which he complained of the "oppressive … silence, this lack of interest and senseless waiting". He added that he was "deeply depressed by it all".[61] Finally, on September 18, Goring received a letter announcing that *The English Convict* was to be published by HMSO. On hearing the news, he wrote back, enquiring if the work was to be published as a "Blue Book". He received the following curt reply: "You are mistaken in your assumption that the work is to be published as a 'Blue Book'. It is to be a Stationery Office publication, which is a very different thing."[62]

Sir Bryan Donkin too, despite his early involvement in the project, spoke out strongly against *The English Convict.* In two highly critical articles written in 1917 and 1919 for the *Journal of Mental Science,* he questioned the fundamental assumptions behind Goring's biometrics-based method: "even correct generalisations … concerning convicted criminals in the mass", he stated bluntly, "are not likely to be of much positive value in the treatment of individuals." He also challenged the Parkhurst doctor's conclusions concerning the central role of heredity in explaining criminal behaviour, emphasising instead the importance of environmental factors. "The only important link between the study of crime and that of biological heredity", he wrote, "is the fact that a considerably larger minority of persons with clearly appreciable mental defect, apparently of a congenital nature, is found among convicted criminals than in the population at large."[63] In his 1919 article, he emphasised that only a small minority of prisoners were irredeemable (a marked contrast with the tenor of his 1908 talk on "The Feeble-Minded Criminal").[64] His experience on the advisory committee at Camp Hill Preventative Detention Prison had taught him that even incorrigible "habituals" were rarely beyond hope of reform.[65]

Dr Charles Mercier, President of the Psychological Section of the British Medical Association, joined the fray with his 1918 book *Crime and Criminals,* in which he echoed Manouvrier's points about the difficulties of constituting a scientifically valid sample of "criminals". Mercier argued that Goring's sample of criminals was flawed in two ways. Firstly, generalisations could not be ventured about the "criminal diathesis", when the statistical data was derived entirely from the *convict* population. Secondly, Goring's statistics only concerned *convicted* criminals, responsible, according to Mercier, for only 15% of all crimes. Thus, Mercier concluded, "Of the 85% of perpetrators of indictable offences we know nothing at all, and the only conjecture we are justified in making with respect to them is that they are probably more intelligent than those from whom Dr Goring's data are drawn."[66]

Sir Evelyn Ruggles-Brise, in contrast, had initially been enthusiastic about Charles Goring's research, seeing it as providing useful support for his ideas about specialised and individualised punishment for "feeble-minded" habitual offenders.[67] However, when he had digested Goring's comments about the "criminal diathesis", he became concerned that the Prison Commission was appearing to sanction the view that *all* criminals were innately predisposed to commit crime, and could not therefore be held responsible for their actions.[68] Thus in his preface to *The English Convict*, Ruggles-Brise accepted that "… the broad and general truth which emerges from this mass of figures and calculations is that the 'criminal' is, to a large extent, a 'defective' man, either physically or mentally", but insisted that Goring's "theory of defectiveness" was not "to be pressed so far as to affect the liability to punishment of an individual for his act." [69]

Ruggles-Brise repeated his conviction that "physical and mental defectiveness" was concentrated among "persons living on a low economic scale"; a "residuum of individuals whose mental and physical state" does not enable them to live up to standards expected by the rest of society. Such a conclusion would, he added,

> … fortify and stimulate all those who desire that there shall be fewer persons suffering from those incapacities which predispose to crime, or that, where incapacity is obvious and can be defined, special steps shall be taken not to expose such a person without care and oversight to the conditions of free life, which are likely to be not only ruinous to himself, but dangerous to the community.

In this way, Ruggles-Brise reached a conclusion which was very different from that elaborated by Goring himself. Whereas the Parkhurst doctor had concluded that crime was "only to a trifling extent (if to any) the product of social inequalities", the President of the Prison Commissioners hinted (in Wiener's "optimistic" mode) that crime could be reduced as a result of intervention aimed at addressing "those incapacities which predispose to crime", presumably a reference to improving those social and economic disadvantages conducive to crime.

In one sense this was an ironic finale to Goring's research. While there was widespread agreement that the Parkhurst doctor had delivered the final *coup de grâce* to Lombrosian criminal anthropology, the reservations expressed by Ruggles-Brise regarding *The English Convict* were precisely the same as those put forward elsewhere by himself and others to explain why the Italian professor's theory of the born criminal-type could not be applied wholesale to the Britain's convict population. True, Goring's "physical, mental and moral type of normal person who tends to be convicted of crime" did not systematically possess Lombroso's check-list of anatomical and physiognomic abnormalities (as the latter had in fact recognised, albeit apparently unbeknown to Goring[70]), but there were nonetheless striking similarities between the conclusions reached by the "anthropological monster" and his slayer. In both cases, crime was considered to be above all a hereditary condition, and one characterised by both "defective physique" and "defective mental capacity". As Marie-Christine Leps has observed, "Finally, no matter how strongly he ridiculed Lombroso, Goring himself ended up with the same results under slightly different labels."[71]

In fact, reactions among Goring's British contemporaries to *The English Convict*'s substantive conclusions were conditioned in large part by how they stood with regard to the eugenics movement in general, a movement with which the Parkhurst doctor had become inextricably linked by his close institutional and personal connections with Professor Karl Pearson and the latter's Biometric Laboratory at University College London. Both Sir Bryan Donkin and Dr Charles Mercier, for example, were well-known opponents of eugenics.[72] At a 1904 session of the newly-formed Sociological Society, chaired by Karl Pearson, Mercier had listened to Francis Galton read a paper called "Eugenics: Its Definition, Scope and Aims".[73] In the ensuing discussion, Mercier had expressed his doubts about the biometric method of the eugenicists, arguing that:

> [B]roadly and generally, and in practice ... we cannot predict from the parentage what the offspring is going to be, and we cannot go back from the offspring and say what the parentage was. If we follow the custom of the Chinese and ennoble the parents for the achievements of their children, are we to hang the parents when the offspring commit murder?[74]

He continued to oppose the dominant hereditary explanation of crime in his evidence to the 1908 Royal Commission on Feeble-Mindedness[75], and in the following decade, spoke out publicly on a number of occasions against those of his profession supporting the eugenicist approach to understanding crime.[76] In a 1917 article in *The Practitioner*, for example, written in response to a previous piece by Dr Alfred Tredgold on "Moral Imbecility", he criticised the latter's notion of "stigmata of degeneracy", describing his notion of "neuropathic stock" as "mere figment".[77] As for Donkin, he also crossed swords with Tredgold, in the letters pages of *The Times*, this time over the issue of the sterilisation of prisoners.[78]

Such comments leave little doubt about the views of Mercier and Donkin, but were they any more representative of opinion among prison doctors, psychiatrists and penal administrators of the period than those of their common sparring partner, the psychiatrist and eugenicist Alfred Tredgold? In short, what precisely *was* the influence of "eugenics" in criminological discourse in this period?

The Eugenics Movement and Crime

The term "eugenics" was not a new one; its etymology goes back to the 1880s, and the ideas behind it even further. The word had been coined in 1883 by Francis Galton. Already a renowned explorer, cartographer and meteorologist, it was, according to his own account, the publication of Charles Darwin's *On the Origin of Species* in 1859 which led Galton to turn his attention to questions of heredity.[79] Galton considered the effect of reading his cousin's book a life-changing experience, what he later called "a marked epoch in my own mental development". He had, he wrote, "devoured" the book's contents, "and assimilated them as fast as they were devoured", a fact that he put down with typical Galtonian logic to the "hereditary bent of mind" that both he and Charles had inherited from their common grandfather, Dr Erasmus Darwin.[80]

The precise reasons for this radical change of direction in Galton's researches remain unclear, high-powered genes not withstanding. Some have seen in his growing obsession with questions of heredity a reflection of his own worries about his infertile marriage[81] or else a desire to banish lingering intellectual self-doubt (he had had to cut short his studies at Cambridge following a nervous breakdown) by including himself among those fortunate souls with an inherited tendency to genius. Intellectual self-doubt may also have contributed to his choice of human heredity as a field of study. Daniel Kevles has pointed to the fact that Galton tended to be drawn to subjects which in scientific terms were somewhat off the beaten track, and thus amenable to solitary—and thus non-competitive—endeavour.[82] The first tangible evidence of his new interest in heredity was an article for *Macmillan's Magazine* in 1865,[83] later expanded into his first book on the subject, *Hereditary Genius*, published in 1869.[84] Although the word "eugenics"—the name Galton gave to what he called the science of improving human stock—would not exist for a further fourteen years[85], the basics of his later theories were already in place.[86]

Of course, Galton was not the only "Darwinian" to deduce from *Origin of Species* that with the mechanism of natural selection apparently in abeyance, there was an urgent need for human intervention to preserve the biological "fitness" of the human race. In this way, one reading of Darwin combined apparently seamlessly with that body of thought, discussed earlier in this book, associated with the work of French alienist B. A. Morel in the late 1850s, emphasising the "degenerative" effects of modern urban life. That such "degeneracy" was endemic in Britain's towns and cities, Galton was in no doubt. In *Hereditary Genius*, he wrote:

> It is perfectly distressing to me to witness the draggled, drudged, mean look of the mass of individuals, especially of women, that one meets in the streets of London and other purely English towns. The conditions of their life seem too hard for their constitutions, and to be crushing them into degeneracy.[87]

Some, like Herbert Spencer, believed that the struggle for survival would ensure that such weakened specimens of the human race would be forced to adapt or die out; some that degeneracy bred infertility thus providing a "natural" solution to the problem. Others—Galton among them—took a less sanguine view of the problem. What then was to be done about the fact that as Galton would later write, "Our human civilised stock is far more weakly through congenital imperfection than that of any other species of animal, whether wild or domestic"?[88] Nature could clearly not be left to its own devices. The complexity of modern English life required more brains than even mid-Victorian England possessed. Galton's book, *Hereditary Genius*, provided part of the answer to this brain shortage, spelling out how, by selective breeding, it would be possible and "quite practicable to produce a highly gifted race of men by judicious marriages during several consecutive generations."[89] In this way, "what Nature does blindly, slowly, and ruthlessly, Man may do providently, quickly and kindly."[90]

It was such a view which had led Galton in 1865 to advocate state-sponsored competitive examinations in hereditary merit, with public ceremonies for the winners, marriages for the chosen few in Westminster Abbey, and public grants to support the genetically-favoured offspring of their unions. Galton had the comforting example of his own family history to support his case here. Whereas his cousin Charles Darwin had married Emma, grand-daughter of pioneering industrialist Josiah Wedgwood,

Galton's own wife Louisa was the daughter of the Reverend George Butler, former headmaster of Harrow and Dean of Peterborough. Louisa's four brothers were all successful academically; one went on to become Master of Trinity College, Cambridge and two others followed their father's example and became headmasters of public schools.[91] The idea of taking steps to encourage the marriage and reproduction of such cerebrally-blessed individuals was what Galton would later refer to as "positive eugenics". Schemes similar to Galton's—such as the awarding of eugenic "stripes" to racially superior World War One veterans in the hope of making them more attractive to potential wives—would remain a mainstay of British eugenics into the first decades of the twentieth century.[92]

Those whose genetic material deserved such cosseting could be identified—or so Galton believed—by measuring their reputation, or that of their families, through such means as biographical dictionaries of "eminence" or by poring over the obituary columns of *The Times*. Eminent families would produce future eminences in their turn. In *Hereditary Genius*, Galton analysed thirty-seven well-known literary figures and their relatives, including Seneca, Madame de Sevigné, Spinoza and Walter Scott, and proved to his satisfaction that "the men who achieve eminence and those who are naturally capable, are, to a large extent, identical."[93] It was such men—Galton put the figure at 1 in 4000 of the British male population—who would constitute the "highly gifted race of men" which the country so desperately needed. Although Galton accepted in principle the notion that the genetically well-endowed were to be found at all levels of the social hierarchy, he confidently assumed that such men would have the intellectual wherewithal to fight their way to positions of eminence. It was therefore natural that as this genetic leavening operated over the centuries, the cerebrally-superior would come to be concentrated in the upper levels of society. *Hereditary Genius* claimed to have provided statistical proof for just such a concentration.[94]

What about those whose services the country could usefully dispense with. How were they to be identified? It was clear in general terms who they were: the shuffling, hollow-eyed Londoners of whom Galton had written in 1869, those "delicate English men and women with narrow chests and weak chins, scrofulous, and otherwise gravely affected" which filled the country's asylums, prisons and hospitals.[95] Galton's interest in anthropometry, intelligence testing and his experiments with "composite photography" can all be seen as part and parcel of his eugenics-based desire to find what he considered to be an *objective* method to sort out the sheep from the goats, to determine by means of mental and physical measurement just who were the members of this degenerate underclass. It was only when such a classification process was complete that thought could be given to the problem of how to stop the proliferation of this "evil, ... eating like a cancer into the constitution of the people".[96]

Time, however, was running short. It was taken as read that the feeble-minded were inconveniently more fecund than their cerebrally-superior brethren. "The weaker the *Intellect*", remarked leading specialist on the subject, Mary Dendy, "... the greater appears to be the strength of the reproductive faculties."[97] Equally alarmist was Dr Alfred Tredgold. In a paper read in 1911 to the Manchester and Salford Sanitary Association on the subject of "The Problem of the Feeble-Minded", he warned:

> It is the steady, persevering, industrious, progressive, and capable members (whatever may be their social status) who are having fewer children; whilst the insane, the feeble-minded, the paupers, the criminals, and the whole parasitic class of the country are continuing to propagate with unabated and unrestricted vigour.[98]

The result was that, as Galton put it in 1909, "a considerable part of the population has already become bearers of germs of degeneracy", representing "a very serious and growing danger to our national efficiency." The situation was thus bad, and getting worse. If let loose on an unsuspecting community, such feeble-minded individuals would inevitably "go to the bad". This was not, Galton added, because of any innate viciousness, "but from the absence of will-power to resist temptations; and [thus they] quickly sink into the pauper and criminal classes." Only some drastic medicine would save Britain's racial stock from such contamination, and the consequent "gradual deterioration and ultimate ruin".[99] The 1908 Royal Commission on the Feeble-Minded had made a good start in identifying the problem, but there was still no statutory power permitting the "compulsory detention" of the mentally defective; no government department to oversee operations. Without such co-ordination, Galton argued, "eugenic victory" would remain elusive.[100]

Galton had been hammering home this message since 1901, returning in old age (he was seventy-nine) to theories he had first developed almost forty years earlier. If Galton's basic ideas had changed little in the intervening period, turn of the century Britain was a very different place from that of his middle years. The country had spent three years and £250 million fighting an inconclusive war against the Boers in South Africa (1899–1902)—a considerable blow in itself to imperial pride—and what is more had been forced to face the unpalatable truth that many of its young men were below the medical standards required to fight in the British Army (three out of five were being rejected as physically unfit, according to a calculations made in Manchester in 1899).[101] "Where to Get Men?", asked a Major General despairingly in an article in the *Contemporary Review* in 1902.[102] Indeed, with such puny specimens of British manhood on the streets of the country's towns and cities, it was not only His Majesty's armed forces and empire which now seemed at risk. How could British industry be expected to compete with the rising stars of the industrial firmament, with the United States, or (particularly) with imperial Germany?[103]

Hereditary degeneration was not of course the only way to explain such deterioration, but that such deterioration had occurred was taken as read. An Inter-Departmental Committee on Physical Deterioration, established in 1903 within the Home Office and the Local Government Board was the government response to these widely-voiced concerns. While those called to give evidence before the committee disagreed on the causes of the phenomenon, "nearly everyone", points out Richard Soloway, "agreed that the evidence of deplorable ill-health and physical incapacity was indisputable".[104] In fact only a minority of witnesses argued that heredity was the prime culprit in the production of "degenerates"; most accorded greater importance to such environmental causes as malnutrition, poor housing, drunkenness, parental neglect and inadequate medical care.[105] The report (published in 1904) conjured up an image of "persons usually of the lowest type, steeped in every kind of degradation and cynically indifferent to the vile surroundings engendered by their filthy habits", a state of affairs which represented "a grave menace to the community". Urgent intervention was required, the report concluded, particularly in the field of child healthcare.[106]

The falling birth rate of this period—down by a fifth since the 1870s[107]—took on an ominous significance in the context of such physical deterioration. Perhaps the poor health of those taking the King's shilling and the dearth of babies was part of the same problem: Britain's racial stock (described significantly as "de-Germanized" by Balfour in 1904[108]) was losing its vigour, increasingly unable to meet the heavy demands being placed on its shoulders by the country's imperial, military and economic responsibilities. It was noted with alarm in 1912 that while Germany's population was increasing at a rate of 900,000 a year, Britain could only manage an annual increment of 111,500. Perhaps the country's fertility levels would soon be rejoining those of France, at that time holder of the European wooden spoon for birth rates. The spectre was thus raised of Britain finding itself in a position where the "number of births [would be] insufficient to maintain the native population."[109] As a *Times* leader of 1913 put it after considering the various explanations of the declining birth rate, "the one question the answer to which all must dread comes uppermost: not whether the birth-rate is falling, but whether the fertility of our people is falling."[110]

It was against this background that the apparent proliferation of the feeble-minded seemed particularly alarming, threatening to engulf the country's "superior stock" in her hour of need. As historian of mental deficiency Mathew Thomson has argued, "Mental defectives became such a potent subject for concern because they provided a symbol which linked these overlapping anxieties about moral, demographic and racial decline".[111] The Royal Commission on the Care and Control of the Feeble-Minded had acted as an important catalyst in the growth and institutionalisation of the British eugenics movement. It is no accident that the movement's campaigning pressure group, the Eugenics Education Society, was set up in 1907 while the Royal Commission was hearing evidence.[112]

For the next five years the Society, whose declared aim was "to modify public opinion and create a sense of responsibility in the respect of bringing all matters pertaining to human parenthood under the domination of eugenic ideals … [to] affect the improvement of the race"[113], lobbied the Liberal government intensively to act on the recommendations of the commission, even coming up with its own "Feeble-Minded Control Bill" when ministers appeared to be dragging their feet. In 1913, the Mental Deficiency Act was passed, setting up a central Board of Control which would oversee the essentially locally-organised provision of institutional care for mental defectives.[114] While some—like Leonard Darwin[115]—were concerned about those categories of criminals beyond the purview of the act, the latter was widely interpreted within the Eugenics movement as a major victory for its programme of radical reform. If there was an element of wishful thinking in this—there was in fact close to universal support for institutional provision for the feeble-minded, supported as it was by the Royal Commission on the Feeble-Minded, a second Royal Commission on the Poor Laws (1909) and the vast majority of expert opinion—this was nevertheless the high point of eugenic influence, and eugenicists could look forward to more sweeping eugenics-inspired (as they saw it) legislation in the future.[116]

Those considered most valuable in the struggle to achieve future "eugenic victory" (Galton's phrase of 1909) were the professional middle classes, precisely those occupational groups most actively involved in the eugenic movement—principally scientists, doctors and university lecturers:

> The eugenic solution to social problems, employing as it would the statisticians' figures, the biologists' studies, the psychologists' tests, the social workers' case reports and ultimately the psychiatrists' custodial care or the surgeons' scalpel, was one which would give potentially full play to the skill of the developing scientific professions.[117]

However, even the growing size and influence of the professions in this period were of no comfort to the dyed-in-the-wool racial pessimists of the eugenics movement, for in their eyes, more professionals simply meant that standards were being lowered as "new" members, recruited from "inferior stock" were joining the previously select few. As for the presence of more middle-class women in their ranks, there was the fear that the Nation's "best women" were thereby "refus[ing] their natural and most glorious burden" for the fripperies of intellectual or worldly endeavour.[118]

Such concerns reflected what Geoffrey Searle sees as being at the heart of British eugenics: a fear about the likely consequences of "differential class fertility".[119] Karl Pearson characteristically put the problem in statistical terms. In a widely-quoted formula, he calculated that 25% of parents were producing 50% of the next generation.[120] What this meant in practice was that by 1911, the doctors, scientists, clergymen and bankers of Classes I and II whose families were complete had an average of 3.4 children, compared with a figure of 6.1 for the labourers, dockers and coal miners at the other end of the social scale. All the contemporary evidence suggested that this class differential would not close. On the contrary.[121] The evidence was ripe for a eugenicist interpretation. In the 1903 Huxley lecture read to the Anthropological Institute, Karl Pearson drew what for many was the patently obvious conclusion: "The mentally better stock in the nation is not reproducing itself at the same rate as it did of old; the less able and the less energetic are more fertile than the better stocks."[122] Or in the more colourful language of Dr Alfred Tredgold, while fertility among the "best elements" was in sharp decline, "the whole parasitic class of the nation" was continuing to reproduce itself "with unabated and unrestricted vigour."[123]

What was needed, according to Havelock Ellis, was for government to concentrate its efforts on "the point of reproduction"; in other words, on "the regulation of sexual selection between stocks and individuals as the prime condition of life".[124] Indeed, concentrating on ameliorative social and economic reform ("the point of production"), was not only a distraction, it threatened to actually make the situation *worse*. As Karl Pearson pointed out in 1900 (indicating that his socialist days were far behind him), "A hundred years ago you hung a rogue if you caught him. Nowadays, you provide him with soup-kitchens and night-shelters up and down the country, and leave him to propagate his kind at will."[125] There was thus something in the left-wing jibe that eugenics was "just now the most fashionable version of *laissez-faire*."[126]

Galton himself placed particular emphasis—as he had always done—on "positive eugenics", as the title of his 1901 return to the eugenics fray, "The Possible Improvement of the Human Breed under the Existing Conditions of Law and Settlement", indicates.[127] In this lecture given to the Anthropological Institute, he did, however, touch on the other strand of eugenics in his discussion of the recent sociological survey of London by Charles Booth (1840–1916). Booth's work, *Life and Labour of the People in London*, of which ten volumes had already been published, attracted a great deal of contemporary interest, and marked the successful marriage of new statistical techniques of sociological inquiry with the older tradition of social exploration described earlier in this book.[128]

Booth had begun his research in the 1880s in the East End of London, later expanding his study to the rest of the Capital. He divided London's population into eight classes (A–H), with classes A–D considered to be below the poverty line. From his researches, Booth calculated that nearly a third (30.7%) of the population in London was living in poverty, a much higher figure than his contemporaries had imagined.[129] At the bottom of Booth's hierarchy was "Class A", comprised of "occasional labourers, loafers and semi-criminals". He describes the members of this class as follows:

> Those I have attempted to count consist mostly of casual labourers of low character, and their families, together with those in a similar way of life who pick up a living without labour of any kind. Their life is the life of savages, with vicissitudes of extreme hardship and occasional excess. Their food is of the coarsest description, and their only luxury is drink. … [From this group] come the battered figures who slouch through the streets, and play the beggar or the bully, or help to foul the record of the unemployed; these are the worst class of corner men who hang round the doors of public-houses, the young men who spring forward on any chance to earn a copper, the ready materials for disorder when occasion serves. They render no useful service, they create no wealth: more often they destroy it.[130]

While Booth was at pains to point out that London's criminals were not drawn entirely from this class ("there are many in class A who are not criminals"[131]), his labelling of this group as "savage semi-criminal" or "vicious", tended to undermine such caveats. He emphasised that this group (which was significantly coloured in black on the maps of London on which he plotted the geographical distribution of each class) was much smaller than in the past, "a small and decreasing percentage, a disgrace, not a danger"[132]:

> This savage semi-criminal class of people had its golden age in the days when whole districts of London were in their undisputed possession. They mainly desire to be let alone, to be allowed to make an Alsatia[133] of their own. Improvements in our eyes is destruction in theirs. Their discontent is the measure of our success. On the other hand, the impression of horror that the condition of the class makes upon the public mind today is out of all proportion to that made when its actual condition was far worse, and consequently the need to deal with the evils involved becomes more pressing. … The outcasts [however, oppose …] dumbly, the efforts of philanthropy or order, their instinct of self-preservation seeks some undisturbed sanctuary where they can herd together, and, secured by the mutual protection of each other's character for evil, keep respectability at bay.[134]

The older tradition of social exploration did not pall in the face of Charles Booth's armoury of tables and coloured maps. On the contrary, it drew on them to provide statistical succour and up-to-the-minute terminology for its own output.[135] Turn-of-the-century social explorers emphasised the gulf separating the residuum from the rest of society. Peter Keating notes the significance of the term "abyss" often used to describe this gap, contrasting it with the image of ethnographic inquiry preferred by Mayhew and his contemporaries:

> You don't journey to an abyss: you descend or fall into it. It is all very well claiming that a Dark Continent lies at one's doorstep but that metaphorically is more welcome than a gaping hole. And what may walk out of an African rain forest is one thing, what *climbs* out of an abyss is quite another.[136]

Thus works like *In Darkest England and the Way Out* (1890) by William Booth, *The People of the Abyss* (1903) by American novelist Jack London, or *From the Abyss* (1902) by Charles Masterman, all depict a brutalised, barely-human residuum at the bottom of society. The emphasis was no longer on individual or family suffering (as in Mayhew), but on the undifferentiated mass of this "submerged tenth" of the urban population: these "weird and uncanny people" now congesting our streets, "emerging like rats from a drain" (Masterman); "beasts of prey in human shape …a population sodden with drink, steeped in vice, eaten up by every social and physical malady" (Booth); or "miserable multitudes, street upon street, [like …] so many waves of a vast and malodorous sea lapping about me and threatening to well up over me" (London).[137]

It may be, as Gareth Steadman-Jones has argued, that this "literature of crisis" represents a belated response to the social and political unrest of the 1880s.[138] Masterman, for one, recalled the time when the residuum had held "the richest city of the world" in the "hollow of their hands" as they "brushed the police away like an elephant dispersing flies."[139] Indeed, in the decade or so before Galton's re-launch of eugenics, there were ambitious plans afoot to physically isolate the residuum from the rest of the community. This was part of that "major re-orientation of middle-class attitudes towards the casual poor" which, according to Steadman-Jones followed the Trafalgar Square Riots of February 1886:

> … fear of the casual residuum played a significant part in provoking the intellectual assault which began to be mounted against laissez faire both from the right and the left in the 1880s. … At a time when the residuum might overrun London, this policy of laissez faire was dangerous. It was urgent that society should take active steps to disperse this class which would otherwise continue to increase and degenerate.[140]

The most popular of the projects aimed at achieving such "dispersal" was broached at the beginning of the 1890s in General Booth's *In Darkest England*. He advocated the creation of "labour colonies" for this underclass, "so incorrigibly lazy that no inducement … will tempt them to work; … so inveterately dishonest that theft is to them a master passion."[141] For this class, "hereditarily wanting in the qualities necessary to enable them to hold their own", the only solution, Booth believed, was "permanent seclusion".[142] General Booth favoured shipping the residuum out to the colonies overseas (what another supporter of the idea called "the wonderful safety valve we possess in our vast colonial empire"[143]); others, like Charles Booth, favoured the creation of labour colonies in the countryside around London, where "their half-fed and half-idle and wholly unregulated life" would be exchanged for "a disciplined existence, with regular meals and fixed hours of work (which would not be short)."[144]

In his 1901 Huxley lecture, Galton quoted with approval remarks by Charles Booth to the effect that "there appears to be no doubt that it [class A] is now hereditary to a very considerable extent", and with regard to habitual criminals came up with a similar suggestion to that urged ten years previously by Booth for the residuum as a whole: "… it would be an economy and great benefit to the country", Galton stated, "if all habitual criminals were resolutely segregated under merciful surveillance and peremptorily denied opportunities for producing offspring."[145]

However, Galton did not elaborate on this point, and soon returned to what he clearly considered to be the main priority for eugenicists, "increasing the productivity of the best stock"; an objective he described as "so noble in its aim that it might well give rise to the sense of a new religious obligation."[146] In similar lofty terms, leading Edwardian eugenicist and Fabian socialist Caleb Saleeby referred to the "Scientific Patriotism" of the eugenics creed. Was it not "well worth society's while that the genius and the saint, the athlete and the artist, should provide posterity, rather than the idiot, the criminal, the weakling, the Philistine"?[147] Indeed, it has been argued that the emphasis of the British eugenics movement as a whole in this period up to the First World War remained principally on the possibilities afforded by "positive eugenics", what Leonard Darwin referred to as "the judicious mating of mankind".[148]

In the USA, in contrast, eugenicists like David Starr Jordan, Harry H. Laughlin and Dr Harry Sharp campaigned vigorously for compulsory sterilisation for the "unfit".[149] In 1907, Indiana was the first US state legislature to introduce a law for the sterilisation of "confirmed criminals, idiots, rapists and imbeciles" if, as the Act put it, "procreation is inadvisable and there is no probability of improvement of the mental condition of the inmate". Even before the law was passed, Dr Sharp, physician to the Indiana State Reformatory at Jeffersonville had performed 465 vasectomies – without anaesthetic – on prisoners in his charge. More than a third were said to have requested this "simple and easy to perform" operation.[150] Between 1907 and 1917, a further eleven American states had enacted sterilisation laws.[151] By the mid-1920s, according to one estimate, over 3,000 habitual criminals had been sterilised. [152]

Although this general distinction between the American and British eugenics movements holds good, there *were* voices active in British eugenics in the early years of the twentieth century urging similar policies to those being pursued across the Atlantic. One of the most vociferous was Dr Robert Reid Rentoul, a medical practitioner from Liverpool, and author of several alarmist works in the early 1900s.[153] In a typical book, *Proposed Sterilisation of Certain Mental and Physical Degenerates* (1903), Rentoul began by noting "the appalling state of physical and mental degeneracy in this country." The problem would not require human intervention, he goes on, were Nature left to get on with its work unhindered. Lunatics would "naturally" commit suicide (thereby bringing a welcome reduction in running costs for the nation's asylums), and physically and mentally unfit couples would gradually succumb to miscarriage and ultimately, to absolute sterility.[154]

Rentoul considered the various options for tackling the problem. Killing the children of degenerate parents was ruled out on the grounds of natural justice (society was to blame, not the "poor victims" themselves), while forbidding marriage between degenerates would merely have led to a surge in degenerate illegitimacy. As for the widely-canvassed option of permanent segregation, that, argued Rentoul, would place an unfair burden on the shoulders of British taxpayers.[155] That left only compulsory sterilisation, the best solution, in the author's view, for those who are "not unfit for citizenship, [but ...] unfit to beget healthy offspring". Rentoul placed in this category the weak-minded, lunatics, epileptics, those suffering from leprosy, cancer, serious heart, lung or kidney problems, or indeed "any specific disease liable to be passed from parent to offspring"; plus "confirmed" tramps, vagrants and criminals. The operation would be a simple one, he concluded cheerfully, and could be sanctioned by a county sterilisation board, composed of medical, psychiatric, legal and penal experts, plus a representative from the local county council.[156]

If Rentoul's was not exactly a lone voice, he was part of a small minority—even among eugenicists—advocating forced sterilisation of the unfit.[157] Among the other members of this select group were Cambridge University physicist W. C. D. Whetham and his wife Catherine. Their 1909 book, *The Family and the Nation: A Study in National Inheritance and Social Responsibility* left no room for equivocation. There was only one way, they argued, to deal with people of "incurably vicious tendencies" and with the feebleminded, and that was to "organise [the] extinction of the tribe."[158] However, this was, if not quite the lunatic fringe, certainly the more extremist wing of the British Eugenics movement.[159]

Even *voluntary* sterilisation never commanded widespread support in this country (though by 1909 Francis Galton was conceding in private that "except by sterilisation, I cannot yet see any way of checking the produce of the unfit who are allowed their liberty and are below the reach of moral control").[160] It is true that the Eugenics Education Society came round to support such a policy in the 1920s—its president Leonard Darwin drafted a voluntary sterilisation bill in 1927—but before the First World War, the socially-conservative British eugenics movement tended to shy away from following the American example. There was a deeply-ingrained worry among British eugenicists that encouraging any kind of birth control would inevitably mean separating the sexual act from the responsibilities of procreation. The radical wing of the movement, represented by writers like Havelock Ellis and George Bernard Shaw, saw nothing but liberation in the freeing of sexual energies that this would entail. However, for mainstream eugenicists, it evoked the spectre of unbridled sexual licentiousness.[161]

There was, moreover, the fear that simply sterilising degenerates would (unlike segregation) do nothing to control the danger they posed to the wider community. Indeed, there was a widespread view – which went well beyond the confines of the Eugenics movement – that the sexual appetites of feeble-minded women were *already* abnormally high, and the situation would simply be exacerbated were mentally-deficient women not held back by the risk of pregnancy.[162] Indeed, one historian has used the term "near hysteria" to describe the tenor of debates on this subject in the Edwardian period.[163]

It could be argued that the key role ascribed to women in the reproduction of the unfit functioned to give female criminality a prominence in Edwardian discourse on crime unthinkable just twenty or thirty years earlier.[164] Mathew Thomson explains why the issue of the sexuality of feeble-minded women carried such a resonance in this period:

> Gradually, mental defect and immorality became so closely associated that it was not uncommon for immorality to be viewed as evidence, rather than the consequence, of mental defect. It was because feeble-minded women were already such an important target for sexual control that eugenic arguments, which were still highly controversial, were accepted so rapidly as an additional justification for control. Since the concern to regulate moral behaviour was so deeply rooted, it brought a much wider constituency of support to the eugenic campaign than it would ever have gained through scientific arguments alone.[165]

An influential contributor to this debate was Dr Thomas Clouston of the Edinburgh Royal Asylum, whom we have already met as a champion of Lombrosian criminology in the 1890s. In his evidence to the Royal Commission on the Care and Control of the Feeble-Minded, Clouston outlined the danger he considered young feeble-minded women to represent. The following quotation from his evidence was reproduced in the Commission's conclusions:

> [S]uch persons in a large city are subject to overwhelming temptations and pressures towards sexual immorality. I find, as a matter of fact, that it is an exception for any of them not to have been sexually tampered with among a certain class of society. Many of them have had illegitimate children, and this often at very early ages. … In a way it is more disgusting and degrading than prostitution or sexual lapses through passion. When illegitimate children are borne by such young women, the chances are enormously in favour of their turning out to be either imbeciles, or degenerates or criminals.[166]

In practice, as Daniel Kevles points out, such reasoning tended "to identify as depravity most sexual expression that fell outside the bounds of prevailing middle class standards."[167] Mary Dendy's evidence to the Royal Commission on the Feeble-Minded puts across this point with stark clarity: "... if a woman comes into the workhouse with an illegitimate child it should be considered evidence of weakness of mind; there is certainly weakness of lack of moral fibre."[168]

An alternative, if eccentric, view which also cautioned against sterilisation was that reflected in a 1906 article by eugenics sympathiser and psychologist William McDougall. Perhaps, he reasoned, criminals were not degenerates at all, but merely non-conformists, and thus, "to sterilise in any way our criminal stocks would be to eliminate our most variable stocks", a most unwise course since "variability is the prime condition of all evolution."[169]

It is true that Havelock Ellis gave his backing to voluntary sterilisation, as later editions of *The Criminal* attest[170], so did Dr Alfred Tredgold[171], and a meeting held in 1904 under the auspices of the Medico-legal Society on "the proposed sterilisation of certain degenerates" also came out in favour.[172] There were equally sporadic calls for sterilisation as a solution to the problem of the feeble-minded or the unfit throughout the period from journalists, churchmen, judges and academics, but unlike their US counterparts, they never succeeded in making significant inroads into political, administrative or medical elite opinion.[173]

Typical of this kind of occasional defence of sterilisation was a book written by prolific Edwardian novelist George Griffith, called *Sidelights on Convict Life* (1903).[174] The book was mainly an illustrated tour of Britain's convict prisons, but in the last chapters, the author turns to his own opinion of the English criminal. Describing the habitual offender as "a noxious weed" and "a by-product which is not only waste, but worse: ... a moral bacillus", Griffith advocated sterilisation "for the obvious reason that he invariably transmits his own moral disease to his offspring, if he has any."[175] He drew on earlier physiognomic stereotypes of the criminal to produce the following physical description of "an unmistakable specimen of 'the habitual' ", encountered in the exercise yard at Holloway Prison:

> ... born of criminal parents, with the brand of crime stamped indelibly like a brand-mark on face and physique. You can see it in every motion of his body, in the sidelong look of his eyes, the motion of his narrow shoulders, even in the way he puts his foot on the ground. He can no more help being a criminal than a man who has inherited consumption can help being consumptive; but the dull brutal law goes on time after time giving him sentence after sentence ...[176]

Even though many senior Edwardian prison doctors and penal administrators probably shared Griffith's belief in the existence of a physical criminal-type, they resisted the eugenicists' tendency to extend the notion of physical and mental degeneracy to *all* criminals—hence their opposition to Charles Goring's conclusions—and they consistently ruled out a policy of sterilisation on both moral and practical grounds. On practical grounds, it was argued that carrying out sterilisation on the inmates of Britain's gaols would undermine order ("... if it were bruited about that doctors were actually mutilating patients ... [there would be] very serious consequences indeed"), and might actually exacerbate certain types of sexual crime (a variant of Thomas Clouston's point about rapacious mentally-deficient women).[177]

In addition, as has been stressed earlier, the dominant ideology at the top of Britain's penal regime emphasised that, but for a small mentally-deficient minority, criminals should be held morally responsible for their acts. The eugenic solution of sterilising large numbers of habitual criminals on the American model seemed to imply that they were a lost cause, for whom the only solution was to lock them up and operate to prevent them passing on their defective genes to the next generation—leopards not changing spots, and so forth. It was not necessary to be a fully paid-up adherent to environmental theories of criminal causation to object to such reasoning.

Dr W. C. Sullivan of Holloway Prison stated this position clearly in his 1909 article for *The Eugenics Review*. Describing the relevance of crime to eugenics as "limited", he pointed out that in general, criminals were not recruited from the "mentally inferior stocks of the proletariat". Indeed, he suggested (in stark contrast to the position defended by Alfred Tredgold in the last chapter) that "skilled criminals are those in which energy and initiative are most abundant". Shutting up such people, he went on, would not serve any eugenic purpose. It was vital, in Sullivan's view, to identify potential career criminals early, and "reclaim" them, via the Borstal system (put in place by Ruggles-Brise from 1903[178]), before they sunk into a pattern of endemic law-breaking. Among this group were criminals "of good stock", "often the best endowed and most promising youths".[179]

Men like Donkin, Mercier and Sullivan were not, in fact, hostile to the notion that some criminals were congenitally predisposed to crime (Sullivan, it will be recalled, had referred to a group of "very dangerous delinquents ... who are congenitally defective"), but the eugenicist project was not about building bridges.[180] In Galton's new secular religion, you were either a believer or a heretic, or as Karl Pearson implied, either you agreed that advances in social and biological knowledge could be achieved only by the statistical methods of biometrics, or your scientific and professional credentials were highly suspect.[181] A good example of Karl Pearson's brusque style can be seen in his opening remarks at the inaugural meeting of the Sociological Society in 1904, at which Francis Galton was to speak. Pearson pronounced himself "sceptical" as to the ability of the Society to "do effective work". He concluded that until a great sociologist came along, "one great thinker"—a Newton, a Descartes (or perhaps a Pearson?)—to lend direction to the discipline, the Society would be like "a herd without a leader"[182]

Moreover, influential professional groups, groups which might have been expected to warm to the technocratic vision of eugenics were more or less openly accused of having aided and abetted the proliferation of the nation's burgeoning population of degenerates. Thus, Medical Officers of Health, Factory Inspectors, educationalists, social reformers and philanthropists were all tarred at various times with this "degenerate-lover" brush, and even the medical profession did not escape implicit criticism. Major Leonard Darwin was grudgingly forced to admit that "medical men must, no doubt, strive to keep the unfit alive"[183], but he reckoned that they therefore had a special obligation "to join us in our efforts to diminish the multiplication of the unquestionably degenerate types".[184] British eugenics was that paradoxical phenomenon, a class-based movement which manifestly failed to attract more than a minority of the class in question.[185]

Such unbending hostility to anyone who did not wholeheartedly share the eugenicist vision does however tend to obscure the points of convergence with mainstream British thinking on crime in this period. It is often necessary to step back from rhetorical pronouncements made in the press or the pages of medical journals to ask just what exactly did separate the eugenicist theories of crime and punishment from those emanating from the medico-psychiatric and penal establishment. Such an approach—similar to that urged by David G. Horn on the question of Franco-Italian debates on the causes of crime in the 1880s and 1890s—reveals that while calls for sterilisation found no echo in the halls of mainstream British criminology, and moves to label all criminals irresponsible "degenerates" were strongly resisted, there *was* considerable support for the eugenicist view expressed by the Malthusian League that for irreclaimable criminals, "non-punitive and non-solitary seclusion … with a view to non-reproduction of the type" was the best way forward, at least as far as feeble-minded prisoners were concerned.[186]

Thus in his 1910 book, *Crime and Criminals 1876–1910*, respected prison doctor R. F. Quinton wrote in favour of secluding incorrigible criminals "for considerable periods" in order to prevent them "for the time being from propagating their kind."[187] In similar fashion, Sir Robert Anderson argued that "It behoves us to take adequate measures to prevent the unfit from preying upon the community or contaminating their associates, and, I would add with emphasis, from reproducing their kind."[188] Dr Sullivan, for his part, described eugenics as "not unimportant" in the specific case of "degenerate" moral idiots.[189] Several of the prison doctors giving evidence to the 1908 Royal Commission on the Feeble-Minded expressed similar sentiments. Dr Smalley, Britain's medical inspector of prisons told the commission that 73% of the mental defectives in the country's prisons were "in the procreative stage of life, *with its obvious corollary*".[190] Eugenics had then found its niche in the British penal establishment, but it was a long way short of the role hoped for it by men like Francis Galton and Karl Pearson.

The problem was that when eugenicists tried to extend the category of the biologically unfit beyond the narrow confines of a feeble-minded minority, or sought to advocate a more muscular policy to control the latter's reproductive capacities than that of segregation—in the form of forced or voluntary sterilisation—they were in effect challenging a number of the fundamental tenets of Edwardian criminology. Not only did the eugenic challenge call into question the assumption that most criminals were "at heart rational, responsible and culpable" in Bill Forsythe's words, and could be punished as such; it also removed any hope for their eventual reform. Such a bleak prognosis ran against the grain of a number of important intellectual developments of the period, which emphasised the capacity of an interventionist State to remould human behaviour.

There were also powerful *professional* reasons to resist eugenics' icy embrace. In 1895, prison doctor Dr David Nicolson had warned that if the criminal anthropologists had their way, his profession would be turned into a corps of white-coated technicians, sorting criminals into boxes on the say-so of the craniometer and the statistical table. Eugenics offered the same professionally unpalatable alternative. That prison doctors and the penal regime more generally did in fact use some of the same boxes as the eugenicists themselves is, in this context, neither here nor there. According to British criminology's seductive self-image, each prisoner deserved a tailor-made penal solution based on a meticulous therapeutic assessment of the causes of his or her criminal behaviour. Galton's "degenerate", just as Lombroso's born criminal-type, left no room for such fine distinctions.

Notes

1 Charles Goring, *The English Convict: A Statistical Study*, London, HMSO, 1913, p. 370.
2 Quoted in Piers Beirne, "Heredity vs. Environment: A Reconsideration of Charles Goring's *The English Convict* (1913)", *British Journal of Criminology*, vol. 28, 1988, p. 335. The following account of Goring's work depends heavily on Beirne's path-breaking article.
3 Victoria Woodhull, *The Rapid Multiplication of the Unfit*, London, 1891, p. 38, quoted in Kevles, *op. cit.*, p. 85.
4 Forsythe, "The Garland Thesis", p. 271.
5 Renneville, "La réception de Lombroso", pp. 120–22; Debuyst, "L'Ecole française", pp. 350–351; Darmon, *Médecins et assassins*, p. 96; Radzinowicz and Hood, *Emergence of Penal Policy*, pp. 19–20; Beirne, *op. cit.*, p. 321.
6 In this context, Manouvrier's original support for the project is somewhat puzzling. Perhaps, as Marc Renneville has suggested, the French anthropologist was caught off balance by the Lombrosians' decision to co-operate with the commission, and he may too have subsequently come to regret a hasty decision to sign up to the research programme when it was far from certain that its results would confirm his own theories ... (Renneville, *op. cit.*, pp. 121–22).
7 Paul Topinard (1887), quoted in Debuyst, *op. cit.*, p. 350.
8 Quoted in Darmon, *op. cit.*, p. 98 [my translation].
9 Griffiths, *Proceedings of the Fourth Congress*, pp. 12–13.
10 Renneville, *op. cit.*, p. 122.
11 Radzinowicz and Hood, *op. cit.*, p. 21; Beirne, *op. cit.*, pp. 321–22.
12 G. B. Griffiths and H. B. Donkin, "Measurements of One Hundred and Thirty Criminals", *Biometrika*, vol. 3, 1904, pp. 60–62.
13 Dr Griffiths went on to become deputy medical officer and assistant governor at Holloway Prison. In this capacity he appeared before the 1908 Royal Commission on the Feeble Minded ("Royal Commission", vol. 2, p. 198).
14 Beirne, *op. cit.*, p. 322; Radzinowicz and Hood, *op. cit.*, pp. 21–22.
15 G. R. Searle states that in reality Pearson's "socialism" did not survive his involvement in the eugenics cause. In the period 1906–14, the latter fiercely criticised the progressive social policies of Herbert Asquith's Liberal government (G. R. Searle, "Eugenics and Class", in Charles Webster (ed.) *Biology, Medicine and Society*, Cambridge, Cambridge University Press, 1981, p. 233). On K. Pearson, see also Kevles, *In Search of Eugenics*, ch. 2. Kevles observes dryly that "Pearson was concerned less with the shape of the new society than with where the Karl Pearsons would fit into it" (p. 24).
16 Gillham, *Life of Sir Francis Galton*, p. 274. Bryan Donkin was also part of this group. At one point in the mid-1880s, both Donkin and Pearson were attracted to South African socialist and close friend of Havelock Ellis, Olive Schreiner (*ibid.*, p. 275).
17 Beirne, *op. cit.*, pp. 323–4.
18 Beirne, *op. cit.*, p. 234, n. 12.
19 Karl Pearson, 1918–19, quoted in Radzinowicz and Hood, *op. cit.*, p. 21.
20 Beirne, *op. cit.*, p. 324, no. 12. In *The English Convict* (p. 27), Goring referred to "the brilliant mathematical researches of one master who has recently reduced to order the previous chaos of statistical science."

21 Charles Goring, "On the Inheritance of the Diatheses of Phthisis and Insanity", *Studies in National Deterioration*, no. 5, London, Biometric Laboratory, 1909.

22 Quoted in Bailey, "English Prisons, Penal Culture", p. 314.

23 Cf. Karl Pearson's remarks: "... in reality nobody really knows whether crime is associated with general degeneracy, whether it is a manifestation of certain hereditary qualities, or whether it is a product of environment or tradition" (Karl Pearson, *Nature and Nurture: The Problem of the Future*, London, Eugenics Laboratory Memoirs, vol. 6, 1910, p. 10) In fact Pearson had already reached his own conclusions on this question (see below).

24 Goring, *The English Convict*, pp. 26–27.

25 Karl Pearson, "Introduction", in Charles Goring, *The English Convict: A Statistical Study*, abridged edition, London, HMSO, 1919, p. xii.

26 In 1909, Pearson wrote that "Lombroso and the school of workers associated with him seem to have totally lacked the scientific spirit. In most cases, starting upon some preconceived hypothesis as to the nature and origins of the criminal, and proceeding always upon the superstitious principle that the mental and physical conditions of man are closely correlated, the chief efforts of the criminal anthropologists have been directed in search of evidence of physical anomalies among imprisoned criminals. Most naturally, almost inevitably, considering the bias of the investigators' minds and the crudity of their methods of research, they soon found the evidence they sought. ... [The criminal anthropologist] did not gather his theories from the criminal: he took his prejudices to the criminal" (University College London, Pearson Papers, 366: "Report upon the aims, methods, progress and results of a statistical investigation now being conducted for the prison commissioners at the Biometric Laboratory, University College" [1909], pp. 3–4, 8).

27 Beirne, *op. cit.*, p. 335.

28 Goring, *op. cit.*, pp. 12–16.

29 Based on Beirne, *op. cit.*, p. 325.

30 Goring, *op. cit.*, pp. 23–24 [my emphasis].

31 *Ibid.*, pp. 22–23.

32 Goring, *op. cit.*, p. 18. Cf. Karl Pearson, *op. cit.*, p. 8: "The conclusions of the old criminology may be true, but being arrived at by unscientific methods, they cannot, without further investigation, be finally accepted" ("Report upon the aims, methods, progress and results").

33 Edwin D. Driver, "Charles Goring", in Hermann Mannheim (ed.), *Pioneers in Criminology*, London, Stephens and Stephens, 1960, pp. 339–340; Beirne, *op. cit.*, p. 327.

34 *Ibid.*, p. 173.

35 *Ibid.*, p. 370.

36 *Ibid.*, frontispiece. Interestingly though, fifteen years later in *The Relation of the Skull and Brain to Crime* (p. 17), Dr William Norwood East would provide a partial defence of the accuracy of Clarke's sketches. Norwood East conceded that Clarke's portraits were "exaggerations of types rarely seen in the convict prisons at that time." However, he added that part of the difference between Clarke's sketches and Goring's photographic portraits lay in the fact that the subjects of the former included "... imbeciles and others now segregated under the Mental Deficiency Acts". Mary Cowling notes that Ellis's selection from among 111 sketches penned

by Vans Clarke was probably influenced by "a penchant for the picturesque and striking" (*The Artist as Anthropologist*, p. 313).

37 *Ibid.*, p. 19.

38 Beirne, *op. cit.*, p. 328.

39 Goring, *op. cit.*, p. 370 [my emphasis].

40 Beirne, *op. cit.*, p. 329.

41 Goring, *op. cit.*, p. 197.

42 *Ibid.*, p. 200.

43 *Ibid.*, p. 372 [my emphasis].

44 Pearson, "Introduction", p. xv; Karl Pearson, *National Life from the Standpoint of Science*, 2nd edition, London, Adam and Charles Black, 1905, p. 19. Cf. Pearson, *Nature and Nurture*, p. 27: "There is no real comparison between nature and nurture; it is essentially the man who makes his environment, and not the environment which makes the man."

45 Beirne, *op. cit.*, p. 317.

46 *Ibid.*, pp. 322–23, 329–31.

47 *Ibid.*, p. 331 and ns. 19 and 20.

48 Goring, *op. cit.*, p. 288.

49 *Ibid.*, p. 368.

50 *Ibid.*, p. 368.

51 *Ibid.*, p. 373 [my emphasis].

52 Radzinowicz and Hood, *Emergence of Penal Policy*, p. 23.

53 Garland, *op. cit.*, p. 12, n. 23; Beirne, *op. cit.*, p. 317, n. 3.

54 Radzinowicz and Hood, *op. cit.*, p. 24, n. 66; Fink, *Causes of Crime*, p. 244.

55 Radzinowicz and Hood, *op. cit*, pp. 23–24.

56 Major Leonard Darwin, "The Habitual Criminal", *The Eugenics Review*, vol. 6, no. 3, October 1914, pp. 207, 209. Darwin was president of the Eugenics Education Society from 1911 to 1928.

57 Pearson, "Introduction", *passim*. Pearson would later recall his disappointment that the book had not made a greater impact in British debates on the causes of crime (Garland, "British Criminology", p. 11).

58 Pearson, *op. cit.*, pp. x–xi.

59 Quoted in Forsythe, *Penal Discipline*, p. 36. See also Radzinowicz and Hood, *op. cit.*, p. 25.

60 Forsythe, *op. cit.*

61 University College London Archives: Pearson Papers : 703/1 (C. Goring to K. Pearson, 21 April 1912).

62 *Loc.cit.* (C. Goring to K. Pearson, 2 October 1912). Presumably the Home Office had second thoughts on this point, for *The English Convict* was indeed published in 1913 as a Blue Book.

63 H. B. Donkin, "Notes on Mental Defects in Criminals", *Journal of Mental Science*, vol. 63, 1917, p. 23. This article prompted a response from Goring, visibly taken aback by the severity of Donkins' criticisms (Charles Goring, "The Aetiology of Crime", *Journal of Mental Science*, vol. 64, 1918, pp. 129–46).

64 H. B. Donkin, "The Factors of Criminal Actions", *Journal of Mental Science*, vol. 65, 1919, pp. 87–96.

65 Forsythe, *op. cit.*, pp. 154–155.

66 Mercier, *Crime and Criminals*, p. 220–23.

67 See Ruggles-Brise, *English Prison System*, ch. XVI.
68 Forsythe, *op. cit.*, p. 154; Bailey, "English Prisons, Penal Culture", p. 314; Radzinowicz and Hood, *Emergence of Penal Policy*, p. 597.
69 Evelyn Ruggles-Brise, "Preface", in Goring, *The English Convict*, p. 8.
70 By the late 1880s, David G. Horn notes, Lombroso had conceded that "fewer than 40 percent of convicted male convicts had any physical anomalies, and still fewer bore the combination of factors (the 'criminal-type') that was considered a reliable predictor of dangerous conduct" (Horn, *The Criminal Body*, p. 16). See also Radzinowicz and Hood, *op. cit.*, p. 26.
71 Leps, *Apprehending the Criminal*, p. 37. See also Beirne, *op. cit.*, pp. 335–36.
72 Forsythe, *op. cit.*, p. 155.
73 Francis Galton, "Eugenics: Its Definition, Scope and Aims", *Sociological Papers I*, London, 1905, pp. 45–79.
74 Discussion following Galton, "Eugenics", p. 55.
75 Jackson, *Borderland of Imbecility*, p. 208.
76 *The Lancet*, 9 August 1913, p. 400; "Moral Imbecility", *The Practitioner*, vol. 99, 1917, pp. 301–308.
77 Quoted in Jackson, *op. cit.*, p. 223.
78 Forsythe, *Penal Discipline*, p. 158.
79 Nicholas Wright Gillham, *A Life of Sir Francis Galton: From African Explorer to the Birth of Eugenics*, Oxford, Oxford University Press, 2001; D. W. Forrest, *Francis Galton: The Life and Work of a Victorian Genius*, New York, Tapling, 1974.
80 Galton, *Memories of My Life*, pp. 287–88.
81 In fact, not only was Galton's own marriage infertile, so were those of his brothers, and his wife's sisters.
82 Forrest, *op. cit.*, p. 85; Daniel J. Kevles, *In the Name of Eugenics: Genetics and the Uses of Human Heredity*, 2nd edition, New Haven, Harvard University Press, 1995, pp. 8–11.
83 Francis Galton, "Hereditary Talent and Character", *Macmillan's Magazine* vol. 22, 1865, pp. 157–66, 318–27.
84 Francis Galton, *Hereditary Genius: An Inquiry into its Laws and Consequences*, London, Macmillan, 1892 [1st edition 1869].
85 Galton wrote in 1883 that it was his intention to "touch on various topics more or less connected with that of the cultivation of race, or, as we might call it, with "eugenic" questions ..." (Galton, *Inquiries into Human Faculty and its Development*, p. 17). In a footnote, he goes on: "That is, with questions bearing on what is termed in Greek, *eugenes*, namely good in stock, hereditarily endowed with noble qualities. ... We greatly want a brief word to express the science of improving stock, ... which especially in the case of man, takes cognisance of all influences that tend in however remote a degree to give to the more suitable races or strains of blood a better chance of prevailing speedily over the less suitable than they otherwise would have had" (*ibid*).
86 Galton's 1865 article was described by his colleague and first biographer Karl Pearson as "an epitome of the great bulk of Galton's work for the rest of his life ..." (Pearson, *The Life, Letters and Labours of Francis Galton*, vol. 2, p. 86).
87 Galton, *Hereditary Genius*, p. 340.
88 Galton, *Inquiries into Human Faculty*, p. 16.
89 Galton, *Hereditary Genius*, p. 1.

90 Francis Galton, *Essays in Eugenics* (1909), quoted in Kevles, *op. cit.*, p. 12.
91 Kevles, *op. cit.*, p. 4; Gillham, *op. cit.*, p. 14; Forrest, *op. cit.*, p. 55.
92 Kevles, *op. cit.*, pp. 91–92; Richard A. Soloway, *Demography and Degeneration: Eugenics and the Declining Birthrate in Twentieth-Century Britain*, 2nd edition, London, University of North Carolina Press, 1995, pp. 63–73.
93 Galton, *op. cit.*, p. 38. In the 1920s, biologist and former eugenicist Raymond Pearl repeated Galton's experiments. He found that only three of the seventy-two poets listed the *Encyclopaedia Britannica* had parents important enough to deserve their own entry. Pearl gives the case of William Shakespeare as a perfect demonstration of the fundamental flaw in Galton's theory. On the Bard's father, Pearl noted: "As a matter of fact [he] was the greengrocer and butcher of the town, doubtless an amiable and useful citizen, but after all probably not greatly different from greengrocers and butchers in general" (quoted in Jonathan Marks, *Human Biodiversity: Genes, Race and History*, New York, Aldine De Gruyer, 1995, pp. 78–79).
94 Gillham, *op. cit.*, p. 158; Kevles, *op. cit.*, pp. 4–5; Soloway, *op. cit.*, pp. 24–25.
95 Galton, *Inquiries into Human Faculty*, p. 16.
96 Francis Galton, "Segregation", in *The Problem of the Feeble-Minded: An Abstract of the Royal Commission on the Care and Control of the Feeble-Minded*, London, P. S. King, 1909, p. 81.
97 Mary Dendy, letter to Francis Galton, February 1909, quoted in Kevles, *In Search of Eugenics*, p. 107.
98 Dr Alfred F. Tredgold, "The Problem of the Feeble-Minded", in Manchester and Salford Sanitary Association, *Proceedings at a Conference on the Care of the Feeble-Minded*, London, Sherratt and Hughes, 1911, pp. 18–19.
99 Galton, *op. cit.*, pp. 81–85.
100 *Ibid.*, pp. 84–85.
101 Soloway, *Demography and Degeneration*, pp. 2, 41–43; Jeffrey Weeks, *Sex, Politics and Society: The Regulation of Sexuality since 1800*, 2nd edition, London, Longman, 1989, p. 125.
102 Major General Sir John Frederick Maurice, quoted in Soloway, *op. cit.*, p. 41.
103 Kevles, *In Search of Eugenics*, pp. 72–73.
104 Soloway, *op. cit.*, p. 45.
105 *Ibid.*, p. 45.
106 Quoted in Pick, *Faces of Degeneration*, p. 185 and Soloway, *op. cit.*, p. 45.
107 Between 1876 and 1901, the birth rate fell from 36.3 per thousand to 28.5 (Harold Perkin, *The Rise of Professional Society: England since 1880*, London, Routledge, 1989, p. 55).
108 Quoted in Soloway, *op. cit.*, p. 54.
109 J. Holt Schooling (1901), quoted in *ibid.*, p. 6.
110 "The Declining Birth-Rate", *The Times*, 31 October 1913, reprinted in Donald Read (ed.), *Documents from Edwardian England*, London, Harraps, 1973, p. 16.
111 Thomson, *Problem of Mental Deficiency*, p. 22.
112 *Ibid.*, p. 33.
113 Quotation from the first issue of the *Eugenics Review* (April 1909), quoted in Soloway, *op. cit.*, p. 32.
114 Radzinowicz and Hood, *Emergence of Penal Policy*, pp. 335–36.
115 Darwin expressed his concern in 1914 about those excluded from the provisions of the Act: "If he can only be proved to be either very stupid, very weak or utterly

worthless, is the man who commits crime after crime to be allowed to go on breeding freely?" ("The Habitual Offender", p. 216).

116 Thomson, *op. cit.*, chs. 1–2.

117 Donald MacKenzie (1978), quoted in Searle, "Eugenics and Class", pp. 218–21. Soloway, *op. cit.*, p. 35 describes the *Eugenics Education Society* as "socially very homogeneous".

118 Searle, *op. cit.*, pp. 236–37; W. C. D and C. D. Whetham, quoted in Kevles, *op. cit.*, p. 89.

119 Searle, *op. cit.*, p. 217. See also Soloway, *op. cit.*, pp. 10–17, 48.

120 Radzinowicz and Hood, *Emergence of Penal Policy*, p. 30; Kevles, *op. cit.*, p. 74; Soloway, *op. cit.*, pp. 12–13.

121 Soloway, *op. cit.*, pp. 11–12.

122 Karl Pearson, "On the Inheritance of the Mental Characters in Man, and its Comparison with the Inheritance of the Physical Characters", *Journal of the Anthropological Institute*, vol. 33, 1903, pp. 179–237.

123 Alfred Tredgold (1911), quoted in Soloway, *op. cit.*, p. 15.

124 Quoted in Weeks, *op. cit.*, p. 129

125 Pearson, *National Life*, p. 101. Cf. Kevles, *op. cit.*, pp. 33–34.

126 Sidney and Beatrice Webb (1911), quoted in Searle, *op. cit.*, p. 233.

127 Francis Galton, "The Possible Improvement of the Human Breed under the Existing Conditions of Law and Settlement", *Nature*, 31 October 1901, pp. 659–65.

128 Charles Booth, *Life and Labour of the People in London*, 10 vols., London, Macmillan, 1892–1897. A second study, this time of the city of York, came to similar conclusions regarding the scale of urban poverty (Seebohm Rowntree, *Poverty: A Study of Town Life*, London, Macmillan, 1901). On the impact of Booth's work, see Steadman-Jones, *Outcast London*, pp. 320–21.

129 Keating, *Into Unknown England*, p. 25.

130 These extracts are reproduced in Keating, *Into Unknown England*, pp. 113–40 (quotation at p. 114).

131 *Ibid.*, p. 140.

132 Quoted in Wiener, *Reconstructing the Criminal*, p. 231. See also Steadman-Jones, *op. cit.*, p. 320.

133 In using this term of criminal slang, Booth is referring to a legal sanctuary for criminal debtors in the London district of Whitefriars (abolished in 1697).

134 Keating, *op. cit.*, p. 139.

135 *Ibid.*, pp. 25, 27.

136 *Ibid.*, p. 21.

137 Quoted in *ibid.*, pp. 241, 147–48, 226. Several commentators have noted the parallel between the inhabitants of this nether-world and the degenerate Morlocks of H. G. Wells' *The Time Machine*, first serialised in 1894–1895 (Wiener, *Reconstructing the Criminal*, p. 183; Pick, *Faces of Degeneration*, pp. 157–59). Interestingly, Wells was present at Galton's 1904 lecture to the Sociological Society and argued that the possibilities for future improvement of the racial stock lay not in "the selection of successes for breeding" (as Galton was urging), but in "the sterilisation of failures" (Galton, "Eugenics: Its Definition, Scope and Aims", discussion, p. 60).

138 Steadman-Jones, *Outcast London*, pp. 312–13.

139 Quoted in Keating, *op. cit.*, p. 241.

140 Steadman-Jones, *op. cit.*, pp. 296–97, 303.

141 Quoted in Leps, *Apprehending the Criminal*, p. 30.
142 Keating, *op. cit.*, p. 172; Leps, *op. cit.*, p. 30.
143 Lord Brabazon (1886), quoted in Steadman-Jones, *op. cit.*, p. 310.
144 Charles Booth (1890), quoted in *ibid.*, p. 307. William Beveridge also proposed the segregation of the "residuum", during a talk to the Sociological Society in 1905 (Harris, *Private Lives, Public Spirit*, p. 243).
145 Galton, *op. cit.*, p. 663.
146 *Ibid.*, pp. 663, 664. A book published in 1921 noted mischievously that even the members of the Eugenics Education Society were in need of the kind of procreative incentives being urged by Galton. The average number of children among the Society's officers was 2.3, and a quarter had no children at all. The members of the 1913 National Birth-Rate Commission fared even worse: the average number of children was only 1.75, and sixteen of the forty-one commissioners were childless (Charles Edward Pell, *The Law of Births and Deaths*, 1921, quoted in Soloway, *op. cit.*, p. 35). Karl Pearson chided the middle classes for their low fertility. "With our modern views as to parental responsibility", he observed, "neither Charles Darwin nor Francis Galton would have been born" (quoted in Kevles, *op. cit.*, p. 33).
147 Caleb W. Saleeby, *Parenthood and Race Culture: An Outline of Eugenics*, New York, Moffat, 1910, p. 30.
148 Darwin, "The Habitual Criminal", p. 218.
149 Elof Axel Carlson, *The Unfit: A History of a Bad Idea*, Cold Spring Harbour NY, Cold Spring Harbour Laboratory Press, 2001.
150 Kevles, *op. cit.*, p. 93.
151 *Ibid.*, p. 218; Rafter, *Creating Born Criminals*, ch. 7–8; James W. Trent Jnr., *Inventing the Feeble Mind: A History of Mental Retardation in the United States*, London, University of California Press, 1994, pp. 194–97; Fink, *Causes of Crime*, pp. 204–9.
152 R. A. Gibbons, "The Treatment of the Congenitally Unfit and of Convicts by Sterilization", *Eugenics Review*, July 1926, vol. 18, no. 2, pp. 100–9.
153 Robert Reid Rentoul, *Proposed Sterilization of Certain Medical and Physical Degenerates: An Appeal to Asylum Managers and Others*, London, Walter Scott, 1903; R. Rentoul, *Race Culture or Race Suicide? A Plea for the Unborn*, London, Walter Scott, 1906.
154 Rentoul, *Proposed Sterilization of Certain Medical and Physical Degenerates*, pp. 3–7.
155 *Ibid.*, pp. 11–13. In 1913, Major Leonard Darwin, president of the Eugenics Education Society, calculated that the State spent £45 million a year on the administration of justice, the police, poor relief, hospitals and asylums. Substantial savings could be made in all these areas if the "unfit were eliminated" (Searle, "Eugenics and Class", p. 234).
156 *Ibid.*, pp. 17–18.
157 Thomson, *Problem of Mental Deficiency*, pp. 181–182; Jackson, *Borderland of Imbecility*, p. 149; Weeks, *Sex, Policy and Society*, pp. 135–136, Kevles, *In the Name of Eugenics*, pp. 93–4; Radzinowicz and Hood, *Emergence of Penal Policy*, p. 324.
158 W. C. D. and C. D. Whetham, *The Family and the Nation: A Study in National Inheritance and Social Responsibility*, London, 1909, p. 212.
159 Soloway, *op. cit.*, p. 64.
160 Francis Galton to Karl Pearson, January 6 1907, quoted in Kevles, *op. cit.*, p. 94.

161 Soloway, *op. cit.*, pp. 94–109. Some eugenicists urged the use of birth control for the "unfit" while condemning its use in the upper echelons of society. That being said, many, like Leonard Darwin, remained sceptical about the ability of the working class to make effective use of contraception (*ibid.*, p. 108). See also Lesley A. Hall, *Sex, Gender and Social Change in Britain since 1880*, London, Macmillan, 2000, p. 66; Kevles, *In Search of Eugenics*, p. 88.

162 Thomson, *op. cit.*, p. 182. A point of view combining elements of eugenics and feminism emphasised the harmful effects of *male* sexual desire (social subjugation of the woman, health risks associated with multiple pregnancies, and the danger of sexually transmitted diseases like syphilis). According to Frances Swiney (who also campaigned for female suffrage), the sexual act had only one useful purpose—procreation. She recommended that an appropriate frequency of sexual relations between husband and wife was about once every four or five years … (Hall, *op. cit.*, pp. 68–69). Lesley A. Hall emphasises that at the outset, nearly 50% of the members of the Eugenics Education Society were women, often single, with a background in the public sector or the professions (*ibid.*, p. 67).

163 H. Simmons (1978), quoted in Sim, *Medical Power in Prisons*, p. 141.

164 Saunders, "Quarantining the Weak-Minded", pp. 290–91.

165 Thomson, *op. cit.*, pp. 22–3. See also Jackson, *Borderland of Imbecility*, p. 146.

166 "Royal Commission", vol. 1, p. 120. The report noted that Clouston had made "a special investigation in regard to this class of feeble-minded women". Cf. Zedner, *Women, Crime and Custody*, ch. 7.

167 Kevles, *In the Name of Eugenics*, p. 107.

168 Quoted in Radzinowicz and Hood, *Emergence of Penal Policy*, p. 328.

169 William McDougall, "A Practicable Eugenic Suggestion", *Sociological Papers*, 1906, p. 57, quoted in Radzinowicz and Hood, *op. cit.*, p. 33 (n. 93).

170 Havelock Ellis, *The Criminal*, 4th edition, London, Walter Scott, 1910; 5th edition, 1914. See also H. Ellis, *The Problem of Race Regeneration*, London, Cassell, 1911.

171 See above, note

172 Sim, *Medical Power in Prisons*, p. 140.

173 Radzinowicz and Hood, *Emergence of Penal Policy*, p. 31–33; Forsythe, *Penal Discipline*, p. 158; Hawkins, *Social Darwinism*, pp. 222–225; Soloway, *Demography and Degeneration*, p. 64.

174 George Griffith, *Sidelights on Convict Life*, London, John Long, 1903. George Chetwynd Griffith-Jones (1857–1906) was known to contemporaries above all for his science-fiction novels, similar in style to those of H. G. Wells.

175 *Ibid.*, pp. 239, 241.

176 *Ibid.*, p. 221.

177 The Superintendent of Broadmoor, quoted in Forsythe, *Penal Discipline*, p. 158. On the dangers of sterilisation, see also the evidence of Dr Mott to the Royal Commission of 1908. Sterilisation would have the effect, according to Dr Mott of creating "outcasts", with men pushed into crime, and women into immorality ("Royal Commission", vol. 2, p. 456). This remained the position of penal administrators and prison doctors when the issue resurfaced in the 1930s. Medical Commissioner Dr Norwood East told the 1933 Departmental Committee on Sterilisation: "It is inconceivable that this country will submit to the eugenic sterilisation of its criminals unless substantial reasons are produced in support of the practice. So far these are lacking … eugenic sterilisation as a means of combating delinquency appears

previous, unwarranted and possibly harmful to the race. As a punitive measure it is outrageous. As a therapeutic measure it is otiose, may incite to sexual crime and lead to a false sense of security in the public mind" (quoted in Forsythe, "The Garland Thesis", p. 270).

178 On the history of this system—outside the scope of this book—see Victor Bailey *Delinquency and Citizenship: Reclaiming the Young Offender*, Oxford, Clarendon Press, 1987; Forsythe, *op. cit.*, ch. 4.

179 Sullivan, "Eugenics and Crime", pp. 118–19.

180 Cf. Searle, *op. cit.*, p. 228: "... as a group, eugenists were not distinguished by their tact."

181 *Ibid.*, p. 223.

182 Galton, "Eugenics: Its Scope and Aims", p. 52.

183 One doctor sympathetic to the eugenics cause, writing in the *British Medical Journal* in August 1913, suggested that surgeons should only save the lives of certain types of "unfit" patients in exchange for a commitment that once well, they would abstain from propagating their deficient germ plasm in the form of children. Such sentiments were hardly likely to rally majority opinion within the medical profession to the eugenics standard (Searle, *op. cit.*, p. 227).

184 Quoted in *ibid.*, p. 225. Darwin did make some conciliatory noises, however. In his 1914 presidential speech to the Eugenics Education Society, he stated: "... increased periods of detention of habitual criminals would produce both immediate social advantages and ultimate improvements in the racial qualities of future generations; and if this be the case, the social reformer and the eugenist ought to be able to march together on this path of criminal reform" (Darwin, "The Habitual Criminal", p. 212).

185 Searle, *op. cit.*, p. 237; Kevles, *In Search of Eugenics*, p. 76.

186 Quoted in Radzinowicz and Hood, *op. cit.*, pp. 32–33.

187 R. F. Quinton, *Crime and Criminals 1876–1910*, London, Longmans, 1910, p. 119.

188 Anderson, *Criminals and Crime*, p. 105.

189 Sullivan, "Eugenics and Crime", pp. 116, 119–20.

190 "Royal Commission", vol. 1 p. 124 [my emphasis]. See also the evidence of Dr Scott (*ibid.*, vol. 2, p. 277).

Conclusion

The lips and hands and arms and legs, which are under our control, are never the only witnesses to the drama which goes on inside—if they keep silent, others will speak.

Hugo Münsterberg,
On the Witness Stand: Essays on Psychology and Crime (1923)[1]

For the fifty or so years covered by this book, lips and hands and arms and legs were in fact conceived as much more than mere silent witnesses to the drama of crime. In an important sense, the criminal body itself was seen as being able to provide vital evidence to corroborate, and even provide initial clues to, its owner's innocence or guilt. Tracing the Criminal in this way involved a double process. First, a route map had to be established, linking particular crimes or indeed deviant behaviour in general to specific *types* of the human body. That generic map or *criminal-type* could then be used to identify the individual culprit, harnessing the body to give evidence against its owner, an unwilling but effective partner in the fight against crime. The criminal body was thus "traced" in both senses of the word.

With crime apparently spiralling out of control in the middle decades of the nineteenth century, and "habituals" frustratingly (if understandably) less than forthcoming about their previous misdeeds, there was an urgent need to find some objective means of identification. The simple amassing of information—verbal and photographic—was to prove woefully unequal to the task. In fact, and here was the paradox, the more plentiful and detailed the data collected on Britain's criminal classes, the more difficult it became to track any given individual through the records. By the mid-1870s, checking the identity of a particular suspect often meant a time-consuming trawl through dozens of registers, and the personal details of tens of thousands of individual criminals, without any certainty of obtaining a positive result at the end.

The collaboration between Sir Edmund Du Cane and Francis Galton in the late 1870s represents a key moment in the search for a faster and more reliable means of identifying criminals. Composite photography would furnish, it was hoped, the means to bypass the unwieldy criminal registers by providing a photographic criminal-type, possibly with variants linking sub-types to particular kinds of crime. However, Du Cane's initiative is interesting not just because it provides a snapshot of contemporary preoccupations with criminal identification, but also because it represents a point of contact with a medico-penal tradition of scientific investigation, based in the convict prison medical service. This tradition, associated with the work of doctors like William Guy, James Bruce Thomson, David Nicolson and George Wilson, was known to Du Cane, and provided him with copper-bottomed scientific support for his belief—clearly articulated in his 1875 talk to the Social Science Association—that there existed a distinctive criminal physiognomy.

Prison doctors were not, however, primarily interested in criminal identification, at least not in the sense the Chairman of the Prison Commissioners understood the phrase. In this sense the label "precursors of Lombroso" sometimes attached to their early research is misleading. They had a different agenda; one determined in large part by the practical demands of the job, requiring rapid diagnoses to be made regarding the "fitness" or otherwise of a prisoner for hard labour or punishment. Diagnosis was made all the more difficult by the extent of the problem of "malingering", one which required medical officers to distinguish between often highly convincing fake symptoms and the real thing. There were thus sound therapeutic reasons for wishing to find convenient markers—physical as well as mental—for a condition which would come to be known as "weak-mindedness". However, to begin with, as Stephen Watson has shown, the term was as much an administrative as a clinical one, enabling a particular convict to avoid hard labour or punishment on medical grounds. Only gradually was this label given an accompanying psychiatric—and physiognomic—content.

That content was not plucked at random out of the ether however. An eclectic mix of intellectual influences structured the priorities accorded by prison doctors to particular kinds of "evidence" when they sought to find objective criteria by which weak-mindedness could be reliably diagnosed. These influences included Darwinian biology, racial anthropology and French psychiatry, together with suppositions drawn from the earlier work of phrenologists and physiognomists. Indeed, with a new, more determinist vision of human nature gradually replacing the voluntarist theories of the first generation of penal reformers, hereditarian explanations of crime, and the physical traits believed to show such transmission in action, took on a new significance.

This diagnostic enterprise was further structured by the ebb and flow of conflicting forces or pressures felt by medical officers and prison administrators when they sought to weigh the evidence concerning the size of the weak-minded component in the convict population. This is not to suggest that mental defect was (or is) merely a figment of the medical imagination; rather that since "what is considered to be abnormal, defective, inferior, and dangerous changes over time, … the definition reveals as much about the definers as the defined."[2] In fact, the latter are doomed to remain a largely elusive quarry for the historian. As Janet Saunders has pointed out, the term "weak-minded" was no doubt in part simply a convenient shorthand for prison officials to describe those prisoners who refused to conform to the model of stoical acceptance demanded of them by the penal regime. By failing to show remorse, such inmates were branded intractable "moral imbeciles". In other cases, such a label may reveal real mental damage brought on by long periods spent in solitary or separate confinement. Then of course there were those prisoners suffering from a variety of forms of mental illness—whether neurological or psychological in origin—and those whose minds had never felt the leavening influence of education, even of the most rudimentary kind. Only a small rump, one suspects, would be diagnosed as congenitally mentally deficient according to modern practice. However, there is simply no way for the historian to reach any substantive conclusions as to the relative proportions of these different groups in the Victorian and Edwardian prison population.[3]

However, in our attempt to understand the "definers", we can make useful reference to the metaphor used in the introduction, that of a series of distorting lenses and coloured filters applied to the magnifying glass of Sherlock Holmes, altering subtly, almost imperceptibly, the perception of the phenomenon under scrutiny. In this case, there were lenses or filters which tended to encourage a grim vision of an endemic—possibly growing—level of mental deficiency; and others which functioned to counsel caution concerning the scale of the problem. Among the forces belonging to the first category was the continuing influence of common sense notions of an in-bred, atavistic "criminal class", cut off from, but constantly threatening to contaminate, the "respectable" working classes. This pessimistic vision of irredeemable criminality also drew strength from the valuable ammunition it provided for beleaguered prison officials. In the 1860s and early '70s, the latter were under mounting pressure from politicians and public alike, who saw before them a penal system apparently incapable of stemming the rising tide of lawlessness (and this despite up-to-the-minute penological theories and copious investment of hard-earned taxpayers' money in the new penitentiary-type prisons). Finally, among those pressures pushing towards an epidemic-like assessment of the weak-mindedness problem, was the professional interest of those prison doctors and psychiatrists seeking to make this category of the prison population the subject of a new medico-penal clinical speciality. For such men, there was an understandable temptation to stretch the evidence on the frequency of the condition to (or perhaps beyond) the limits of the statistical evidence, an exercise made easier by the imprecise nature of official definitions of the condition. Dr Smalley's from 1901 is typical. "Weak-mindedness", he wrote, encompassed "many varying types and degrees of mental weakness or disorder, yet all being persons of imperfect or impaired responsibility, unfit for ordinary penal treatment, but not capable of being certified as insane."[4] With such a "loose and pliable" definition, trying to count the numbers of the mentally deficient was thus akin to "measure[ing] with an elastic ruler", with all the room for personal judgment which such a metaphor implies.[5] Opting for a figure from the higher range of possible estimates offered the tantalising prize of creating an object of study of major importance to the prison medical service, and perhaps to psychiatric medicine as a whole. A comparison can be drawn here with what might be termed the "feeble-mindedness industry" in the Edwardian period. Psychiatrists and charity workers specialising in this field—people like Dr Alfred Tredgold and Mary Dendy—consistently disagreed with other experts (including prison medical officers) about the scale of the problem, often alleging that virtually all deviant behaviour could be explained in terms of this form of mental deficiency.

In the case of prison doctors and administrators, there were, however, also forces pulling in the other direction, away from a tendency to equate all crime with irreversible mental defect. Prison doctors were after all an integral part of the disciplinary machinery of the Victorian prison, and like other criminal justice professionals of the period, they generally had few moral qualms about the quintessentially punitive character of the institutions in which they worked. Though assuming responsibility for the health needs of prisoners might occasionally bring medical officers into conflict with the demands of prison management, they had no wish to call into question the regime's fundamental right to impose hard labour and punishment—including corporal punishment—on its inmates. Severity and lenity were, as Martin Wiener has pointed out, two sides of the same penal coin as far as medical officers were concerned. The prison was there to punish; reform, for much of the nineteenth century at least, was a secondary consideration. Only in this way, it was argued, could the Prison effectively deter potential offenders, tempted by the easy pickings of a criminal career.

Prison officials and medical personnel thus had little sympathy for one version of the positivist creed which considered all habitual criminals—or worse, *all criminals*—to be programmed from birth to wrongdoing, their hereditary defect clearly identifiable by means of standardised anatomical and physiological stigmata. If the prison population could be subsumed entirely in such a description, prisons would need to be converted *en masse* to "moral hospitals" or perhaps benevolent labour colonies for the terminally criminal, and deterrence of any kind would fall into dangerous abeyance. Moreover, if such institutions saw the light of day, they would require a new kind of specialist, the "criminal anthropologist", able to assess the extent to which particular offenders conformed to one of a range of criminal types or sub-types, before assigning them to the appropriate institution for "treatment". This was Dr David Nicolson's nightmare scenario for the future, with the prison doctor reduced to a mere technician with clipboard and ruler, measuring offenders against an unchanging check-list of criminal stigmata before sorting them like coloured beads into one of several degenerate categories.

Late-Victorian and Edwardian criminology in Britain chose to define its practice in very different terms, stressing the importance of differentiation and individuation. Though to a certain extent this agenda would remain a better guide to *aspirations* than to the clinical nuts and bolts of forensic medicine in this country (a distinction Marshal de Saxe would have appreciated), this discourse did allow Britain's medico-penal Establishment to accommodate the "filtered" reality to which they had access, while securing for themselves a pivotal role in the punishment process. The painstaking clinical unravelling of the multifarious causes of a particular case of criminal conduct gave a central diagnostic and therapeutic role to prison doctors similar to that enjoyed by their medical colleagues on the outside, putting them in the forefront of advances in psychiatric practice. Systematic reference to a catch-all criminal-type—the equivalent of the phrenological head of previous years—would not have allowed doctors to brandish their hard-won and jealously-guarded professional expertise in the same way. Thus, as Marie-Christine Leps points out, "Lombroso's theory of atavism introduced elements of chance and fatality in hereditary influences, which dangerously restricted the power base of the established authorities."[6] Such Foucauldian motives do not on their own explain the rejection of criminal anthropology by the British medico-penal Establishment, but the grim spectre of deskilling no doubt added provided a powerful additional reason to reject the Lombrosian creed.

The criminal-type was to prove remarkably resilient, however. It did not disappear; rather it morphed, changing slowly, almost imperceptibly from a blanket description of large swathes of the prison population (in the 1860s and '70s) into a well-defined psychiatric and physiognomic sub-type at the century's end, applicable to only a small number of offenders. This meant that most prison inmates were considered capable of reform, a view which was more in keeping with the voluntarist mood in late-Victorian and Edwardian medicine, and at the same time chimed with powerful intellectual currents of the period which accorded a significant role to benevolent state intervention, implemented by a new cadre of middle-class professionals. Indeed right at the end of the nineteenth century there was something of a revival of the idea that a humanised prison regime—shorn of the worst aspects of the Du Cane years—could effect the kind of moral reformation of which the early Victorians had dreamed. It was no longer a question of isolating and masking prisoners to leave them alone with their God to contemplate the enormity of their crimes, but of individualised, medicalised treatment for each category of prisoners, according to the latest developments in psychiatric and psychological science.

The strength of these more optimistic intellectual currents, emphasised in the work of Victor Bailey and William Forsythe, would function to limit the degree of common ground between the ethos of the British prison system and the radical agenda of the Edwardian Eugenics movement. There was what I described in the last chapter as a precarious bridge linking these two ostensibly antagonistic approaches in the specific area of policy concerned with the feeble-minded offender. The Eugenicists' apocalyptic vision of a country overrun with a sexually deviant and highly fertile underclass of intractable petty criminals, a vision that fed on widespread contemporary fears about Britain's place in a changing industrial and colonial world order, helped propel the "care and control of the feeble-minded" towards the top of the policy makers' agenda. This sense of urgency, if not necessarily the solutions put forward by the Eugenics movement, rubbed off on Britain's criminological establishment.

In this context, the reliable identification of feeble-minded offenders—and, crucially, *potential* feeble-minded offenders (a new outing for the notion of *precrime*)—became a matter of more than merely academic interest. This is where the "physical stigmata" of crime remained important.

With reliable intelligence testing still several decades in the future, visible, outward signs of a "weak-minded" criminal disposition continued to play a valuable role in corroborating the psychiatric diagnosis of the medical practitioner. Indeed, there was near-consensus among criminal justice professionals in Edwardian England that this sub-group of feeble-minded prisoners could be characterised not only by clinically-observable psychiatric symptoms, but also by distinct (and photographable) inherited physical "stigmata". That such stigmata tapped into long-standing and implicitly accepted theories of the "typical" criminal physiognomy, back beyond Lombroso to Lavater and Gall, only served to lend them greater credence.

By 1914 then, criminologists could pride themselves on having discovered the physical criminal type which had eluded Francis Galton in his photographic experiments with "composite portraiture" in the late 1870s. There was no question, of course, of calling it a "criminal-type" (not, at least, unless you were called Dr Alfred F. Tredgold), just as the term "instinctive criminal" was rejected in favour of the more anodyne "moral imbecile". But when you force your way through this thicket of terminological and conceptual caveats, what you find on the other side is something not very different from Cesare Lombroso's *delinquente nato*. Thus while British criminologists high-mindedly eschewed the clip-board and craniometer in favour of the individualised psychiatric profile, they *were* still prepared to reach generalisations about the mentally deficient habitual offenders in their charge, and offer solutions that were, in some respects, similar to those of the Eugenics movement.

That being said, the rope bridge between the two camps could only take so much strain, and it broke altogether when eugenicists ventured to suggest that the reasoning applied to the feeble-minded should be extended to the criminal population as a whole. For a variety of reasons, British penal officials and prison doctors were determined not to make such a conceptual leap. This is why the Home Office dragged its feet before publishing *The English Convict*, despite its impeccable anti-Lombrosian credentials. It also explains why representatives of mainstream criminological opinion like Doctors Donkin, Mercier and Sullivan vigorously resisted efforts to tar the whole criminal population with the "unfit" brush, and steadfastly refused to sanction the eugenic policies—including sterilisation—advocated for stopping them from passing on their supposedly "degenerate" seed to future generations.

A majority of British criminologists were in fact prepared to conceive that that *some* criminals were beyond the reach of medical science (though in their more optimistic moments some British practitioners, like Sir Evelyn Ruggles-Brise and Sir Bryan Donkin, would claim that there was hope even in this area). Most, however, would have concurred with the view expressed trenchantly by Dr Charles Mercier, that beer, skittles and Sophocles were no more effective than the barbarous punishments of the past in effecting the permanent reform of a certain class of habitual criminal. In this restricted sense, then, a physical and mental "criminal-type" continued to operate in late-Victorian and Edwardian British criminology, a fact which tends to be obscured by the rhetoric of the anti-Lombrosian position.

* * *

Increasingly, of course, mental deficiency would be defined in *psychological* rather than physiognomic terms. New, apparently "objective", markers of mental defect, drawn from the nascent science of intelligence testing, would come to replace the anthropometric stigmata of old. It may be thought for this reason that theories of a physical criminal-type would soon be confined to the introductory "historical background" chapters of criminology textbooks. In fact, he past is not, so hermetic. It is true that no self-respecting criminologist or forensic psychologist today would advocate the measurement of brain capacity or facial angle as a reliable guide to criminal propensities. This does not mean, for all that, that the criminal body has become an empty vessel, drained of any capacity to signify the innocence or guilt of the individual inhabiting it.

In the 1930s and '40s, American researchers like Ernest Hooton and William Sheldon continued to base their theories of criminal behaviour on essentially Lombrosian assumptions.[7] Thus after a study of some 10,000 criminal subjects, Hooton was able to conclude that "within every race, it is the biologically inferior, the organically inadaptable, the mentally and physically stunted and warped, and the sociologically debased—who are responsible for the majority of crimes committed."[8] Both Hooton and Sheldon argued that only a strict eugenicist policy of controlling the reproduction of "the weakest and least gifted", as the latter put it, could solve the crime problem.[9] As late as the 1970s, Sheldon's division of the criminal population into three body forms or "somotypes" was still being taken seriously in some quarters.[10]

If such theories have now been pushed firmly (one hesitates, on past experience, to say *definitively*) beyond the boundaries of academically respectable criminology, it remains the case that implicit assumptions concerning the physical appearance of a "typical" criminal continue to persist.

In fact, research evidence has indicated that physiognomic stereotypes—not so very different from those found in the works of Lavater and Gall—continue to exert an influence on the behaviour of the police, legal professionals, and juries. Clinical experiments conducted by social psychologists R. H. C. Bull and J. Green at the end of the 1970s indicated a striking degree of continuity with some of the Victorian criminal stereotypes discussed in the pages of this book.[11] Their research revealed that many people continue to associate particular kinds of crime with a distinctive "criminal" physiognomy; stereotypes found in all social groups, genders and among criminal justice professionals as well as the general public. A sample of adult members of the public, together with a number of police officers, were shown photographs of ten 27–33 year-old men, all wearing the same expression, and all taken in similar conditions of dress, lighting, background etc. The participants were then given a list of offences and asked to say which of the ten individuals portrayed had committed each. It was found that irrespective of gender, and of the police/civilian split, the choices made were far from random. When the participants in the experiment were asked to choose a likely suspect for the crimes of mugging, robbery with violence, company fraud, soliciting, car theft, illegal drug possession, and gross indecency, particular faces were repeatedly picked out.[12]

The two British psychologists go on to put forward what they admit to be a somewhat "far-fetched" hypothesis, namely that the way society reacts to and treats children and adults with an "unattractive" face *can actually cause them to become criminals.* In other words, the unfortunate possessors of such aesthetically-challenged features find themselves the victims of discrimination and social exclusion because their appearance does not correspond to dominant cultural norms. The latter structure our expectations as to what a law-abiding face should look like, and so particular individuals are stigmatised as potential criminals, irrespective of their actual behaviour. Excluded as a result from conventional channels to pursue economic and social success, some at least of these individuals, it is postulated, find themselves turning to crime. Thus,

> … not only may we judge an individual's likely antisocial behaviour by the way he looks, but that in behaving towards children in this way we may create in them certain predispositions which then result in the existence of self-fulfilling prophesies.[13]

But is there any evidence that criminals as a whole are any more likely to be caught in possession of a disagreeable physiognomy than their law-abiding fellows? Bull & Green refer to an American study from 1939 that purported to show that members of the public "could fairly often but by no means always" predict the type of crime committed after being shown a photographic portrait of the person responsible.[14] They also cite a more recent German study to support their argument. This research, carried out in the 1960s, started by dividing 730 criminal mug-shots into sixteen categories according to the type of crime committed. Using Francis Galton's technique of composite photography, it was found that there was a "statistically significant dependence of the resultant physiognomic character upon the respective category of crime from which the criminal pictures had been taken." Bull & Green conclude tentatively that "there may be some relationship between physical appearance and criminality."[15]

Their conclusion may not in fact be tentative enough. Neither successful identifications which occur "fairly often", nor the highly subjective nature of the evidence derived from the study of criminal composites (a failing seen in Galton's own work) offer a solid basis for such conjecture. Indeed, on the face of it, it seems unlikely that such a labelling process could push people into crime with anything like systematic frequency, though the existence of exceptional cases where physiognomic stigmatisation—in combination with other factors—helps account for criminal behaviour cannot be ruled out.

Bull & Green are on firmer ground when they cite a range of clinical studies in the psychological literature which suggest that when teachers are faced with a written report of two identical cases of youthful wrongdoing, they are more likely to interpret the misdemeanour as "temporary misbehaviour" in the case of physiognomically well-endowed children, while the same act is labelled "persistent naughtiness" or "anti-social behaviour" in the case of their less attractive classmates. In the same way, when witnesses pick out an individual from an identity parade, there may be a temptation to choose a suspect merely because he or she provides the closest match to pre-existing expectations of what a certain type of criminal should look like. Equally, the judgments reached by judges and juries, and the severity of the sentences handed down by the former may be conditioned, at least in part, by similar criteria.[16]

However such research does not by any means exhaust the possibilities for those seeking to demonstrate a biological component to crime.[17] Criminological research continues to try and pin down the inherited component of criminal behaviour by studying family trees, twins and, most recently, adopted children. There has also been interest in a possible "crime gene", in the role of physical injury or exposure to toxic substances before birth, in hormone imbalance and even how dietary deficiency may lead individuals to commit crime.[18]

While many of the sweeping claims made for such "biosocial criminology" find little favour with the wider scientific community, few mainstream criminologists would go as far as rejecting outright *any* role for inherited characteristics. As the authors of a respected American criminology text-book put it, in language that recalls the aphorisms coined by Professor Alexandre Lacassagne of Lyons, "It may be ... that criminality is a heritable trait, but one that becomes manifest only when triggered by particular environmental conditions (such as poverty, parental neglect or abuse, or living in a crime-ridden neighbourhood)."[19]

But can that "heritable trait" be pinned down, measured, and even take visual shape? Many Victorians and Edwardians clearly thought so, and some researchers still believe it to be within our grasp. Prison medical officer James Devon, writing in the 1910s, dismissed the work of the criminal anthropologists as nothing more than "new phrenology". Interestingly, the same phrase has been used recently to describe research by criminologists seeking to harness up-to-date technology to scan the brains of convicted criminals for signs of recurring cerebral anomalies or electrical activity corresponding to "guilty thoughts", in the hope that what amounts to a neurological criminal-type can be identified.[20] Indeed, there are already plans in the pipeline to use electroencephalogram technology to scan queues of passengers waiting to board a flight to see if they contain in their ranks individuals whose brains show signs of "violent tendencies", and therefore represent a potential security risk.[21]

More generally, criminologist Nicole Hahn Rafter has recently noted that "the idea that the cause of crime may lie in brain defects (or genes that lead to brain defects) seems today to be making a comeback"[22]; a trend which has both fed off, and fed, other technological breakthroughs in criminal identification, notably the development of DNA typing since the 1980s.[23] Indeed, the heady enthusiasm which often accompanies discussion of this genetic technology in law enforcement circles, strongly resembles the mood surrounding discussions of criminal photography and anthropometry in the 1860s–1870s and dactyloscopy at the turn of the century.

Historian Simon A. Cole provides a useful framework for observing these continuities. He points out that all efforts to harness science for the purposes of criminal identification consist of three related modes of inquiry: *forensic identification* (linking a specific criminal act to a specific criminal body); *archival identification* (linking a particular criminal body to itself across space and time); and finally, *diagnostic identification* (seeking to read the signs of past or future criminal behaviour in the body itself).[24] This typology can be applied equally to the criminal photographic portrait, anthropometry, fingerprinting, and to the latest genetic techniques. "In the past", he adds,

> diagnostic identification always foundered eventually, and law enforcement agencies settled for forensic and archival applications of the technology. The debate over the expansion of DNA databases, however, has been largely conducted in ignorance of this history.[25]

It is not surprising then that the DNA sample has been vaunted in some quarters as a potential marker of actual or future criminality, though the existence of any such sure-fire predictive capacity flies in the face of criminological orthodoxy, and, it might be added, common sense. Even if we take on board Curran & Renzetti's conclusion that heredity has a role to play in the generation of criminal behaviour, it is a big step to extrapolate that a particular inherited trait or traits can effectively *predict* future wrongdoing. However, if certain identifiable hereditary traits—perhaps written in the DNA code or visible on a brain scan—could be shown to significantly increase the probability of an individual turning to crime, it is not impossible to conceive of circumstances in which such screening would become mandatory: when recruiting for the security services for example, or perhaps even for jobs which involve working with children?

The film, *Minority Report*, memorably raises the question of whether "*precrime*", even if shown to be an entirely reliable indicator of future wrongdoing (and it is a big "if", as the film implies), can really be called "crime" in any meaningful sense. It is not beyond the bounds of possibility that future generations of policy-makers and legislators will be required to reach a judgment on this question. Can we be sure that the basic human rights of such potential "criminals" will not be considered of lesser importance than the wellbeing (and perhaps the very lives) of their future "victims"?

Parallels may also be drawn between the Du Cane/Galton experiments with composite photography and some recently-developed computer software capable of using CCTV footage taken in public places—car parks, shopping centres, football stadiums, etc.—and comparing the facial characteristics of large numbers of unwitting "suspects" against a database composed of mug-shots of known criminals. A pilot scheme carried out in the London borough of Newham in 1998 claimed to have brought a significant fall in the crime rate as a result of such facial recognition technology, though the precise contribution of successful "hits" established thanks to the new software, as distinct from a general deterrent effect, is not clear.[26] Perhaps a comparison with Alphonse Bertillon's *portrait parlé* is more appropriate in this case than with the composite portrait. Like the Frenchman, this new technology seeks to establish a match between a "suspect" with no known criminal antecedents, and specific, named offenders with a recorded past of illegal activity (Cole's *forensic identification*).

As anthropometry has given way to biometry, however, the potential scale of application of this idea has increased beyond all recognition. Whereas Bertillon was limited to comparing the anthropometric vital statistics of those arrested by the Paris police, or at least suspected of having committed a crime, against his bank of signaletic cards, in the case of the new "faceprint" technology (or indeed DNA typing), there is virtually no limit to the number of individuals who can be screened, and in the case of facial identification, screened without their knowledge. The vast majority, inevitably, will be found to have not the slightest connection with any form of wrongdoing; a state of affairs which raises important questions about where to draw the line between the need to protect fundamental civil liberties and the wider concerns of crime prevention and detection. Facial identification technology would seem to have shifted the balance significantly away from individual liberty towards collective security. Some may consider this a trade-off worth making (particularly in the wake of the 9/11 attacks), but it is important to remember that there are losses as well as gains in the adoption of such technologies.

In the new phrenology, DNA testing, and the faceprint then, some of the assumptions underlying the work of Sir Edmund Du Cane, Francis Galton and Alphonse Bertillon live on, albeit in new forms. In this sense, Leon Radzinowicz and Roger Hood's Whiggish description of how modern criminology approaches the ideas of its Lombrosian forebears erects a misleading barrier between a blinkered past and an enlightened (criminological) present:

> It is like moving about in a bewildering, fantastic antique shop, out of this world, and even the elements of truth which were the fruits of the anticipation and perceptions of superior minds, are submerged or distorted by an incongruous amalgamate of hypotheses, comparisons, generalisations, and illogical conclusions.[27]

If the ideas of the Victorian and Edwardian criminologists are to be considered as "antiques", it must be conceded that they remain very much part of our mental furniture in the twenty-first century. To understand their origins is surely the necessary preliminary to any sophisticated understanding not only of our collective past, but of our present as well.

Notes

1 Hugo Münsterberg, *On the Witness Stand: Essays on Psychology and Crime*, New York, Clark Boardman, 1923, p. 114.
2 Rafter, *Creating Born Criminals*, p. 237.
3 Saunders, "Quarantining the Weak-Minded", pp. 279–80. See also Radzinowicz & Hood, *Emergence of Penal Policy*, p. 548 for this point.
4 "Report of the Commissioners of Prisons, etc. for 1900–1901", quoted in Radzinowicz & Hood, *Emergence of Penal Policy*, p. 319.
5 *Ibid.* Their reference is to the concept of "feeble-mindedness", but the point is applicable here.
6 Leps, *Apprehending the Criminal*, p. 66.
7 Ernest Hooton, *The American Criminal,* Cambridge, Mass., Harvard University Press, 1939; William Sheldon, *Varieties of Delinquent Youth*, New York, Harper and Brothers, 1949. For the background, see Nicole Hahn Rafter, "Ernest A. Hooton and the Biological Tradition in American Criminology", *Criminology*, vol. 42, no. 3, Aug. 2004, pp. 735–37.
8 Hooton, *op. cit.*, p. 33.
9 Sheldon, *op. cit.*, p. 836.
10 Daniel J. Curran & Claire Renzetti, *Theories of Crime*, 2nd edition, London, Allyn & Bacon, 2001, pp. 39–40.
11 R. H. C. Bull & J. Green, "The Relationship Between Physical Appearance and Criminality", *Medicine, Science, and the Law*, vol. xx, 1980, pp. 79–83.
12 *Ibid.*, pp. 81–2. The crimes of arson, rape and burglary did not generate statistically significant results.
13 *Ibid.*, p. 81.
14 *Ibid.*, p. 80.
15 *Ibid.*
16 *Ibid.*, pp. 79–81.
17 For an overview of this "biosocial" approach to criminology, written by one of its supporters, see Anthony Walsh, *Biosocial Criminology: Introduction and Integration*, London, Matthew Bender & Co., 2001.
18 Based on Curran & Renzetti, *op. cit.*, pp. 40–54.
19 *Ibid.*, p. 46.
20 *Ibid.*, pp. 54–56. The phrase, with the same derogatory implication as in Devon's usage, forms the title to W. R. Uttal's *The New Phrenology*, Cambridge, Mass., MIT Press, 2001.
21 Davie, "Identifier les tueurs-nés", p. 31.
22 Rafter, "The Murderous Dutch Fiddler", p. 86.
23 Cole, *Suspect Identities*, p. 305.
24 *Ibid.*, p. 305.
25 *Ibid.*, p. 306.
26 Davie, *op. cit.*
27 Radzinowicz & Hood, *op. cit.*, p. 5.

Bibliography

A. Primary Sources

1. Archive Sources

Bodleian Library, Oxford:
Mss. Eng. Hist. 648–49: Correspondence and official papers of Sir Edmund Du Cane, 1870–1890.

Public Record Office, Kew, London:
HO 45: Home Office Correspondence, 1841–1909.
HO 144: Home Office, Supplementary Archives, 1868–1959.
PCOM 7: Prison Commission Archives, 1838–1938.

Parkhurst Prison, Isle of Wight:
Case Book No. 800, Parkhurst Lunatic Asylum, 1904–1911.
Bound Volume of Correspondence, Prison Medical Officers, 1838–1883.
Prison Medical Officer's Journal, 1855–1882.

Archives of University College, London:
Galton Papers, 152/6A, 158/1B: Sir Francis Galton correspondence.
Galton Papers, 159: Sketches by Dr Vans Clarke, 1877–1878.
Pearson Papers, 703/1: Correspondence between Karl Pearson and Charles Goring, 1912–1918.
Pearson Papers, 366: "Report Upon the Aims, Methods, Progress and Results of a Statistical Investigation Now Being conducted for the prison commissioners at the Biometric Laboratory, University College" [1909 ?].

2. Government Reports

"Reports of the Directors of Convict Prisons", 1860–1914, *Parliamentary Papers*, 1861–1915.

"Report from the Select Committee of the House of Lords on the Present State of Discipline in Gaols and Houses of Correction" [Carnarvon Commission], *Parliamentary Papers*, 1863, vol. 9.

"Report of the Royal Commission on Transportation and Penal Servitude", *Parliamentary Papers*, 1863, vol. 21.
"Report of the Royal Commission into the Working of the Penal Servitude Acts" [Kimberley Commission], 2 vols., *Parliamentary Papers*, 1878–1879, vol. 37–38.
"Report of a Committee appointed by the Secretary of State to inquire into the best means available for identifying Habitual Criminals", *Parliamentary Papers*, 1893–1894, vol. 72, pp. 209–91.
"Report from the Departmental Committee on Habitual Offenders, Vagrants, Beggars, Inebriates and Juvenile Delinquents [Scotland]", *Parliamentary Papers*, 1895, vol. 37.
"Report from the Departmental Committee on Prisons" [Gladstone Committee], *Parliamentary Papers*, 1895, vol. 56.
"Report of a Committee Appointed by the Secretary of State to Inquire into the Method of Identification of Criminals by Measurements and Finger Prints", London, Wyman & Sons, 1901.
"Report of the Royal Commission on the Care and Control of the Feeble-Minded", *Parliamentary Papers*, 1908, vol. 35 & 39.
Report to the Secretary of State for the Home Department on the Proceedings of the Fourth Congress of Criminal Anthropology, Held at Geneva in 1896, by Major Arthur Griffiths, London, HMSO, 1896.

3. Books and Articles Published before 1930

Adam, Hargrave L., *The Police Encyclopaedia*, 8 vols., London, Waverley, 1911.
—— *Women and Crime*, London, Werner Laurie, 1914.
Adshead, Joseph, *Prisons and Prisoners*, London, 1845.
Anderson, Sir Robert, "Our Absurd System of Punishing Crime", *Nineteenth Century and After*, vol. 55, 1901, pp. 268–84.
Anderson, Sir Robert, *Criminals and Crime: Some Facts and Suggestions*, London, James Nisbet, 1907.
Baker, John, "Some Points Connected with Criminals", *Journal of Mental Science*, vol. 38, 1892, pp. 364–69.
Beddoe, John, *The Races of Britain: A Contribution to the Anthropology of Western Europe*, Bristol, 1885.
Beggs, Thomas, *Repression and Prevention of Crime*, London, 1868.
Bertillon, Alphonse, *L'Identité des récidivistes et la loi de relégation*, Paris, 1883.
—— *La Photographie judiciaire*, Paris, 1890.
Bridges, Frederick, *Criminals, Crimes and their Governing Laws, as Demonstrated by the Sciences of Physiology and Mental Geometry*, London, 1860.
Broca, Paul, *Instructions générales pour les recherches anthropologiques à faire sur le vivant*, Paris, 1879 [1st edition 1864].
Brougham, Lord, "Opening Address", *Transactions of the National Association for the Promotion of Social Science*, Edinburgh, 1863, p. 1–26.
Booth, Charles, *Life and Labour of the People in London*, 10 vols., London, 1892–1897.
Bourne Taylor, Jenny & Shuttleworth, Sally (eds.), *Embodied Selves: An Anthology of Psychological Texts 1830–1890*, Oxford, Oxford University Press, 1998.
Campbell, John, *Thirty Years Experience of a Medical Officer in the English Convict Service*, London, 1884.

Congrès international de l'anthropologie criminelle: travaux du IVe session … Genève, 1896, Geneva, 1897.

Chesterton, George Laval, *Revelations of Prison Life, with an Enquiry into Prison Discipline and Secondary Punishments*, 2 vols., London, 1856.

Clouston, T.S., "The Developmental Aspects of Criminal Anthropology", *Journal of the Royal Anthropological Institute of Great Britain and Ireland*, vol. 33, 1894, pp. 215–25.

Combe, George, *Essays on Phrenology*, Edinburgh, 1819.

—— *The Constitution of Man and its Relation to External Objects*, Edinburgh, 1828.

—— *Notes on the United States of North America during a Phrenological Visit in 1838–9–40*, 3 vols., Edinburgh, 1841.

Combe, George, "Instances of Successful Moral Treatment of Criminals", *Phrenological Journal*, vol. 18, 1845, pp. 205–9.

Combe, George & Mittermaieri, C. J. A., "On the Application of Phrenology to Criminal Legislation and Prison Discipline", *Phrenological Journal*, vol. 16, 1843, pp. 1–19.

Commission Internationale Pénale et Pénitentiaire, *Prisons and Reformatories at Home and Abroad, being the Transactions of the International Penitentiary Congress, held in London , July 3–13, 1872*, ed. Edwin Pears, Maidstone, H. M. Prison, 1912 [1872].

Corre, Armand, *Les Criminels: caractères physiques et psychologiques*, Paris, 1889.

Crofton, Sir Walter, *The Immunity of Habitual Criminals, with Proposals for Reducing their Number*, London, 1861.

—— "The Criminal Classes", *Transactions of the National Association for the Promotion of Social Science*, 1868, pp. 299–311.

Dallemagne, Jules, *Les Stigmates anatomiques de la criminalité*, Paris, 1894.

Darwin, Charles, *On the Origin of Species by Means of Natural Selection or the Preservation of Favoured Races in the Struggle for Life*, London, 1859.

—— *Descent of Man, and Selection in Relation to Sex*, 2nd edition, London, 1882.

—— *Charles Darwin's Letters: A Selection*, ed. Frederick Burkhardt, Cambridge, Cambridge University Press, 1996.

Darwin, Major Leonard, "The Habitual Criminal", *The Eugenics Review*, no. 6, 1914–15, pp. 214–18.

Dixon, William Hepworth, *The London Prisons*, London, 1850.

Dendy, Mary, *Feebleness of Mind, Pauperism and Crime*, Glasgow, Provincial Committee for the Permanent Care of the Feeble-Minded, 1901.

Devon, James, *The Criminal and the Community*, London, John Lane/Bodley Head, 1912.

Donkin, Sir Bryan, "The State Punishment of Crime", *British Medical Journal*, 2 Aug. 1913, pp. 234–36.

Du Cane, Edmund, "Address on the Repression of Crime", *Transactions of the National Association for the Promotion of Social Science*, 1875, pp. 271–78.

Du Cane, Sir Edmund, *The Punishment and Prevention of Crime*, London, 1885.

Dugdale, Richard L., '*The Jukes*': *A Study in Crime, Pauperism, Disease and Heredity*, New York, 1877.

East, William Norwood, "Physical and Moral Insensitivity in the Criminal", *Journal of Mental Science*, vol. 47, 1901, pp. 737–58.

—— *The Relation of the Skull and Brain to Crime*, Edinburgh, Oliver & Boyd, 1928.

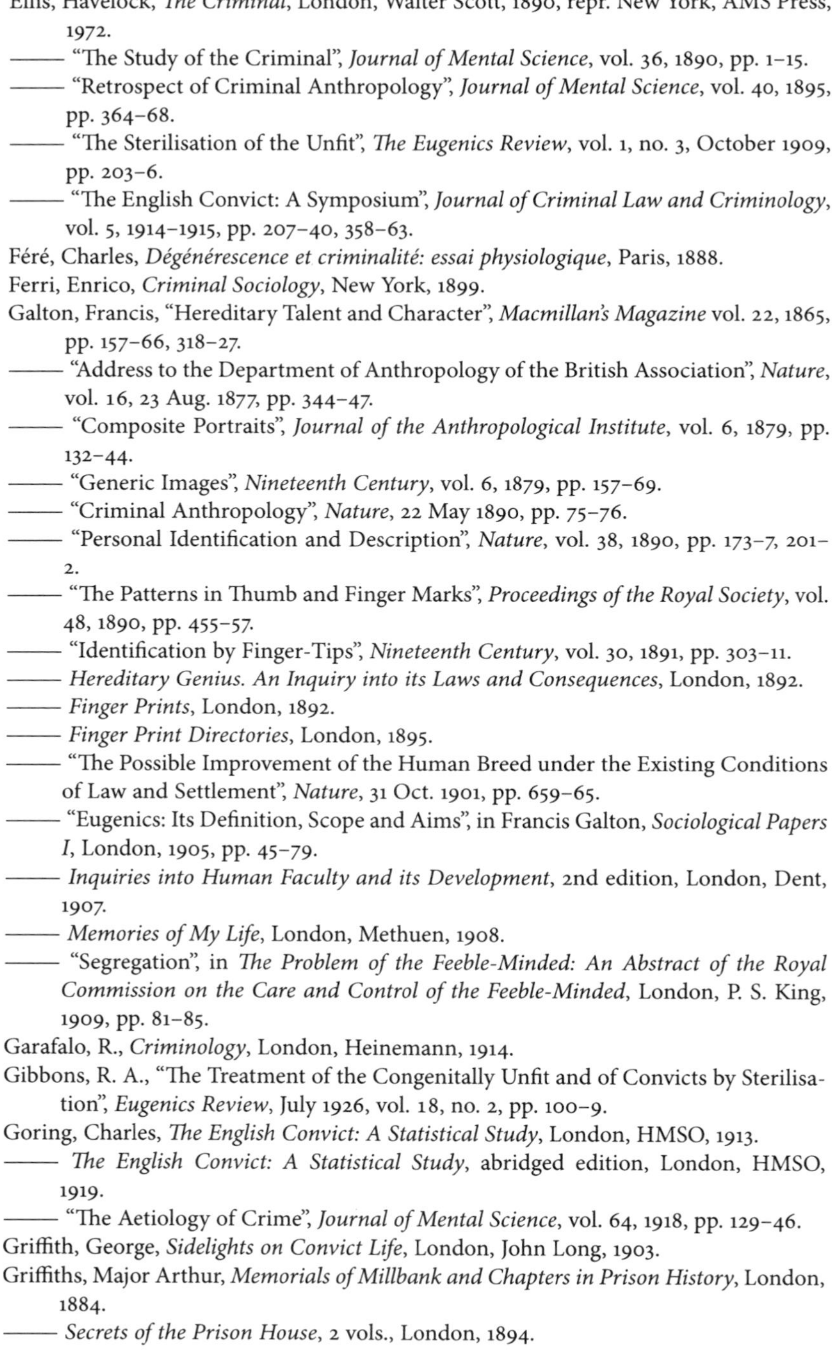

Ellis, Havelock, *The Criminal*, London, Walter Scott, 1890, repr. New York, AMS Press, 1972.

—— "The Study of the Criminal", *Journal of Mental Science*, vol. 36, 1890, pp. 1–15.

—— "Retrospect of Criminal Anthropology", *Journal of Mental Science*, vol. 40, 1895, pp. 364–68.

—— "The Sterilisation of the Unfit", *The Eugenics Review*, vol. 1, no. 3, October 1909, pp. 203–6.

—— "The English Convict: A Symposium", *Journal of Criminal Law and Criminology*, vol. 5, 1914–1915, pp. 207–40, 358–63.

Féré, Charles, *Dégénérescence et criminalité: essai physiologique*, Paris, 1888.

Ferri, Enrico, *Criminal Sociology*, New York, 1899.

Galton, Francis, "Hereditary Talent and Character", *Macmillan's Magazine* vol. 22, 1865, pp. 157–66, 318–27.

—— "Address to the Department of Anthropology of the British Association", *Nature*, vol. 16, 23 Aug. 1877, pp. 344–47.

—— "Composite Portraits", *Journal of the Anthropological Institute*, vol. 6, 1879, pp. 132–44.

—— "Generic Images", *Nineteenth Century*, vol. 6, 1879, pp. 157–69.

—— "Criminal Anthropology", *Nature*, 22 May 1890, pp. 75–76.

—— "Personal Identification and Description", *Nature*, vol. 38, 1890, pp. 173–7, 201–2.

—— "The Patterns in Thumb and Finger Marks", *Proceedings of the Royal Society*, vol. 48, 1890, pp. 455–57.

—— "Identification by Finger-Tips", *Nineteenth Century*, vol. 30, 1891, pp. 303–11.

—— *Hereditary Genius. An Inquiry into its Laws and Consequences*, London, 1892.

—— *Finger Prints*, London, 1892.

—— *Finger Print Directories*, London, 1895.

—— "The Possible Improvement of the Human Breed under the Existing Conditions of Law and Settlement", *Nature*, 31 Oct. 1901, pp. 659–65.

—— "Eugenics: Its Definition, Scope and Aims", in Francis Galton, *Sociological Papers I*, London, 1905, pp. 45–79.

—— *Inquiries into Human Faculty and its Development*, 2nd edition, London, Dent, 1907.

—— *Memories of My Life*, London, Methuen, 1908.

—— "Segregation", in *The Problem of the Feeble-Minded: An Abstract of the Royal Commission on the Care and Control of the Feeble-Minded*, London, P. S. King, 1909, pp. 81–85.

Garafalo, R., *Criminology*, London, Heinemann, 1914.

Gibbons, R. A., "The Treatment of the Congenitally Unfit and of Convicts by Sterilisation", *Eugenics Review*, July 1926, vol. 18, no. 2, pp. 100–9.

Goring, Charles, *The English Convict: A Statistical Study*, London, HMSO, 1913.

—— *The English Convict: A Statistical Study*, abridged edition, London, HMSO, 1919.

—— "The Aetiology of Crime", *Journal of Mental Science*, vol. 64, 1918, pp. 129–46.

Griffith, George, *Sidelights on Convict Life*, London, John Long, 1903.

Griffiths, Major Arthur, *Memorials of Millbank and Chapters in Prison History*, London, 1884.

—— *Secrets of the Prison House*, 2 vols., London, 1894.

—— *Report to the Secretary of State for the Home Department on the Proceedings of the Fourth Congress of Criminal Anthropology, Held at Geneva in 1896*, London, HMSO, 1896.

—— *Fifty Years of Public Service*, London, Cassel, n.d. [1904].

Guy, William A., *The Evils of England, Social and Economic*, London, 1846.

—— "On Some Results of a Recent Census of the Populations of the Convict Prisons of England and Wales", *Transactions of the National Association for the Promotion of Social Science*, 1863, pp. 569–74.

—— "On Insanity and Crime, and on the Plea of Insanity in Criminal Cases", *Journal of the Statistical Society of London*, vol. 32, no. 2, June 1869, pp. 159–91.

—— *Results of the Census of the Population of the Convict Prisons in England, Taken in 1862 and 1873*, London, HMSO, 1875.

Hill, Frederic, *Crime: Its Amount, Cause and Remedies*, London, 1853.

Holford, George, *An Account of the General Penitentiary at Millbank*, London, 1828.

Holmes, Thomas, *London's Underworld*, London, Dent & Sons, 1912.

Horsley, J. W., *How Criminals are Made and Prevented: A Retrospect of Forty Years*, London, Fisher Unwin, 1913.

Hoyle, William, *Crime in England and Wales in the Nineteenth Century: An Historical and Critical Retrospect*, London, 1876.

Lacassagne, Alexandre, "Préface", in Emile Laurent, *Le Criminel aux points de vue anthropologique, psychologique et social*, Paris, Vigot Frères, 1908.

Lauvergne, Hubert, *Les Forçats considérés sous le rapport physiologique moral et intellectuel*, Paris, 1841.

Lilly, W. S., "Criminals and the Criminal Class", *Nineteenth Century and After*, vol. 66, 1912, pp. 371–81.

Lombroso, Cesare, *L'Uomo delinquente*, Milan, Hoepli, 1876.

—— *L'Homme criminel—criminel né, fou moral, épileptique*, Paris, 1887.

—— *L'Anthropologie criminelle et ses récents progrès*, Paris, 1890.

—— *Nouvelles recherches de psychiatrie et d'anthropologie criminelles*, Paris, 1892.

—— *Crime, causes et remèdes*, Paris, 1899.

—— *Crime: Its Causes and Remedies*, Boston, Little Brown & Co., 1911.

Lombroso, Cesare & Ferrero, Guglielmo, *The Female Offender*, London, 1895.

—— *Criminal Woman, the Prostitute and the Normal Woman*, trans. & ed. Nicole Hahn Rafter & Mary Gibson, Durham & London, Duke University Press, 2004 [1893].

Mackintosh, D., "Comparative Anthropology of England and Wales", *The Anthropological Review*, no. 12, January 1866, pp. 1–21.

McDowall, William, *The Mind in the Face: An Introduction to the Study of Physiognomy*, London, 1882.

Maudsley, Henry, *The Physiology and Pathology of the Mind*, London, 1867.

—— *Body and Mind*, London, Macmillan, 1873.

—— *Responsibility in Mental Disease*, London, King, 1874.

—— "Remarks on Crime and Criminals", *Journal of Mental Science*, vol. 34, 1889, pp. 159–67.

—— *The Pathology of Mind*, London, Macmillan, 1895.

Mayhew, Henry, *London Labour and the London Poor*, 4 vols., London, 1851–1862.

—— *London's Underworld, Being Selections from 'Those That Will Not Work', the Fourth Volume of 'London Labour and the London Poor' by Henry Mayhew*, ed. Peter Quennell, London, Spring Books, 1950 [1862].

Mayhew, Henry & Binny, John, *The Criminal Prisons of London and Scenes of Prison Life*, London, Griffin & Co., 1862, repr. London, Frank Cass, 1971.
Mercier, Charles, "Moral Imbecility", *The Practitioner*, vol. 99, 1917, pp. 301–8.
—— *Crime and Criminals: Being the Jurisprudence of Crime, Medical, Biological and Psychological*, London, University of London Press, 1918.
Meredith, Susanna, *A Book about Criminals*, London, 1881.
Morel, B. A., *Traité des dégénérescence physiques, intellectuelles et morales de l'espèce humaine*, 2 vols., Paris, 1857.
Morrison, W. Douglas, "Reflections on the Theories of Criminality", *Journal of Mental Science*, vol. 35, 1889, pp. 14–23.
—— *Crime and its Causes*, London, 1891.
—— "The Increase of Crime", *Nineteenth Century*, vol. 31, June 1892, pp. 950–57.
—— "Are our Prisons a Failure?", *Fortnightly Review*, vol. 61, April 1894, pp. 459–69.
—— *Juvenile Offenders*, London, 1896.
—— "The Interpretation of Criminal Statistics", *Journal of the Royal Statistical Society*, vol. 60, no. 1, March 1897, pp. 1–32.
—— "Prison Reform: Prisons and Prisoners", *Fortnightly Review*, vol. 69, May 1898, pp. 781–89.
Nicolson, David, "The Morbid Psychology of Criminals", *Journal of Mental Science*, vol. 19, 1873, pp. 222–32; 398–409; vol. 20, 1874, pp. 20–37, 167–85, 527–51; vol. 21, 1875, pp. 18–31, 225–50.
—— "Presidential Address", *Journal of Mental Science*, vol. 41, 1895, pp. 567–91.
Nihill, Reverend Daniel, *Prison Discipline in its Relations to Society and Individuals in Deterring from Crime, and as Conducive to Personal Reformation*, London, 1839.
Pare, William, *A Plan for the Suppression of the Predatory Classes*, London, 1862.
Pearson, Karl, "On the Inheritance of the Mental Characters in Man, and its Comparison with the Inheritance of the Physical Characters", *Journal of the Anthropological Institute*, vol. 33, 1903, pp. 179–237.
—— *National Life from the Standpoint of Science*, 2nd edition, London, Adam & Charles Black, 1905.
—— *Nature and Nurture: The Problem of the Future*, London, Eugenics Laboratory Memoirs, vol. 6, 1910.
—— *The Life, Letters and Labours of Francis Galton*, 3 vols., Cambridge, Cambridge University Press, 1914–1930.
Plint, Thomas, *Crime in England: Its Relation, Character and Extent*, London, 1851.
Pritchard, H. Baden, "At Pentonville Penitentiary", in *idem.*, *The Photographic Studios of Europe*, London, 1882, pp. 119–23.
Quinton, R. F., *Crime and Criminals 1876–1910*, London, Longmans, 1910.
Rentoul, R. R., *Proposed Sterilization of Certain Medical and Physical Degenerates: An Appeal to Asylum Managers and Others*, London, Walter Scott, 1903.
Robinson, Frederick William, *Prison Characters Drawn from Life, With Suggestions for Prison Government*, 2 vols., London, 1886.
Rowntree, Seebohm, *Poverty: A Study of Town Life*, London, Macmillan, 1901.
Ruggles-Brise, Sir Evelyn, *Proceedings of the Fifth International Penitentiary Congress, Held at Paris in 1895*, London, HMSO, 1895.
—— *The English Prison System*, London, Macmillan, 1921.

Rumsey, Henry W., "On a Progressive Physical Degeneracy of Race in the Town Populations", *Transactions of the National Association for the Promotion of Social Science*, 1870, pp. 466–72.

Rylands, L. Gordon, *Crime: Its Causes and Remedy*, London, 1889.

Saleeby, Caleb W., *Parenthood and Race Culture: An Outline of Eugenics*, New York, Moffat, 1910.

Sampson, Marmaduke B., *Criminal Jurisprudence Considered in Relation to Mental Organisation*, London, 1841.

—— *Rationale of Crime, and its Appropriate Treatment; Being a Treatise on Criminal Jurisprudence Considered in Relation to Cerebral Organisation*, ed. Eliza Farnham, New York, 1846.

Scougal, Francis, *Scenes from a Silent World or Prisons and their Inmates*, Edinburgh, 1889.

St John, Arthur, "Criminal Anthropology and Common Sense", *The Sociological Review*, vol. 5, 1912, pp. 65–67.

Spearman, Edmund R., "Known to the Police", *Nineteenth Century*, vol. 36, 1894, pp. 356–70.

Spencer, Herbert *The Study of Sociology*, London, 1873.

Strahan, S. A. K., "Instinctive Criminality: Its True Character and National Treatment", *Report of the British Association for the Advancement of Science*, London, 1891, pp. 811–13.

Sullivan, W. C., "Eugenics and Crime", *The Eugenics Review*, vol. 1, no. 2, July 1909, pp. 112–20.

Sutherland, J. F., *Recidivism: Habitual Criminality and Habitual Petty Delinquency: A Problem in Sociology, Psycho-Pathology and Criminology*, Edinburgh, William Green, 1908.

Tarde, Gabriel, *La Criminalité comparée*, Paris, Félix Altan, 1924 [2nd edition, 1890].

Thomson, J. Bruce, "The Effects of Prison Discipline on the Body and Mind", *Journal of Mental Science*, vol. 12, 1866, pp. 340–48.

—— "The Hereditary Nature of Crime", *Journal of Mental Science*, vol. 15, 1869, pp. 487–98.

—— "The Psychology of Criminals", *Journal of Mental Science*, vol. 16, 1870, pp. 321–50.

Tredgold, A[lfred] F., "The Feeble-Minded—A Social Danger", *The Eugenics Review*, vol. 1, no. 2, July 1909, pp. 97–104.

—— *Mental Deficiency (Amentia)*, 2nd edition, London, Ballière, Tindall & Cox, 1914.

Tristan, Flora, *Flora Tristan's London Journal, 1840*, trans. Denis Palmer & Giselle Pincentl, London, George Prior, 1980.

Whetham, W. C. D. & C. D., *The Family and the Nation: A Study in National Inheritance and Social Responsibility*, London, 1909.

B. Secondary Sources

Anderson, Clare, *Legible Bodies: Race, Criminality and Colonialism in south Asia*, Oxford, Berg, 2004.

Badinter, Robert, *La Prison républicaine 1871–1914*, Paris, Fayard, 1992.

Bailey, Victor (ed.), *Policing and Punishment in Nineteenth Century Britain*, London, Croom Helm, 1981.

—— *Delinquency and Citizenship: Reclaiming the Young Offender*, Oxford, Clarendon Press, 1987.

—— "The Fabrication of Deviance?: 'Dangerous Classes' and 'Criminal Classes' in Victorian England", in John Rule & Robert Malcolmson (eds.), *Protest and Survival: The Historical Experience*, London, Merlin Press, 1993, pp. 221–57.

—— "English Prisons, Penal Culture and the Abatement of Imprisonment, 1895–1922", *Journal of British Studies*, July 1997, pp. 285–324.

Barringer, Tim, "Images of Otherness and the Visual Production of Difference: Race and Labour in Illustrated Texts 1850–1865", *in* West (1996), pp. 34–52.

Barry, John Vincent, *Alexander Maconochie of Norfolk Island*, London, Oxford University Press, 1958.

—— "Alexander Maconochie 1787–1860", in Mannheim (1972), pp. 84–106.

Beirne, Piers, "Heredity vs. Environment: A Reconsideration of Charles Goring's *The English Convict* (1913)", *British Journal of Criminology*, vol. 28, 1988, pp. 315–39.

Blankaert, Claude, "Des sauvages en pays civilisé: l'anthropologie des criminels (1850–1900)", in Mucchielli (1994), pp. 55–88.

Bolt, Christina, *Victorian Attitudes to Race*, London, Routledge, 1971.

Brown Janet, "Darwin and the Face of Madness", in W. F. Bynum *et al.* (eds.), *The Anatomy of Madness: Essays in the History of Psychiatry*, vol. 1, London, Routledge, 1985, pp. 151–65.

Bull, R. H. C. & Green, J., "The Relationship Between Physical Appearance and Criminality", *Medicine, Science, and the Law*, vol. 20, 1980, pp. 79–83.

Bynum, W. F., Porter, Roy, & Shepherd, Michael (eds.), *The Anatomy of Madness: Essays in the History of Psychiatry*, vol. III, London, Routledge, 1988.

Carlson, Elof Axel, *The Unfit: A History of a Bad Idea*, Cold Spring Harbour N. Y., Cold Spring Harbour Laboratory Press, 2001.

Cole, Simon A., *Suspect Identities: A History of Fingerprinting and Criminal Identification*, Cambridge, Mass., Harvard University Press, 2001.

Collins, Philip, *Dickens and Crime*, London, Macmillan, 1962.

Cooter, Roger, *The Cultural Meaning of Popular Science: Phrenology and the Organisation of Consent in Nineteenth Century Britain*, Cambridge, Cambridge University Press, 1984.

Creese, Richard *et al.* (eds.), *The Health of Prisoners: Historical Essays*, Amsterdam, Rodopi, 1995.

Curran, Daniel J. & Renzetti, Claire, *Theories of Crime*, London, Allyn & Bacon, 1994.

Cowling, Mary, *The Artist as Anthropologist: The Representation of Type and Character in Victorian Art*, Cambridge, Cambridge University Press, 1989.

Davie, Neil, "Identifier les tueurs-nés", *Le Monde Diplomatique*, December 2002, p. 31.

—— "Criminal Man Revisited? Continuity and Change in British Criminology, c. 1865–1918", *Journal of Victorian Culture*, vol. 8, no. 1, 2003, pp. 1–32.

—— "'Une des défigurations les plus tristes de la civilisation moderne': Francis Galton et le criminel composite", in Michel Prum (ed.), *Les Malvenus: Race et sexe dans le monde anglophone*, Paris, L'Harmattan, 2003, pp. 191–220.

—— *Les Visages de la criminalité: à la recherché d'un criminel-type scientifique en Angleterre*, 1860–1914, Paris, Kimé, 2004.

—— "Criminology", in Tom & Sara Pendergast (eds.), *Grolier Encyclopedia of the Victorian Era*, 4 vols., Danbury, Connecticut, Grolier Academic Press (forthcoming).

Davis, J., "The London Garotting Panic of 1862: A Moral Panic and the Creation of a Criminal Class in Mid-Victorian England", in V. A. C. Gatrell *et al.* (eds.), *Crime and the Law: The Social History of Crime in Europe since 1500*, London, Europa, 1980, pp. 190–213.

Debuyst, Christian *et al.* (eds.), *Histoire des savoirs sur le crime et la peine*, vol. 2: *La Rationalité pénale et la naissance de la criminologie*, Paris, De Boeck Université, 1998.

De Guistino, David, *Conquest of Mind: Phrenology and Victorian Social Thought*, London, Croom Helm, 1975.

De Maré, Eric, *Victorian London Revealed: Gustave Doré's Metropolis*, London, Penguin, 2001 [1973].

Desmond, Adrian, *The Politics of Evolution: Morphology, Medicine and Reform in Radical London*, Chicago, Chicago University Press, 1989.

Desmond, Adrian & Moore, James, *Darwin: The Life of a Tormented Evolutionist*, New York, Warner Books, 1991.

Driver, Edwin D., "Charles Goring", in Mannheim, (1972), pp. 429–42.

Edwards, Elizabeth (ed.), *Anthropology and Photography 1860–1920*, New Haven, Yale University Press, 1992.

Emsley, Clive, *Crime and Society in England 1750–1900*, 2nd edition, London, Longmans, 1996.

—— *The English Police: A Political and Social History*, 2nd edition, London, Longmans, 1996.

Evans, Robin, *The Fabrication of Virtue: English Prison Architecture 1750–1840*, Cambridge, Cambridge University Press, 1982.

Fink, Arthur E., *Causes of Crime: Biological Theories in the United States 1800–1915*, New York, A. S. Barnes, 1962 [1st edition 1938].

Forrest, D. W., *Francis Galton: The Life and Work of a Victorian Genius*, New York, Tapling, 1974.

Forsythe, William J., *The Reform of Prisoners 1830–1900*, London, Croom Helm, 1987.

—— *Penal Discipline, Reformatory Projects and the English Prison Commission*, Exeter, Exeter University Press, 1991.

—— "The Garland Thesis and the Origins of Modern English Prison Discipline", *The Howard Journal*, vol. 34, no. 3, August 1995, pp. 259–73.

Foucault, Michel, *Discipline and Punish: The Birth of the Modern Prison*, London, Penguin, 1977.

—— "The Eye of Power", in Sylvère Lotringer (ed.), *Foucault Live: Collected Interviews, 1961–1984*, New York, Semiotext(e), 1996, pp. 226–40.

Frizot, Michel, "Body of Evidence: The Ethnophotography of Difference", in *idem.* (ed.), *A New History of Photography*, Cologne, Könemann, 1998, pp. 258–71.

Garland, David, *Punishment and Welfare: A History of Penal Strategies*, Aldershot, Gower, 1985.

—— "The Criminal and his Science", *British Journal of Criminology* vol. 25, no. 2, April 1985, pp. 109–37.

—— "British Criminology Before 1935", *British Journal of Criminology*, vol. 28, no. 2, Spring 1988, pp. 1–18.

—— "Criminological Knowledge and its Relation to Power", *British Journal of Criminology*, vol. 32, no. 4, Autumn 1992, pp. 403–22.

—— "Of Crimes and Criminals: The Development of Criminology in Britain", in Mike Maguire *et al.* (eds.), *The Oxford Handbook of Criminology*, 3rd edition, Oxford, Oxford University Press, 2002, pp. 7–50.

Gatrell, V[ictor] A. C., "Crime, Authority and the Policeman State", in F. M. L. Thompson (ed.), *The Cambridge Social History of Britain, 1750–1950*, 3 vols., vol. 3: *Social Agencies and Institutions*, Cambridge, Cambridge University Press, 1990, pp. 243–310.

—— *The Hanging Tree: Execution and the English People, 1770–1868*, Oxford, Oxford University Press, 1994.

Gernsheim, Helmut, *The History of Photography*, 2nd edition, London, Thames & Hudson, 1969.

Gibson, Mary, *Born to Crime: Cesare Lombroso and the Origins of Modern Criminology*, Praeger, Westport, Conn., 1992.

Gillham, Nicholas W., *A Life of Sir Francis Galton: From African Explorer to the Birth of Eugenics*, Oxford, Oxford University Press, 2001.

Gilman, Sander L. (ed.), *The Face of Madness: H. W. Diamond and the Origin of Psychiatric Photography*, New York, Brunner/Mazel, 1976.

Gould, Stephen J., *The Mismeasure of Man*, 2nd edition, London, Penguin, 1997.

Green, David, "Veins of Resemblance", *Oxford Art Journal*, vol. 7, no. 2, 1985, pp. 3–16.

Hall, Lesley A., *Sex, Gender and Social Change in Britain since 1880*, London, Macmillan, 2000.

Hamilton, Peter & Hargreaves, Roger, *The Beautiful and the Damned: The Creation of Identity in Nineteenth Century Photography*, London, Lund Humphries/ National Portrait Gallery, 2001.

Hardy, Ann, "Development of the Prison Medical Service", in Creese *et al.* (1995), pp. 59–82.

Harris, José, *Private Lives, Public Spirit: Britain 1870–1914*, Harmondsworth, Penguin, 1994.

Hartley, Lucy, *Physiognomy and the Meaning of Expression in Nineteenth-Century Culture*, Cambridge, Cambridge University Press, 2001.

Hawkings, David T., *Criminal Ancestors: A Guide to Historical Criminal Records in England and Wales*, Stroud, Alan Sutton, 1992.

Hawkins, Mike, *Social Darwinism in European and American Thought: Nature as Model and Nature as Threat*, Cambridge, Cambridge University Press, 1997.

Himmelfarb, Gertrude, *The Idea of Poverty: England in the Early Industrial Age*, London, Faber, 1984.

Horn, David G., *The Criminal Body: Lombroso and the Anatomy of Deviance*, London, Routledge, 2003.

Humpherys, Anne, *Travels into the Poor Man's Country: The Work of Henry Mayhew*, Athens, University of Georgia Press, 1977.

Ignatieff, Michael, *A Just Measure of Pain. The Penitentiary in the Industrial Revolution*, London, Macmillan, 1978.

—— "State, Civil Society and Total Institutions: A Critique of Recent Social Histories of Punishment", in Stanley Cohen & Andrew Scull (eds.), *Social Control and the State*, Oxford, Robertson, 1983, pp. 75–105.

Jackson, Mark, *The Borderland of Imbecility: Medicine, Society and the Fabrication of the Feeble Mind in Later Victorian and Edwardian England*, Manchester, Manchester University Press, 2000.

Jayewardine, C. H. S., "The English Precursors of Lombroso", *British Journal of Criminology*, vol. 4, no. 1, July 1963, pp. 164–70.

Jones, Greta, *Social Darwinism and English Thought: The Interaction between Biological and Social Theory*, Hassocks, Harvester, 1980.

Keating, Peter (ed.), *Into Unknown England: Selections from the Social Explorers*, Manchester, Manchester University Press, 1976.

Kelves, Daniel J., *In the Name of Eugenics: Genetics and the Use of Human Heredity*, Cambridge, Harvard University Press, 1995.

Leps, Marie-Christine, *Apprehending the Criminal: The Production of Deviance in Nineteenth-Century Discourse*, Durham & London, Duke University Press, 1992.

Lightman, Bernard (ed.), *Victorian Science in Context*, London, University of Chicago Press, 1997.

Lorimer, Douglas A., "Race, Science and Culture: Historical Continuities and Discontinuities", in West (1996), pp. 12–33.

—— "Theoretical Racism in Late-Victorian Anthropology, 1870–1900", *Victorian Studies*, vol. 31, no. 3, Spring 1988, pp. 405–30.

MacKenzie, Donald "Eugenics in Britain", *Social Studies of Science*, vol. 6, 1976, pp. 503–18.

Mannheim, Herman (ed.), *Pioneers in Criminology*, 2nd edition, Montclair NJ, Patterson Smith, 1972.

McConville, Sean, *A History of English Prison Administration: Volume I 1750–1877*, London, Routledge, 1981.

—— *English Local Prisons 1860 to 1900: "Next Only to Death"*, London, Routledge, 1994.

—— "The Victorian Prison, England 1865–1965", in Morris & Rothman (1998), pp. 117–50.

McGowen, Randall, "The Well-Ordered Prison, England 1780–1865", in Morris & Rothman (1998), pp. 71–116.

Manser, Brian, *Behind the Small Wooden Door: The Inside Story of Parkhurst Prison*, Freshwater, Isle of Wight, Coach House Publications, 2000.

Marks, Jonathan, *Human Biodiversity: Genes, Race and History*, New York, Aldine De Gruyer, 1995.

Morris, Norval, *Maconochie's Gentlemen: The Story of Norfolk Island and the Roots of Modern Prison Reform*, Oxford, Oxford University Press, 2002.

Morris, Norval & Rothman, David (eds.), *The Oxford History of the Prison: The Practice of Punishment in Western Society*, Oxford, Oxford University Press, 1998.

Mucchielli, Laurent (ed.), *Histoire de la criminologie française*, Paris, L'Harmattan, 1994.

—— "Hérédité et 'Milieu Social', le faux-antagonisme franco-italien, la place de l'école de Lacassagne dans l'histoire de la criminologie", in *idem*. (1994) pp. 189–214.

Nye, Robert A., *Crime, Madness and Politics in Modern France*, Princeton, Princeton University Press, 1984.

—— "The Rise and Fall of the Eugenics Empire: Recent Perspectives on the Impact of Biomedical Thought in Modern Society", *Historical Journal*, vol. 36, no. 3, 1993, pp. 687–700.

Peel, J. D. Y., *Herbert Spencer: The Evolution of a Sociologist*, London, Heinemann, 1971.

Perrot, Michelle, *Les Ombres de l'histoire: Crime et châtiment au* XIX*e siècle*, Paris, Flammarion, 2001.

Petit, Jean-Jacques *et al.*, *Histoires des galères, bagnes et prisons* XIII*e*–XX*e siècles*, Toulouse, Bibliothèque Historique Privat, 1991.

Phéline, Christian, *L'Image accusatrice*, Les Cahiers de la Photographie, no. 17, 1985.

Philips, David, "Crime, Law and Punishment in the Industrial Revolution", in Patrick O'Brien & Roland Quinault (eds.), *The Industrial Revolution and British Society*, Cambridge, Cambridge University Press, 1993, pp. 156–82.

Pick, Daniel, *Faces of Degeneration: A European Disorder, c. 1848–1918*, Cambridge, Cambridge University Press, 1989.

Porter, Roy, *Bodies Politic: Disease, Death and Doctors in Britain, 1650–1900*, London, Reaktion, 2001.

Priestley, Philip, *Victorian Prison Lives: English Prison Biography 1830–1914*, 2nd edn., London, Pimlico, 1999.

Radzinowicz, Leon & Hood, Roger, *The Emergence of Penal Policy in Victorian and Edwardian England*, Oxford, Clarendon Press, 1990 [first published as vol. 5 of *A History of English Criminal Law*, London, Stevens & Sons, 1986].

Rafter, Nicole Hahn, *Creating Born Criminals*, Urbana, University of Illinois Press, 1997.

—— "Seeing and Believing: Images of Heredity in Biological Theories of Crime", *Brooklyn Law Review*, vol. 67, no. 1, Autumn 2001, pp. 71–99.

—— "Ernest A. Hooton and the Biological Tradition in American Criminology", *Criminology*, vol. 42, no. 3, Aug. 2004, pp. 735–71.

—— "The Unrepentant Horse-Slasher: Moral Insanity and the Origins of Criminology", *Criminology*, vol. 42, no. 4, Nov. 2004, pp. 977–1006.

—— "The Murderous Dutch Fiddler: Criminology, History and the Problem of Phrenology", *Theoretical Criminology*, vol. 9, no. 1, Feb. 2005, pp. 65–96.

Renneville, Marc, "La réception de Lombroso en France (1880–1900)", in Mucchielli (1994), pp. 107–35.

—— *Le Langage des crânes: une histoire de la phrénologie*, Paris, Institut d'Edition Sanofi-Synthélabo, 2000.

Rhodes, Henry Taylor Fowkes, *Alphonse Bertillon, Father of Scientific Detection*, London, Harrap, 1956.

Ryan, James R., *Picturing the Empire: Photography and the Visualisation of the British Empire*, London, Reaktion Books, 1977.

Sahlins, Marshall, *Waiting for Foucault, Still*, Chicago, Prickly Paradigm Press, 2002.

Saunders, Janet, "Quarantining the Weak-minded: Psychiatric Definitions of Degeneracy and the Late-Victorian Asylum", in W.F . Bynum *et al.* (eds.), *The Anatomy of Madness: Essays in the History of Psychiatry*, vol. 3, London, Routledge, 1988, pp. 273–96.

Searle, G. R., "Eugenics and Class", in Charles Webster (1981), pp. 217–42.

Schlicke, Paul (ed.), *Oxford Reader's Companion to Dickens*, Oxford, Oxford University Press, 1999.

Sekula, Allan, "The Body and the Archive", *October*, no. 39, 1986, pp. 3–64.

Sim, Joe, *Medical Power in Prisons: The Prison Medical Service in England 1774–1989*, Buckingham, Open University Press, 1990.

Soloway, Richard A., *Demography and Degeneration: Eugenics and the Declining Birthrate in Twentieth-Century Britain*, 2nd edition, London, University of North Carolina Press, 1995.

Smith, Philip Thurmond, *Policing Victorian London: Political Policing, Public Order and the London Metropolitan Police*, London, Greenwood Press, 1985.

Smith, Richard, "History of the Prison Medical Services", *British Medical Journal*, vol. 287, 10 Dec. 1983, pp. 1786–88.

Stedman-Jones, Gareth, *Outcast London: A Study in the Relationship Between Classes in Victorian Society*, Oxford, Clarendon Press, 1971.

Stepan, Nancy, *The Idea of Race in Science: Great Britain 1800–1860*, London, Macmillan, 1982.

Stern, Madeline B., "Matthew Brady and the 'Rationale of Crime': A Discovery in Daguerreotypes", *Quarterly Journal of the Library of Congress*, vol. 31, 1974, pp. 127–35.

Stocking, George W. Jnr., *Victorian Anthropology*, New York, The Free Press, 1987.

Tagg, John, *The Burden of Representation: Essays on Photography and Histories*, London, Macmillan, 1988.

Taylor, David, *Crime, Policing and Punishment in England, 1730–1914*, London, Macmillan, 1998.

Thomas, Donald, *The Victorian Underworld*, London, John Murray, 1998.

Thomas, Ronald A., *Detective Fiction and the Rise of Forensic Science*, Cambridge, Cambridge University Press, 1999.

Thomson, Matthew, *The Problem of Mental Deficiency: Eugenics, Democracy and Social Policy in Britain, c. 1870–1959*, Oxford, Oxford University Press, 1998.

Tort, Patrick, "L'Histoire naturelle du crime", in *idem.*, *La Raison classificatoire*, Paris, Aubier, 1989, pp. 469–535.

—— *Darwin et la science de l'évolution*, Paris, Gallimard, 2000.

Trent, James W. Jnr., *Inventing the Feeble Mind: A History of Mental Retardation in the United States*, London, University of California Press, 1994.

Tucker, Jennifer, "Photography as Witness, Detective and Impostor: Visual Representation in Victorian Science", in Lightman (1997), pp. 378–408.

Turner, Trevor, "Henry Maudsley: Psychiatrist, Philosopher and Entrepreneur", in W. F. Bynum *et al.* (eds.), *The Anatomy of Madness: Essays in the History of Psychiatry*, vol. 3, London, Routledge, 1988, pp. 151–89.

Urry, James, *Before Social Anthropology: Essays in the History of British Anthropology*, Chur (Switzerland), Harwood, 1993.

Walkowitz, Judith R., *Prostitution and Victorian Society: Women, Class and the State*, Cambridge, Cambridge University Press, 1980.

Watson, Stephen, "Applying Foucault: Some Problems Encountered in the Application of Foucault's Methods to the History of Medicine", in Colin Jones & Roy Porter, eds., *Reassessing Foucault: Medicine and the Body*, London, Routledge, 1994, pp. 132–51.

—— "'Malingers', the 'Weakminded' and the 'Moral Imbecile': How the English Prison Medical Officer Became an Expert in Mental Deficiency", in Michael Clark & Catherine Crawford (eds.), *Legal Medicine in History*, Cambridge, Cambridge University Press, 1994 , pp. 223–41.

Webster, Charles (ed.), *Biology, Medicine and Society 1840–1940*, Cambridge, Cambridge University Press, 1981.

West, Shearer (ed.), *The Victorians and Race*, Aldershot, Scholar Press, 1996.

Wetzell, Richard F., *Inventing the Criminal: A History of German Criminology, 1880–1945*, Chapel Hill & London, University of North Carolina Press, 2000.

Wiener, Martin, *Reconstructing the Criminal: Culture, Law and Policy in England, 1830–1914*, Cambridge, Cambridge University Press, 1990.

—— "The Health of Prisoners and the Two Faces of Benthamism", in Creese *et al.* (1995), pp. 44–58.

Wilson, David, "Millbank, The Panopticon and Their Victorian Audiences", *The Howard Journal*, vol. 41, no. 4, September 2002, pp. 364–81.

Wolfgang, Marvin E., "Cesare Lombroso", in Mannheim (1972), pp. 232–91.

Zedner, Lucia, *Women, Crime and Custody in Victorian England*, Oxford, Clarendon Press, 1991.

—— "Wayward Sisters", in Morris & Rothman (1998), pp. 295–324.

Index

The numbers in italics indicate references to photographic plates.